POLITICAL THOUGHT AND
INTERNATIONAL RELATIONS

Political Thought and International Relations

Variations on a Realist Theme

Edited by
DUNCAN BELL

OXFORD
UNIVERSITY PRESS

OXFORD

UNIVERSITY PRESS

Great Clarendon Street, Oxford, OX2 6DP,
United Kingdom

Oxford University Press is a department of the University of Oxford.
It furthers the University's objective of excellence in research, scholarship,
and education by publishing worldwide. Oxford is a registered trade mark of
Oxford University Press in the UK and in certain other countries

Published in the United States of America by Oxford University Press
198 Madison Avenue, New York, NY 10016, United States of America

British Library Cataloguing in Publication Data

Data available

Library of Congress Control Number: 2008027680

ISBN 978–0–19–955627–4

Acknowledgements

I would like to thank the Centre of International Studies, University of Cambridge, and the British International Studies Association (BISA), for helping to fund the conference on 'Tragedy, Justice, and Power: Realism as Political Theory' (2005) at which a number of the following chapters were first presented. I would also like to thank the Semenenko Foundation and the journal *Millennium* for permission to print, in modified form, essays originally published under their auspices. Dominic Byatt at Oxford University Press has been an exemplary editor. Above all, I thank the contributors to this volume for their patience, good humour, and commitment to the project.

Contents

List of Contributors

Duncan Bell is a Leverhulme Early Career Fellow at the Centre of International Studies, University of Cambridge, and a Fellow of Christ's College

Joshua Foa Dienstag is a Professor of Political Science at UCLA

Ze'ev Emmerich is a PhD candidate in the Department of Politics, University of Cambridge

Richard Ned Lebow is the James O. Freedman Presidential Professor of Government at Dartmouth College

Seán Molloy is a Lecturer in Politics at the University of Edinburgh

Patricia Owens is a Senior Lecturer in Politics at Queen Mary, University of London

N. J. Rengger is a Professor of Political Theory and International Relations at the University of St. Andrews

Andrea Sangiovanni is a Lecturer in Philosophy, King's College London

William E. Scheuerman is a Professor of Political Science at Indiana University (Bloomington)

Roger Spegele is an Associate Professor of Politics at Monash University

Vibeke Schou Tjalve is a Senior Research Fellow at the Danish Institute for Military Studies, Copenhagen

Stephen Turner is Graduate Research Professor of Philosophy, University of South Florida

1

Introduction: Under an Empty Sky—Realism and Political Theory

Duncan Bell

Nobody loves a political realist.[1]

1.1. INTRODUCTION

Realism is a term with multiple meanings. It is employed in different and some-times antagonistic ways across the fields of art, literature, epistemology, jurispru-dence, metaphysics, moral philosophy, and politics. This volume explores realism as a mode of, or theme in, political thought. To be a realist, in everyday language, is to assume a certain attitude towards the world, to focus on the most salient dimensions of a given situation, whether or not they conform to our prefer-ences or desires. It implies the will, and perhaps even the ability, to grasp that 'reality'—however this might be understood—and not to be misled by ephemera. It also suggests wariness of easy answers, and of unreflective optimism. This sense carries over into its usage in politics, where it has resonant but ambivalent connotations.[2] Realism is frequently employed as a term to describe approaches that focus on the sources, modalities, and effects of power. As such, it is compatible with a wide range of positions, ranging from conservatism through to radical forms of political critique. The following chapters analyse some of the ways in which realism has shaped, and can shape, political theorizing about international relations.

Realist arguments stand at the intersection of two discrete, though often inter-secting, literatures. The first emerges from the field of International Relations (IR), and in particular the writings of the 'classical realists' of the mid-twentieth cen-tury, a group that includes E. H. Carr, Hans Morgenthau, and Reinhold Niebuhr.[3] The other literature is more nebulous, spreading across the history of Western political and philosophical reflection. Its motto could be, to paraphrase Bernard Williams, the 'priority of politics to morality'.[4] Here we find reference to a rich array of sources, most notably Thucydides, Machiavelli, Hobbes, Rousseau, Marx, Nietzsche, and Weber. Classical realism can be seen, in part, as an attempt to employ their insights to try and understand the horrors of twentieth-century (international) politics.

Realism is often associated with a crude form of *realpolitik*, a deeply conservative position that fetishizes the state and military power, and disdains progressive change in the international order. On this view, it can be seen as an outgrowth of the *machtpolitik* of the nineteenth-century German state theorists—the political philosophy translated into action by Bismarck.[5] For many political theorists, realism is the antithesis of ethical reflection, not a species of it. According to Marshall Cohen, realists 'argue that international relations must be viewed under the category of power and that the conduct of nations is, and should be, guided and judged exclusively by the amoral requirements of the national interest'. Jürgen Habermas, meanwhile, states that realism constitutes the 'quasi-ontological primacy of brute power over law'.[6] *Realpolitik* has, of course, had adherents in the corridors of power and in academia; Henry Kissinger, straddling both domains, exemplifies this position. But *realpolitik* does not exhaust 'realism'; indeed it has little in common with sophisticated understandings of it.

The idea that realism is amoral has been reinforced by the trajectory of post-war IR. Many contemporary IR scholars view their work as detachable from normative issues. Kenneth Waltz, a leading 'neorealist' scholar, pinpointed this separation in identifying and celebrating a transition from 'realist thought' to 'realist theory', the former shot through with normative concerns, the latter supposedly stripped of them.[7] This simplistic narrative implies both a conception of scientific progress and a division of academic labour. Following the 'behavioural revolution' of the 1960s, realism, it suggests, could finally move beyond its pre-scientific age and emerge into the bright sunlight of proper, normal science. IR theorists could then focus their energy on explaining the dynamics of the world as it is, while political theorists could be left to argue about how it should be.[8] This belief still structures much of the debate in IR theory. The post–Cold War fortunes of realism have been mixed. While they dominated IR during the Cold War, realists were forced onto the back-foot during the 1990s, chiefly as a result of their perceived inability to predict or adequately explain the collapse of the Soviet Union.[9] A sense of optimism pervaded public political debate. Globalization was purportedly transforming the international order, and the final triumph of democratic capitalism, even the 'end of history', was proclaimed.[10] In this 'new world order', realism was seen as morally bankrupt and intellectually flawed, its adherents defending, whether implicitly or explicitly, a world of cynical great power politics. It belonged to another, more primitive age. Yet the optimism soon faded. Genocide in Rwanda, vicious ethnic conflict in Somalia, East Timor, and the former Yugoslavia, and then, at the dawn of the new millennium, 9/11 and the subsequent wars in Afghanistan and Iraq, all illustrated the continuing vitality of state power and the horrors of political violence. The gross inequalities generated by neo-liberal capitalism exposed the dark side of globalization. Realism was partly rehabilitated, albeit in a more pluralistic form.[11] Meanwhile, the consistent realist hostility to the Iraq War rekindled interest in the normative dimensions of realism.[12]

Political Thought and International Relations addresses three main issues. First, it offers innovative interpretations of key classical realists, notably Carr, Morgenthau, and Niebuhr. As such, it contributes to a growing literature that has sought to elucidate the complex history of twentieth-century realist political thinking.[13] Second, it widens the lens through which realism is usually examined, identifying patterns of similarity and difference in the writings of Hannah Arendt, Martin Heidegger, and Leo Strauss, among others. Finally, a number of chapters explore how realism can contribute to contemporary debates in (international) political theory. In the remainder of this introduction, I discuss different interpretations of the realist tradition (Section 1.2), identify some of the key contexts for understanding the development of twentieth-century realist thought (Section 1.3), and discuss realism in relation to radical political theory and liberalism (Section 1.4).

1.2. REALISM AND POLITICAL THEORY: TRADITIONS

A maxim for the twenty-first century might well be to start not by fighting evil in the name of good, but by attacking the certainties of people who claim always to know where good and evil are to be found.[14]

There is no agreement over the scope and content of realism. Indeed William Scheuerman concludes Chapter 3 in this volume by asking whether, given the sheer diversity of positions it encompasses, the term 'realism' is a 'misnomer'.[15] This is an important question, albeit one that can be directed at many different kinds of political theorizing. Any sufficiently complex body of thought will be impossible to capture neatly and to delineate clearly from other positions. While they share much in common, including a sceptical sensibility, the varieties of realism discussed in this section, and in the following chapters, differ in many important respects. They exhibit a family resemblance, rather than cohering into a unified theoretical structure. If anything, realism is best understood negatively— in terms of what realists fear, what they seek to avoid, and what they criticize as dangerous or misguided. Suspicious of utopianism, and of optimistic visions of self and society, realists of different stripes concentrate on power, violence, and irreducible conflicts over meaning, interests, and value. But the conclusions they draw from this focus—and their political projects—vary greatly. This volume does not seek to identify an 'authentic' realism; instead, it probes some of the diverse expressions of realism found in modern political thought.

One common view of realism is that it embodies 'timeless wisdom' about politics. This wisdom is often traced back to the ancient world, and especially to the historian Thucydides.[16] It is a commonplace in IR that the 'Melian Dialogue' in Thucydides's *History of the Peloponnesian War* is an emblematic statement of the general principles of realism, and in particular the triumph of might over right, of power over justice. But more complex readings of Thucydides are available. Richard Ned Lebow, for example, interprets Thucydides as an exponent of Greek tragedy, and contends that the Melian Dialogue serves to *condemn* the folly of power politics. Thucydides insisted on the necessary interweaving of power and ethics, not their ineluctable alienation.[17] In Chapter 2 in this volume, Lebow argues that in the writings of Aeschylus, Sophocles, Thucydides, and Plato, we find a subtle recognition of the social bases of power and a sophisticated account of the conditions necessary for securing justice. They offer, he maintains, a more compelling way of understanding the relationship between self, community, and politics than does much contemporary social science. Realists today, then, would do well to return to their roots.

It is not only IR scholars who have turned to Thucydides for inspiration. Nietzsche once argued that Western philosophy went awry with Plato, and that it would have been better off following the example of Thucydides. This insight has been defended by two contemporary advocates of political realism, Bernard Williams and Raymond Geuss. Geuss argues that there were two main reasons why Nietzsche looked to Thucydides as an antidote to Plato. First, he had a much more sophisticated understanding of the plurality of human motivations. And second, he lacked Plato's naïve optimism, an optimism that has infected much of the history of Western philosophy:

First of all, traditional philosophers assumed that the world could be made cognitively accessible to us without remainder: it was in principle possible to come to know every part of the world as it really was. Second, they assumed that when the world was correctly understood, it would make moral sense to us. Third, the kind of 'moral sense' which the world made to us would be one that would show it to have *some* orientation toward the satisfaction of some basic, rational human desires or interests, that is, the world was not sheerly indifferent to or perversely frustrating of human happiness. Fourth, the world is set up so that for us to accumulate knowledge and use our reason as vigorously as possible will be good for us, and will contribute to making us happy. Finally it was assumed that there was a natural fit between the exercise of reason, the conditions of healthy individual human development, the demands of individuals for the satisfaction of their needs, interests, and basic desires, and human sociability. Nature, reason, and all human goods, including human virtues, formed a potentially harmonious whole.

In comprehensively rejecting this view, Thucydides conveyed an 'attitude toward the world which is realistic, values truthfulness, and is lacking in the shallow "optimism" of later philosophy'.[18] This 'attitude' links realists of different stripes.

Other scholars prefer to trace realism to the Renaissance or to the politics of early modern Europe; the anointed figures here are Machiavelli and Hobbes.[19] Realism, on this view, emerges out of the incessant warfare of the Italian city-states, and reaches maturity in the 'Westphalian' interstate system. As such, it is coeval with—and indeed a legitimation of—the modern international order. An alternative way of plotting this narrative is to view realism as a theory of modern politics in general, not simply of interstate relations. Michael Williams, for example, has identified the lineaments of a 'wilful realist' position in the thought of Hobbes, Rousseau, and Morgenthau. Seeking to map the 'politics of modernity', its proponents are united by three key elements: *scepticism* (the rational questioning of the limits of reason); *relationality* (a recognition that selves are dynamic and mutually constituted); and *power politics* (a focus on the pervasiveness of power, encompassing both its generative and dangerous dimensions). 'Wilful realism', Williams argues, 'is deeply concerned that a recognition of the centrality of power in politics does not result in the reduction of politics to pure power, and particularly to the capacity to wield violence.' Instead, it seeks 'a politics of limits that recognizes the destructive and productive dimensions of politics, and that maximizes its positive possibilities while minimizing its destructive potential'.[20] Realism, then, aims to tame and channel positively the inherent conflict that structures the human world.

Still others prefer to interpret political realism chiefly as an ideological product of the long twentieth century, albeit one that draws extensively on the philosophical (and psychological) insights of the 'Thucydidean' and 'Westphalian' readings.[21] Political realism is seen best, then, as a constellation of arguments that were shaped by, and responded to, the cultural, intellectual, and political forces of two major conjunctures: first, the murderous cataclysms that shook the world during the first half of the century, and second, the geopolitical dynamics of the Cold War, and above all the evolution of nuclear weapons. Realism, as such, is an ethico-political response to the visceral combination of industrial warfare, mass democracy, mechanized genocide, nationalism, global capitalism, and the development of unprecedented technologies of mass destruction—technologies that for the first time threaten the destruction of humanity as a whole, of exterminating the very possibility of species-being. Here the key figures shaping realist thought include Marx, Nietzsche, Weber, Freud, Kelsen, Mannheim, and Schmitt.

These narratives each offer a different—though not necessarily mutually exclusive—account of what realism embodies and the targets it challenges. In the most sophisticated expositions of the Thucydidean narrative, realism is a philosophical sensibility or disposition, an 'attitude towards the world'. Although the structure of the sensibility varies across time and space, and between individual thinkers, realists have in general tended to focus on the causes and effects of the irresolvable conflicts of meaning, value, and interest that structure human interaction, as well as expressing scepticism about the scope of reason and the motive power of morality in a hostile, disenchanted world. They insist, moreover, that political theorists and moral philosophers should attend first to the 'only certainly universal material of politics: power, powerlessness, fear, cruelty'. In short, the 'universalism of negative capabilities'.[22] This attitude is also a constitutive feature of the other two narratives, although they each add historical and political specificity. In the 'Westphalian' narrative, the focal point is the emergence of the sovereign state. What we might call the modernist narrative emphasizes elements only seen in fateful combination during the long twentieth century (and beyond). Moreover, it was during this period that 'realism' as a self-conscious body of political thought emerged, and it did so primarily, though certainly not exclusively, in the context of the disciplinary development of the modern human sciences, and especially IR.[23] This adds a further element of institutional novelty.

What are we to make of these contending narratives? In order to shed light on this question, it is useful to consider the idea of 'tradition' in the interpretation of political thought. We can distinguish between two ideal–typical conceptions, 'expansive' and 'restrictive'.[24] They differ along three main dimensions: abstraction; selectiveness; and agential self-understanding. An expansive conception of tradition, then, is characterized by:

1. The (very) high level of *abstraction* employed to link the specified elements—individual arguments, texts, and thinkers—of political thought across time and space. Thus, Thucydides, Machiavelli, Hobbes, and Weber can be seen as realists because, despite the profound differences between their ideas and the contexts in which they were produced, they all recognized the centrality of power and violence in political life, the fragility of moral norms, and the selfishness of human nature.

2. A high degree of *selectiveness* in appropriating arguments, texts, and thinkers. Proponents of expansive interpretations tend to focus narrowly on (limited) parts of the general corpus of arguments produced by the individuals or movements they seek to connect. Realists concentrate mainly on Thucydides's Melian Dialogue, elements of Machiavelli's *Il Principe*, Hobbes's discussion of the logic of the state of nature in *Leviathan*, and Weber's views on the state and the 'ethics of responsibility'.

3. A lack of interest in the *self-understandings* of historical agents. None of these thinkers saw themselves as belonging to a distinct 'realist' tradition, although they often felt affinity with, or were inspired by, at least some of the others (for example, Hobbes translated Thucydides).

Expansive traditions are, typically, retrospectively imposed analytical frames created to identify and align certain core themes, and link them across historical time and space. The key questions to ask of such narrative constructions are what purposes—ideological, pedagogical, theoretical—do they serve? And do they occlude more than they illuminate? These questions cannot be answered *a priori*.[25] Some expansive interpretations of realism, for example those elaborated by Richard Ned Lebow and Michael Williams, are based on careful close reading and offer subtle interpretations to support their case. But many attempts lack such subtlety, and instead represent crude appeals to authority or the unreflective repetition of scholarly dogma.

The modernist narrative is, of course, the interpretation that fits most closely with the restrictive conception of realism. At the core of this narrative stands what is now called (rather confusingly) 'classical realism'. This label encompasses a diverse group of thinkers who came to prominence in the mid-twentieth century, including the marxisant historian E. H. Carr, the émigré scholar Hans Morgenthau, the theologian Reinhold Niebuhr, the polymath Raymond Aron, and the diplomat-cum-scholar George Kennan.[26] They helped to shape the post-war study of international politics, providing some of the most influential—if not always the most sophisticated—articulations of the realist disposition in the twentieth century. It is to this topic that I now turn.

1.3. REALISM AND POLITICAL THEORY: CONTEXTS

The general tenor and tone of much mid-century political theorizing in the Anglo-phone world was profoundly influenced by the catastrophic impact of 'total war, totalitarianism, and the holocaust'.[27] German political experience and intellectual traditions played a central role in shaping the thought of the period. The study of political theory (and international relations) was redirected by the influx of émigré scholars, including Theodor Adorno, Leo Strauss, and Hannah Arendt. According to one's intellectual tastes, political theorizing then either began a long and painful descent or was positively reinvigorated by the infusion of innovative ideas.[28] IR was similarly affected. Classical realism was a discourse of disillusionment, motivated by the attempt to understand the horrors of the twentieth century. It represented a key element in the transformation of the human sciences in post-war America, a topic that is now the subject of a lively historical debate, albeit one in which IR plays little role.[29] This context is, however, vital for interpreting the evolution of post-war theorizing about international politics, for it illuminates both the concerns that motivated the realists and the methods they adopted.

While the classical realists differed over many issues, they were nevertheless united in their criticism of certain modes of theorizing politics, most notably forms of moralizing and legalistic liberalism. It was this so-called idealism that Carr had targeted in *The Twenty Years' Crisis* (1939), one of the founding documents of twentieth-century realism, although he also insisted on the necessity of dialectically combining 'utopianism' and 'realism' in any defensible account of politics.[30] The purported optimism of nineteenth and early twentieth-century liberals was, so the classical realists argued, not only naïve but also positively dangerous. The danger resided in both the blindness of liberals (of this kind) to the grim realities of power politics and the temptation—too often acted upon—to insist that liberal values should be universalized, and that peace and prosperity would result. This was, and is, a standard critique of liberal thought. Morgenthau saw this form of political myopia embodied in the 'nationalistic universalism' driving the foreign policies of both the United States and the Soviet Union. It was a dangerous mistake, he wrote, to identify 'the moral aspirations of a particular nation with the moral laws that govern the universe'.[31] A related concern, generated especially by the fate of democratic politics in Weimar, focused on the ostensible inability of liberalism to deal aggressively with anti-liberal forms of politics; once again, this was seen to flow from a profound failure to grasp the character of politics itself. In mid-twentieth century political thought, this was often characterized as the problem of 'relativism'. 'Decadent liberalism', as he labelled it, was a central theme in Morgenthau's deeply pessimistic *Scientific Man versus Power Politics* (1946). The shadow of Hitler haunted his dystopian vision. The dangers inhering in each liberal vice were amplified by the onset of the nuclear confrontation.

The arguments of Morgenthau and his contemporaries expressed a strain of historical pessimism, often couched in the language of tragedy.[32] This was a function, among other things, of the 'enduring presence of evil in all political action'.[33] Following Weber, and with Nietzschean undertones, much of his work can be seen as an attempt to map the difficulties (and even the impossibility) of escaping the disenchanted condition of the modern world. 'Nations', Morgenthau wrote once, 'meet under an empty sky from which the Gods have departed.'[34] The point of moral and political reflection was to identify the most appropriate ways of thinking and acting after the death of God and the end of illusions—in light, that is, of what Bernard Williams has called the 'negative narrative of Enlightenment'.[35] This was the subject of some of the most powerful (and desolate) political theorizing of the twentieth century, culminating in Adorno and Horkheimer's *Dialectic of Enlightenment* (1947).[36] There was always the danger that realism could descend into paralysing fatalism—something of which realists have at times been guilty, as too were the first generation of critical theorists[37]—but this need not be the case. In his contribution to this volume, Joshua Foa Dienstag explores the idea of pessimism. He identifies a 'pessimistic tradition' in modern thought, encompassing Schopenhauer, Nietzsche, and Freud, among others, and he probes the overlaps between this tradition and twentieth-century realism in IR. He argues that there are both clear similarities and significant differences between them. If anything, realists—and in particular neorealists—are not pessimistic enough. 'Pessimism should not disguise itself as realism nor should realism be insulted by means of pessimism. Rather, pessimism invites realism to extend its skepticism even further, to the point where even its own laws of anarchy are brought into question. Then and only then will we have a realism that is appropriately—realistically—pessimistic.'[38] Pessimism, Dienstag avers, can be liberating, and it remains a necessary attitude to adopt in a disenchanted universe.

The recent outpouring of scholarship on Morgenthau has painted a rich picture of the complexity of his thought, highlighting in particular the way in which his work was imprinted by the intellectual and political currents of the Weimar years. Yet while this act of intellectual recovery is most welcome, there is little agreement on the character of his political vision. We now have almost as many Morgenthaus as there are interpreters of him, and he has been presented as everything from an arch-conservative to a critical theorist. On the one hand, this should come as little surprise, for Morgenthau was a sophisticated thinker whose writing career spanned six decades, three languages, and two continents. It would be peculiar if we discovered absolute consistency in his views. But there is more to it than this, for as William Scheuerman notes, one of the chief problems with recent attempts to classify Morgenthau's thought—of seeking to identify the 'real' Morgenthau—is that scholars often do a 'disservice to the astonishingly creative and exploratory character' of much of his early work.[39] During the 1920s and 1930s in particular, Morgenthau was an intellectual magpie, attempting to grasp the dynamics of the international order with whatever theoretical tools seemed most promising at the time. We will search in vain for a singular interpretation of such an itinerant intellect. The best that can be done is to anatomize the structures of his thought at specific times, identifying the different vectors of influence, while attempting to track *both* the continuities and the ruptures in his thinking.

Philip Mirowski contends that Morgenthau translated the precepts of 'reactionary modernism' from interwar Germany into post-war American conservatism.[40] Following Jeffrey Herf, he argues that reactionary modernism was a complex of ideas that fused *Technik* and *Kultur*, the modernist fascination with the transformative powers of technology and conservative strains of nationalistic romanticism. It encompassed figures as diverse as Werner Sombart, Oswald Spengler, Martin Heidegger, Carl Schmitt, and Ernst Jünger, all of whom castigated individualism, materialism, parliamentarianism, and rationalism—in short, liberalism. Morgenthau was their heir.

There are two main problems with this intriguing line of argument. The first is that it does not help us to make sense of Morgenthau's own intellectual formation in Weimar. In Chapter 3 in this volume, William Scheuerman demonstrates how Morgenthau moved in left-wing circles during the 1920s and 1930s, developing a 'normatively sympathetic but socially critical interpretation of international law'. It was only after his move to the United States, Scheuerman continues, that Morgenthau's political thought lost its radical edge, becoming increasingly 'intellectually troublesome and politically conservative'.[41] The chief reason for this is that Morgenthau moved away from his previous attempt to develop a critical sociology of international law, and instead focused on the power-seeking propensity of individual humans; his realism then took 'its foundational bearings primarily from psychology and philosophical anthropology'. Post-war realism, concludes Scheuerman, 'was forced to pay a high price' for this move. Second, the 'reactionary modernist' argument underestimates the degree to which Morgenthau can be seen as a Weberian, a theme elucidated by Stephen Turner in Chapter 4. The reactionary modernists disdained the relativism, and the focus on means–ends rationality, that they associated with Weber.[42] Yet for Turner, Morgenthau was 'largely a consistent Weberian', and he argues that once this is understood it can clarify some 'puzzles about his thought, and enables us to correct some mis-impressions'. In particular, it sheds light on some of the key elements in Morgenthau's writings, including his conception of social scientific methodology, his understanding of the relationship between politics and ethics, and his focus on leadership and 'moral purpose' in politics. His obsession with leadership is, Turner suggests, 'perhaps the distinguishing mark of Morgenthau's realism, and the aspect of his thought that is at once the most compelling and challenging'.[43]

Weimar is not the only context important for understanding the development of classical realist theorizing. Theological concerns also played a role. The most significant figure in realist political theology is Reinhold Niebuhr—a thinker whose impact continues to resonate widely, especially in American political culture.[44] Niebuhr sought to develop a theology that was more praxis-oriented and worldly than that offered by the social gospel movement, while nevertheless avoiding the anti-liberal path trodden by Karl Barth and his followers.[45] Christian realism, often characterized in terms of Augustinian awareness of human finitude, retains a significant place in debate over international ethics, notably in the writings of Jean Bethke Elshtain.[46] Moreover, a number of important realists (including Morgenthau) drew on religious themes, while others can be seen as Christian political thinkers, including Herbert Butterfield and Martin Wight, the latter a powerful anatomist of power politics and a pacifist conscientious objector during World War II.[47] The religious sources of (certain forms of) realism provide a fertile and underdeveloped topic for study.

Vibeke Schou Tjalve argues in Chapter 10 that both Morgenthau and Niebuhr were exponents of 'enchanted scepticism'. In response to totalitarianism and the disenchantment of the world, they sought to 'initiate a spiritual public rebirth' comprising three main elements: 'a recovery of transcendent purpose in civic discourse; a redefinition of patriotism as deliberative dissent against conformist consensus; and finally, a reconstitution of leadership as the potential stimulus of agonistic and dissenting debate rather than stifled and uniform compromise.' Fearing that the loss of meaning heralded by the death of God eliminated the foundations for ethical action, and the resources necessary to defend liberal democracy, they argued for a public philosophy that reinscribed meaning in the world 'without lapsing into renewed delusions of grandeur'.[48] Tjalve suggests that the contemporary left has much to learn from this attempt.

If realism is understood as an 'attitude towards the world' of a truth-seeking kind, then some of the standard interpretations of realism (especially those prevalent in IR) lose plausibility. The most significant of these concerns the role of the state. Realism in IR, whether in its 'classical' or 'neo' guises, is routinely defined in terms of its state-centrism. For 'neorealists', the state is seen both as the central unit in world politics and as a unitary rational actor; indeed Deborah Boucoyannis suggests that this is 'the only assumption now shared by the multifarious versions of the theory'.[49] Yet this assumption does not capture the thinking of the leading classical realists; nor does it fit with realism as an 'attitude towards the world'. At certain times and in certain places, the state may be the most significant actor in world politics, but this may change. Failure to adapt to such change would represent a failure of *realism* about the world. It is arguable that realism today demands a frank recognition of the potentially catastrophic dangers presented by global climate change, and the development of radically new political institutions to face this crisis. It would also suggest that, given the prevailing structures of power in the international system, it will be extremely hard, even impossible, to motivate the necessary transformation. Yet the key point remains: realism is not theoretically committed to any particular type of political association. Morgenthau, for one, was alive to this issue, writing in the introduction to *Politics Among Nations* (1948) that '[n]othing in the realist position militates against the assumption that the present division of the political world into nation states will be replaced by units of a quite different character, more in keeping with the technical potentialities and the moral requirements of the contemporary world'.[50] The development of nuclear weapons provided the spur for classical realist thinking about the future of the modern state. Many of the leading realists grappled with the political consequences of this radical new technology, and some of them, including Herz and Morgenthau, argued that it demanded a fundamental rethinking of the value and purpose of the state. It was not uncommon in realist circles to argue, albeit hesitantly and ambivalently, that the state had been rendered obsolete, and that new transnational forms of political order—even a world state—were either necessary or inevitable.[51]

Chapters 5, 6, 7 and 8 by Seán Molloy, Patricia Owens, Nicholas Rengger, and Roger Spegele, respectively, also examine aspects of mid-twentieth century political thinking. Molloy dissects the divergent ethical visions elaborated by Carr and Morgenthau. He concludes that Carr was a 'pragmatist' who focused on the 'social construction of norms and ethics in international society', while Morgenthau, who was heavily critical of Carr's conception of ethics, insisted instead on a 'transcendent perspective on matters of political morality, a perspective located outside of politics and rooted in a moral philosophy of the lesser evil'.[52] Realism, on this view, is neither anti-moral nor does it presuppose a singular conception of ethical judgement. Patricia Owens grapples with the writings of Hannah Arendt, sparring partner, colleague, and friend of Morgenthau at Chicago. She argues that Arendt developed 'a form of "realism" in which attentiveness to reality itself and the cultivation of a character trait in which to face and enlarge one's sense of reality are ends in themselves with serious ethical implications'. Here she confronts one of the most important—but also most elusive—themes in assessing realist political thought: the character of the 'reality' to which realism must orient itself to deserve the name.[53] In Chapter 8 Nicholas Rengger addresses another Chicago professor, the ever-controversial Leo Strauss. He argues that Strauss was a realist in so far as he viewed war as a tragically ineliminable aspect of the human condition, but that he reached this conclusion via a route that marked his distance from the self-proclaimed realists. What differentiated him was chiefly the way in which he focused on particular types of regime, above all democracy.[54] Roger Spegele, meanwhile, turns to Martin Heidegger, one of the key intellectual influences on Arendt and Strauss. He discusses three main themes: the destructiveness of technology, the pervasiveness of tragedy, and the impossibility of adequately reconciling theory and practice. From this reading, inspired by Heidegger and echoed by themes in the work of Morgenthau, he argues for the need to formulate a 'compassionate' realism. Such a formulation 'makes capacious space for poetry (in the larger sense), classical political thought, history and commonsense...It is anti-theoretical and anti-metaphysical and insists on the need to draw "lessons" from history and the concrete doings of men and women rather than to construct "models" of human behaviour from which inferences are drawn'.[55]

1.4. THE POLITICS OF REALISM

There is no escaping that politics is about power and there is consequently no escaping that good political theory needs to give plausible accounts of what is entailed, in the broadest sense, by political thinking relevant to power.[56]

Realism is often seen as a form of conservatism. Many conservatives have indeed been realists, and it is certainly arguable that a coherent conservatism demands adherence to some form of realism. This is one of the reasons why the 'neoconservatives' look so strange from a traditional conservative perspective.[57] But it does not follow that all realists are conservative; realism—especially as disposition—is compatible with manifold political and ethical orientations. Realism is not (in any of its usual variants) a fully fledged political ideology, with coherent and determinate positions on a wide range of moral and political issues.[58] It does not offer a comprehensive alternative to liberalism, socialism, conservatism, social democracy, Marxism, or the plethora of hybrid ideological formations that dominate the contemporary political landscape.

Realism is also often seen as antithetical to liberalism. In terms of IR theory, this distinction is deeply problematic.[59] When it comes to political theory, it is hopelessly misguided. There is no antithesis between realism and liberalism *per se*. Realism may be incompatible with certain forms of liberal political theory, but many realists have been liberals of one sort or another, including Morgenthau, Niebuhr, Aron, and Herz. While they argued against what they routinely called 'utopianism' or 'idealism'—and sometimes, rather confusingly, simply 'liberalism'— they nevertheless defended liberal values and sought the flourishing and further development of liberal democratic states. Their liberalism was similar in form to that of Isaiah Berlin, Karl Popper, and Judith Shklar; it was, in Skhlar's words, chiefly a 'liberalism of fear'.[60] Jan-Werner Müller offers a succinct summary of this position: 'it was a liberalism that asked two famous Kantian questions—*Was kann ich wissen? Was sol ich tun?*—and changed the phrasing of the third: *Was muss ich fürchten?*'

Put differently, this liberalism began with what one might call an epistemological foundation, or, if you like, a 'politics of knowledge'—the question about the bases and limits of political knowledge. It then sought to advance a conception of political action that was informed by the knowledge about the limits of political knowledge; and, finally, it concentrated on the future dangers to be feared, and on avoidance, rather than positive projects...their concern was to avoid the *summum malum*, not the realization of any *summum bonum*.[61]

Morgenthau was deeply sceptical about the power of human reason to transcend the tragic character of politics. In *Scientific Man versus Power Politics*, he indicted many liberals for their purported belief that reason alone—expressed in what he saw as an unwarranted veneration of science—provided the means to solve the problems of modern politics.[62] This scepticism flowed from his critique of positivism, his hostility to the idea that politics could be understood and controlled by utilizing methods modelled on those used in the natural sciences.

Why have liberalism and realism so often been viewed as stark alternatives? Part of the answer lies in the disciplinary formation of IR; another aspect concerns the *type* of political theory that the classical realists elaborated. IR is a field which has been remarkably 'adept at creative forgetting'.[63] As such, we are often presented with highly distorted accounts of disciplinary history. Probably the most glaring example of this concerns the character of interwar international political thought. The standard account of this period, shaped by Carr's polemical critique, sees it as populated by deeply naïve 'idealists' who sought an end to war through the creation of international institutions, and who were proven catastrophically wrong by World War II. This story has shaped the self-image of the field ever since. While it is not without truth, it presents a crude caricature of the variety and richness of liberal internationalism.[64] This caricature has had a pernicious effect on how many IR theorists have come to understand the genealogy of the field, and hence the relationship between liberalism and realism.[65]

Realism itself has been a victim of disciplinary amnesia. Craig Murphy argues that contemporary radical approaches in IR have three main ('democratically inspired') precursors in the twentieth century: the *fin de siècle* anti-imperial radicalism of J. A. Hobson and his contemporaries; the interwar realism of Niebuhr and Carr, understood as an element of the 'international theory of the left'; and the early 1960s peace research programme. This radical realism was eclipsed during the Cold War, he suggests by the anti-democratic 'realism of the national-security experts'.[66] In Chapter 3 Scheuerman plots a similar trajectory for Morgenthau, identifying a move from a 'critical realist' position to a more conservative one. This transition, Scheuerman concludes, represents a theoretical 'missed opportunity' for those seeking to develop critical theories of international politics. But it represents an opportunity nevertheless.

A further reason why realism and liberalism are sometimes regarded as antithetical relates to the evolution—and self-image—of post-Rawlsian liberal political philosophy. Following the early lead of Rawls, its exponents tended to focus on the domestic dimensions of states, although in recent years 'global justice' has moved to the centre of debate. As Thomas Nagel writes, the 'need for workable ideas about the global or international case presents political theory with its most important current task'.[67] Many analytical philosophers regard political philosophy as 'a branch or application of *moral* philosophy'.[68] They have focused above all (though not exclusively) on the elaboration and justification of the principles necessary for living in a just society, whether domestic or global in scope. This has resulted in the dominance of a type of theorizing that Amartya Sen has labelled 'transcendental', concentrating as it does on 'identifying perfectly just societal arrangements'.[69] This vision has been tied to an account of the trajectory of political thought. It is, as Müller notes, an 'almost universally accepted narrative' about Anglophone political theory that the field was moribund, even dead, before it was resuscitated by the publication of Rawls's *A Theory of Justice* (1971).[70] This narrative—another example of creative amnesia—consigns the work of Adorno, Marcuse, Popper, Arendt, Voegelin, Hayek, Oakeshott, Berlin, Shklar, Wolin, and a host of other figures, to the dark ages. And the political thinking of the classical realists is relegated with them. Yet as R. G. Collingwood once wrote, in another context, '[w]e call them the dark ages, but all we mean is that we cannot see.'[71] In so far as none of these thinkers (and their followers) engaged in 'transcendental theorizing', or saw the primary role of political theory as the elaboration of theories of social justice, then the narrative is not wholly incorrect. But it is a fundamental mistake to equate or conflate political theory with one particular species of moral philosophy. Despite their many differences, the political theorists of the time—and many of their heirs today—tended to view the 'irreplaceable contribution' of political theorizing as highlighting 'the fundamental features of human life in general and political life in particular, exposing bad arguments, attacking seductive but inherently unrealizable ideological projects, standing guard over the integrity of the public realm, and clarifying the prevailing form of political discourse'. Most of them, moreover, 'thought that political philosophy was primarily concerned to understand rather than to prescribe, that it operated at a level which prevented it from recommending specific institutions and policies, and that it could never become a *practical* philosophy'.[72] This is the relevant intellectual milieu for interpreting the mode of political theorizing engaged in by many of the classical realists.

What, if anything, can realism contribute to contemporary (international) political theory? Is it anything more than a symptom of the 'age of extremes'?[73] One answer lies in opening up space for radical political thought. The emphasis on power has provided realism with a radical edge, and with the resources for forms of critical theorizing about society and international politics. A number of the classical realists attacked Marxism as a species of political thinking (in this way similar to liberalism) that sought to reduce politics to economic or social factors. In one way or another, most realists have argued for the autonomy, or at least the semi-autonomy, of the political.[74] Yet the parallels between Marxist modes of analysis and realism are also striking, and it should come as no surprise that they often intersect.[75] As one British Marxist historian recently wrote of John Mearsheimer's arch-realist *The Tragedy of Great Power Politics* (2001), the '[l]eft has more to learn from it than from any number of treatises on the coming wonders of global governance'.[76] A 'post-Marxist' realist account of international politics can be found in the work of Chantal Mouffe. Drawing on Schmitt and Derrida, Mouffe argues that cosmopolitan political theories cannot accommodate the global 'pluriverse', the cornucopia of antagonistic identities and affiliations that characterize contemporary global politics. The main problem with the 'diverse forms of cosmopolitanism is that they all postulate, albeit in different guises, the availability of a form of consensual governance transcending the political, conflict and negativity. The cosmopolitan project is therefore bound to deny the hegemonic dimension of politics.' Given this, it is necessary to 'pluralize hegemony'— to seek to eradicate or transcend it, she argues, is a fantasy—by creating an equilibrium between federated regional power blocs. This 'multipolar' world would be held together, in agonistic equilibrium, by the balance of power.[77] Similar themes can be seen in the writings of the self-professed realist Italian political philosopher Danilo Zolo.[78]

Chapters 11 and 12, by Ze'ev Emmerich and Andrea Sangiovanni, also investigate the relevance of the realist disposition for contemporary political theory, though they reach different conclusions. Emmerich examines the idea of a 'realistic spirit' which 'denotes an attitude characterised by sensitivity to the details of "surface phenomena" coupled with a propensity to accept the limits of theorisation, in our case, the limits of theorising about politics'. He argues that realism, on this view, requires us to regard humans as 'historical beings', in a manner alien to Rawls and Habermas, and he concludes by suggesting that any adequate political theory must be able to plot the complex interplay of sentiment and reason in capitalist modernity.[79] Sangiovanni, on the other hand, offers a robust defence of the 'project of normative political theory'. He assesses the various criticisms levelled by realists—and in particular Bernard Williams—against the (basically Rawlsian) project, and argues that many of them fail. However, he continues, the 'insights' embedded in the liberalism of fear can 'help us to rethink how to go about doing' normative theory. Due to the fundamental importance of history and context, it is a mistake—one commonly found in contemporary political philosophy—to 'think of institutions and practices solely as instruments for the realization of moral values whose justification is given independently of them'.[80] Instead it is necessary to focus more thoroughly on the relationship between political practice and ethical judgement.

Another question that has figured prominently in recent scholarship concerns the relationship between realism and republican political theory. Ian Shapiro has defended a modified version of containment in foreign policy.[81] He argues that there are pragmatic reasons for adopting such a strategy, but he also offers a principled defence, stating that containment 'flows naturally out of the democratic understanding of nondomination'. Containment is inherently anti-imperial and for 'centuries it has been a staple of republican political theory that empires invariably become overextended and collapse. Kennan and the other architects of containment built on this intellectual legacy, however unwittingly.' He also insists that this view is compatible with cosmopolitanism.[82] Here the republicanism is muted, even unconscious. Michael Williams, meanwhile, has suggested that Morgenthau's thought exhibits many of the characteristics defining the 'Atlantic republican tradition'. Morgenthau, he contends, exhibits 'a keen concern with the maintenance of a vital, democratic public sphere as the basis for a politics of responsibility, [that seeks] to foster and support [the] construction of a vibrant and yet self-limiting politics in both domestic and foreign policy'. Virtue, prudence, balance, and the pursuit of the common good shape his political thought. For Daniel Deudney, on the other hand, realism (like liberalism) is but a fragment of an older, more complex body of republican political theory, a mode of thinking about the organization of politics which has its roots in ancient Greece but which was profoundly transformed by the American revolution. Realism, on this view, is insightful but radically incomplete.[83]

In Chapter 10 Tjalve also highlights the republican dimensions of Niebuhr and Morgenthau. She maintains that while some realists, like Kennan, defended a stifling form of communitarianism, Morgenthau and Niebuhr developed positions that were participatory, individualist, and pluralistic in orientation. They challenged conformity and nationalism, elaborating a conception of patriotism that placed dissent and criticism at its core. Morgenthau practised what he preached, most notably in relation to the Vietnam War, of which he was an early, consistent, and vitriolic critic.[84] He thought that the role of the intellectual was to uphold an 'ethos of permanent criticism'.[85] Echoes of this position can be seen in the widespread realist opposition to the war in Iraq. Realism provided critical intellectual ammunition for those seeking inspiration for a plausible alternative to the imperialism of the Bush administration, as well as tools to analyse the power political dynamics involved.[86] The disastrous course of the war also led some neoconservatives—both repentant and practising—to drape themselves in the rhetorical cloak of realism.[87] These developments highlight both the malleability of the term realism and its powerful rhetorical force.

We can, then, discern a variety of different realist orientations. One defends the status quo, prioritizing great power stability and order above the pursuit of other values. It is a form of international conservatism, insisting that the immutable character of politics renders significant change undesirable, even dangerous. *Realpolitik* flows from this position. Liberal realism also focuses on the importance of order, but does so to defend the conditions necessary for the flourishing of liberal states in a brutally competitive world. It strives to balance 'Lockean' politics on 'Hobbesian' foundations—a delicate task, always vulnerable in the face of the ineliminable dangers of political life. It can be seen as an international variant of the 'liberalism of fear', although it is in principle compatible with a more fully fledged defence of social democracy than that offered by Shklar. A third, more radical understanding of realism does not tie it to any particular political project, but instead focuses chiefly on unmasking power relations, and exposing self-interest, hypocrisy, and folly, whether in domestic or international politics. This is realism as a critical 'attitude towards the world'—a sceptical disposition about the scope of reason and the influence of morality in a world in which power, and the relentless pursuit of power, is a pervasive feature. It can be seen as an expression of the 'hermeneutics of suspicion'. Morgenthau, for one, oscillated between all three positions. The key question for contemporary realists is whether it is possible to develop coherent and compelling—if not morally edifying—political visions given the intellectual resources available, and, if not, what might be done to improve upon the attempts of the past.

ACKNOWLEDGEMENTS

I thank Ze'ev Emmerich, Nicholas Rengger, Casper Sylvest, Sarah Fine and Stephen Turner for their helpful comments on this essay.

NOTES

1. Robert Gilpin, 'Nobody Loves a Political Realist', *Security Studies*, 5 (1996), pp. 3–28.
2. See, for example, the discussion in R. N. Berki, *On Political Realism* (London: J. M. Dent, 1981), ch. 1.
3. Following convention, I refer to the academic field as International Relations (IR), and the object of study as international relations.

4. Williams, In the Beginning was the Deed: Realism and Moralism in Political Argument, ed. Geoffrey Hawthorn (Princeton: Princeton University Press, 2005), pp. 1–18. See also, Andrea Sangiovanni, 'Justice and the Priority of Politics to Morality', *Journal of Political Philosophy*, 16 (2008), pp. 137–64.

5. On which see Friedrich Meinecke, *Machiavellism: The Doctrine of Raison D'etat and its Place in Modern History*, trans. Douglas Scott (London: Routledge, 1957), Bk III.

6. Cohen, 'Moral Skepticism and International Relations', in Charles Beitz, Marshall Cohen, and A. John Simmons (eds.), *International Ethics* (Princeton: Princeton University Press, 1985), p. 4; Habermas, *The Divided West*, trans. Ciaran Cronin (Cambridge: Polity, 2006), p. 161.

7. Waltz, 'Realist Thought and Neorealist Theory', *Journal of International Affairs*, 44 (1990), pp. 21–38. Cf. Stacie Goddard and Daniel Nexon, 'Paradigm Lost? Reassessing *Theory of International Politics*', *European Journal of International Relations*, 11 (2005), pp. 9–61.

8. For the general context, see the essays in Robert Adcock, Mark Bevir, and Shannon Stimson (eds.), *Modern Political Science: Anglo-American Exchanges Since 1880* (Princeton: Princeton University Press, 2006); and George Steinmetz (ed.), *The Politics of Method in the Human Sciences: Positivism and its Epistemological Others* (Durham: Duke University Press, 2005). On some of the philosophical problems with this view, see Patrick Thaddeus Jackson, 'Foregrounding Ontology: Dualism, Monism, and IR Theory', *Review of International Studies*, 34 (2008), pp. 129–53.

9. Richard Ned Lebow and Thomas Risse-Kappen (eds.), *International Relations Theory and the End of the Cold War* (New York: Columbia University Press, 1996). Cf. Michael Cox, 'Hans J. Morgenthau, Realism, and the Rise and Fall of the Cold War', in Michael Williams (ed.), *Realism Reconsidered: The Legacy of Hans J. Morgenthau in International Relations* (Oxford: Oxford University Press, 2007), pp. 166–95.

10. See especially Francis Fukuyama, *The End of History and the Last Man* (New York: Free Press, 1992). See also, Arthur Melzer, Jerry Weinberger, and M. Richard Zinman (eds.), *History and the Idea of Progress* (Ithaca: Cornell University Press, 1995).

11. Richard Ned Lebow, 'Texts, Paradigms, and Political Change', in Williams (ed.), *Realism Reconsidered*, pp. 241–69. On developments in realist theorizing, see, for example, Stephen Brooks, 'Dueling Realisms', *International Organization*, 51 (1997), pp. 445–77. Realism in IR is today divided between a variety of schools, many of them overlapping, including 'offensive', 'defensive', and 'neo-classical' variants. For a sampling, see Michael E. Brown, Sean Lynn-Jones, and Steven Miller (eds.), *The Perils of Anarchy: Contemporary Realism and International Security* (Cambridge, MA: MIT Press, 1995).

12. For an illustrative example, see the section on 'Realism Then and Now' published in the critical theory journal *Constellations* in December 2007.

13. On the intellectual history of realism, see Campbell Craig, *Glimmer of a New Leviathan: Total War in the Realism of Niebuhr, Morgenthau, and Waltz* (New York: Columbia University Press, 2003); W. D. Clinton (ed.), *The Realist Tradition and Contemporary International Relations* (Baton Rouge: LSU Press, 2007); Benjamin Frankel (ed.), *Roots of Realism* (London: Frank Cass, 1996); Stefano Guzzini, *Realism in International Relations and International Political Economy: The Continuing Story of a Death Foretold* (London: Routledge, 1998); Jonathan Haslam, *No Virtue Like Necessity: Realist Thought in International Relations since Machiavelli* (London: Yale University Press, 2002); Richard Ned Lebow, *The Tragic Vision of Politics: Ethics, Interests, and Orders* (Cambridge: Cambridge University Press, 2003); Seán Molloy,

The Hidden History of Realism: A Genealogy of Power Politics (Basingstoke: Palgrave, 2006); Alistair Murray, *Reconstructing Realism: Between Power Politics and Cosmopolitan Ethics* (Edinburgh: Keele University Press, 1997); Joel Rosenthal, *Righteous Realists: Political Realism, Responsible Power, and American Culture in the Nuclear Age* (Baton Rouge: LSU Press, 1986); Michael Joseph Smith, *Realist Thought from Weber to Kissinger* (Baton Rouge: LSU Press, 1986); Roger Spegele, *Political Realism in International Theory* (Cambridge: Cambridge University Press, 1996); Vibeke Schou Tjalve, *Realist Strategies of Republican Peace: Niebuhr, Morgenthau, and the Politics of Patriotic Dissent* (Basingstoke: Palgrave, 2008); and Michael C. Williams, *The Realist Tradition and the Limits of International Relations* (Cambridge: Cambridge University Press, 2005).

14. Tzetvan Todorov, *Hope and Memory: Reflections on the Twentieth Century*, trans. David Bellos (London: Atlantic Books, 2003), p. 195.

15. Scheuerman, 'A Theoretical Missed Opportunity?', p. 57.

16. Barry Buzan, 'The Timeless Wisdom of Realism', in Ken Booth, Steve Smith, and Marysia Zalewski (eds.), *International Theory: Positivism and Beyond* (Cambridge: Cambridge University Press, 1996), pp. 47–65.

17. Lebow, *The Tragic Vision of Politics*, chs. 3–4. For cogent accounts of Thucydides as a realist, see David Boucher, *Political Theories of International Relations* (Oxford: Oxford University Press, 1998), chs. 2–3; and Michael Doyle, *Ways of War and Peace: Realism, Liberalism, and Socialism* (New York: W. W. Norton, 1997), Pt. I. Thucydides represents realism in Michael Walzer, *Just and Unjust Wars: A Moral Argument with Historical Illustrations* (New York: Basic Books, 1977), ch. 1. On the genealogy of realism, see also R. W. Dyson, *Natural Law and Political Realism in the History of Political Thought: Volume 1, From the Sophists to Machiavelli* (New York: Peter Lang, 2005).

18. Geuss, 'Thucydides, Nietzsche, and Williams', in his *Outside Ethics* (Princeton: Princeton University Press, 2005), pp. 223 and 225 (italics in original). Geuss notes that Nietzsche's most highly praised trait was '*Tatsachen-Sinn*', a 'sense for the facts' (p. 220). See also Williams, *Shame and Necessity* (Berkeley: University of California Press, 1993), pp. 163–4; Geuss, *Philosophy and Real Politics* (Princeton: Princeton University Press, 2008); and John Dunn, *The Cunning of Unreason: Making Sense of Politics* (London: Harper Collins, 2000).

19. See, for example, Haslam, *No Virtue Like Necessity*. Hobbes stands in as the archetypical realist in Charles Beitz, *Political Theory and International Relations* (Princeton: Princeton University Press, 1979), Pt. I. Cf. Noel Malcolm, 'Hobbes's Theory of International Relations', in his *Aspects of Hobbes* (Oxford: Oxford University Press, 2002), pp. 432–57. On the interpenetration of the modern state and the global capitalist economy, see Istvan Hont, *Jealousy of Trade: International Competition and the Nation-State in Historical Perspective* (Cambridge, MA: Harvard University Press, 2005).

20. Williams, *The Realist Tradition and the Limits of International Relations*, p. 7.

21. Nicholas Rengger, *International Relations, Political Theory, and the Problem of Order: Beyond International Relations Theory?* (London: Routledge, 2000), pp. 39–40; and Molloy, 'E. H. Carr vs. Hans J. Morgenthau', p. 83 in this volume. This narrative is nearest to my own position.

22. Bernard Williams, 'The Liberalism of Fear', *In the Beginning was the Deed*, p. 59.

23. On the origins of the American social sciences, see Thomas Haskell, *The Emergence of Professional Social Science: The American Social Science Association and the Nineteenth-Century Crisis of Authority* (Urbana: University of Illinois Press, 1977);

and Dorothy Ross, *The Origins of American Social Science* (Cambridge: Cambridge University Press, 1991). On political science, see Adcock and Bevir (eds.), *Modern Political Science*; Nicolas Guilhot (ed.), *The Invention of International Relations Theory* (forthcoming); John Gunnell, *Imagining the American Polity: Political Science and the Discourse of Democracy* (Philadelphia: Pennsylvania State University Press, 2004); and Brian Schmidt, *The Political Discourse of Anarchy: A Disciplinary History of International Relations* (Albany: SUNY Press, 1998). The British context had its own peculiarities, shaded by the memories of appeasement: Ian Hall, 'Power Politics and Appeasement: Political Realism in British International Thought, c. 1935–1955', *British Journal of Politics and International Relations*, 8 (2006), pp. 174–92.

24. For further discussion, see Duncan Bell, *On Liberalism and Empire* (Princeton: Princeton University Press, forthcoming). For related commentary, see John Gunnell, 'The Myth of Tradition', *American Political Science Review*, 72 (1978), pp. 122–34; and Renee Jeffrey, 'Tradition as Invention: The "Traditions Tradition" and the History of Ideas in International Relations Theory', *Millennium*, 34 (2005), pp. 57–84.

25. The answers given to these questions will also depend, crucially, on the method of historical interpretation adopted. 'Contextualist' thinkers, for example, are likely to be wary of claims about transhistorical traditions, while Straussians posit them as the necessary foundation for mature reflection on politics. For the former position, see especially Quentin Skinner, *Visions of Politics, Vol. 1: Regarding Method* (Cambridge: Cambridge University Press, 2002). For a Straussian reading of the history of international thought, see Peter Ahrensdorf and Thomas Pangle, *Justice among Nations: On the Moral Basis of Power and Peace* (Lawrence: University of Kansas Press, 1999). On Strauss and realism, see Nicholas Rengger's Chapter in this volume.

26. Other classical realists include Arnold Wolfers, Georg Schwarzenberger, Nicholas Spykman, Walter Lippmann, Martin Wight, and John Herz. Some of these scholars are long overdue a scholarly re-examination. For example, John Herz, an émigré German, has received surprisingly little attention. Influential in IR for his work on the 'security dilemma', he was a self-declared 'liberal realist', a pioneer in the study of environmental political theory and 'human security', and an early social constructivist. See Herz, *Political Realism and Political Idealism: A Study in Theories and Realities* (Chicago: University of Chicago Press, 1951); and Herz, *International Politics in the Atomic Age* (New York: Columbia University Press, 1959). See also Peter Stirk, 'John H. Herz: Realism and the Fragility of the International Order', *Review of International Studies*, 31 (2005), pp. 285–306; Christian Hacke and Jana Puglierin, 'John H. Herz: Balancing Utopia and Reality', *International Relations*, 21 (2007), pp. 367–82; and Casper Sylvest, 'John H. Herz and the Resurrection of Classical Realism', unpublished paper, University of Southern Denmark, January 2008.

27. Ira Katznelson, *Desolation and Enlightenment: Political Knowledge after Total War, Totalitarianism, and the Holocaust* (New York: Columbia University Press, 2003).

28. For the story of declension, see John Gunnell, *The Descent of Political Theory: The Genealogy of an American Vocation* (Chicago: University of Chicago Press, 1993); and Gunnell, *Imagining the American Polity*, ch. 6. See also Robert Adcock and Mark Bevir, 'The Remaking of Political Theory', in Adcock and Bevir (eds.), *Modern*

Political Science, pp. 209–33. On the intellectual émigrés, see Bernard Bailyn and Donald Fleming (eds.), *The Intellectual Migration: Europe and America, 1930–1960* (Cambridge, MA: Harvard University Press, 1969); and Jean-Michel Palmier, *Weimar in Exile: The Anti-Fascist Emigration in Europe and America*, trans. David Fernbach (London: Verso, 2006).

29. For an excellent overview, see Joel Isaac, 'The Human Sciences in Cold War America', *Historical Journal*, 50 (2007), pp. 725–46.

30. Carr, *The Twenty Years' Crisis, 1919–39* (London: Macmillan, 1939). Carr's brief defence of appeasement was dropped in the 1946 edition. On Carr, see Jonathan Haslam, *The Vices of Integrity: E. H. Carr, 1892–1982* (London: Verso, 1999); Charles Jones, *E. H. Carr and International Relations: A Duty to Lie* (Cambridge: Cambridge University Press, 1998); Michael Cox (ed.), *E. H. Carr: A Critical Appraisal* (Basingstoke: Palgrave, 2000), and Molloy's Chapter 5 in this volume.

31. Morgenthau, *Politics among Nations: The Struggle for Power and Peace* (New York: Knopf, 1948), p. 10.

32. For a discussion of tragedy, see Lebow, *The Tragic Vision of Politics*; and the exchange between Lebow, Rengger, Meryvn Frost, James Mayall, J. Peter Euben, and Chris Brown in vols. 17 (2003), 19 (2005), and 21 (2007) of *International Relations*. See also Roger Spegele's Chapter 7 in this volume.

33. Morgenthau, *Scientific Man vs. Power Politics* (Chicago: University of Chicago Press, 1946), pp. 201–2. In Chapter 4 in this volume (p. 64), Stephen Turner suggests that Morgenthau's book can be seen as a 'characteristic emigration document'.

34. Morgenthau, *Politics Among Nations*, p. 249.

35. Williams, 'There are Many Kinds of Eyes', in Williams, *A Sense of the Past: Essays in the History of Philosophy*, ed. Myles Burnyeat (Princeton: Princeton University Press, 2007), p. 329. The impact of Nietzsche on Morgenthau's thought is highlighted in Frei, *Hans J. Morgenthau*, yet it is hard to specify with any precision. He owed a far clearer debt to Weber. See here Williams, *Realism and the Limits of International Relations*; Tarak Barkawi, 'Strategy as a Vocation: Weber, Morgenthau, and Modern Strategic Studies', *Review of International Studies*, 24 (1998), pp. 159–84; Stephen Turner and G. O. Mazur, 'Morgenthau as a Weberian Methodologist', *European Journal of International Relations* (forthcoming); and Turner's Chapter 4 in this volume.

36. Theodor Adorno and Max Horkheimer, *Dialectic of Enlightenment*, trans. John Cumming (London: Verso, 1999 [1947]). For an interesting analysis of the wider philosophical engagement with evil, see Susan Neiman, *Evil in Modern Thought: An Alternative History of Philosophy* (Princeton: Princeton University Press, 2002), esp. ch. 4. See also, Richard J. Bernstein, *Radical Evil: A Philosophical Interrogation* (Cambridge: Polity, 2002). In certain respects, classical realism can be seen as an attempt to grapple with the problem of evil, exemplified in the horrors of the twentieth century.

37. Simone Chambers comments on the 'pessimistic immobility' of early critical theory in 'The Politics of Critical Theory', in Fred Rush (ed.), *The Cambridge Companion to Critical Theory* (Cambridge: Cambridge University Press, 2004), p. 229.

38. Dienstag, 'Pessimistic Realism and Realistic Pessimism', p. 173. See also, Dienstag, *Pessimism: Philosophy, Ethic, Spirit* (Princeton: Princeton University Press, 2006).

39. Scheuerman, 'A Theoretical Missed Opportunity?', p. 43.

40. Mirowski, 'Realism and Neoliberalism: From Reactionary Modernism to Postwar Conservatism', in Guilhot (ed.), *The Invention of International Relations Theory*. See Jeffrey Herf, *Reactionary Modernism: Technology, Culture and Politics in Weimar and the Third Reich* (Cambridge: Cambridge University Press, 1984).

41. Scheuerman, 'A Theoretical Missed Opportunity', p. 56. Scheuerman notes that Morgenthau penned a scathing (unpulished) attack on Jünger's *Deutschen Kriegsphilosophie* in 1931 (p. 42). On Morgenthau and international law, see also Oliver Jütersonke, 'Hans J. Morgenthau on the Limits of Justiciability in International Law', *Journal of the History of International Law*, 8 (2006), pp. 181–211; Jütersonke, 'The Image of Law in *Politics Among Nations*', in Williams (ed.), *Realism Reconsidered*, pp. 93–117; and Koskeniemmi, *The Gentle Civilizer of Nations*, ch. 6.

42. See also David Cooper, 'Reactionary Modernism', in Anthony O'Hear (ed.), *German Philosophy Since Kant* (Cambridge: Cambridge University Press, 1999), pp. 291–304. The general realist distrust of technology is discussed in Rosenthal, *Righteous Realists*, pp. 154–68.

43. Turner, 'Hans J. Morgenthau and the Legacy of Max Weber', pp. 66, 79.

44. As political theorist William Galston has argued, in the context of the war on Iraq, '[a]fter a period of neglect, Reinhold Niebuhr is the man of the hour.' During the presidential election campaign of 2007–8, Hilary Clinton, John McCain, and Barack Obama all declared that they had been influenced by Niebuhr's ideas. Benedicta Cipolla, 'Reinhold Niebuhr is Unseen Force in 2008 Election', *The Pew Forum on Religion and Public Life: Religion News*, 27 September 2007.

45. I thank Nicholas Rengger for discussion on this point. From a vast literature on Niebuhr, see Richard W. Fox, *Reinhold Niebuhr: A Biography* (New York: Pantheon, 1985); Charles C. Brown, *Niebuhr and His Age: Reinhold Niebuhr's Prophetic Role and Legacy* (Harrisburg: Trinity Press, 2002); and Robin Lovin, *Reinhold Niebuhr and Christian Realism* (Cambridge: Cambridge University Press, 1995).

46. Elshtain, *Just War Against Terror: The Burden of American Power in a Violent World* (New York: Basic Books, 2003); Elshtain, *New Wine in Old Bottles: International Politics and Ethical Discourse* (Notre Dame: University of Notre Dame Press, 1998); and Elshtain, *Augustine and the Limits of Politics* (Notre Dame: University of Notre Dame Press, 1995). Cf. 'Forum: Jean Bethke Elshtain's *Just War Against Terror*', *International Relations*, 21 (2007).

47. Ian Hall, 'History, Christianity and Diplomacy: Sir Herbert Butterfield and International Relations', *Review of International Studies*, 28 (2002), pp. 719–36; and Hall, *The International Thought of Martin Wight* (Basingstoke: Palgrave, 2006). On religion and realism, see also Charles Jones, 'Christian Realism and the Foundations of the English School', *International Relations*, 17 (2003), pp. 371–87; Michael Loriaux, 'The Realists and Saint Augustine: Skepticism, Psychology, and Moral Action in International Relations Thought', *International Studies Quarterly*, 36 (1992), pp. 401–20; and Murray, *Reconstructing Realism*.

48. Tjalve, 'Realism and the Politics of (Dis)Enchantment', p. 182.

49. Boucoyannis, 'The International Wanderings of a Liberal Idea, or Why Liberals Can Learn to Stop Worrying and Love the Balance of Power', *Perspectives on Politics*, 5 (2007), p. 713.

50. Morgenthau, *Politics among Nations: The Struggle for Power and Peace*, 6th edn. (New York: Knopf, 1985 [1948]), p. 10.

51. Craig, *Glimmer of a New Leviathan*; Daniel Deudney, *Bounding Power: Republican Security Theory from the Polis to the Global Village* (Princeton: Princeton University

Press, 2005), Pt. III. For the general context, see Paul Boyer, *By the Bombs Early Light: American Thought and Culture at the Dawn of the Atomic Age* (New York: Pantheon, 1985); and Duncan Bell and Joel Isaac (eds.), *The Cold War in Pieces* (forthcoming).

52. Molloy, 'E. H. Carr versus Hans Morgenthau', p. 83.

53. One answer has been the transhistorical reality of 'human nature', a theme commonly associated with classical realism. For Jack Donnelly, Morgenthau's focus on 'human nature' exemplifies a 'biological' strain of realism. Donnelly, *Realism and International Relations* (Cambridge: Cambridge University Press, 2000), ch. 2. However, this is misleading as the conception of human nature found among realists was very rarely strictly biological. In Morgenthau's case, it was (arguably) derived from Nietzsche and Freud; for Niebuhr, it was theological. It is an important question as to whether a thick account of human nature—or perhaps, in Arendtian terms, the human condition—is necessary for a coherent realist political theory. Cf. Annette Freyberg-Inan, *What Moves Man: The Realist Theory of International Relations and its Judgement of Human Nature* (Albany: SUNY Press, 2004); Ulrich Enemark Petersen, 'Breathing Nietzsche's Air: New Reflection on Morgenthau's Concepts of Power and Human Nature', *Alternatives*, 24 (1999), pp. 83–118; Brian Leiter, 'Classical Realism', *Philosophical Issues*, 11 (2001), pp. 244–67; and Robert Schuett, 'Freudian Roots of Political Realism: The Importance of Sigmund Freud to Hans J. Morgenthau's Theory of International Power Politics', *History of the Human Sciences*, 20 (2007), pp. 53–78.

54. On the similarities and differences between Strauss and realism, see also Michael Williams, 'The Neoconservative Challenge in International Relations Theory', *European Journal of International Relations*, 11 (2005), pp. 307–37.

55. Spegele, 'Towards a More Reflective Realism', p. 123.

56. Michael Freeden, 'What Should the "Political" in Political Theory Explore?' *Journal of Political Philosophy*, 13 (2005), p. 116. Freeden argues that most political theorists, and especially analytic liberals, 'shy away from exploring and understanding power'.

57. Williams, 'The Neoconservative Challenge in International Relations Theory'. For a conservative realist riposte, see Jonathan Clarke and Stefan Halper, *America Alone: The Neo-Conservatives and the Global Order* (Cambridge: Cambridge University Press).

58. For a discussion of modern ideologies, see Michael Freeden, *Ideologies and Political Theory: A Conceptual Approach* (Oxford: Oxford University Press, 1996), Part I. On the normative indeterminacy of contemporary IR realism, see Duncan Bell, 'Political Realism and Global Justice', working paper, University of Cambridge, January 2008. To suggest that something is normatively indeterminate does not, of course, mean that it lacks a normative dimension.

59. Boucoyannis, 'The International Wanderings of a Liberal Idea'; Deudney, *Bounding Power*.

60. Shklar, 'The Liberalism of Fear' [1989], in Stanley Hoffmann (ed.), *Political Thought and Political Thinkers* (Chicago: University of Chicago Press, 1998), pp. 3–28; Bernard Yack (ed.), *Liberalism Without Illusions: Essays on Liberal Theory and the Political Vision of Judith N. Skhlar* (Chicago: University of Chicago Press, 1996); and Williams, 'The Liberalism of Fear'. Cf. Corey Robin, *Fear: The History of a Political Idea* (Oxford: Oxford University Press, 2004), pp. 144–52.

61. Müller, 'Fear and Freedom: On "Cold War Liberalism"', *European Journal of Political Theory*, 7 (2008), p. 48, and Sangiovanni's Chapter 12 in this volume.

62. For commentary, see William Scheuerman, 'Was Morgenthau a Realist? Revisiting *Scientific Man versus Power Politics*', *Constellations*, 14 (2007), pp. 506–30.

63. Mark Neufeld, 'What's Critical about Critical International Relations Theory', in Richard Wyn Jones (ed.), *Critical Theory and World Politics* (Boulder: Lynne Rienner, 2001), p. 135.

64. On interwar thought, see Lucian Ashworth, *Creating International Studies: Angell, Mitrany, and the Liberal Tradition* (Aldershot: Ashgate, 1999); Casper Sylvest, *Making Progress? British Liberal Internationalism 1880–1930* (Manchester: Manchester University Press, forthcoming); Schmidt, *The Political Discourse of Anarchy*; and David Long and Peter Wilson (eds.), *Thinkers of the Twenty Years' Crisis: Interwar Idealism Re-assessed* (Oxford: Clarendon, 1995). See also, Duncan Bell, 'Political Theory and the Functions of Intellectual History', *Review of International Studies*, 29 (2003), pp. 151–60.

65. The caricature is reiterated in John Mearsheimer, 'E. H. Carr vs. Idealism: The Battle Rages On', *International Relations*, 19 (2005), pp. 139–52.

66. Craig Murphy, 'Critical Theory and the Democratic Impulse: Understanding a Century-Old Tradition', in Wyn Jones (ed.), *Critical Theory and World Politics*, pp. 61–78. See also William Scheuerman, 'Realism and the Left: The Case of Hans Morgenthau', *Review of International Studies*, 34 (2008), pp. 5–27; Scheuerman's Chapter 3 in this volume; and Richard Falk, 'The Critical Realist Tradition and the Demystification of State Power: E. H. Carr, Hedley Bull and Robert W. Cox', in Stephen Gill (ed.), *Innovation and Transformation in International Studies* (Cambridge: Cambridge University Press, 1997), pp. 39–55. On the democratic potential of realism, see also Alan Gilbert, *Must Global Politics Constrain Democracy? Great Power Realism, the Democratic Peace, and Democratic Internationalism* (Princeton: Princeton University Press, 1999).

67. Nagel, 'The Problem of Global Justice', *Philosophy & Public Affairs*, 33 (2005), p. 113.

68. A. John Simmons, *Political Philosophy* (Oxford: Oxford University Press, 2007), p. 2 (italics in original); Williams, 'Realism and Moralism in Political Theory'; and Wayne Norman, 'Inevitable and Unacceptable? Methodological Rawlsianism in Contemporary Anglo-American Political Philosophy', *Political Studies*, 46 (1998), pp. 276–94.

69. Sen, 'What do We Want from a Theory of Justice?' *The Journal of Philosophy*, ciii (2006), p. 216. Cf. Sangiovanni's Chapter 12 in this volume.

70. Müller, 'Fear and Freedom', p. 46.

71. Collingwood, *The Idea of History* (Oxford: Clarendon, 1946), p. 218.

72. Bhikhu Parekh, 'Political Theory: Traditions in Political Philosophy', in Robert Goodin and Hans-Dieter Klingemann (eds.), *A New Handbook of Political Science* (Oxford: Oxford University Press, 1996), pp. 505–6. Adapting a term from Wolin, Adcock and Bevir label American political theory in this vein 'epic political theory': 'The Remaking of Political Theory', pp. 217–24.

73. Eric Hobsbawm, *Age of Extremes: The Short Twentieth Century, 1914–1991* (London: Michael Joseph, 1994).

74. The idea of 'the political' has generated considerable interest among political theorists since World War II. Carl Schmitt has been a controversial source. On Morgenthau's complex engagement with Schmitt, see Williams, *The Realist Tradition and the Limits of International Relations*; William Scheuerman, *Carl Schmitt: The End of Law* (Lanham: Rowman and Littlefield, 1999), ch. 9; Koskenniemi, *The Gentle Civilizer of Nations*, ch. 6; and the chapters by Scheuerman, Jütersonke, and

Brown in Williams (ed.), *Realism Reconsidered*. For an alternative conception of the political, focusing on Arendt and Wolin, see Emily Hauptman, 'A Local History of "The Political"', *Political Theory*, 32 (2004), pp. 34–60.

75. Brian Leiter lists Marx, with Nietzsche and Freud, as an exemplar of realism in moral and political theory. For a powerful naturalist reading of these figures, see Leiter, 'The Hermeneutics of Suspicion: Recovering Marx, Nietzsche, and Freud', in Leiter (ed.), *The Future of Philosophy* (Oxford: Oxford University Press, 2004), pp. 74–105. See also Leiter 'Classical Realism'.

76. Peter Gowan, 'A Calculus of Power', *New Left Review*, 16 (2002), p. 67.

77. Mouffe, *On the Political* (London: Routledge, 2005), p. 106. On the connections between post-structuralism and realism, see also Williams, *The Realist Tradition and the Limits of International Relations*, ch. 4; and Francis Beer and Robert Hariman (eds.), *Post-Realism: The Rhetorical Turn in International Relations* (Minneapolis: University of Minnesota Press, 1996).

78. Zolo, *Cosmopolis: Prospects for World Government*, trans. David Mckie (Cambridge: Polity, 1997); and Zolo, *Invoking Humanity: War, Law, and Global Order*, trans. Gordon Pool (London: Continuum, 2002). Zolo, like Mouffe, draws creatively on Schmitt. An issue that requires more detailed analysis concerns the role of gender within realist theorizing. Thus far, this has been a deeply problematic issue, and further work remains to be done. For an early intervention, see Jean Bethke Elshtain, 'Reflections on War and Political Discourse: Realism, Just War, and Feminism in a Nuclear Age', *Political Theory*, 13 (1985), pp. 39–57.

79. Emmerich, 'Political Theory and the Realistic Spirit', p. 196.

80. Sangiovanni, 'Normative Political Theory: A Flight from Reality?', pp. 235, 234; see also his, 'Justice and the Priority of Politics to Morality'.

81. The idea is associated mainly with George Kennan. See Anders Stephanson, *Kennan and the Art of Foreign Policy* (Cambridge: Harvard University Press, 1989); Bruce Kucklick, *Blind Oracles: Intellectuals and War from Kennan to Kissenger* (Princeton: Princeton University Press, 2006); and Richard Russell, *George F. Kennan's Strategic Thought: The Making of an American Realist* (Westport: Praeger, 1999).

82. Shapiro, *Containment*, pp. 102, 33; see also Shapiro, 'Containment and Democratic Cosmopolitanism', working paper, Department of Political Science, Yale University, January 2008.

83. Williams, *The Realist Tradition and the Limits of International Relations*, p. 84; Deudney, *Bounding Power*.

84. Morgenthau, *Vietnam and the United States* (Washington: Public Affairs Press, 1965); and Morgenthau, *Truth and Power: Essays of a Decade, 1960–1970* (London: Pall Mall Press, 1970). See also Jennifer W. See, 'A Prophet Without Honor: Hans Morgenthau and the War in Vietnam, 1955–1965', *Pacific Historical Review*, 70 (2001), pp. 419–48; Gilbert, *Must Global Politics Constrain Democracy?*, ch. 2.

85. Murielle Cozette, 'Reclaiming the Critical Dimension of Realism: Hans J. Morgenthau on the Ethics of Scholarship', *Review of International Studies*, 34 (2008), p. 27. Cozette also suggests that 'the realist *project* is therefore best understood as a critique of the powers-that-be'. Italics in original.

86. Shapiro, *Containment*; John Hulsman and Anatol Lieven, *Ethical Realism: A Vision for America's Role in the World* (New York: Pantheon, 2006); John Mearsheimer, 'Hans Morgenthau and the Iraq War: Realism vs. Neoconservatism', *Open Democracy*. http://www.opendemocracy.net/content/articles/PDF/2522.pdf (accessed October 2007); and Robert Gilpin, 'War is Too Important to Be Left to

Ideological Amateurs', *International Relations*, 19 (2005), pp. 5–18. On what this means for realism as 'value neutral' social science, see Rodger Payne, 'Neorealists as Critical Theorists: The Purpose of Foreign Policy Debate', *Perspectives on Politics*, 5 (2007), pp. 503–14.

87. Charles Krauthammer calls his warmed-over neoconservatism 'democratic realism': *Democratic Realism: An American Foreign Policy for a Unipolar World* (Washington: AEI Press, 2004). Francis Fukuyama is now calling for a 'Realistic Wilsonianism': *America at the Crossroads: Democracy, Power, and the Neoconservative Legacy* (London: Yale University Press, 2006).

2

The Ancient Greeks and Modern Realism: Ethics, Persuasion, and Power

Richard Ned Lebow

2.1. INTRODUCTION

There is widespread recognition that the realist tradition reached its nadir in neo-realism. In his unsuccessful effort to transform realism into a scientific theory, Kenneth Waltz, father of neorealism, denuded the realist tradition of its complexity and subtlety, appreciation of agency, and understanding that power is most readily transformed into influence when it is both masked and embedded in a generally accepted system of norms. Neorealism is a parody of science.[1] Its key terms like power and polarity are loosely and haphazardly formulated and its scope conditions are left undefined. It relies on a process akin to natural selection to shape the behaviour of units in a world where successful strategies are not necessarily passed on to successive leaders and where the culling of less successful units rarely occurs. It more closely resembles an unfalsifiable ideology than it does a scientific theory, and its rise and fall has had little to do with conceptual and empirical advances. Its appeal lay in its apparent parsimony and superficial resemblance to science; something that says more about its adherents that it does about the theory. Its decline was hastened by the end of the Cold War, which appeared to many as a critical test case for a theory that sought primarily to explain the stability of the bipolar world. The end of the Cold War and subsequent collapse of the Soviet Union also turned scholarly and public attention to a new range of political problems to which neorealism was irrelevant.

The decline of neorealism has encouraged many realists to return to their roots. In doing so, they read with renewed interest the works of great nineteenth- and twentieth-century realists like Max Weber, E. H. Carr, and Hans Morgenthau in search of conceptions and insights relevant to contemporary international relations. Weber and Morgenthau in turn were deeply indebted to the Greeks, as is the broader tradition of classical realism. In *The Tragic Vision of Politics* (2003), I sought to recapture the wisdom of that tradition through a close reading of the texts of Thucydides, Carl von Clausewitz, and Morgenthau.[2] My project here is less ambitious, and is limited to describing the fifth-century Greek understanding of power and using it to critique modern conceptions, especially those associated with realism.

My argument draws on the writings of Aeschylus, Sophocles, Thucydides, and Plato. They differ in many ways, but give voice to a set of largely shared understandings about human nature and social relations. They have much to teach us about the nature of community, how it is held together by affection and friendship, the role of dialogue and persuasion in creating these bonds, and the ways in which the exercise of power can reinforce or undermine them. Their arguments, and mine, rely on the particularly rich Greek lexicon, which allows a more sophisticated analysis of such concepts as power, hegemony, and persuasion. This lexicon, and the manner in which they developed and deployed it, can enrich our understanding of power in several important ways. It highlights the links between power and the purposes for which it is employed, as well as the means used to achieve these ends. It also provides a conceptual framework for distinguishing enlightened from narrow self-interest, identifies strategies of influence associated with each, and their implications for the long-term survival of communities.

2.2. CONTEMPORARY CONCEPTIONS

In the field of International Relations, power has been used interchangeably as a property and a relational concept.[3] This elision reflects a wider failure to distinguish material capabilities from power, and power from influence. Classical realists—unlike many later theorists—understood that material capabilities are only one component of power, and that influence is a psychological relationship. Hans Morgenthau insisted that influence is always relative, situation specific, and highly dependent on the skill of actors.[4] Stefano Guzzini observes that this political truth creates an irresolvable dilemma for realist theory.[5] If power cannot be defined and measured independently from specific interactions, it cannot provide the foundation for deductive realist theories.

Liberal conceptions also stress material capabilities, but privilege economic over military power. Some liberal understandings go beyond material capabilities to include culture, ideology, and the nature of a state's political-economic order; what Joseph Nye, Jr. calls 'soft power'. Liberals also tend to conflate power and influence. Many assume that economic power—hard or soft—automatically confers influence.[6] Nye takes it for granted that the American way of life is so attractive, even mesmerizing, and the global public goods it supposedly provides so beneficial, that others are predisposed to follow Washington's lead.[7] Like many liberals, he treats interests and identities as objective, uncontroversial, and given.[8]

Recent constructivist writings differentiate power from influence, and highlight the importance of process. Habermasian accounts stress the ways in which argument can be determining, and describe a kind of influence that can be fully independent of material capabilities. They make surprisingly narrow claims. Thomas Risse considers argument likely to be decisive only among actors who share a common 'lifeworld', and in situations where they are uncertain about their interests, or where existing norms do not apply or clash.[9] Risse and other advocates of communicative rationality fail to distinguish between good and persuasive arguments—and they are by no means the same. Nor do they tell us what makes for either kind of argument, or how we determine when an argument is persuasive without reasoning backwards from an outcome. Thicker constructivist approaches build on the ancient Greek understanding of rhetoric as the language of politics, and consider the most persuasive arguments those that sustain or enable identities. According to Christian Reus-Smit, 'all political power is deeply embedded in webs of social exchange and mutual constitution—the sort that escapes from the short-term vagaries of coercion and bribery to assume a structural, taken-for-granted form—ultimately rests on legitimacy.'[10]

Like thick constructivist accounts, the Greeks focus our attention on the underlying causes of persuasion, not on individual instances.[11] They offer us conceptual categories for distinguishing between different kinds of argument, and a politically enlightened definition of what constitutes a good argument. The Greeks appreciated the power of emotional appeals, especially when they held out the prospect of sustaining identities. More importantly, they understood the transformative potential of emotion; how it could combine with reason to create shared identities; and with it, a general propensity to cooperate with or be persuaded by certain actors.

2.3. PERSUASION AND POWER

We need to distinguish the goal of persuasion from persuasion as a means. As noted above, efforts at persuasion (the goal) rely on the persuasive skills of actors (the means) to offer suitable rewards, make appropriate and credible threats, or marshal telling arguments. Aeschylus, Sophocles, Thucydides, and Plato recognize the double meaning of persuasion, and like their modern counterparts, devote at least as much attention to persuasion as a means as they do to it as an end. Unlike many contemporary authorities, their primary concern is not with tactics (e.g. the best means of demonstrating credibility) but with ethics. They distinguish persuasion brought about by deceit (*dolos*), false logic, coercion, and other forms of chicanery from persuasion (*peithō*) achieved by holding out the prospect of building or strengthening friendships, common identities, and mutually valued norms and practices. They associate persuasion of the former kind (*dolos*) with those sophists who taught rhetoric and demagogues who sought to win the support of the assembly by false or misleading arguments for selfish ends. *Peithō*, by contrast, uses dialogue to help actors define who they are, and this includes the initiating party, not just the actor(s) it seeks to influence. *Peithō* constructs common identities and interests through joint understandings, commitments, and deeds. It begins with recognition of the ontological equality of all the parties to a dialogue, and advances beyond that to build friendships and mutual respect. *Peithō* blurs the distinction between means and ends because it has positive value in its own right, independently of any specific end it is intended to serve.

Some of the Greek authors I examine—Sophocles in particular—treat *peithō* and *dolos* as diametrically opposed strategies. This reflects the tendency of Greek tragedy to pit characters with extreme and unyielding commitments to particular beliefs or practices against each other in order to illustrate their beneficial and baneful consequences. I do the same while recognizing, as did the Greeks, that pure representations of any strategy of influence are stereotypes. *Peithō* and *dolos*, like other binaries I describe, have something of the character of ideal types. Actual strategies or political relationships approach them only to a certain degree and, in practice, can be mixed.

Sophocles, Thucydides, and Plato consider *peithō* a more effective strategy than *dolos* because it has the potential to foster cooperation that transcends discrete issues, builds and strengthens community, and reshapes interests in ways that facilitate future cooperation. For much the same reason, *peithō* has a restricted domain; it cannot persuade honest people to act contrary to their values or identities. *Dolos* can sometimes hoodwink actors into behaving this way. In contrast to *peithō*, it treats people as means not ends—a Kantian distinction implicit in Sophocles and explicit in Plato. In *Gorgias*, he has Socrates maintain that rhetoric, as practised by sophists, treats others as means to an end, but dialogue treats them as ends in themselves and appeals to what is best for them.

Dolos is almost always costlier in a material sense because it depends on threats and rewards. States whose power is primarily capability-based, and whose influence is largely exercised through *dolos*—the Greeks referred to such a political unit as an *archē*—often felt driven to pursue foreign policies intended to augment their capabilities. Like Athens, they may try to expand beyond the limits of their capabilities. *Peithō*, by contrast, encourages self-restraint.

Dolos is most often a strategy of the powerful, as they have the resources to employ it most effectively. For the playwrights and Thucydides, *dolos* is also associated with the domination of *archē*. Along with violence, it is the quintessential expression of this kind of rule. It can also be used by the weak to subvert the authority of the powerful. In Euripides's *Hecuba*, the Trojan queen Hecuba tricks her enemy Polymestor in order to tie him up. His Medea is at a double disadvantage because she is a barbarian as well as a woman, but triumphs over Jason by means of chicanery.

My analysis points to an interesting and complex relationship between power and ethics. While recognizing that might often makes for right, it reveals that right can also make might. Of equal importance, it provides a discourse that encourages the formulation of longer-term, enlightened self-interests predicated on recognition that membership and high standing in a community is usually the most efficient way to achieve and maintain influence. Such commitments also serve as a powerful source of self-restraint. For all of these reasons, ethical behaviour is conducive—perhaps even essential—to national security.

2.4. ARCHĒ

The Greeks generally used two words to signify power: *kratos* and *dunamis*. For Homer, *kratos* is the physical power to overcome or subdue an adversary from such action. Although fifth-century Greeks did not always make a clear distinction between these words, they tended to understand *kratos* as the basis for *dunamis*. It is something akin to our notion of material capability. *Dunamis*, by contrast, is power exerted in action, like the concept of force in physics.

Archē—rule over others—is founded on *kratos* (material capabilities) and, of necessity, sustains itself through *dunamis* (displays of power). Superior material capability provides the basis for conquest or coercion. Influence is subsequently maintained through rewards and threats. Such a policy makes serious demands on resources, and encourages an *archē* to increase its resource base. Athens did this through territorial and commercial expansion, but even more through the extraction of tribute, which permitted a major augmentation of its fleet.

Archē is always hierarchical. Control will not admit equality, and an authoritarian political structure is best suited to the downward flow of central authority and horizontal flow of resources from periphery to centre. Once established, the maintenance of hierarchy becomes an important second-order goal, for which those in authority are often prepared to use all resources at their disposal. Athenians explicitly acknowledged that Melian independence, by challenging that hierarchy, would encourage more powerful allies to assert themselves, which could lead to the unraveling of their empire. The Soviet Union, another classic *archē*, periodically intervened in Eastern Europe for the same reason. Successful *archē* requires impressive material capabilities and also self-restraint. There are diminishing returns to territorial expansion and resource extraction. At some point, further predation encourages active resistance and makes maintenance of *archē* even more dependent on displays of resolve, suppression of adversaries, and the maintenance of hierarchy. All these responses require greater resources, which in turn encourages more expansion and resource extraction. For political, organizational, and psychological reasons, self-restraint is extraordinarily difficult for an *archē*. Hierarchy without constitutional limits or other restraints—the political basis for *archē*—makes it easier to ignore the interests and desires of domestic opinion and client states, isolates those in authority from those whom they oppress, and narrows the focus of the former on efforts to maintain or enhance their authority. Over time, it can produce a ruling class—like Athenian citizens, slave owners in the American antebellum South, the former Soviet *nomenklatura*, or the present day Chinese Communist Party—whose socialization, life experiences, and expectations make the inequality on which all *archē* is based seem natural, and for whom rapacity and suppression of dissent has become the norm.

Thucydides offers the political equivalent of what would become Newton's third law of motion: an *archē* is likely to expand until checked by an opposite and equal force. Imperial overextension—*dunamis* beyond that reasonably sustained by *kratos*—constitutes a serious drain on capabilities, especially when it involves an *archē* in a war the regime can neither win nor settle for a compromise peace for fear of being perceived as weak at home and abroad. In this circumstance, leaders become increasingly desperate and may assume even greater risks because they can more easily envisage the disastrous consequences to themselves of not doing so. Athens threw all caution to the winds and invaded Sicily, not only in the expectation of material rewards but also in the hope that a major triumph in *Magna Grecia* would compel Sparta to sue for peace. In our age, Austria–Hungary invaded Serbia to cope with nationalist discontent at home, Japan attacked the United States hopeful that a limited victory in the Pacific would undermine resistance in China, and Germany invaded Russia when it could not bring Britain to its knees. All of these adventures ended in disaster.

2.5. PERSUASION

As I noted in the introduction, the ancient Greeks distinguished between persuasion based on deceit (*dolos*), false logic, and other forms of verbal chicanery, from persuasion (*peithō*) based on honest dialogue. *Peithō* is characterized by frankness and openness and accomplishes its goal by promising to create or sustain individual and collective identities through common acts of performance. As a form of influence, it is limited to behaviour others understand as supportive of their identities and interests. It is nevertheless more efficient than *archē* because it does not consume material capabilities in displays of resolve, threats, or bribes.

The contrast between the two strategies is explored in Aeschylus's *Oresteia*. In *Agamemnon*, the first play of the trilogy, Clytemnestra employs *dolos* to trick her husband, just back from the Trojan War, into walking on a red robe that she has laid out before him. She wraps him up in the robe to disable him so she can kill him with a dagger. In the next play, *Libation Bearers*, Orestes resorts to *dolos* to gain entrance to the palace and murder Clytemnestra and her consort, Aegisthus. In the final play, the *Eumendides*, Athena praises *peithō* and the beneficial ends it serves and employs it to end the Furies' pursuit of Orestes, terminate the blood feuds that have all but destroyed the house of Atreus, and replace tribal with public law (lines 958–74). *Dolos* is clearly linked to violence and injustice. Even when used to achieve justice in the form of revenge it entails new acts of injustice that perpetuate the spiral of deceit and violence. The only escape from the vicious cycles is through *peithō* and the institutional regulation of conflict, which have the potential of transforming the actors and their relationships. This transformation is symbolized by the new identity accepted by the Furies—the *Eumenides*, or well-wishers—who, at the end of the play, are escorted to their new home in a chamber beneath the city of Athens.

Although the trilogy is ostensibly about the house of Atreus and the regulation of family and civic conflict, it is also about international relations. Many of the major characters are central figures in the Trojan War. Helen is married to Menelaus, and her seduction and abduction by Paris triggers the war. Menelaus's honour can only be redeemed by the recapture of Helen and destruction of the city that has taken her in. Agamemnon, his brother and king of Argos, leads the Greek expedition against Troy. The *Oresteia* opens with his return to Argos after a ten-year absence. In the interim, his wife Clytemnestra has taken Aegisthus, son of Thyestes, for a consort. Among her motives for murdering her husband is his earlier sacrifice at Aulis of their daughter Iphigenia in response to the prophecy that it was necessary to secure favourable winds for the departure of the Greek fleet to Troy.

The curse of the Atridae and the Trojan War are also closely connected in their origins: both are triggered by serious violations of guest friendship (*xenia*), one of the most important norms in heroic age Greece. In Aeschylus's version, the troubles of the Atridae clan begin with Thyestes's seduction of his brother Atreus's wife. This violation of the household is followed by another more terrifying one. Atreus pretends to forgive Thyestes and allows him to return home where he is invited to attend a feast. In the interim, Atreus has murdered two of Thyestes's three children and put them in a stew which he then serves to Thyestes. This gives Aegisthus, the surviving son, a motive for seducing Clytemnestra and assisting her in the murder of Agememnon, the son of Atreus. The curse of the Atridae and the Trojan War unfold as a series of escalating acts of revenge. If the curse of the Atridae can be resolved through *peithō* and institutional regulation, this might be possible for the internecine conflicts among the community of Greeks, as they arise from the same causes and are governed by the same dynamics.

Peithō is also central to Sophocles's *Philoctetes*, produced in 409 BCE, five years before Athens's defeat in the Peloponnesian War. Greek tragedy was deeply affected by two decades of war, the plague, the breakdown of Athenian civic culture, and the re-emergence of intense factional conflict. Sophocles and Euripides are less convinced than Aeschylus, writing more than a generation earlier, that reason and dialogue can successfully overcome, or at least, mute conflict. Their plays suggest that civic conflicts are multiple, cross-cutting, and endemic, and correspondingly more difficult to resolve. They nevertheless search for some way of restoring a civilizing discourse in the intensely partisan and conflictual environment of late-fifth-century Athens.

Like many tragedies, the *Philoctetes* is set during the Trojan War. Philoctetes's father had been given Heracles's bow because he had lit that hero's funeral pyre. Philoctetes inherited the bow, and trained himself to become a master archer. En route to Troy, he was bitten in the leg by a snake and left with a foul-smelling, suppurating wound. The resulting stench, and Philoctetes's repeated cries of pain, led the Greeks to abandon him on the island of Lemnos while he slept. After years of inconclusive warfare, the Greeks receive a prophecy that Troy will only be conquered when Philoctetes and his bow appear on the battlefield. They dispatch Odysseus and Achilles's son Neoptolemus to retrieve archer and bow, and the play opens with their arrival on the island.

Odysseus lives up to his reputation as a trickster; he resorts to soft words (*logoi malthakoi*) to persuade Neoptolemus to go along with his scheme to pretend friendship with Philoctetes in order to steal the bow. He does this by creating a seemingly irreconcilable conflict between two important components of his identity: the honourable man who would rather fail than resort to dishonesty and deceit, and the Greek committed to the defeat of Troy. Odysseus presents his argument at the very last moment, giving Neoptolemus no time for reflection.

Philoctetes is an honourable, friendly, and generous person, with whom Neoptolemus quickly establishes a genuine friendship. When Philoctetes grows weak from his wound, he gives his bow to Neoptolemus for safekeeping, and when he awakes from his feverish sleep is delighted to discover that Neoptolemus has kept his word and not abandoned him. In the interim, the chorus had pleaded unsuccessfully with Neoptolemus to sneak off with the bow. Neoptolemus then half-heartedly tries to persuade Philoctetes to accompany him to Troy on the spurious grounds that he will find a cure there for his wound. Philoctetes sees through this deceit, and demands his bow back. Neoptolemus initially refuses, telling himself that justice, self-interest, and, above all, necessity demand that he obey his orders to bring the bow back to Troy. Philoctetes is disgusted, and Neoptolemus's resolve weakens. Odysseus returns and threatens to force Philoctetes to board their ship, or to leave him on the island without his bow. Odysseus appears to have won, as he and Neoptolemus depart with the bow. However, Neoptolemus, who has finally resolved his ethical dilemma, returns to give back the bow because he recognizes that what is just (*dikaios*) is preferable to that which is merely clever (*sōphos*). Odysseus threatens to draw his sword, first against Neoptolemus, and then against Philoctetes. Neoptolemus refuses to be intimidated, as does Philoctetes, who draws his bow and aims an arrow at Odysseus. Neoptolemus seizes his arm and tells him that violence would not reflect honour on either of them. Philotetes then agrees to proceed voluntarily with Neoptolemus and Odysseus to Troy.

Odysseus fails to grasp the essential truth that our principal wealth is not material, but social and cultural. It consists of the relationships of trust we build with neighbours and friends through honest dialogue, and the communities which this sustains. Odysseus is willing to use any means to accomplish his ends because he lacks any definition of self beyond the ends he can accomplish. He is incapable of interrogating those ends or the means by which they might be obtained. His attempts to exercise power through deceit and threats fail, leaving him something of an outcast.[12] Odysseus comes close to imposing his will on both his protagonists, and fails only because Neoptolemus and Philoctetes have established a friendship based on mutual trust and respect. His emotional attachment puts Neoptolemus back in touch with his true self and the values that make him who he is, and give him the resolve and the courage to return to Philoctetes with his bow, apologize for having obtained it dishonourably, and face down an enraged Odysseus. The emotional bond Neoptolemus and Philoctetes establish also leads Philoctetes to imagine an encounter between himself and Heracles, who tells him that it is his fate to go to Troy with Neoptolemus and there win glory. He agrees to proceed because he too has been restored as a full person through his relationship with Neoptolemus.

Gorgias (circa 430 BCE) described language (*logos*) as a 'great potentate, who with the tiniest and least visible body achieves the most divine works'. When employed in tandem with persuasion (*peithō*), it 'shapes the soul as it wishes'.[13]

Thucydides exalts the power of language and its ability to create and sustain community, but recognizes how easily it can destroy that community when employed by clever people seeking selfish ends. I have argued elsewhere that one of the key themes of his text is the relationship between words (*logoi*) and deeds (*erga*).[14] Speech shapes action, but action transforms speech. It prompts new words and meanings, and can subvert existing words by giving them meanings diametrically opposed to their original ones. The positive feedback loop between *logoi* and *erga*—the theme of Thucydides's 'Archeology'—created the *nomoi* (conventions, customs, rules, norms, and laws) that made Greek civilization possible. His subsequent account of the Peloponnesian War shows how the meaning of words was twisted and transformed to encourage and justify deeds that defied *nomos*, and how this process was responsible for the most destructive forms of civil strife (*stasis*) that consumed Hellas.[15] For Thucydides, *dolos* was an important cause of war. It is pronounced in the opening speeches of the text (1.32–44): the appeals of Corcyraeans and Corinthians to the Athenian assembly to persuade and dissuade it from entering into a defensive alliance with Corcyra.

Words are the ultimate convention, and they too succumb to *stasis* in the sense that civilized conversation is replaced by a fragmented discourse in which people disagree about the meaning of words and the concepts they support, and struggle to impose their meanings on others—as Odysseus did with Philoctetes. Altered meanings changed the way people thought about each other, their society, and obligations to it, and encouraged barbarism and violence by undermining long-standing conventions and the constraints they enforced. Thucydides (3.82) attributes this process to 'the lust for power arising from greed and ambition; and from these passions proceeded the violence of parties once engaged in contention'. Leaders of democratic and aristocratic factions

sought prizes for themselves in those public interests which they pretended to cherish, and, recoiling from no means in their struggles for ascendancy, engaged in the direct excesses; not stopping at what justice or the good of the state demanded, but making the part caprice of the moment their only standard, and invoking with equal readiness the condemnation of an unjust verdict or the authority of the strong arm to glut the animosities of the hour.

Thucydides gives us few examples of *peithō*. Arguably, the most significant is Pericles's funeral oration, which turns a solemn recognition of the sacrifices of the fallen into an uplifting commemoration of Athens and its values, and how they are maintained by the love, sacrifice, and self-restraint of its citizens. Pericles speaks in a forthright manner, acknowledging that the Athenian empire has come in some ways to resemble a tyranny. It nevertheless retains its *hēgemonia* and achieves excellence (*aretē*) by demonstrating generosity (*charis*) to its allies (2.34.5). 'In generosity', he tells the assembly, 'we are equally singular, acquiring our friends by conferring not by receiving favours' (2.40.4). *Charis* encouraged loyalty, self-restraint, and generosity based on the principle of reciprocity. With *philia* (friendship), it was the foundation of interpersonal, civic, and inter-polis relations.

To this point in the argument, I have stressed the beneficial consequences of *peithō* and the negative consequences of *dolos*. Are there circumstances in which *dolos* may be necessary or beneficial, and *peithō* damaging? The ending of *Philoctetes* leaves us with the thought that *peithō* and *dolos* may be usefully combined. Heracles tells Achilles that he cannot capture Troy without the assistance of Philoctetes, but working together like twin lions hunting, they shall overcome Ilium. Philoctetes will use Heracles's bow to kill Paris and Odysseus, as readers of Homer knew, would devise the scheme of the 'Trojan horse' to gain the Greeks entry into the City.

Thucydides's Mytilenian debate is sometimes cited as a less ambiguous example of the benefits of *dolos*. In this episode, Diodotus convinces the Athenian assembly not to execute all Mytilenian adult males, but only a limited number of aristocrats who can be held responsible for the rebellion. He openly acknowledges that it is no longer possible to defend a policy in the name of justice; Athenians will only act on the basis of self-interest. He carries the day by using his considerable rhetorical skill to mask an appeal based on justice in the language of self-interest (3.36–49). Modern examples abound. Franklin Roosevelt has been almost uniformly praised by historians for the rhetorically dishonest, but strategically effective, way he committed American naval forces to engage German submarines in the Atlantic before America entered the war. Modelling himself on Roosevelt, Lyndon Johnson campaigned as the peace candidate and promptly exploited an alleged attack on American naval vessels in the Gulf of Tonkin to intervene militarily in Vietnam. As that war ended in disaster, historians condemn Johnson's deception. George W. Bush and his advisors made multiple false claims to gain public and congressional approval for an invasion of Iraq. It is too early to offer a definitive judgement, but it seems highly likely that history will judge Bush's *dolos* at least as critically as it has Johnson's.

Leaders routinely believe that they know better than public opinion what is good for their countries, and feel justified to use *dolos* to achieve their policy goals. Even when their policies are in the national interest, they risk exacerbating the political problem by making the public less responsive to honest, and inevitably more complicated, arguments in the future. Thucydides uses the sequence of Pericles's funeral oration, the Mytilenian and Sicilian debates to track this decline. More often than not, *dolos* is simply a political convenience; leaders use it because it is the only way, or at least the easiest way, of gaining popular support.

Plato's opposition to *dolos* was unyielding for these reasons. He understood that rhetoric was at the heart of politics, and sought to develop dialogue as an alternative to speeches that so easily slipped into reliance on *dolos*. Quite apart from dialogue's ability to produce consensual outcomes through reason, the free exchange of ideas among friends and the give-and-take of discussion had the potential to strengthen the bonds of friendship and respect that were the foundation of community. Plato portrays Socrates's life as a dialogue with his polis, and his acceptance of its death sentence as his final commitment to maintain the coherence and principle of that dialogue. Plato structures his dialogues to suggest that Socrates's positions do not represent any kind of final truth. His interlocutors often make arguments that Socrates cannot fully refute, or chooses not to, which encourages readers to develop a holistic contemplation of dialogue that recognizes that unresolved tensions can lead to deeper understandings and form the basis for collaborative behaviour.

The Socratic emphasis on dialogue has been revived in the twentieth century, and is central to the thought and writings of figures as diverse as Mikhail Bakhtin, Hans-Georg Gadamer, and Jürgen Habermas. Bakhtin suggests that even solitary reflection derives from dialogues with others against whom or with whom we struggle to establish ourselves and our ideas.[16] Habermas's 'critique of ideology' led him to propose a coercion-free discourse in which participants justify their claims before an extended audience and assume the existence of an 'ideal speech situation', in which participants are willing to be convinced by the best arguments.[17] Greek understandings of *peithō* have much in common with, but are not entirely the same as, Habermas's conception of communicative rationality. Habermas puts great emphasis on reasoned argument among equals, and its ability to persuade—an outcome so essential to democracy. *Peithō* values reason, but less for its ability to convince than its ability to communicate openness and honesty. These values help to build the trust and friendship on which the underlying propensity to cooperate and be persuaded ultimately depend.

Gadamer's conception of dialogue is closer to the Greeks. For Gadamer, dialogue 'is the art of having a conversation, and that includes the art of having a conversation with oneself and fervently seeking an understanding of oneself'.[18] It is not so much a method, as a philosophical enterprise that puts people in touch with themselves and others and reveals to them the prior determinations, anticipations, and imprints that reside in their concepts. Experiencing the other through dialogue can lead to *exstasis*, or the experience of being outside of oneself. By this means, dialogue helps people who start with different understandings to reach a binding philosophical or political consensus. Critical hermeneutics in its broadest sense is an attempt to transgress culture and power structures through a radical break with subjective self-understanding.[19]

This framing of persuasion has important implications for the theory and practice of power and influence. In contrast to *archē*, which is created and sustained by violence, threats, and *dolos*, *hēgemonia* is created and sustained by *peithō* and rewards. It is only possible within a community whose members share core values, and is limited to activities that are understood to support common interests and identities. *Peithō* can also help to bring such a community into being. While it is the strategy of influence associated with *hēgemonia*, it is largely independent of material capabilities. However, it can help to sustain those capabilities because it does not require the constant exercise of *dunamis*.

Classical realists like Hans Morgenthau were also aware that power is most effective when least apparent. 'Man is born to seek power', he wrote in his first postwar book, 'yet his actual condition makes him slave to the power of others.'[20] Human beings repress this unpleasant truth, and those who want to exercise power, he wrote, must help them do so. Clever leaders come up with justifications or invoke ideologies that make 'interests and power relations...appear as something different than what they actually are'. Whenever possible, they must convince others who must submit to their will that they are acting in their own interest or that of the community.[21] For all of these reasons, Morgenthau insisted that '[w]hat is required for mastery of international politics is not the rationality of the engineer but the wisdom and moral strength of the statesman'.[22]

2.6. POWER AND ETHICS

In modern discourses, ethics and behaviour are generally considered distinct subjects of enquiry because they are understood to derive from different principles. Many modern realists consider these principles antagonistic; not all the time to be sure, but frequently enough to warrant the establishment of a clear hierarchy with interest-based considerations at the apex. For the Greek tragedians, there was no dramatic separation between ethics and interest. Their writings show how individuals or states that sever identity-defining relationships enter a liminal world where reason, freed from affection, leads them to behave in self-destructive ways. The chorus in *Antigone*, proclaims in the first stasimon (lines 267–9): 'When he obeys the laws and honours justice, the city stands proud...But when man swerves from side to side, and when the laws are broken, and set at naught, he is like a person without a city, beyond human boundary, a horror, a pollution to be avoided.'

Like the chorus in Antigone, Thucydides—arguably, the last of the great tragedians—recognized the extraordinary ability of human beings to harness nature for their own ends, and their propensity to destroy through war and civil violence what took them generations to build. His writings explore the requirements of stable orders, but reveal pessimism about the ability of the powerful to exercise self-restraint. Like Aeschylus, he saw a close connection between progress and conflict. He understood that violent challenges to the domestic and international orders are most likely in periods of political, economic, social, and intellectual ferment.

Thucydides was a friend of Sophocles and Euripides, and wrote what might be called a tragedy.[23] Tragedy in many ways provides the vision of the world that underlies what has come to be known as classical realism. Hans Morgenthau, its preeminent modern exemplar, is very much in this tradition. In the late eighteenth century, German intellectuals turned to tragedy as a model for reconstituting ethics and philosophy. Morgenthau was intimately familiar with the corpus of ancient and modern literature and philosophy. His intellectual circle included his colleague and fellow émigré Hannah Arendt, who had studied with Heidegger, wrote about tragedy and applied its lessons to contemporary politics.[24] Morgenthau came to understand tragedy, he wrote to his British colleague, Michael Oakeshott, as 'a quality of existence, not a creation of art'.[25] His postwar writings, beginning with *Scientific Man vs. Power Politics*, repeatedly invoke tragedy and its understanding of human beings as the framework for understanding contemporary international relations. The principal theme at which he hammers away is the misplaced faith in the powers of reason that have been encouraged by the Enlightenment. But he is equally wary of emotion freed from the restraints of reason and community. 'The *hybris* of Greek and Shakespearean tragedy, the want of moderation in Alexander, Napoleon, and Hitler are instances of such an extreme and exceptional situation.'[26] Although he never used the Greek word, *sōphrosunē* (prudence and self-restraint), his German and English writings and correspondence make frequent use of its equivalents: *Urteilskraft* [sound judgement] and prudence. He offers them, as did the Greeks, as the antidotes to hubris. Tragedy, and its emphasis on the limits of human understanding, also shaped his approach to theory. Like politics, it had to set realistic goals, and recognize the extent to which its vision was shaped and constrained by its political and social setting.

Thucydides and Morgenthau understood that foreign policy at odds with the accepted morality of the age—or at least the community to which actors belong—undermines the standing, influence, and even the hegemony of great powers. The Anglo-American invasion of Iraq might be cited as the latest example of this age-old phenomenon. The national security elite of the United States still considers its country 'the indispensable nation' to whom others look for leadership. Public opinion polls of its closest allies—countries like Canada, Japan, and the countries of Western Europe—indicate that the United States has lost any *hēgemonia* it may once have had, and is overwhelmingly perceived as an *archē*, and one that many people believe is the greatest threat to the peace of the world.[27] In the run up to the invasion of Iraq, it surely behaved as an *archē*; the Bush administration's duplicitous claims about weapons of mass destruction and false claims that the purpose of an invasion was to remove these weapons and introduce democracy to Iraq were a quintessential exercise in deceit (*dolos*). Its subsequent occupation began with efforts to protect only those assets of strategic or economic value to the Bush regime (e.g. the oil ministry and refineries), and was followed by the installation of an American proconsul, unwillingness to share authority with any international organization, and the denial of contracts for the rebuilding of Iraqi infrastructure to companies from countries that had not supported the war. Such behaviour is typical of an *archē* who can no longer persuade but must coerce and bribe; and, Blair's Britain aside, this is the basis of the so-called coalition of the willing.

At least as far back as Homer, the Greeks believed that people only assumed identities—that is, became people—through membership and participation in a community. The practices and rituals of community gave individuals their values, created bonds with other people and, at the deepest level, gave meaning and purpose to peoples' lives. Community also performed an essential cognitive function. To take on an identity, people not only had to distinguish themselves from others but also 'identify' with them. Without membership in a community, they could do neither, for they lacked an appropriate reference point to help determine what made them different from and similar to others. This was Oedipus's problem; because of his unknown provenance, he did not know who he was or where he was heading. His attempt to create and sustain a separate identity through reason and aggression was doomed to failure.

For the Greeks, this pathology extended beyond individuals to cities. There is reason to believe that Sophocles intended Oedipus as a parable for Periclean Athens. Like Oedipus, Athens's intellectual prowess became impulsiveness, its decisiveness thoughtlessness, and its sense of mastery, intolerance to opposition. Oedipus's fall presages that of Athens, and for much the same reasons.[28] The United States would do well to consider the extent to which the unilateral foreign policies that it has pursued since the end of the Cold War are taking it down the same path as Oedipus and Athens. Its unilateral foreign policies, often accompanied by aggressive rhetoric, have opened a gulf between itself and the community of democratic nations that has previously allowed it to translate its power into influence in efficient ways. Once outside this community, and shorn of the identity it sustained, Washington must increasingly use threats and bribes to get its way, and like Athens and Oedipus, the goals it seeks are likely to become increasingly short-sighted and irrational. If this comes to pass, it will be another tragic proof of arguably the most fundamental truth of politics: that friendship and persuasion create and sustain community, and community in turn enables and sustains the identities that allow rational formulation of interests. In the last resort, justice and power are mutually constitutive.

NOTES

1. An earlier version of this chapter appeared under the title 'Power and Ethics' in a special issue of *Millennium*, 33/3 (2005), on power and international relations.
2. Lebow, *The Tragic Vision of Politics: Ethics, Interests and Orders* (Cambridge: Cambridge University Press, 2003).
3. Robert Dahl, 'Power', in David L. Sills (ed.), *International Encyclopedia of the Social Sciences, Vol 12* (New York: Free Press, 1968), pp. 405–15; Steven Lukes, *Power: A Radical View*, 2nd edn. (New York: Macmillan, 2004); and Stefano Guzzini, 'Structural Power: The Limits of Neorealist Power Analysis', *International Organization*, 47/3 (1993), pp. 443–78.
4. Morgenthau, *Politics Among Nations: The Struggle for Power and Peace* (New York: Knopf, 1948), pp. 14ff, 270–4.
5. Guzzini, 'The Enduring Dilemmas of Realism in International Relations', *European Journal of International Relations*, 10 (2004), pp. 533–68.
6. For example, Dahl, 'Power'.
7. Nye, *Soft Power: The Means to Success in World Politics* (Washington: Public Affairs Press, 2004); and Nye, 'The Decline of America's Soft Power', *Foreign Affairs*, 83 (May/June 2004), pp. 16–21.
8. Reus-Smit, *American Power and World Order* (London: Polity, 2004), pp. 64–5.
9. Risse, ' "Let's Argue!": Communicative Action in World Politics', *International Organization*, 54 (2004), pp. 1–40. On Habermas, see also Ze'ev Emmerich's Chapter 11 in this volume.
10. Reus-Smit, *American Power and World Order* (London: Polity, 2004).

11. For a thick constructivist account, see Martha Finnemore and Stephen J. Toope, 'Alternatives to "Legalization": Richer Views of Law and Politics', *International Organization*, 55 (2001), pp. 743–58.

12. Bernard Knox, *The Heroic Temper: Studies in Sophoclean Tragedy* (New York: Cambridge University Press, 1982), ch. 5; and James Boyd White, *Heracles' Bow: Essays on the Rhetoric and Poetics of the Law* (Madison: University of Wisconsin Press, 1985), pp. 3–27.

13. Frg. 82, BII, in Hermann Diels and Walther Kranz (eds.), *Die Fragmente der Vorsokratiker*, 7th edn. (Berlin: Weidmannsche Verlagsbuchhandlung, 1956), pp. 8, 13–14.

14. Lebow, *The Tragic Vision of Politics*, ch. 4.

15. James Boyd White, *When Words Lose Their Meaning: Constitutions and Reconstitutions of Language, Character, and Community* (Chicago: University of Chicago Press, 1984); and Lebow, *The Tragic Vision of Politics*, ch. 4.

16. Bakhtin, *Problems of Dostoevsky's Poetics* (Minneapolis: University of Minnesota Press, 1984).

17. Habermas, *The Theory of Communicative Action*, 2 vols., trans. Thomas McCarthy (Boston: Beacon Press, 1984–7); and Habermas, *Moral Consciousness and Communicative Action*, trans. Christian Lenhardt and Shierry Weber Nicholsen (Cambridge: M.I.T. Press, 1990).

18. Gadamer, 'Reflections on My Philosophical Journey', in Lewis Edwin Hahn (ed.), *The Philosophy of Hans-George Gadamer* (Chicago: Open Court, 1997), p. 33.

19. See also Gadamer, 'Plato and the Poets', in *Dialogue and Dialectic*, trans. P. Christopher Smith (New Haven: Yale University Press, 1980), pp. 39–72; Gadamer, *Truth and Method*, 2nd edn., trans. Joel Weinsheimer and Donald G. Marshall (New York: Crossroad, 1989); and Gadamer, 'Reflections on My Philosophical Journey', pp. 17, 27.

20. Morgenthau, *Scientific Man vs. Power Politics* (London: Latimer House, 1946), p. 145.

21. Morgenthau, *Politics in the Twentieth Century*, Vol I of *The Decline of Democratic Politics* (Chicago: University of Chicago Press, 1962), p. 59.

22. Morgenthau, *Politics Among Nations*, 3rd edn. (New York: Knopf, 1960), p. 172.

23. Lebow, *The Tragic Vision of Politics*, pp. 126–41.

24. On Heidegger and Arendt, see Chapters 7 and 6 by Spegele and Owens in this volume.

25. Letter to Michael Oakeshott, 22 May 1948, Morgenthau Papers, Library of Congress, Washington, D.C., B-44.

26. Morgenthau, *Scientific Man vs. Power Politics*, p. 135.

27. Lebow, *The Tragic Vision of Politics*, pp. 314–5.

28. Bernard Knox, *Oedipus at Thebes* (New York: Norton, 1970); and J. Peter Euben, *The Tragedy of Political Theory: The Road Not Taken* (Princeton: Princeton University Press, 1990), pp. 40–1.

3

A Theoretical Missed Opportunity? Hans J. Morgenthau as Critical Realist

William E. Scheuerman

3.1. INTRODUCTION

When Richard K. Ashley suggested twenty-five years ago that Hans J. Morgenthau's realism contained rudiments of a critical theory of international relations, his claim met with widespread scepticism.[1] How could Henry Kissinger's mentor and the father of post-war US international relations theory have possibly contributed to an emancipatory theory heralding fundamental transformations to the existing state system? Understandably perhaps, Ashley's thesis faced a hostile reception not only among mainstream realist and neo-realist thinkers with a vested professional interest in preserving the conventional portrait of Morgenthau but also scholars on the left. Richard Falk, for example, conceded the existence of a tradition of what he called 'critical realism', which conceives of international relations as 'a matter of historical evolution arising from the play of social, economic, and ideological forces'.[2] Falk notably refused to classify Morgenthau as a representative of this subterranean current of realist thinking, however, suggesting that Morgenthau reified existing interstate relations by failing to acknowledge their historically alterable character. Critical realism, Falk posited, was open to the possibility of significant reforms to the existing international system, whereas conventional realists like Morgenthau—as well, presumably, as most of his more recent progeny—ultimately denied this possibility. So intent on beating up on the bogeyman of idealism, Morgenthau and his followers obscured the dynamic character of interstate relations and *a priori* excluded the feasibility of a superior alternative global order.

In the meantime, a significant body of literature has refurbished Morgenthau's credentials as someone to whom contemporary critical-minded theorists might turn for inspiration.[3] In general agreement with this line of enquiry, I argue in this chapter that some of Morgenthau's early writings contain the outlines of an alternative version of realism never fully developed by him and in fact in deep tension with his mature theory. For reasons I outline below, this competing version of realism not only can be interpreted as offering a socially critical account of international politics, but it also lacks many of the more intellectually troublesome and politically conservative features of the brand of realist theory endorsed by Morgenthau in the immediate aftermath of World War II. Although I can only speculate here about why the mature Morgenthau abandoned his early contributions to an identifiably *critical* version of realism, in my view it represents a *theoretical missed opportunity* with potential relevance for those of us who believe that critical international political theory can gain from sustained engagement with some versions of realist theory. Unfortunately, the reputation garnered by Morgenthau as a result of the publication of *Politics Among Nations* (1948) and *In Defense of the National Interest* (1951) not only distorts our picture of his intellectual legacy but also leaves post-war political science with a less defensible version of realism than can be found in Morgenthau's pre-war reflections.

3.2. IN SEARCH OF REALISM: MORGENTHAU'S EARLY WRITINGS

A considerable cottage industry on Morgenthau's pre-World War II writings has emerged in recent years, with scholars offering vivid accounts of the competing intellectual and political influences that came together between 1929 and 1940. We now know that Morgenthau not only contributed creatively to a series of lively debates among international lawyers before 1940, but he was also profoundly influenced by Friedrich Nietzsche, Max Weber, and Carl Schmitt.[4] He also exerted substantial energy in the mid-1930s developing an immanent critique of the most prominent continental liberal legal theorist of the interwar period, Hans Kelsen, writing one book and a handful of articles in which Kelsen was an object of sympathetic yet astute criticisms.[5] While doing so, Morgenthau familiarized himself with the main ideas of another prominent Weimar legal theorist, Hermann Heller, from whom he probably drew some of his criticisms of Kelsen.[6] Archival materials suggest a surprising fascination with the controversial right-wing author Ernst Jünger, whose highly eroticized glorification of (masculine) experience on the battlefield riveted bourgeois Weimar public opinion and generated a devastating response from Morgenthau in an unpublished 1931 book.[7] While in politically and intellectually progressive Frankfurt in the late 1920s and early 1930s, he also encountered the ideas of Sigmund Freud and even began writing a work in Freudian political theory.[8]

Although neglected by the recent revival of interest in his early writings, Morgenthau was fascinated by the development of moral philosophy from Kant to Nietzsche and Dilthey, penning a lengthy unpublished 1935 manuscript in which he chronicled the decline of ambitious universalistic moral philosophy and its replacement by a brand of moral subjectivism which, Morgenthau pessimistically insisted, went hand-in-hand with the increasingly nihilistic character of Western modernity.[9] His famous post-war reflections on 'the decline of international morality' stem, it turns out, from a deep engagement with modern moral philosophy. Last but by no means least (as we will see), Morgenthau was well versed in innovative methods in the sociology of law, having spent three years in Frankfurt working under the tutelage of Hugo Sinzheimer, a well-known Social Democrat, architect of the Weimar Constitution's social rights clauses, and prominent labour lawyer, who pioneered left-wing interwar legal sociology.[10]

Yet the existing secondary literature tends to suffer from a serious flaw. Obsessed with explaining the origins of Morgenthau's post-war realism, it offers both anachronistic and overly partisan readings of his early writings. Commentators dig around in search of parallels to post-war arguments and ideas in his pre-war reflections, typically focusing on precisely those pieces of the puzzle which, not surprisingly, confirm their own evaluations of Morgenthau's post-war realist theory. Those hostile to Morgenthau and the 'official' version of post-war realist theory delight in underscoring his debts to reactionary German ideas of *Realpolitik* or right-wing authoritarian thinkers like Schmitt, struggling to show how their impact on Morgenthau supposedly left permanent scars on his thinking.[11] In contrast, those sympathetic to Morgenthau tend to neglect the roots of his thinking in right-wing authoritarianism, at most alluding to the impact of respectable liberal figures like Weber.[12] For their part, the US international relations mainstream simply ignores the pre-war European roots of Morgenthau's theory altogether, thereby implicitly buttressing the (US-oriented) social scientific, anti-philosophical, and positivist credentials of post-war realist theory. Any suggestion that we should turn to interwar continental political and legal thought to understand realism necessarily unsettles those political scientists for whom the history of the discipline begins not with Thucydides and Plato, but instead with David Truman and Sidney Verba.

Most commentators on Morgenthau's early writings commit another error as well: they miss the deeply experimental character of his wide-ranging writings from 1929 to 1940, exaggerating their programmatic coherence while interpreting them as nothing more than a stepping stone to Morgenthau's post-war realism. They do disservice to the astonishingly creative and exploratory character of Morgenthau's early reflections, in which he tackled a stunning range of issues in international law, political and moral philosophy, and legal theory, as well as an equally impressive diversity of interlocutors, in order to diagnose the failings of mainstream international law and begin to outline an alternative to it. The young Morgenthau's central thematic preoccupation was indeed the *pathologies of existing international law and the dominant positivist approach to analysing it*, and thus the need to formulate what he always described as an alternative *'realist' vision of international law and method*. However, his pre-war writings consist of disparate and arguably tension-ridden ideas about what *precisely* constitutes a 'realist' theory of international law, as Morgenthau borrowed from the deeply conflicting ideas of Freud, Kelsen, Schmitt, Sinzheimer, Weber, and others. The young Morgenthau offered competing interpretations of realism, only some components of which remained constitutive parts of his post-war theory.

At some points, the young Morgenthau defines realism as nothing more than a method, in sharp contrast to legal positivism, which pays proper respect to the 'real' social facts of international political life and refuses to conflate the normative

wishes of reform-minded international jurists with them. But even when rely-
ing on this elementary definition, Morgenthau oscillates in his interpretation of
which social facts matter, at times casting a wide net to include a vast range of
political, social, and economic power relations, while elsewhere sharply delimiting
the range of analytically relevant social facts.[13] At times, Morgenthau insists that
realist theory must build on an agonistic 'concept of the political' according to
which politics represents an autonomous sphere of activity governed by distinct
laws,[14] while at still others he associates realism with the quest to explain political
life, in terms borrowed from Freudian psychology, as the expression of deeply
rooted human drives.[15] A theory of human nature or philosophical anthropology, it turns out, constitutes the chief identifying feature of realist theory, in
contrast to influential views of international law which ignore human nature:
only philosophical anthropology explains the historically unchanging (e.g. 'real'
or foundational) character of political action. A careful reading of the full range
of Morgenthau's early writings shows that his realism was very much a *work in
progress*, and that it never fully crystallized into a complete (let alone dogmatic)
theory of international relations along the lines we find in his post-war writings.
Even though the young Morgenthau repeatedly implied that he could provide a
coherent framework for the seemingly disparate pieces of his puzzle, the fact that
he was more than willing to discard some of those pieces along the way shows
that he was intellectually honest enough to recognize both its experimental and
tension-ridden shape. His early fascination with Schmitt and Freud was thus soon
replaced by scepticism, and even the appreciative and deferential analysis of Kelsen
found in an important 1934 book was periodically replaced by deep hostility.

The intellectually playful yet probably incongruent character of Morgenthau's
early ideas about realism justifies, or so it seems to me, the next step in my argument: without ignoring the complexity of Morgenthau's early writings, we can
legitimately suggest that *one* version of his early rendition of realist theory deserves
our special attention. Subsequently I will try to demonstrate that Morgenthau
abandoned this unfairly neglected but potentially fruitful variant of *critical realism*
in part because he opted to underscore competing ideas about realism found in his
early writings. He underlined those rival elements because he ultimately believed
that a realistic approach to international law and politics should take its foundational bearings primarily from psychology and philosophical anthropology. By
doing so, post-war realism was forced to pay a high price.

3.3. MORGENTHAU AS CRITICAL REALIST?

The international lawyer Francis Anthony Boyle was justified in 1985 not only
in describing Morgenthau's 1940 article 'Positivism, Functionalism, and International Law' as 'one of the most stimulating ever published in the *American Journal
of International Law*' but also in claiming that it delineated an impressive research
programme subsequently abandoned after 'the horrors of World War II'.[16]

Because Boyle was apparently unfamiliar with many of Morgenthau's early writings, however, he failed to do justice to their programmatic potential, and he ultimately offered up a pale version of what Morgenthau describes in the essay as his 'functionalist' method in international law. Morgenthau embraced the term functionalism not, as Boyle claimed, because he had yet to embrace realism, but chiefly because of the term's potentially misleading connotations in the 1930s.[17] But Morgenthau's use of the phrase 'functionalism' hardly entailed a rejection of what since 1929 he had repeatedly described as the quest for an identifiably *realist* alternative to mainstream international law: 'realist jurisprudence is, in truth, "functional" jurisprudence'.[18] Morgenthau simply understood what he described here, as in his other pre-war writings, as a realist *or* 'sociological' approach to legal scholarship differently from what it came to mean after World War II.[19] This early variant of Morgenthau's realism not only diverges sharply from Morgenthau's subsequent theorizing, but it also marks out a path for an alternative critical realism never pursued in his post-war writings.

Morgenthau employs the potentially misleading term functionalism in the 1940 *AJIL* article because it astutely captures a constitutive feature of his early understanding of realism. As he underscores in many pre-war writings, the relationship between law and social reality is fundamentally tension-ridden: social relations are dynamic and ever-changing, and law consequently always tends to lag behind social change. Law must try both to mesh with and to fruitfully channel a specific constellation of social forces. Much of modern private law, for example, is modelled in accordance with the necessities of a capitalist private property-based economy. The constantly changing contours of modern social life, however, inevitably pose deep challenges to the quest to achieve a relatively stable and predictable legal system. Especially in the international arena, where we lack what Morgenthau as early as 1929 had described as 'dynamic' devices for adjusting law to evolving social relations, the gap between legal and social reality is likely to prove especially troublesome.[20] While municipal law typically possesses an elastic normative-legal framework by means of which legal relations can be recalibrated in accordance with altered social needs (e.g. new legislation), international law codifies the political and social status quo without typically establishing effective mechanisms for updating the machinery of international law. As Morgenthau noted in 1929, '[t]he development of international law stopped at precisely that juncture where the most fundamental function of a legal system commences.'[21] Explosive conflicts tend to emerge in international politics precisely because of the structural misfit between the relatively static character of international law and the unavoidably dynamic contours of social existence. A less dramatic but no less urgent consequence of this misfit is that the normative framework of international law may appear formally unchanged, while in reality it serves novel political and social *functions*. Because formal alterations to international law are difficult to achieve, social actors typically outfit standing rules with new functions as a way of establishing some rough equilibrium between law and social reality. Particularly in the international arena, legal rules may serve new purposes or gain unexpected meanings rarely anticipated by those who engineered them.

Thus, one is able, for instance, to distinguish three different periods in the history of the Treaty of Locarno. Those three periods are characterized by three significant changes in the normative content of the rules, resulting from changes in the political [or social] context, although the wording of the rules remained unchanged. The Covenant of the League of Nations, as a whole, as well as particular provisions...have been submitted to similar modifications as a result of factual sociological developments and not of legislative changes.[22]

This understanding of functionalism was a commonplace among the left-wing Frankfurt legal sociologists who influenced the young Morgenthau.[23] Recent commentators have misconstrued or simply ignored it only because that tradition has been pretty much forgotten today.

Most striking perhaps, Morgenthau's 1940 *AJIL* essay lacks many of the most problematic features of his post-war realism. Although alluding to the necessity of paying heed to the 'psychological laws' of politics, Morgenthau draws at best a tentative link between realism and philosophical anthropology.[24] This gap is likely to lighten the hearts of present-day neo-realists, who have long rejected the claim that realism must be grounded in some conception of human nature.[25] Yet Morgenthau's offspring will be surprised to learn that their intellectual grandfather simultaneously refused to endorse other familiar ideas central to his post-war theory. They will search in vain for both the concept of the 'national interest', for example, and for the telltale signs of the deep nostalgia for the traditional Westphalian state system that sometimes colored his reflections after 1945. The only reference to the balance of power, for example, occurs in the context of the observation that because the interstate arena lacks a shared sovereign, the adjustment of law to changing social conditions is determined by the free interplay of political forces. 'Where there is neither community of interests nor balance of power, there is no international law' because it then lacks effective sanctions.[26] No trace of his anti-democratic post-war claims about the dangers of mass public opinion in foreign affairs, typically coupled with a romanticized view of traditional diplomacy, can be detected here either. The *AJIL* article perceptively underscores the frailties of existing models of ambitious legal reform at the international level, but nothing in Morgenthau's exposition excludes the possibility of fundamental changes to the international system. In fact, his own recourse to a brand of legal sociology, in which *social change* takes on a pre-eminent analytic and explanatory role, not only meshes well with Falk's definition of critical realism as resting on a view of international politics as 'a matter of historical evolution arising from the play of social, economic, and ideological forces' but also deviates from the ubiquitous tendency among neo-realists to downplay the significance of recent transformations to the Westphalian system.

Most important perhaps, missing from the essay is the mature Morgenthau's heavy-handed polemics against the so-called moralist–legalist approach to international politics.[27] Still writing in 1940 *as an international lawyer*, albeit one who clearly believed that the admirable quest to minimize international violence by legal means can only be advanced by drastically breaking with legal orthodoxy, he offers a surprisingly sympathetic account of many of its features. Morgenthau's main target is legal positivism and not, as his post-war reflections sometimes imply, modern international law or even liberalism *in toto*. Even though the article begins with the polemical comment that 'great humanitarians and shrewd politicians [who] to reorganize the relations between states' represent nothing more than 'sorcerers of primitive ages' who 'exorcise social evils by the indefatigable repetition of magic formulae', Morgenthau by no means intends to discard modern international law's fundamental quest for world peace.[28] Instead, his main point is that only a realist or sociological interpretation of international law can better accomplish that goal than legal positivism, whose intellectual pathologies allegedly plague the real-life operations of the interwar international order.

With some justification, Morgenthau accuses positivists like Kelsen of mapping out a distorted picture of legal reality, in which law is artificially separated, on the one hand, from ethics and mores and, on the other hand, from the factual realities of social power. In his appropriately labelled 'pure theory of law', Kelsen had argued that if the autonomy of law were to be appropriately theorized, legal analysis would have to break radically with ethics and politics on one side and the social sciences on the other. Too often, the pre-eminent interwar representative of legal positivism argued, legal science had been subordinated to problematic moral theories and crude modes of social analysis so as to have transformed it into nothing more than a cheap weapon for competing political ideologies.[29] Although deeply appreciative of this basic methodological move, Morgenthau argues that it is overstated, and he builds on his earlier 1934 study of Kelsen's theory, *The Reality of Norms*, in order to relativize the strict positivist divisions between law and morality, on one side, and law and social reality, on the other side.[30] Without *collapsing* law into morality or ethics, or *disfiguring* law's significance as a relatively *independent* normative system operating in society, a realistic analysis recognizes two crucial points. First, law is indeed basically separate from morality and ethics yet 'the intelligibility of any legal system depends upon the recognition of ... fundamental principles which constitute the ethical substance of the legal system'.[31] Second, the actual operations of law can only be fully understood 'within the sociological context of economic interests, social tensions, and aspirations for power', or, alternately, 'the social sphere, comprehending the psychological, political, and economic fields'.[32] Not only must a realistic (and hence *realist*) study of international law acknowledge the basic moral ideals motivating international law, but it must also focus on the complex ways in which law as a system of norms interacts with a constantly changing environment constituted by competing social interests struggling for power. Only this approach, Morgenthau asserts, can explain the actual realities of international law and help guide fruitful international reform.

In this formulation, realism offers *a normatively minded sociology of international law*. It maintains the characteristically neo-Kantian tension between *Sein* [is] and *Sollen* [ought], but in some contrast to neo-Kantians like Kelsen, refuses to hypostasize that tension. By doing so, Morgenthau implies, his version of realism can successfully acknowledge the normative core of international law without reducing legal science to the pursuit of pie-in-the-sky utopian schemes. It also avoids the opposite danger of recognizing the harsh social realities of international political life at the price of interpreting law, along the lines of crude Marxism or reductive versions of legal sociology, as a mere superstructural plaything of the dominant political and social forces.

In particular, the second *sociological* facet of this conception of realism takes on special significance for the young Morgenthau; no wonder that he repeatedly described his own work as belonging to the genre of legal sociology. International legal practice and science remain underdeveloped, he asserts, because they analyse legal reality in isolation from the social conditions of international political life. In contrast, '[n]obody would ever endeavor to grasp the legal meaning of economic legislation without making economic interests and conflicts part of their reasoning.' But international jurists commit just this mistake, and thus they necessarily distort their object of enquiry. At the municipal level, one still encounters remnants of a 'decadent [positivist] legal science' which occludes legal reality by ignoring the ways in which 'new economic and social needs' alter the functions played by seemingly unchanged legal rules.[33] This decadence is both more pervasive and potentially more destructive at the international level, however. At the level of municipal law, the state 'has developed not only an overwhelming power apparatus, but also highly refined mechanisms of legislative and judicial readjustment, which lead the social forces into certain channels without disrupting the legal and social continuity'. Under optimal conditions, municipal law has been able to achieve a 'temporarily stabilized society where there was approximately no tension between law and sociological context'.[34] But the international arena lacks a system of shared sovereignty able to calibrate law in accordance with social life, or, alternately, funnel social change into existing legal channels. Because no universal or world state exists or seems likely to emerge in the near future,[35] peaceful social and legal change in the international arena is vastly more difficult to accomplish than in the domestic sphere. Changed social and political conditions internationally risk resulting in explosive conflicts and violence. How else might states hoping to modify the international status quo bring about change in light of the fact that the possibility of peaceful legal evolution has been foreclosed to them, and that the existing rules of the game tend to favour the powerful states which established them? Nonetheless, the push for change is irrepressible given both the dynamism of social life and the fact that rising states inevitably challenge status quo powers. When struggles between rising states and beneficiaries of the legal status quo occur, the lack of a common sovereign means that a ruthless and potentially violent 'competitive contest for power will determine the victorious social force, and the change of the existing legal order will be decided, not through a legal procedure ... but through a conflagration of conflicting social forces which challenge the legal order as a whole'.[36]

Even when conflict occurs *within* the confines of an unchanged legal order, positivism misconstrues this process because its exclusion of social factors from the proper domain of legal science prevents it from explaining how apparently constant forms of law can undergo far-reaching 'modifications as a result of factual sociological changes'. Changing social and political conditions, as noted, can lead even a seemingly clear general norm to take on a surprising multiplicity of evolving and potentially competing functions. Not surprisingly, Morgenthau's *AJIL* essay concludes with a call for international lawyers to abandon their fidelity to conventional notions of legal interpretation. Traditional modes of interpretation, he claims, are poorly equipped to deal with 'the peculiar relationship between social forces and rules of international law' because they ignore the possibility that an unmodified legal norm can perform a diversity of political and social functions, and that gaps repeatedly emerge between a formal rule and the 'real' rule of law.[37] This lacuna poses problems in the context of municipal law as well. Nonetheless, jurists there for the most part can get away with ignoring it without doing disservice to the law: the existence of a sovereign state works to minimize the existence of extreme disjunctures between legal and social reality. In the international realm, however, where no single sovereign exists and the free interplay of political and social power determines the authoritative meaning of legal material, rules undergo dramatic functional changes even within a relatively short period of time. Traditional interpretative devices are destined to fail because the real meaning of an international treaty may very well be obscured by its language: 'it is only from the social context that the treaty will receive its meaning'.[38]

A number of attributes of Morgenthau's early version of realism deserve closer scrutiny. In stark contrast to some recent versions of legal sociology or 'socio-legal studies', his approach to analysing international law, as noted above, takes its core *moral and normative aspirations* seriously. The most basic justification for describing Morgenthau's early theoretical interventions as representing a brand of critical realism is that its normative starting point is modern international law's *own* underlying quest to minimize violent conflict: even when Morgenthau criticizes influential positivist ideas about international law, he does so from the same implicit normative standpoint as his positivist opponents. In short, the young Morgenthau can be read as offering an *immanent critique* of modern international law which aims to preserve its valuable normative kernel while insisting that it can only be realized in novel ways.[39] A second reason why Morgenthau's early realism can be faithfully described as critical is downplayed somewhat in his 1940 *AJIL* essay but is stated more clearly elsewhere. To the extent that he continues to hold open the possibility of a *dynamic* system of international law better able to recalibrate law with social relations, he at least implicitly accepts what he explicitly stated in his first 1929 book: only a 'relatively just and for all parties valid' international legal order can provide, as the municipal legal order periodically has under modern conditions, effective elastic mechanisms for legal and social change.[40] In the domestic arena, legal systems which failed to offer sufficient opportunities for the underprivileged to bring about peaceful reform face the spectre of violent revolution. Rising social groups may be forced to overthrow ruling groups by force. This peril has only been warded off by the establishment of a relatively just legal and social order where ascendant groups (e.g. the industrial working class in early twentieth-century Europe) possess a real chance to achieve social and political reform by peaceful legal means.[41] Since the main pathologies of international law derive from its lack of dynamism, the only way to overcome them is by establishing an elastic or adaptable international legal system. Until the international order can realize a basic modicum of political and social justice, however, it will prove unable to do so.

Unfortunately, the reader searches Morgenthau's early writings in vain for an adequate discussion of the interplay between justice and a workable system of legality; he simply failed to address some of the more difficult quagmires generated by his own analysis. His views here, as in his post-war writings, about the likelihood of radical change to the existing state system are sober and hard-headed, in contrast to those of the naïve legal reformers he delights in mocking. By the same token, it would be a mistake to downplay his position's far-reaching political ramifications. As Morgenthau was well aware, the achievement of liberal democracy and basic social reforms in some corners of the globe, for example, took many centuries and cost countless lives. In a similar vein, Morgenthau repeatedly highlighted, the achievement of a just international order would require far more than wishful thinking on the part of international lawyers or grandiose plans for utopian legal reform. For this reason perhaps, he always underscored the potential virtues of a 'world state' as well as its unfeasibility for the immediate future. But the crux of the matter remains that he refused to exclude *a priori* its possibility, and that his own diagnosis of the ills of the existing international order implicitly called for establishing a global legal order substantially more just than the status quo.

This interpretation is buttressed by a second crucial feature of Morgenthau's youthful realism. According to Justin Rosenberg, a major failing of realism is that it perceives 'that the modern state seeks to mobilize the economy, but not that the economy is also part of a transnational whole which produces important *political* effects independently of the agency of the state'.[42] Realists interpret economic resources as an instrument of state power in a competitive system, but they ignore global capitalism as a structural reality with far-reaching implications for a broad array of power relations.

This represents an astute criticism of contemporary mainstream realism, but not of Morgenthau's early rendition of it. Recall again that Morgenthau calls for the investigation of 'the sociological context of economic interests, social tensions, and aspirations for power', or, in a related formulation, 'the social sphere, comprehending the psychological, political, and economic fields'. At least in principle, this version of realism implies the necessity of a broad range of empirical analyses of power and inequality at the global level. In fact, in an unpublished 1931 manuscript, Morgenthau argued that only major economic changes could counteract the self-destructive enthusiasm for warfare which had resulted in so many millions suffering the horrors of the World War. Unless new possibilities for creative and self-affirming activity were available in everyday economic life, war would disastrously continue to seem like an attractive escape from an increasingly routinized and rationalized social world:

In the economic sphere the change in conditions must be total. Because of modern wage slavery; because of the closing of every opportunity for the masses to prove themselves and improve their station according by regular methods; because of the impossibility for the overwhelming majority of men to be able to complete something responsibly and by full employment of their personality about which they might say, here is my achievement, my work; because of the degradation of the human being to an object...because of their irrevocable damnation to a depersonalized machine...Because of these conditions a leaden and tired hopelessness has emerged, the true sister to an explosive desperation, which sees war as a savior, as a great uplifting force. To change this situation and to bring about a renewal is a task which the best men of our times have taken upon themselves as their fate.[43]

The purpose of such investigations would have been to offer a rigorous analysis of those power relations shaping international law with an eye towards achieving legal reform. Critical realism presupposes not only a more nuanced and multi-faceted analysis of power than its mainstream competitors, but the crucial subtext of Morgenthau's argument is that *legal, political, and social reform at the global level must go hand-in-hand.* The lack of a system of shared sovereignty is the most obvious source of many of the irrationalities of the existing international order. Yet pathologies resulting from the decentralized manner in which international law is presently enforced are aggrandized by vast inequalities which make a mockery of even modest types of international law. Amid dramatic power inequalities, the potentially egalitarian and protective functions of general law risk taking a back seat to its exploitation by the great powers. General law then tends to operate as an additional instrument for the powerful rather than a meaningful check on them. For this reason, the young Morgenthau's animus by the late 1930s was primarily directed, as noted, against positivists like Kelsen who, despite his own socially reformist impulses, encouraged legal analysts to ignore the concrete social conditions which undermine international law's operations. For Morgenthau, positivism blinded legal scholars and humanitarian reformers to power inequalities that worked to convert normatively attractive modes of general law into weapons of a handful of the great powers who typically interpret and enforce them.

In light of the familiar portrayal of Morgenthau as a student of counter-enlightenment thinkers like Nietzsche, Weber, or Schmitt, my reading of him as a critical realist must seem surprising and perhaps untenable. Yet the conventional picture is misleadingly one-sided, as it ignores Morgenthau's many debts to leftist Weimar legal sociology. Although the story is a complicated one, we now know that Morgenthau was shaped by one of the Weimar Republic's most famous left-wing legal practitioners and scholars, Hugo Sinzheimer, under whom he worked as a legal *Referendar* in Frankfurt for nearly three years.[44] Morgenthau later described Sinzheimer as 'passionately and eloquently devoted to the legally defined interests of the underdog—the worker exploited and abused and the innocent helplessly caught in the spider web of criminal law'.[45] He was personally and intellectually close to Sinzheimer, under whose mentorship he published his first articles as well as a book on international law and became 'life-long friends' with 'a group of distinguished people [who] worked in that [e.g. Sinzheimer's] office'—including the socialist lawyers Ernst Fraenkel, Franz L. Neumann, and Otto-Kahn Freund, all of whom worked hard to synthesize Marxian political economy and Weberian legal sociology.[46] When Morgenthau was forced to flee Europe for the United States, Sinzheimer saw him off from the docks of Antwerp.[47] In a brief unpublished note from 1935 penned in honour of his mentor's sixtieth birthday, Morgenthau accurately summed up the core intuition underlying his theory: 'at its base is the legal theoretical insight that the abstract concepts of freely and equally contracting persons that dominate German civil law no longer accord with the changed structure of capitalist society', and, consequently, such legal forms must fail given the real-life 'dependence of the industrial worker'. As a result, 'new legal forms' must be achieved in order to realize meaningful freedom and equality for the working classes. Morgenthau noted that Sinzheimer had long been fascinated by the gap between the 'abstract individualism of bourgeois law' and the 'realistic, that is, social relations-oriented' facts of legal experience. For this reason, he noted, Sinzheimer was a pioneer in the field of realist or sociological legal scholarship.[48] His left-wing students advanced that methodological agenda, typically criticizing legal positivism for its refusal both to ignore law's moral or ethical connotations and grapple systematically with the harsh social realities in which law operates.[49] Like Sinzheimer, they repeatedly homed in on the many ways in which changing social conditions forced standing legal rules to undertake novel functions.

Many elements of Morgenthau's early writings suggest that he sought creatively to apply Sinzheimer's ideas and sociological method to international law. Not surprisingly, his ideas sometimes mirror those of Sinzheimer and his left-wing protégés. Like Morgenthau, they placed special weight on the historical or dynamic nexus between social reality and law. For example, Fraenkel and Neumann argued in the 1930s that the changing contours of capitalist development transformed the significance of the traditional liberal defence of general law. In classical capitalism, general law was not only morally desirable but also economically rational since individual legal interventions violated the principle of equal competition. When massive economic concentrations determine production, this alliance between general law and economic life is obliterated:

In a monopolistically organized system the general law cannot be supreme. If the state is confronted only by a monopoly, it is pointless to regulate this monopoly by general law. In such a case the individual measure is the only appropriate expression of the sovereign power.[50]

The young Morgenthau's observations about the pathologies of existing modes of international law in the context of an unjust global order echo this thesis. In the spirit of his Weimar-era legal colleagues, Morgenthau's account of international law openly acknowledged the noble moral aspirations of the idea of general law. Yet he also followed them in arguing that those normative aspirations were typically distorted in the context of social inequality. For Morgenthau as for his left-wing lawyer friends, the quest for legal reform unavoidably called out for significant shifts in social and political power.

3.4. MORGENTHAU'S POST-WAR REALISM

Morgenthau never fully developed the version of critical realism intimated in some of his pre-war writings and discussed most cogently in 'Positivism, Functionalism, and International Law'. As Boyle speculated, 'by the time the horrors of World War II were fully revealed, he and others like him had become thoroughly disillusioned over the chances of international law and organizations ever playing a meaningful role in the regulation of international conflict'.[51] When *Scientific Man vs. Power Politics* (1946) mocked the legalistic liberal belief 'that man is able to legislate at will, that is, to realize through the means of law whatever aims he pursues', Morgenthau was engaging in self-criticism to a greater extent than either openly admitted by him or apparent to English-speaking readers unfamiliar with his mostly French and German pre-war writings.[52] Although Morgenthau had always criticized positivist visions of international reform, he previously had accepted the possibility of constructive legal reforms that better funnel social change. In contradistinction, a decisive feature of Morgenthau's mature realism was its deeply sceptical view of international law, especially when considered as a device for challenging the great powers or reforming international politics. As Boyle pointed out, Morgenthau's post-war writings contributed to the 'decisive break between international political science and international legal studies' that has plagued most subsequent scholarship.[53] Despite Morgenthau's prescient criticisms of post-war US policy in Vietnam and elsewhere, the anti-legalistic overtones of post-war realism also deleteriously influenced US foreign policy, as generations of policymakers internalized its hostility to international law and condoned great power unilateralism.[54]

Morgenthau's famous list of the six principles of realism, first included in the 1954 edition of *Politics Among Nations* and since memorized by generations of cramming undergraduates, contrasts sharply with the programmatic agenda of the 1940 *AJIL* essay. Revealingly, the principles neglect international law. They similarly fail to make any reference to the need for a wide-ranging sociologically minded analysis of power. To be sure, the second and third principles declare that 'the concept of interest defined in terms of power' is crucial to realism, and that 'realism does not endow its key concept of interest defined as power with a meaning that is fixed once and for all'.[55] Morgenthau also notes that 'power covers all social relationships . . . from physical violence to the most psychological ties by which one mind controls another'.[56] However, the pivotal result of these reflections for the mature Morgenthau seems to have chiefly been the insight that the state's pursuit of the 'national interest' takes different forms and relies on a multiplicity of power instruments.[57] Rosenberg's criticism that realism conceives of economic power as little more than one instrument of state power in a competitive system probably applies to Morgenthau's post-war writings. For the mature Morgenthau, economic power potentially contributes to the effective pursuit of the national interest. Yet he shows little if any interest in the question of how capitalism independently shapes and conditions modern political experience— including the state system—as a whole. His early reflections about the complex relationship between legality and morality also vanish from the later story. Instead, Morgenthau's fourth principle emphasizes, in the spirit of Weber's ethic of responsibility, the moral paradoxes of political action, while the fifth principle warns of the perils of identifying 'the moral aspirations of a particular nation with the moral laws that govern the universe'.[58] However sound, his Weberian political ethics lacks some of the intellectual gems we find in his pre-war writings, where Morgenthau struggled with the puzzles of modern moral philosophy and jurisprudence to figure out how morality was both separate from and simultaneously linked to legality.

Nonetheless, the first principle, in which Morgenthau famously declares that 'politics, like society in general, is governed by objective scientific laws that have their roots in human nature', clearly hearkens back to his 1940 comments about the need for realist scholarship to recognize 'psychological laws'.[59] The sixth principle, which asserts 'the autonomy of the political sphere', also builds on elements of his pre-war writings.[60] A 1933 book, for example, was devoted to the relevance of the 'concept of the political' for international law, and as early as 1929, Morgenthau evinced a certain fascination with Schmitt's controversial ideas about politics.[61] Although my discussion of Morgenthau's critical realism in the previous section unavoidably downplayed this fact, his pre-war writings include numerous assertions about the autonomous logic of politics and its basis in human psychology. In his post-war writings, these elements rapidly became decisive features of Morgenthau's realism, whereas his understanding of it as a critical sociological-minded interpretation of international law, in which law's own normative aspirations are taken seriously, generally fell to the wayside. Realism increasingly was associated in Morgenthau's mind with the effort to identify *historically constant* patterns of political experience resting on the 'real' (e.g. primordial) basis of human nature. Realism of this second type no longer chiefly referred to the real (e.g. existing but alterable) historical and social facts surrounding international law, but instead to more-or-less permanent features of politics whose roots could be located in human nature and psychology. One implication of this conceptual shift was that many of the familiar enigmas of international politics were now subsequently portrayed by Morgenthau as deriving from unchanging elements of human nature. Politics 'is governed by objective laws that have their root in human nature', which 'has not changed since the classical philosophies of China, India, and Greece'.[62] Inevitably perhaps, one tendency in Morgenthau's post-war thinking was implicitly if not always explicitly to attribute a sense of necessity to key components of the existing international system, in some contrast to his pre-war ideas about their potential alterability.[63] Even if his periodical assertions that 'nothing in the realist position militates against the assumption that the present division of the political world ... will be replaced by larger units of a quite different character' occasionally seem reminiscent of his pre-war pursuit of international reform, it was hardly accidental that realism soon became correlated with a deep scepticism about the prospects of reform.[64]

Boyle was probably justified in attributing this shift at least in part to the traumas of World War II. However, its internal theoretical roots can be highlighted by returning briefly to Morgenthau's pre-war writings. As we have seen, the young Morgenthau repeatedly described himself as a practitioner of legal sociology, and when citing some of his own works in the 1940 *AJIL* article, he classified them as part of this genre. However, those studies which Morgenthau himself placed under this rubric tend to reproduce a shared but highly problematic line of enquiry.[65] After espousing the virtues of an approach to international law grounded in the changing dynamics of social reality, Morgenthau typically leaps to a second step: he argues that the realist or sociological method requires a careful investigation of the immanent dynamics of political conflict, and thus sustained reflection about what he always described as the 'concept of the political'. However conceptually plausible, the result of this move within Morgenthau's internal argumentation was a troublesome tendency to reduce, even in his most creative pre-war theoretical writings, a potentially wide-ranging critical and normatively sensitive sociology of international law to a philosophically minded analysis of politics. To be sure, a plausible version of critical realism would have required, if systematically pursued, clear ideas about the nature of political experience. Yet this otherwise sensible move leads Morgenthau to short-circuit the broader project of what I have described as his critical realism in favour of an analysis of the (for him) unchanging dynamics of political conflict. A realistic sociology of law becomes, in effect, a rather one-sided realist political theory centered on an agonistic model of politics.

Typically, a second jump then follows. Having analysed or at least alluded to the unchanging dynamics of conflict-laden politics, Morgenthau insists that we locate the roots of political life in human nature and psychology since they best illuminate the 'real' or primordial roots of human action. As noted earlier, some writings from the early 1930s borrow substantially from Freud. Yet even when Freud fades from the scene, Morgenthau frequently draws a close analytic link between a realistic or sociological account of international law and psychology.[66] Once again, this move initially seems sound: a persuasive version of critical realism might plausibly make use of psychology or philosophical anthropology. Unfortunately, even in Morgenthau's early writings, it tends to reinforce a tendency to delimit the rich analytic and explanatory possibilities otherwise found there. Critical realism, as articulated most forcefully in 'Positivism, Functionalism, and International Law', remains untapped as a programmatic agenda, while Morgenthau repeatedly gets waylaid by his preoccupation with rooting political action in a theory of psychological 'drives'. A realist psychology, in this final move, tends to supplant both the sociology of law and political theory.

Let me reiterate that a fully developed critical realism might legitimately have built on both political theory and psychology or philosophical anthropology. In the case of Morgenthau, however, they apparently distracted him from pursuing the more innovative intellectual pathways mapped out by his own early reflections. By the 1940s, they also encouraged him to jettison what originally was a complex but potentially critical theory of international law for an increasingly conservative brand of realism which traced the so-called objective laws of politics to human nature. The underdeveloped and aphoristic character of Morgenthau's post-war reflections on psychology and human nature, in some contrast to his creative Freudian reflections from the 1930s, only added to the conceptual weaknesses of Morgenthau's post-war realism. Their Freudian moorings dropped, Morgenthau's post-war psychology and philosophical anthropology often appeared intellectually dogmatic and even simplistic.[67]

3.5. CONTEMPORARY RAMIFICATIONS

This chapter has tried to demonstrate that the young Morgenthau pointed to the possibility of a surprisingly sophisticated version of *critical realism*, whose normatively sympathetic but socially critical interpretation of international law diverged sharply from the brand of realism linked to his name after World War II. For those contemporary scholars who hope to weld critical theory to realism, Morgenthau's early reflections may not be a bad place to start. To be sure, much about those theoretical considerations remains underdeveloped and even problematic. His comments about the need for a just international order remain vague. Even though he points the way to a multifaceted critical analysis of global power relations, he says too little about what intellectual traditions and methods might be employed in undertaking that analysis. This gap probably stems from the idiosyncrasies of Morgenthau's Weimar intellectual background. Although influenced by left-wing scholars like Sinzheimer, and even though his ideas sometimes parallel those of Sinzheimer's students, Morgenthau breaks with the tradition of leftist Frankfurt legal sociology in at least one decisive respect: while they tried to synthesize the ideas of Marx and Weber,[68] Morgenthau 'learned a great deal from Marx' but could never 'abide that particular type of Marxist who considers Marxism to be a closed system'.[69] Since so much of the sociological approach refigured by Morgenthau into realist international theory borrowed heavily from Marxism, however, a certain theoretical lacuna necessarily plagues his thinking. Morgenthau's scepticism about orthodox Marxism was undoubtedly justified, yet it nonetheless engendered immanent theoretical weaknesses.

The story I have told here also sheds fresh light on widely noted tensions in Morgenthau's mature theory. Commentators have pointed out that Morgenthau's thought was always more complex and contradictory than typically described by textbook-like attempts to pigeonhole him into the category of 'classical realist'. Richard Rosecrance sees a dualism in Morgenthau's theory: he was both a theorist of a static and historically unchanging 'drive for power' *and* an astute historically sensitive analyst of major changes in the state system.[70] Marcus Raskin speaks of the implicit 'idealism' of Morgenthau's realism.[71] More recently, Campbell Craig has vividly explained how the terrifying spectre of nuclear war encouraged Morgenthau during the 1960s to reconsider basic realist theses and embrace views he once had disdainfully dubbed 'idealistic'.[72] My attempt to uncover strands of critical realism within Morgenthau's pre-war writings can perhaps help us understand the source of these tensions. As a young scholar, Morgenthau was deeply immersed in critical intellectual traditions, and for some time was open to the possibility of large-scale reforms to the global order. Morgenthau's early critical realism was by no means hostile to international law's 'idealistic' quest to minimize the brutality of state violence by legal means. The fact that Morgenthau's mature theory *always* included *both* idealist *and* realist elements, *both* a deep appreciation of the role of social change *and* a rigid insistence on the static character of human nature and psychology, implies that he never fully discarded vestiges of his early critical realism.

One final implication can be drawn as well. It is by no means only Morgenthau's realism that is deeply conflicted. Even a cursory glance at recent debates about foreign policy reveals that realists repeatedly come down on opposing sides of the great issues of the day. Washington neoconservatives recently claimed the realist mantle as a cover for their imperial misadventures in Iraq and elsewhere, while some of the most astute criticisms of the US invasion of Iraq have come from the realist scholarly camp. Interestingly, we seem to be witnessing a replay of the Vietnam War, when realists like Kissinger played a significant role in the ugliest moments of the US effort, while Morgenthau and others bluntly accused the Johnson and Nixon Administrations of committing war crimes. Of course, nothing should surprise us about this general phenomenon. Every rich intellectual tradition is open to multiple and even conflicting interpretations; fidelity to an abstract theory hardly provides easy answers to tough political questions. Nonetheless, the account I have provided here suggests that a deeper enigma may be at hand. The conventional contrast of 'realism vs. idealism' is obviously too simplistic. One might also draw upon my arguments here to suggest that the term 'realism' itself is a misnomer. If we can locate deeply conflicting ideas about realism in the writings of a single major author, can the term realism (even when modified by 'neo' or 'offensive' or some other adjective) really get us very far? How much substantial overlap in fact exists between Morgenthau's early critical reflections and his post-war ideas? The thematic continuities are real, but the deviations remain at least as far-reaching. By the same token, does it make sense to group thinkers as diverse as E. H. Carr and Henry Kissinger, or Reinhold Niebuhr and Kenneth Waltz, under the same realist rubric? As every introductory textbook smugly declares, the commonalities among realist writers remain significant. But can we be so sure that the intellectual concord is deeper or at least more revealing than the discord?

NOTES

1. Richard K. Ashley, 'Political Realism and Human Interests', *International Studies Quarterly*, 25 (1981), pp. 204–36; Ashley, 'The Poverty of Neorealism', *International Organization*, 38 (1984), pp. 225–86.
2. Richard Falk, 'The Critical Realist Tradition and the Demystification of State Power: E. H. Carr, Hedley Bull and Robert W. Cox', in Stephen Gill (ed.), *Innovation and*

Transformation in International Studies (Cambridge: Cambridge University Press, 1997), pp. 39–55. My use of the term 'critical realism' is inspired by Falk, though my conception of it here is shaped, in contrast to his, by the ideas of the left-wing Weimar sociologists of law who exercised a deep influence on the young Morgenthau.

3. See especially Michael C. Williams, *The Realist Tradition and the Limits of International Relations* (Cambridge: Cambridge University Press, 2004). Also, Ken Booth, 'Security in Anarchy: Utopian Realism in Theory and Practice', *International Affairs*, 15 (1989), pp. 527–45; Sean Molloy, *The Hidden History of Realism: A Genealogy of Power Politics* (New York: Palgrave, 2006). I use the term critical theory here broadly as referring to a variety of competing critical approaches in international political theory. What they all minimally share, in my view, is a commitment to the necessity of a fundamental transformation of the present Westphalian system of states and the quest to achieve an egalitarian alternative to it. I realize that this is a rather open-ended definition of critical theory, but for the purposes of my argument here, it suffices.

4. On Nietzsche and Morgenthau, see Christoph Frei, *Hans J. Morgenthau: An Intellectual Biography* (Baton Rouge: Louisiana State University Press, 2001); on Weber, Hans-Karl Pichler, 'The Godfathers of "Truth": Max Weber and Carl Schmitt in Morgenthau's Theory of Power Politics', *Review of International Studies*, 24 (1998), pp. 185–200, and the excellent essay by Stephen Turner in this volume; Michael Joseph Smith, *Realist Thought from Weber to Kissinger* (Baton Rouge: Louisiana State University Press, 1986); on Schmitt, see Jan Willem Honig, 'Totalitarianism and Realism: Hans Morgenthau's German Years', in Benjamin Frankel (ed.), *Roots of Realism* (London: Frank Cass, 1996), pp. 283–313; Martti Koskienniemi, *The Gentle Civilizer of Nations: The Rise and Fall of International Law, 1870–1960* (Cambridge: Cambridge University Press), pp. 412–509; William E. Scheuerman, *Carl Schmitt: The End of Law* (Oxford: Rowman & Littlefield, 1999), pp. 225–51; and Scheuerman, 'Carl Schmitt and Hans J. Morgenthau: Realism and Beyond', in Michael C. Williams (ed), *Realism Reconsidered: The Legacy of Hans J. Morgenthau in International Relations* (Oxford: Oxford University Press, 2007), pp. 62–92. More generally on Morgenthau and the German right, also Alfons Söllner, 'German Conservatism in America: Morgenthau's Political Realism', *Telos*, 72 (1987), pp. 161–72.

5. The key published text here is *La Réalité des Normes, en particulier des Norms du Droit International* (Paris: Felix Alcan, 1934). For useful discussions of Morgenthau and Kelsen, see Niels Amstrup, 'The "Early" Morgenthau: A Comment on the Intellectual Origins of Realism', *Cooperation and Conflict*, 3 (1978), pp. 163–75; Oliver Jütersonke, 'The Image of Law in *Politics Among Nations*', in Williams (ed.), *Realism Reconsidered*, pp. 93–117; and G. O. Mazur, 'Confirming the Geopolitics of Primitive Law', in Mazur (ed.), *One Hundred Year Commemoration to the Life of Hans Morgenthau* (New York: Semenenko Foundation, 2004), pp. 237–51.

6. Morgenthau, *Genfer Antrittsvorlesung* (Geneva, unpublished manuscript, 1932) (HJM-B110, Library of Congress). Morgenthau's argument about both Kelsen and Schmitt parallels Heller's. For a useful recent discussion of Heller, see David L. Dyzenhaus, *Legality and Legitimacy: Carl Schmitt, Hans Kelsen, and Hermann Heller in Weimar* (Oxford: Oxford University Press, 1997).

7. Morgenthau, *Selbstmord mit gutem Gewissen. Zur Kritik des Pazifismus und der neuen deutschen Kriegsphilosophie* (Frankfurt, unpublished manuscript, 1931) (HJM-B96, Library of Congress).

8. Morgenthau, *Über die Herkunft des Politischen aus dem Wesen der Menschen* (Frankfurt, unpublished manuscript, 1931) (HJM-B151, Library of Congress). In his 'Fragment of an Autobiography: 1904–32', in Kenneth Thompson and Robert J. Myers (ed.), *Truth and Tragedy: A Tribute to Hans J. Morgenthau* (New York: Transaction Books, 1984), p. 14, Morgenthau discusses his early fascination with Freud. Morgenthau apparently attended lectures at the Institute for Social Research, where Freud was heatedly discussed by Erich Fromm, Max Horkheimer, and others.

9. Morgenthau, *Die Krise der metaphysichen Ethik von Kant bis Nietzsche* (Geneva, unpublished manuscript, 1935) (HJM-B112, Library of Congress).

10. William E. Scheuerman, 'Realism and the Left: The Case of Hans J. Morgenthau', *Review of International Studies*, 34 (2008), pp. 29–51.

11. See, for example, Honig, 'Totalitarianism and Realism: Hans Morgenthau's German Years', as well as some of my own earlier essays in which I focus on Schmitt and Morgenthau.

12. For example, the excellent studies by Richard Lebow, *The Tragic Vision of Politics: Ethics, Interest, and Order* (Cambridge: Cambridge University Press, 2003); and Smith, *Realist Thought from Weber to Kissinger*. Morgenthau's European roots are only alluded to in Greg Russell, *Hans J. Morgenthau and the Ethics of American Statecraft* (Baton Rouge: Louisiana State University Press, 1990).

13. See my discussion below.

14. See especially the 1933 *La Notion du 'Politique' et la Theorie des Differends Internationaux* (Paris: Libraire du Recueil Sirey, 1933).

15. Morgenthau frequently discusses the 'concept of the political', but he links it most closely to Freudian psychology in the unpublished (1931) *Über die Herkunft des Politischen aus dem Wesen der Menschen*.

16. Francis Anthony Boyle, *World Politics and International Law* (Durham: Duke University Press, 1985), p. 12. The article in question appeared in the *American Journal of International Law* [*AJIL*], 34 (1940), pp. 260–84. It brings together many of Morgenthau's key ideas from the pre-war period. A neglected discussion of the changing nature of neutrality written about the same time offers a clear application of the ideas sketched out in the *AJIL* essay (Morgenthau, 'The Problem of Neutrality', *University of Kansas City Law Review*, 7 [1939], pp. 109–28).

17. It was associated, as Morgenthau notes, with the far-reaching legal scepticism of American Legal Realism ('Positivism, Functionalism, and International Law', p. 273). As Morgenthau must have been aware, some Nazi international lawyers were also describing their method as 'realistic'.

18. Morgenthau, 'Positivism, Functionalism, and International Law', p. 274.

19. In 'Positivism, Functionalism, and International Law', as throughout his pre-war publications, he uses these terms interchangeably, describing his own earlier works as contributions to legal sociology (see, for example, p. 264, ft. 12).

20. Morgenthau, *Die internationale Rechtspflege, ihr Wesen und ihre Grenzen* (Leipzig: Universitätsverlag von Robert von Noske, 1929).

21. Morgenthau, *Die internationale Rechtspflege*, p. 75. All translations from the German are my own.

22. Morgenthau, 'Positivism, Functionalism, and International Law', p. 271.

23. They probably built on Karl Renner's influential ideas about the 'functional transformation of private law', in *The Institutions of Private Law and Their Social Functions* (London: Routledge, 1949), which was originally published in German in 1929.

24. Morgenthau, 'Positivism, Functionalism, and International Law', p. 283.

25. Kenneth N. Waltz, *Man, the State, and War: A Theoretical Analysis* (New York: Columbia University Press, 1954). In the same vein, but more recently, see John J. Mearsheimer, *The Tragedy of Great Power Politics* (New York: Norton, 2001).

26. Morgenthau, 'Positivism, Functionalism, and International Law', p. 275.

27. See especially his *In Defense of the National Interest: A Critical Examination of American Foreign Policy* (New York: Knopf, 1951).

28. Morgenthau, 'Positivism, Functionalism, and International Law', p. 260.

29. Hans Kelsen, *Reine Rechtslehre* (Darmstadt, Ger.: Scientia Verlag 1985 [1934]).

30. Morgenthau, *La Réalité des Normes*; also, *Genfer Antrittssvorlesung*.

31. Morgenthau, 'Positivism, Functionalism, and International Law', p. 268.

32. Morgenthau, 'Positivism, Functionalism, and International Law', p. 269, 283.

33. Morgenthau, 'Positivism, Functionalism, and International Law', p. 270.

34. Morgenthau, 'Positivism, Functionalism, and International Law', pp. 275, 272.

35. Morgenthau, *La Réalité des Normes*, pp. 229–30.

36. Morgenthau, 'Positivism, Functionalism, and International Law', pp. 275–76.

37. Morgenthau, 'Positivism, Functionalism, and International Law', p. 282.

38. Morgenthau, 'Positivism, Functionalism, and International Law', p. 282.

39. The method of immanent critique looms large in various forms of social criticism. For a general discussion, see Michael Walzer, *The Company of Critics: Social Criticism and Political Commitment in the Twentieth Century* (New York: Basic Books, 1988). On its role within recent neo-Marxism, see Seyla Benhabib, *Critique, Norm, and Utopia: A Study of the Foundations of Critical Theory* (New York: Columbia University Press, 1986).

40. Morgenthau, *Die internationale Rechtspflege*, p. 150.

41. Morgenthau, *Die internationale Rechtspflege*, pp. 73–6.

42. Rosenberg, *The Empire of Civil Society: A Critique of the Realist Theory of International Relations* (London: Verso, 1994), p. 13.

43. Morgenthau, *Selbstmord mit gutem Gewissen*, pp. 47–8.

44. The *Referendariat* entailed a legal apprenticeship under the auspices of a senior lawyer.

45. Morgenthau, 'Fragment of an Intellectual Autobiography', p. 10.

46. See Scheuerman, 'Realism and the Left'. Fraenkel (1898–1975) became a prominent political scientist in post-war Germany; Neumann (1900–54) was the resident political and legal theorist of the Frankfurt School when based in New York; Kahn-Freund (1900–53) was a leading progressive labour and comparative lawyer in the UK. Although Weberian Marxists, it was Weber's legal sociology that most appealed to them, and neither Weber's political ethics nor his famous defence of German power politics. This is probably true of Morgenthau's early writings as well, in contrast to some later writings in which Weber's political ethics looms large.

47. Frei, *Hans J. Morgenthau*, p. 61.

48. This untitled piece appears to have been unsuccessfully submitted to a legal journal (HJM-B110, Library of Congress).

49. See, for example, Neumann's comments on Kelsen in *Behemoth: The Structure and Practice of National Socialism* (New York: Oxford University Press, 1944), pp. 46–7.

50. Neumann, 'The Change in the Function of Law', in William E. Scheuerman (ed.), *The Rule of Law Under Siege: Selected Essays of Franz L. Neumann and Otto Kirchheimer* (Berkeley: University of California Press, 1996), p. 126. For Fraenkel's version of the argument, see 'Die Krise des Rechtsstaats und die Justiz', *Die Gesellschaft*, 8 (1931), pp. 327–41.

51. Boyle, *World Politics and International Law*, p. 12.
52. Morgenthau, *Scientific Man vs. Power Politics* (Chicago: University of Chicago Press, 1946), pp. 116–7.
53. Boyle, *World Politics and International Law*, p. 12.
54. A recent study of the influence of intellectuals on post-war US foreign policy describes Morgenthau as 'the leading realist thinker ... an anomalous ally who barely walked in the corridors of power but who had a pervasive influence': Bruce Kuklick, *Blind Oracles: Intellectuals and War from Kennan to Kissinger* (Princeton: Princeton University Press, 2006).
55. Morgenthau, *Politics Among Nations: The Struggle for Power and Peace*, 2nd edn. (New York: Alfred Knopf, 1954), pp. 5–9.
56. Morgenthau, *Politics Among Nations*, p. 8.
57. Morgenthau, *In Defense of the National Interest*.
58. Morgenthau, *Politics Among Nations*, p. 10.
59. Morgenthau, *Politics Among Nations*, p. 4.
60. Morgenthau, *Politics Among Nations*, p. 10.
61. Morgenthau's *La Notion du 'Politique' et la Theorie des Differends Internationaux* (1933) contains a lengthy critical discussion of Schmitt, as does the 1929 *Die internationale Rechtspflege, ihr Wesen und ihre Grenzen*. I discuss the exchange between Schmitt and Morgenthau at length in my *Carl Schmitt*, pp. 225–51. The Morgenthau archival collection at the Library of Congress (HJM-B110) includes additional unpublished writings on Schmitt.
62. Morgenthau, *Politics Among Nations*, p. 4.
63. Critics of Morgenthau's post-war work have accordingly worried about its conservative overtones: it tends to reify unfortunate facets of contemporary international politics and rests on an exaggerated hostility to even modest forms of international reform. See, for example, Falk, 'The Critical Realist Tradition and the Demystification of State Power'.
64. Morgenthau, *Politics Among Nations*, p. 9.
65. He describes the 1933 *La Notion du 'Politique' et la Theorie des Differends Internationaux*, for example, as a 'sociological' work which deepens the analysis provided by his earlier 1929 study of international dispute resolution. Yet its main novelty, at least in terms of Morgenthau's own theoretical development, probably lies in its extended reflections about 'the political'. In this pre-war work, as in many others, the crucial fact of social life is politics, and thus his discussion of the complex facticity of social power ultimately takes the form of an analysis of 'the political'.
66. Even in his 1929 *Die internationale Rechtspflege, ihr Wesen und ihre Grenzen*, p. 74, Morgenthau concludes his reflections on the concept of the political by arguing that it requires recourse to a theory of basic 'drives'. The clearest argument for the link is probably made in *La Notion du 'Politique' et la Theorie des Differends Internationaux* and the unpublished *Über die Herkunft des Politischen aus dem Wesen der Menschen* (1931). As Koskenniemi accurately points out, these early works describe the political as a sociological fact. 'But '[w]hat is common to such sociological facts is that they all have their basis, as a psychological factor, in the will to power' ... Facts about states, too, are ultimately determined by the psychology of individuals. In social life the principle of desire is translated into the lust for power' constitutive of political experience (*The Gentle Civilizer of Nations*, p. 454). The translated passage comes from *La Notion du 'Politique' et la Theorie des Differends Internationaux*, p. 43.

Political conflict is best understood, it appears, on the basis of the deep psychological drives generating it.

67. Morgenthau's post-war writings are filled with bold assertions about human nature, but he rarely provides much grounding for them.

68. See William E. Scheuerman, *Between the Norm and the Exception: The Frankfurt School and the Rule of Law* (Cambridge: MIT Press, 1994).

69. Morgenthau, 'Fragment of an Intellectual Biography', p. 13.

70. Rosecrance, 'The One World of Hans Morgenthau', *Social Research*, 48 (1981), pp. 749–65.

71. See, for example, Raskin, 'Morgenthau: The Idealism of a Realist', in Thompson and Myers (eds.), *Truth and Tragedy*, pp. 85–94.

72. Craig, *Glimmer of a New Leviathan: Total War in The Realism of Niebuhr, Morgenthau, and Waltz* (New York: Columbia University Press, 2003), pp. 54–73.

4

Hans J. Morgenthau and the Legacy of Max Weber

Stephen P. Turner

4.1. INTRODUCTION

To begin to understand Max Weber's significance for Hans Morgenthau, it is necessary to read Morgenthau in the light of the situation of the émigré scholar in the 1940s.[1] Many of the emigrants failed to adapt, while others thrived, and thrived spectacularly, in their new setting. Morgenthau was one of the success stories, but it is important to see what success consisted in, and what needed to be done to succeed, especially at the crucial point of his transformation into an American scholar writing in English.[2] For almost all of the most successful emigrants, it rested in both the utilization and the transformation of the skills and ideas which they had acquired in Germany, very often in a different academic discipline.

The required transformations were multiple: not only was the American setting one with a strong disciplinary structure, with less deference to the Professor, but it also was an academic setting in which different forms of writing were prized, which involved a different structure of academic publishing and demanded a different kind of book. But most important was the fact that the common points of reference between writer and reader were dissimilar. Communicating with an American audience required appealing to a new set of philosophical, literary, and historical sources, as well as historical experiences. Ironically, though not irrelevant to the discussion of political morality, one of the pre-existing common points of reference between Germany and the United States was the literature of intellectual Protestantism. German immigrants of earlier generations had preserved their ties to the theological language and traditions of Germany, and in several cases, had become prominent American theologians.

If one considers merely a few individuals closely related to Morgenthau himself, one can see some patterns in the process of transformation. A standard strategy was to give a series of lectures in English at the New School. Lectures of this kind, and there were many, were the means by which European, primarily German scholars, began or resumed an academic career in the new and not terribly hospitable setting of the American university. They were documents of

Americanization, in which the key scholarly ideas of the lecturer were presented in a cleansed, de-Germanized, form. Morgenthau's *Scientific Man vs. Power Politics* (1946) is in many respects a characteristic emigration document.[3] The book was based on a series of lectures at the New School. It represents Morgenthau's critical encounter with American foreign policy thinking, yet also performed the necessary task of shedding the German roots or form of his thinking and finding an alternative set of historical references and examples in support of his arguments. Recruiting Lincoln, and counterposing him to other figures often invoked in the discussion of foreign policy, such as Wilson, gave Morgenthau a means of expressing for an American audience ideas which otherwise would have been associated with the German enemy. *Politics Among Nations* (1948), which began life as a series of lectures at the University of Chicago, continued this process of Americanization, as did many of the essays that Morgenthau wrote in this period, such as his review of the books of E. H. Carr.[4]

This process of transformation is especially important to understand in relation to Morgenthau's use of Weber. Weber's thought came to have a somewhat different role in academic discourse at the time Morgenthau wrote *Politics Among Nations*. Although it was a role of quite extraordinary prestige, Weber's political writings, from which Morgenthau drew, were largely unknown among American academics. Only a few of them had been translated in Gerth and Mills's influential *From Max Weber* (1946), and they did not suffice to give a sense of the political thought of Weber as a connected whole. Instead, during the post-war period and through the early 1950s, Weber appeared as a founding father of sociology whose greatest text was *The Protestant Ethic and the Spirit of Capitalism* (1958), which in turn was understood as an alternative to the Marxist account of the origins and consequently the moral nature of capitalism.[5] The demotic Weber (one might even say the Harvard Weber, since it was under the influence of Talcott Parsons that this image of Weber flourished in the curriculum) was Weber as a sociologist and godfather of the emerging specialization of political sociology.[6]

Weber's ideas about value-freedom in social science, similarly, were imported and at the same time transformed into another support for American social science disciplines' self-definition in terms of objectivity and the post-war quest for a 'behavioural science' stripped of its lingering pre-war reformism. In the course of this transformation, Weber's ideas were shorn of much of their moral content, and especially their tragic and quasi-nihilistic or Nietzschean elements, elements that of course Leo Strauss stressed in his *Natural Right and History* (1953).[7] As Allan Bloom recalled in *The Closing of the American Mind* (1987), the atmosphere in the social sciences at Chicago was suffused with Weber, who was taught in the famous Social Science sequence in the College, and he had this influence in mind.[8] Yet at the University of Chicago, people close to Morgenthau, such as Edward Shils, who is thanked in the preface to *Politics Among Nations*, were well aware of the whole of Weber. In the 1940s, Shils was producing his translated selections from Weber's *Wissenschaftslehre*, including the crucial paper on value-neutrality, which outlines his value ideas.[9] Strauss, of course, delivered the lectures that were the basis of *Natural Right and History*: Weber and the radicalization of Weber represented by Heideggerianism are the central antagonists. Max Rheinstein, who was producing his translation of Weber's writings on the sociology of law at the time that *Politics Among Nations* was written, also knew the political side of Weber very well. Frank Knight, the doyen of the Department of Economics and the founder of Chicago sociology, was an admirer of Weber, translated his *General Economic History* in the 1920s, and brought Weber's last assistant to the University. Knight was thanked for his help with *Scientific Man and Power Politics*. Chicago, in short, was the setting in which the greatest knowledge of Weber was concentrated.

The role of Weber in Morgenthau's thought, however, is not apparent to the casual reader until much later. In the early editions of *Politics Among Nations*, Weber is not mentioned explicitly. In the first chapter of the fifth edition of *Politics Among Nations*, however, we find one of Weber's best known sayings: 'Interests (material and ideal), not ideas, dominate directly the actions of men. Yet the "images of the world" created by these ideas have often served as switches determining the tracks on which the dynamism of interests kept actions moving.'[10] The 'interests' quotation is an easily interpreted clue to the sources of Morgenthau's thought. But Morgenthau was never tagged with the label 'Weberian', and from the point of view of the conventional, student-oriented understanding of Weber before Morgenthau's death, the quotation and its source—indeed its meaning— must have been something of a puzzle to many of Morgenthau's readers. Weber is not discussed further in the text itself. The quotation is from Weber's writings on the sociology of religion, rather than his political writings, though it is from a passage on worldliness and religion that is central to his understanding of the nature of politics, and is indeed one of the most central and powerful expressions of his thinking on those relationships between politics and morality. His peers at Chicago would have known this. But none of this would have been apparent to Morgenthau's ordinary American readers, and, in this period, Weber was a standard source neither in political theory nor in international relations.

Morgenthau's own understanding of Weber, of course, owed nothing to the American reception of Weber. His was an understanding of the original texts in the context of their political origin. Moreover, Morgenthau had a special kind of introduction to the thinking of Weber, and this bears directly on the problem of understanding his relation to Weber. Morgenthau tells us that while preparing for his first legal examination in Munich, 'I attended Professor Rothenbücher's seminar on Max Weber's political and social philosophy, based upon the latter's political writings', that is the recently collected *Politische Schriften* (1921), which in the first edition contained not only published material but also letters, some of which proved to be too strong for the tastes of the editors of the 1950s version. 'It was a great experience', Morgenthau says. 'Weber's political thought possessed all the intellectual and moral qualities I had looked for in vain in the contemporary literature inside and outside of the universities.'[11] The fact that he encountered Weber in a seminar meant that he began his encounter with Weber in a synthetic mode. He did not pick up scraps here and there, or read isolated texts. He was guided by Rothenbücher, whom Morgenthau admired, into a synthetic grasp of Weber as a political thinker.[12]

In what follows, I will discuss *seriatim* some of the Weberian ideas that are the sources of Morgenthau's thought by considering what Weber said and explaining how these ideas appear in a transformed way in Morgenthau's writings. My aim is not to consider 'influence', though I think it will be evident that there is a great deal of influence, but to provide materials for the understanding of aspects of Morgenthau's thought and politics that have proven so puzzling, especially to American scholars who have attempted to locate his thought within the coordinates of American liberalism and American foreign policy thinking and politics. I will do this informally, by explaining the Weberian ideas that Morgenthau had access to in the texts that Morgenthau tells us influenced him, and by showing how they reappear in Morgenthau. The transformation that Morgenthau was compelled to make to establish these ideas in the American setting was immense, his sources were various, and Weber was one source among many. But Morgenthau, I will suggest, was largely a consistent Weberian, and this clarifies some puzzles about his thought, and enables us to correct some mis-impressions. I do not want to point fingers at specific erroneous interpretations of Morgenthau here. But the impressions that I will try to correct are each found in the secondary literature on Morgenthau, often in prominent places.[13] What I will not do is to engage in the misleading procedure of matching quotations from Weber with quotations from Morgenthau. Morgenthau's experience of Weber was Weber as a systematic and coherent thinker. So in what follows I will describe the systematic structure of Weber's thinking as it bears on various issues, and explain how Morgenthau's thought may be understood in relation to it.

4.2. A NOTE ON THE SOURCES

At the time Morgenthau was a student, during the early Weimar era, certain writings of Max Weber had achieved the status of touchstone in the intellectual controversies of the time. His speech 'Science as a Vocation' (1917), which has echoes in both Morgenthau's writing on scientism in *Scientific Man and Power Politics* and his later *Science: Servant or Master* (1972), was perhaps the most important of these texts.[14] It was reprinted as a pamphlet and widely circulated, and became the subject of anguished reactions and responses by the Frankfurt School and by Heidegger, who regarded it as a disappointment—and Max Scheler, who quipped that Weber was the representative of his time, but that these were the worst of times[15]—and which produced its own rather interesting literature of critique and response. Weber had clearly struck a nerve with this speech. It was interpreted by most of his hearers as a failure or refusal on Weber's part as a scientist or a scientific leader to provide a resolution to the master questions of the time, especially what was known as the Crisis of the Sciences. It is an anti-scientistic text, a denial that science has the capacity to resolve the master questions of the time. But it is also a rejection of the idea that some sort of over-arching intellectual synthesis could be provided by philosophy or *Wissenschaft* in the broadest sense. The message was instead that specialization was the condition of advance in the sciences, and that specialization precluded the offering of world views.

The companion to this speech was 'Politics as a Vocation' (1919), another post-war lecture to students, which Morgenthau also knew well.[16] More will be said about this speech below, but its form is very striking. Like 'Science as a Vocation', it is a text which dashes the hopes of its audience, in this case hope for a new kind of politics that would provide an escape from the moral dilemmas of political life. Much of it is taken up with a general historical characterization of politics, focusing on parties and the deep (and pre-democratic) roots of party politics and party rule. Weber told a story about the development of liberal democracy that omitted the constitutive notions of liberal democracy. It was not the story of rights, or popular sovereignty, or the fulfilment of ideals. It was instead a lesson in the tough and deeply rooted realities of political action, explicitly directed against any kind of utopian optimism. It was a brutal assault on the idealism of its student audience, and was received as such. It instructed them in what political leadership consists, and the qualities of genuine leaders. The text con-cluded with the argument that neither science nor biblical morality can deliver us from the necessity of fundamental and fundamentally irrational value-decisions in politics, and with the suggestion that the pursuit of national values was the only remaining ennobling or meaningful this-worldly political choice in the present.

A third text was Weber's newspaper writing, towards the close of the war, about the post-war constitution.[17] The text is a classic of constitutional thinking, but it is oriented to a very specific problem, the question of who in the German polity can be used as a reliable resource in the pursuit of the national interest. The essay includes an extended reflection on Bismarck and his constitutional role and the unfortunate consequences of this role for constitutional development—a string of mediocre successors incapable of serving the national interest and a collection of party politicians unable or unwilling to either articulate or prosecute the national interest, and a bureaucracy that produced 'leaders' who were incapable of making the kind of decisions that pursuit of the national interest required, and incapable of legitimating their decisions with the public. The aspect of this important text that bears on Morgenthau in particular may be put in the form of a question, the question which implicitly loomed for Weber, who recognized that the constitu-tional structure of the future regime had to be fundamentally democratic, namely, how is it possible to defend and pursue the national interest in a democratic polity?

Weber played with fire in his discussion of leadership, in that he believed that a national interest–oriented constitutional solution for Germany required the maximization of the possibilities for charismatic leadership. Weber believed that only a President who could rise above the parties and come to office in an election that tested his charisma could overcome the bureaucracy's limited capacity for decision and the limited vision of interest-oriented parties and interest-driven domestic politics. Weber's political anxieties were closely related to this. As Weber surveyed the various class parties for their capacity for producing leaders, a capacity that a post-war democratic constitutional settlement would depend on, he was unremittingly pessimistic. The missing element in each was what he called the Catalinarian energy of the deed—the drive for power and willingness to act that he took to be necessary for the defence of national interests. As he repeatedly comments, what was needed was leaders who were genuinely political, rather than merely spokespersons for the short-term interests of the groups that their parties represented. But the bureaucracy would not produce real leaders either. And this meant that national interests could not be served.

In addition to these texts, Morgenthau knew at least parts of Weber's *Sociology of Religion*, including the 'Die Wirtschaftethik der Weltreligionen' from which the 'interests' quotation was taken, and would also have known something of the methodological writings, including 'The Meaning of "Ethical Neutrality" in Sociology and Economics', which presents Weber's views on the relation of theory to practice and the limitations of science in connection with policy.[18] We can assume that he would have known, as a good student would have known, the contents of the first edition of the *Politische Schriften*, including 'Between Two Laws', which discussed the notion of national responsibility, and had been written for a newspaper in response to a contribution by a Swiss pacifist, which contrasts, and places in radical opposition, the law of the Gospel and 'our responsibility in the face of history'.[19]

It is perhaps also important to note what Weber's political writings do not include, and what they include alternatives to. Weber was not an adherent to the standard account of the rise of liberal democracy—to Whig history. The political writings point to an alternative but never fully articulated account of the development of modern politics, in which the various elements of the modern state arise in different historical periods and come together with the modern phenomenon of mass society to produce the need for a certain modern kind of demagogy in the framework of parliaments and parties. Not 'the people', but parties and their evolution, and the practical ineliminability of parties, is the focus of the bulk of the text of 'Politics as a Vocation'. One can see from this emphasis alone why the text was a disappointment to those of its hearers who aspired to an escape from politics into a post-political *Gemeinschaft*. For Weber then, the rise of mass democracies is not a matter so much of noble sentiment and the virtues of public discussion as a product of successful and ineliminable organizational forms, notably state and party bureaucracies. Politics in the present is necessarily party politics, and to become a leader one must make one's way in a party. Even the SPD (German Social Democratic Party), as Weber's friend and associate Robert Michels famously put it, was subject to the Iron Law of Oligarchy, in contrast to, and in spite of, its egalitarian aims—a revealing example of the problem of realism and utopianism.[20]

4.3. UTOPIANISM, FUNDAMENTALISM, AND RESPONSIBILITY

In Weber's methodological writings, as well as in the Vocations essays, he developed a complex conception of the nature of value choices and the interplay between value choices and facts.[21] 'Ultimate Values', a term that Morgenthau also used, cannot be grounded in facts, justified factually, and are not matters of scientific truth—they must be decided for or committed to. Nevertheless, reason and fact is relevant, in several ways. If one is attempting to reconcile one's commitments, whether they can be reconciled is a factual matter. It is also a factual matter as to how and whether one's values are achievable in this world. Science can contribute causal knowledge, which is also knowledge about the relation between real world means and real world ends. Causal knowledge thus enables one to distinguish that which is a this-worldly or a realizable ultimate value and that which is not.

Because the achievement of many ultimate values requires the achievement of various steps in the causal process, or has many causal conditions, there are intermediate ends that are also, in effect, values or interests, and some of these intermediate ends, notably the values of the legal sphere, are intermediate ends that are shared by many people who have different ultimate ends. Political stability and action thus do not require agreement on ultimate values, or a common ideology. The nation-state is the locus of common intermediate ends, as is the law—a stable legal order is a condition for the achievement of many ultimate values, but of course it may conflict with many ultimate values as well. Weber (like his follower the legal theorist Gustav Radbruch) was fascinated with the case of the consistent anarchist, the Tolstoyan Christian who rejects the state, and with similar cases, for these were instances of ultimate values outside of and in conflict with the intermediate values of the state, and indeed with politics itself. These are not people who are confused about the realizability of their ideals in this world. Theirs is an ethic of conviction or intention, whose standards are not this-worldly success. Historically, of course, as Weber's own *Protestant Ethic* showed, the pursuit of such ideals can have powerful this-worldly consequences. And the Lutheran 'here I stand, I can do no other', which is the classic assertion that one must sometimes act in ways that do not bring success in this world, is relevant to politics as well. It appears at the end of 'Politics as a Vocation' to make a point about leadership and political morality—that deep conviction, even if it leads to failure, may be a personal condition of political greatness.

Weber's critique of the political alternatives of the time were directed at the sorts of positions, such as Christian pacifism, that mixed up this-world ends with other-world ends, and promoted delusory notions, such as the idea that from good acts only good comes. He professed genuine admiration for consistent other-worldly moralists, such as the anarchist who acknowledged that bomb-throwing would not end the state, or the Christian saint who left the consequences to God. This is the context for the many references in Morgenthau to the notion that leaders, who are responsible for the this-worldly good of the nation, cannot act justly and let the skies fall, and for the comments he makes on E. H. Carr's attempt—probably inspired by R. H. Tawney's contemporary writings—to reconcile idealism and realism. By its very nature, if idealism is other-worldly and realism is this-worldly, there can be no mixture which in the end sacrifices the this-worldly ends to the other-worldly ones. To be a Christian statesman whose Christianity gets in the way of his statesmanship is simply to risk failure.

The nation, in Weber's terms, can be an ultimate value as well as being an intermediate end, a necessity for those pursuing other ends. Indeed, in principle there is no limit on what can be an ultimate value, though of course some values—Weber gave free trade as an example—are ridiculous as 'ultimate' value choices. One of the themes of 'Politics as a Vocation' was the consideration of what, now, is a possible political value choice that is not illusory, ignoble, or other-worldly, and Weber's answer (which implies that it is the only ennobling answer) was the nation. The nation is a this-worldly goal. Ethical positions that have this-worldly goals Weber called ethics of responsibility, because they imply that the agent is responsible for the this-worldly consequences of his actions. It is, *de facto*, because of its centrality as an intermediate goal, the locus of an unusually powerful set of consequential relationships. We cannot have this-worldly goals and ignore the central causal significance of the fact of the nation-state. Yet the character of the state, and of the political, is morally problematic. The thing that states have in common is not ends, a point that Morgenthau also underlined,[22] but the means of violence. And here the Tolstoyans are right: to engage in politics, as Weber said, is to contract with diabolical powers. Politics is morally dangerous, precisely because it is intrinsically connected with the means of violence. With the means of violence, one cannot be sure that the consequences of one's actions will be entirely good: the achievement of good ends is mixed up with bad consequences. The tragic character of politics is a result of the *pacte diabolique* that the political agent makes with the intrinsically violent power of the state. This is not, however, a plea for 'power politics'. On the contrary, power is a means, or an intermediate end. When taken as a goal (by a politician, for example), Weber said, it 'leads nowhere and is senseless'.[23]

Morgenthau used different terms to deal with these distinctions, but much of what he said maps on to Weber exactly. He used the Weberian language of ultimate values, a language which makes sense as ethical theory only in the context of a particular concept of valuation as a matter of decision.[24] In an unpublished 1937 paper, he reiterated Weber's notion that in our time, having eaten the fruit of the tree of knowledge, as he put it, we are faced with the fact that there can be no metaphysical foundation of morality, but that we must choose. As Morgenthau put it, 'We live in a crisis of metaphysical consciousness . . . This insight bans morality into that realm within which it alone can still exist in objectivity today: the human soul.'[25] For both of them, decision is necessitated by the antinomic character of the choices—between power and the absolutism of the Christian Gospels for Weber (in 'Between two Laws' and in 'Politics as a Vocation'), between 'Love and Power' and 'natural aspirations' and the Christian Gospels for Morgenthau.[26] The distinction between realism and utopianism in Morgenthau worked to make the same point that Weber made—that particular 'goals' and programmes appear to their followers to be realistic and this-worldly, but are in fact utopian escapes from the realities of politics. Morgenthau, it might appear, has a much more restrictive conception of what goals are realistic—so restrictive that there are, for great powers, no real options in international politics: every nation is bound to pursue its interests through power politics or fail. But this is a misreading, as will become evident in the next section.

Morgenthau was obliged to comment on a number of other traditions as well, notably those that were foundational to American liberal democracy. Needless to say, it would have been self-defeating to announce himself as a philosophical critic of these foundations: prudence required something else. So we do not find among Morgenthau's works anything like the dramatic texts in which Weber presented his views. But the views are nevertheless given explicitly, as when he said that 'the moral problem of politics resolves itself into the question: Given the essential incompatibility between politics and Christian ethics, how must moral men act in the political sphere?'[27] Morgenthau's answer was not quite the same as Weber's, who stressed the conflict more than the resolution. Morgenthau's answer was 'to try to choose the lesser evil' and do 'as little violence to the commands of Christian ethics' as one can. The dilemma is nevertheless the same for both, and the difference in Morgenthau's response is not one that necessarily has any practical significance. The political 'sphere'—the term is used by both men— is governed by its own considerations, notably the this-worldly consideration of consequences. Moreover, it is unclear precisely what 'ultimate or absolute' status Christian morality can have for a thinker who affirms the reality of the antinomian conflicts, resolvable only by decision, that both Weber and Morgenthau placed in the centre of ethical consideration.

Morgenthau seemed to have adopted the solution of his colleague Leo Strauss and his followers, of treating the dogmatic foundations of liberal democracy and the adherence of the American people to them, in a utilitarian way, as a *donné* of history which is better left publicly unquestioned.[28] Morgenthau found a surrogate for the acceptance of liberal dogmatism in a Herder-like notion of the purpose of American politics, an exercise that resembles comments by Weber on the civilizational differences between France and Germany, which Weber said cannot be rationally judged or decided between, but are like different gods. Morgenthau did not say this. Instead he discussed a distinction between 'the absolute good' and 'the relative good' that allowed him to bracket the question of absolute good—leaving it, as he said, 'to a seminar in political philosophy', and to speak in a utilitarian manner about the political effectiveness of communist and democratic ideology in the setting of actual political contestation. He suggested that a fascination with the idea of 'the truth' in politics, combined with a 'disregard for the actual aspirations of human beings' gets in the way of political success, much as, one might say, Christian doctrine gets in the way of sound political action.[29] In 'the sphere of political action' itself, Morgenthau suggested, we must accept that 'there is no such thing as one and the same truth for everyone', and that good policies, those which respond to people's aspirations, are the condition for the success of propaganda, not the other way around.[30]

4.4. INTERESTS, POWER, AND 'PRAGMA'

The 'interests' quotation in *Politics Among Nations* is *not* an affirmation of some sort of reductive thesis to the effect that a small set of *particular* (power-political) interests rule the world. It is the opposite—'ideal' interests are 'real' interests as well, and they include the ideals of a culture, religious ideals, and, indeed, all the goals that it could possibly to fall in either the category of ideal or material interests. So a theory of international politics based on the idea that there are common human interests would not be a Weberian one. Yet this is precisely the idea that has often been thought to define 'realism', and to define Morgenthau himself as a 'human nature realist'. But it has often puzzled commentators that Morgenthau repeatedly contradicted this claim. His use of this quotation and the related commentary indicates that he took the same view that Weber did on the matter: political goals of all kinds—ideal and material—have been the object of states and leaders. Weber defined states not in terms of ends, which he said have, historically, been exceedingly various, but in terms of means: the use of physical force and the successful creation of a monopoly of legitimate violence. It is no accident that the same language appears in Morgenthau. But there is another issue, that Weber spoke of under the heading of the *pragma* of power, that qualifies this diversity of possible ends. The state, as an intermediate end to the achievement common of virtually all actions—to the individual goal of getting rich as well as the goal of helping the poor—is governed by considerations of power that seem to be autonomous.

4.5. LAWS OF POLITICS, SCIENTISM, POLICY SCIENCE, AND VERSTEHENDE SOZIOLOGIE

One area in which Weber and Morgenthau seem to be radically different, indeed poles apart, is in respect to the possibilities of social science as a discoverer of 'laws' of social life. There is also what is at least a puzzle about the notion of a policy science. Morgenthau's model of international relations theory and advice seems to be a form of policy science; Weber fought a pivotal struggle against policy science and the policy of the German Historical School of Economics, which was also fond of the language of 'laws', in a dispute over value-freedom in the *Verein für Sozialpolitik*. In his methodological writings on Röscher and Knies, he went out of his way to attack two thinkers of the older generation of the Historical School, in part because their use of the language of laws, in the context of laws of development, was historicist and epistemic.[31] The so-called laws, he argued, were teleological constructions that mixed up fact and value and represented the historical perspective of their authors, a critique that resembled Butterfield's critique of the Whig conception of history. He went on to argue that the terms of description of the historical events that interest us are necessarily and intrinsically laden with the values of our culture, and that the idea of a final or scientific vocabulary for the historical sciences was an illusion. A chemistry or astronomy of social life, as he put it, even if it could be constructed, would fail to answer the questions that interest us, precisely because it would not explain the facts that we want to explain, which come in the language of life, which is intrinsically valuative, or as we would now say, cultural.

Weber also had a related argument about abstraction, which suggested that supposed laws, such as the abstractions of economics, were better understood as ideal-types than as representations of reality. Their first purpose is to aid in the understanding of action, and they are only secondarily of interest for their predictive power. Like Morgenthau, he was trained in the continental legal tradition, and his notion of abstraction reflected his background: the application of the abstract categories, as in the law, was, as he put it, a matter of casuistry. The notion of causality he employed was also drawn from the legal tradition, and it was not the causality of scientific 'law' but of causal responsibility, which he understood in terms of an increase in the probability of an outcome that could be attributed to some act by comparing the (necessarily hypothetical) probable outcome without the act to the probable outcome with the act. Models of rational action (which he regarded as ideal-types as well) were valuable for explicating action, or making it understandable, even when the point of the analysis was to show how emotion and error produced the outcome.

This was Weber's *Verstehende Soziologie*. His view of policy science was that policy could never be 'scientifically' grounded. For Weber, the younger German Historical School, especially such figures as Gustav Schmoller, who served as government advisors and sought in the *Verein* to do studies that provided direct advice based on a scientific consensus with respect to policy, were committing a kind of fraud because they mixed up fact and value and presented conclusions as 'scientific' which were necessarily valuative. In this case, a particular set of values was concealed—values which he himself did not share, and which he argued served to promote the bureaucratization of human life and the parcelling out of the human soul that bureaucratization produced.

Morgenthau, it would appear, was by contrast an anti-relativist with respect to social science and an anti-historicist who believed in 'laws' of power in the politics of nations, rooted in universal truths about human nature, that not only can be discovered or identified but also can ground a policy science, or as he put it, the 'rational principles of sound foreign policy'.[32] Advising the state on policy, and independently criticizing policy when necessary on the basis of knowledge of the laws of power, is the proper business of the International Relations specialist. Morgenthau's listing of the Six Principles of Political Realism is certainly unlike any list to be found in Weber. Though Weber was also fond of lists, the lists were typically of types or causal conditions, consistent with his general methodological ideas, not lists of principles or laws.

Nevertheless there are some important surface commonalities that point to a possible resolution of the apparent conflict. Both Weber and Morgenthau opposed the kind of single-factor law that writers like Marx, in Weber's case the energeticist Wilhelm Ostwald, and in Morgenthau's case E. H. Carr, represented.

They opposed these as reductivisms, particularly attempts to reduce politics to something outside the sphere of politics. This was another way of saying that the sphere of politics had a kind of *de facto* autonomy, that to explain politics required considerations special to politics. And in this special context, Weber himself, in his political writings, spoke of laws, as when he said that 'whatever participates in the achievements of the power-state, is entangled with the laws of the "power-pragma" that rules over all political history'.[33] This is a remarkable formulation. It seems to at least open the door to precisely the kind of interpretation Morgenthau later developed.

Morgenthau's theoretical constructions, of which the discussion of the balance of power in *Politics Among Nations* is perhaps the paradigm case, are 'universal' in a peculiar sense. They more closely resemble Weber's ideal-typifications—which after all represent causal processes, as well as casual processes taken together to represent phenomena such as the state, or systemic forms, such as the Greek city-state—than they do laws of physics or principles of engineering. They do not explain and predict in an unconditional way, as 'scientific' laws do. Statesmen routinely fail to act in accordance with them: otherwise there would be no point to advising them and no occasion for criticizing them for failing to act in accordance with these laws.

From the point of view of Weber's own methodological writing, the phrase 'the laws of the "power-pragma" that rules over all political history' is anomalous. It of course appears not in an academic text but a wartime newspaper exchange on pacifism. Nevertheless, it is intriguing to raise the question of consistency. If one does not make too much, or the wrongly scientistic thing, of the language of 'laws', it can be reconciled to Weber's general methodological position in a way that also sheds some light on Morgenthau. If we consider the 'power-pragma' as the more or less stable realities of state action, and consider, in the light of the discussion of intermediate ends above, that there is a common ground of intermediate ends or interests which come together in the 'power-pragma' facts of the state's ability to act, and we further grant that the problem of preserving and producing the effective state has complex ramifications that are distinctive to states and to the sphere of the political, it makes sense to say, as Weber said, that participating in the achievements of the *Machtstaat* entangles one in these causal and moral realities and thus in the complex ramifications that they produce. The anarchist, or the consistent Tolstoyan, whom Weber had discussed a few lines before the phrase appeared, is right to think that with respect to the *Machtstaat* one is in for a penny, in for a pound, and cannot free oneself from the entanglement of consequences implied by any 'participation in the achievements'.

The stable complexity of these power-pragma allows us to typify them. For Weber, this would mean that we could reason about the typifications as though power pragma belonged to the domain of fact. He would nevertheless remind us of the valuative or cultural conditions of our construction of this domain as meaningful. It is a construction that reflects our practical and valuative interests, and a selection from the infinite complexity of reality which has no transhistorical validity. This is as real as it gets in the social sciences, and enough 'reality' for us to speak, loosely, about 'laws', at least in a non-scholarly context. And it is reasonable to think that in the special context in which Morgenthau operated, the policy-oriented domain of international relations, which as Weber would have said takes the basic elements of international politics as presuppositions, this use of the notion of law is also unproblematic. It only becomes problematic when we forget how the domain was constructed and treat it transhistorically.

But here, in a central part of Morgenthau, we do find a striking (though again practically insignificant) difference with Weber. Although much has been written about Weber's implicit philosophical anthropology or conception of man, there are few texts in which Weber made transhistorical generalizations about man as such. One of them is a comment to the effect that the desire for freedom is part of fundamental humanity. Morgenthau, however, went far beyond this by asserting that the desire for power is universal.[34] Weber was more cautious, and indeed, in his constitutional writings, emphasized the problem of putting into authority people who had the necessary power-instincts.

What are we to make of this? It is difficult to see what sort of account can be given of Morgenthau's theoretical constructions other than one that is consistent with Weber's form of historicism: they are not transhistorical, if only because they presuppose state-forms that are not universal. They are policy-relevant only because they are not true in the sense that laws of physics are true. When Morgenthau spoke of 'uncertainty', he was using a term derived from his colleague Frank Knight at the University of Chicago, who famously distinguished uncertainty (randomness with unknowable probabilities) from risk (randomness with knowable probabilities). The term is appropriate. In a practical sense, international relations as an area of expertise operates in a domain of uncertainty, just as statesmen do, in part because the *de facto* causal autonomy of the political sphere is always incomplete, so the political is not a domain with fully knowable probabilities, and thus not capable of being made fully subject to predictive laws, even of a probabilistic kind. Weber captured this feature with his notion of ideal-type.

Morgenthau, not surprisingly, used a different language to make the point in a way that had the same practical implications. Nevertheless, Morgenthau himself appears to endorse the kind of interpretation I have given here, when he said, that, because of uncertainty, we can only judge correctness retrospectively, and that this inherent feature of the subject matter

> ...erects insuperable limits to the development of a rational theory of international relations. It is only within these limits that theoretical thinking on international relations is theoretically and practically fruitful. Within these limits, a theory of international relations performs the function any theory performs, that is, to bring *order and meaning* into a mass of unconnected material and to increase knowledge through the logical development of certain propositions empirically established.[35]

The two-step phrasing of this account of the function of theory, beginning with meaning and continuing to empirical propositions, is suggestive of Weber's model of *Verstehende Soziologie,* and in the following paragraph Morgenthau expanded on this hint in a striking way:

While this theoretical function of a theory of international relations is no different from the function *any social theory* performs, its practical function is peculiar to itself. The practical function of a theory of international relations has this in common with all political theory that it depends very much on the political environment in which it operates. In other words, political thinking is, as German sociology puts it, '*standortgebunden*', that is to say, it is tied to a particular social situation.[36]

Treating international relations as a social theory and making political theory a subcategory of social theory bound to specific historical situations, and emphasizing that 'science conveys not only objective knowledge but also the image of a meaningful world worth knowing selected from the many available',[37] brings us back to the model of ideal-types in Weber, which perform, for a particular historical epoch with particular cultural constitutive interests, the function of organizing a mass of material—a selection from the infinity of facts, as Weber said, and also provide a means of making empirical sense of the facts.

Morgenthau's philosophical anthropology, however, particularly his ideas about the universality of power-seeking, takes us beyond Weber. Weber framed the kinds of fundamental conflicts that Morgenthau addressed in 'Love and Power' in his sociology of religion in terms of what he called the religious rejection of the world, and he associated rejection of the world with the problem of theodicy. In 'Politics as a Vocation', he argued that anything short of complete abstention or saintliness produced entanglement. Morgenthau was more philosophically ambitious, or incautious, when he attempted to argue that love and power have a common root in the desire, impossible to fulfil, to overcome loneliness.[38] And he went on, intriguingly, to characterize the relation of charismatic subject and ruler in terms of love.[39] This is a real difference. But what is the practical significance of the difference? It is difficult to find any. For the statesman, who lives in the world of power pragma and consequences, the ethic of love of the Gospel is not an option.

4.6. LEADERS AND STATESMEN

Any consideration of the nature of statesmanship presupposes a consideration of the nature of the political and political choice. We may summarize the results of Weber's account of political choice as follows. Pure power politics leads nowhere and is senseless, since power is at most an intermediate end, or a means, rather than an end in itself. This is true for the domestic politician, but it is equally true for national leaders and for national policy. If each beneficiary of the power-state is entangled in its power-pragma, the statesman is most entangled of all. Although, in theory, the leader is free to choose whatever ultimate value he wishes, and to try his programme out on the field of charismatic competition with other potential leaders, the complex ramifications of the consequences of political action have the effect of limiting possible political programmes or international policies very sharply. The category defined by what is both meaningful and achievable is very limited: this is why the nation, understood in a particular sense to be something beyond a machine of power, comes to be the single answer to the question 'what should I choose?' that Weber can offer at the close of 'Politics as a Vocation'.

The notion of responsibility, together with the need for goals to be other than mere power, points the leader who is governed by the this-worldly consequences of his actions towards a particular relation with the nation in its larger sense as a bearer of a cultural contribution to the world, its legacy or message. It was of course a major element of the German identity at the time, contained in the 'Ideas of 1914', that Germany was the land of poets and thinkers.[40] Along with this went a belief in the inferiority of other national cultures, notably that of the 'nation of shopkeepers' and its 'night-watchmen state'. Weber reviled the 'Ideas of 1914' and was largely free of the illusion of cultural superiority in its extreme forms. He would never have written a book like Sombart's *Heroes and Hawkers* (1915).[41] Nevertheless, he did believe that Germany had a special contribution to make to world culture, and preserving this contribution implied that international political struggle was the 'responsible' course of action. As he put in a much quoted passage:

Future generations, our own descendants in particular, will not blame the Danes, the Swiss, the Dutch, the Norwegians if, without a struggle, the rule over the world—and that ultimately means the determination of the character of the civilization of the future—should be divided between the ordinances of Russian officials on one side and the conventions of Anglo-Saxon society on the other—perhaps with some touch of Latin *raison* added for good measure.[42]

The phrasing recalls a contemporary discussion, in which Weber participated, of the profound historical consequences of the battle of Marathon.[43] Implicitly, the magnitude of the consequences—the determination of the character of civilization—have the effect of dictating the task of the leader and his value 'choice'. His task is to take on the burden of these consequences and to commit to the fulfilment of the nation's historical responsibility as his own value. To succeed requires that this be done in a way that attracts the kind of public support that enables him to succeed—and in the modern setting this means attracting a following with one's charisma. Since charisma is dying at the moment of its birth, always and inevitably collapsing into a system of payoffs to followers, which limits the leader's range of action, the moment of effective action has to be seized. Moreover, it is characteristically the case that the leader needs to be ahead of the led. The leader can only lead by taking chances, committing himself to some goal, and pulling the followers along. The character of the leader is thus critical. His commitment may well need to take on the same emotional character as the utopian in order to persuade his followers to follow, and to act with sufficient resolution in the face of danger and uncertainty.

One can scarcely trace out this logic without thinking of Bismarck, and of course neither Weber, the son of a National Liberal politician in the era of Bismarck, nor Morgenthau, who told us that he was impressed by Oncken's seminar on Bismarck's diplomacy, thought about leadership without thinking about the Iron Chancellor. Bismarck was the model of successful leadership. He knew what his goal was, and when the opportunity arose he seized the moment, saw beyond the limitations of the political situation he was in, attracted support and cowed his parliamentary opponents through the success of his bold actions, and showed that political forms—parliament—and legalities could be overcome by the plebiscitary leader who derived support directly from public legitimation. Weber's constitutional writings, which were designed to create a space for a plebiscitary strong President who could act above the heads of the parties, were an attempt to take the lessons of Bismarck and use them to overcome the problems with Bismarck himself—notably the catastrophic consequences of his rule for the development of successor leaders. Weber saw this as a direct consequence of Bismarck's sidelining of parliament, which prevented it from serving as a nursery for leaders. The later Chancellors, who came from the bureaucracy, not only lacked his political instincts, but they had the deficiencies of the bureaucratic mentality as well, despite being competent experts from a much-admired bureaucratic system.

Weber's conception of leadership is contained in his discussion of the question of what sort of person has the inner qualities to have the calling of the genuine politician. It was, in a sense, a description of a Bismarck without the flaws. But it was composed out of elements that were part of his ongoing wartime polemics against the Pan-Germans to whom he was politically opposed, and employed much of the same language.[44] The three pre-eminent qualities are 'passion, a feeling of responsibility, and a sense of proportion' where 'passion as devotion to a "cause" makes responsibility to this cause a guiding star of action', which in turn requires a sense of proportion, and an 'ability to let realities work upon him with inner concentration and calmness'.[45] 'Lack of distance *per se* is one of the deadly sins of every politician' and the one to which intellectuals in politics are most susceptible.

These notions reappear in Morgenthau's discussions of the qualities of statesmen and in his critical comments on political leaders. In the case of 'proportion', the same term was used in a discussion of the American obsession with the trial of Cardinal Mindszenty and in the reactions to the acquisition of the atomic bomb by the Soviets.[46] What Weber called 'distance', Morgenthau, quoting Churchill, called the absence of illusions.[47] Passion, in Weber's sense, is largely what is meant by Morgenthau's many remarks on moral purpose, and have the same structural place in their arguments: for Weber, passionate devotion to a cause is what lifts the politician above the pointless pursuit of power for its own sake, as 'moral purpose' does for Morgenthau.[48]

Morgenthau's complaints about American self-aggrandizement are parallel to Weber's similar comments about the Pan-Germans. His specific critiques of various politicians, such as Kennedy, whom he faulted for vacillation and unwillingness to lead, and diplomats, such as Dulles, and even of the work-products of the state department bureaucracy, call to mind Weber's critiques of the bureaucratic mentality and of the personal diplomacy of Wilhelm II.[49] But the parallels are especially evident in Morgenthau's discussions of Lincoln. Morgenthau organized his material on Lincoln in terms of Lincoln's personal qualities, and used much of Weber's own language in his characterizations, such as 'objectivity and detachment', 'the union as the ultimate value', and he touches on themes familiar from Weber, including Lincoln's humility or freedom from vanity, what Weber would call his sense of proportion, toughness, practicality, his sense of the nation's uniqueness, and of course, his passionate devotion to the cause.[50]

Much could be said about the judgements involved here, and the differences in shading between the two. But even to construct the problem of statesmanship or leadership in this way reflects the acceptance of a common model for the problem of leadership, a problematic that is itself unusual, and points to a more basic commonality. The great theme of Weber's political thinking, which appears most fully in his constitutional writings, is the problem of conducting an effective foreign policy in the face of the *de facto* reality of democracy—the reality that without broad public support no policy can be effective. This is Morgenthau's great theme as well, and the place it leads him is the same: to the problem of leadership understood as a problem of character and a problem of overcoming the temptation to capitulate to the short-term advantages of domestic politics, represented for Weber by the parliamentary parties, and for Morgenthau by the American constitutional structure itself.

The focus on leadership, shared with Weber, is perhaps the distinguishing mark of Morgenthau's realism, and the aspect of his thought that is at once the most compelling and challenging. Morgenthau was very far from thinking of the realm of international politics as a depersonalized security system governed by mechanical laws or rational choice calculations. The problem of leadership that occupied Weber also occupied Morgenthau. That Morgenthau reflected on Lincoln for forty years, eventually reading and analysing his letters with an eye to assessing his character and virtues as a leader, without a definite agenda for publication, but out of an almost obsessive concern with making sense of the morality of great leadership itself, speaks volumes. Morgenthau's realism was about understanding the concrete world—and the inner world—of flesh-and-blood humans who were faced with responsibility before history.

NOTES

1. This chapter is an abridged and modified version of 'Morgenthau as a Weberian' originally published in G. O. Mazur (ed.), *One Hundred Year Commemoration to the Life of Hans Morgenthau (1904–2004)* (New York: Semenenko Foundation, 2004), pp. 88–114.

2. On the importance of the émigré experience for classical realism, see Duncan Bell's introduction to this volume.

3. Morgenthau, *Scientific Man vs. Power Politics* (Chicago: University of Chicago Press, 1946).

4. Morgenthau, *Politics among Nations: The Struggle for Peace and Power* (New York: Knopf, 1948); Morgenthau, 'The Political Science of E. H. Carr', *World Politics*, 1

(1948), pp. 127–34. For Morgenthau's views on Carr, see Molloy's Chapter 5 in this volume.

5. Weber, 'The Introduction to the Sociology of Religions', in H. H. Gerth and C. W. Mills (eds. and trans.), *From Max Weber: Essays in Sociology* (New York: Oxford University Press, 1946 [1915]), pp. 267–301; Weber, 'Science as a Vocation' [1917] in Gerth and Mills, *From Max Weber*, pp. 129–56; and Weber, *The Protestant Ethic and the Spirit of Capitalism*, trans. Talcott Parsons (New York: Scribner's, 1958 [1904–5]).

6. See William Buxton, *Talcott Parsons and the Capitalist Nation State: Political Sociology as a Strategic Vocation* (Toronto: University of Toronto Press, 1985).

7. Strauss, *Natural Right and History* (Chicago: University of Chicago Press, 1953).

8. Bloom, *The Closing of the American Mind* (New York: Simon and Schuster, 1987).

9. Weber, *The Methodology of the Social Sciences*, trans. E. Shils and H. Finch (New York: The Free Press, 1949).

10. Morgenthau, *Politics Among Nations: The Struggle for Peace and Power*, 5th edn. (New York: Knopf, 1978), p. 9.

11. Morgenthau, 'An Intellectual Autobiography', *Society*, 15 (1978), p. 64.

12. Rothenbücher and his relation to Weber are described in Stephen P. Turner and Regis Factor, *Max Weber and the Dispute over Reason and Value* (London: Routledge, 1984), p. 169.

13. The literature that mentions these issues is both large and growing. See, for example, William Bain, 'Deconfusing Morgenthau: Moral Inquiry and Classical Realism Reconsidered', *Review of International Studies* 26 (2000), pp. 445–64; Christoph Frei, *Hans J. Morgenthau: An Intellectual Biography* (Baton Rouge: LSU, 2001); Jim George, *Discourses of Global Politics: A Critical (Re)Introduction to International Relations* (Boulder: Lynne Rienner, 1994); Stefano Guzzini, *Realism in International Relations and International Political Economy: The Continuing Story of a Death Foretold* (London: Routledge, 1998); Robert Jervis, 'Hans Morgenthau, Realism, and the Scientific Study of International Politics', *Social Research*, 61 (1994), pp. 853–76; Joseph Kruzel and James Rosenau, *Journeys through World Politics: Autobiographical Reflections of Thirty-Four Academic Travelers* (Lexington: Lexington Books, 1989); Benjamin Mollov, *Power and Transcendence: Hans J. Morgenthau and the Jewish Experience* (Lanham: Rowman & Littlefield, 2002); A. J. H. Murray, 'The Moral Politics of Hans Morgenthau', *The Review of Politics*, 58 (1996), pp. 81–107; Ido Oren, *Our Enemies and Us: America's Rivalries and the Making of Political Science* (Ithaca: Cornell University Press, 2003); Greg Russell, *Hans J. Morgenthau and the Ethics of American Statecraft* (Baton Rouge: LSU, 1990); Michael Smith, *Realist Thought from Weber to Kissinger* (Baton Rouge: LSU, 1986), pp. 134–65; Alfons Soellner, 'Hans J. Morgenthau—Ein Deutscher Konservativer in Amerika? Eine Fallstudie zum Wissenstransfer durch Emigration', in Rainer Erb and Michael Schmidt (eds.), *Antisemitismus und juedische Geschichte: Studien zu Ehren von Herbert A. Strauss* (Berlin: Wissenschaftlicher Autorenverlag, 1987); Kenneth Thompson (ed.), *A Collection of Essays: Truth and Tragedy: A Tribute to Hans J. Morgenthau* (Washington: New Republic, 1985); Robert Tucker, 'Professor Morgenthau's Theory of Political Realism', *American Political Science Review*, 46 (1952), pp. 214–24. I am grateful to Christian Büger for identifying several of these sources for me.

14. Weber, 'Science as a Vocation' [1917], in Gerth and Mills (eds.), *From Max Weber*, pp. 129–56.

15. Max Scheler, in Maria Scheler (ed.), *Schriften zur Soziologie und Weltanschauugslere*, 2nd edn. (Munich: Francke Verlag, 1963), p. 15.

16. Weber, 'Politics as a Vocation' [1919], in Gerth and Mills (eds.), *From Max Weber*, pp. 77–128.

17. Weber, 'Parliament and Government in Germany under a New Political Order' [1918], in Peter Lassman and Ronald Speirs (eds.), *Political Writings* (Cambridge: Cambridge University Press, 1994), pp. 130–71.

18. Weber, *Gesammelte Aufsätze zur Religionssoziologie*, 3 vols. (Tübingen: Mohr, 1988 [1920]); and Weber, 'The Meaning of "Ethical Neutrality" in Sociology and Economics' [1917], in Edward A. Shils and Henry Finch (eds. and trans.), *The Methodology of the Social Sciences* (New York: The Free Press, 1949), pp. 1–47.

19. Weber, 'Between Two Laws' [1916], trans. C. W. Mackauer, in John W. Boyer and Jan Goldstein (eds.), *Readings in Western Civilization: Twentieth-Century Europe* (Chicago: The University of Chicago Press, 1987), p. 151.

20. A useful brief discussion of the problem of mass society and politics in Weber can be found in Sven Eliaeson, 'Constitutional Caesarism: Weber's Politics in Their German Context', in Stephen P. Turner (ed.), *The Cambridge Companion to Weber* (Cambridge: Cambridge University Press, 2000), pp. 131–48.

21. The best treatment of the topic of Weber's value theory remains H. H. Brunn, *Science, Values and Politics in Max Weber's Methodology* (Copenhagen: Munksgaard, 1972). As it happens, Bruun spent his career as a Danish Diplomat.

22. Morgenthau, *Politics among Nations: The Struggle for Peace and Power*, 5th edn., p. 9.

23. Weber, 'Politics as a Vocation', p. 116.

24. Morgenthau, *The Purpose of American Politics* (New York: Knopf, 1960), p. 343.

25. Morgenthau, 'Kann in unserer Zeit eine objektiv Moralordnung aufgestellt werden?', unpublished ms. Geneva 1937, quoted in Hans-Karl Pichler, 'The Godfathers of "Truth": Max Weber and Carl Schmitt in Morgenthau's Theory of Power Politics', *Review of International Studies*, 24 (1998), p. 191.

26. Morgenthau, *The Restoration of American Politics* (Chicago: University of Chicago Press, 1962), pp. 7–18. For a discussion of 'Love and Power', see also Molloy's Chapter 5 in this volume.

27. Morgenthau, *The Restoration of American Politics*, p. 16.

28. See also the discussion of Morgenthau's America in Vibeke Schou Tjalve's Chapter 10 in this volume.

29. Morgenthau, *The Restoration of American Politics*, p. 243.

30. Morgenthau, *The Restoration of American Politics*, p. 244.

31. Weber, *Röscher and Knies* (New York: The Free Press, 1975).

32. Morgenthau, *Truth and Power: Essays of a Decade, 1960–1970* (New York: Praeger, 1970), p. 44.

33. Weber, 'Between Two Laws', p. 151.

34. There is a literature attributing Morgenthau's ideas on these subjects to Nietzsche and Freud. Frei, in his *Hans J. Morgenthau*, makes the case for Nietzsche's influence, a case which must be approached with some caution. Cf. Stephen Turner and G. O. Mazur, 'Morgenthau as a Weberian Methodologist', *European Journal of International Relations*, forthcoming. The case for Freudian influence is made by Robert Schuett, 'Freudian Roots of Political Realism: The Importance of Sigmund Freud to Hans J. Morgenthau's Theory of International Politics', *History of the Human Sciences*, 20 (2007), pp. 53–78.

35. Morgenthau, *The Decline of Democratic Politics* (Chicago: University of Chicago Press, 1962), p. 72. Emphasis added.

36. Morgenthau, *The Decline of Democratic Politics*, pp. 72–3. Emphasis added.

37. Morgenthau, *Science: Servant or Master* (New York: New American Library, 1972), p. 16.
38. Morgenthau, *The Restoration of American Politics*, pp. 8–9.
39. Morgenthau, *The Restoration of American Politics*, pp. 12–13.
40. Wolfgang Natter, *Literature at War, 1914–1940: Representing the Time of 'Greatness' in Germany* (New Haven: Yale University Press, 1999).
41. Sombart, *Händler und Helden: Patiotsche Besinnungen* (Munich: Dunkler and Humboldt, 1915).
42. Weber, *Politische Schriften*, pp. 139–42, trans. and quoted in Boyer and Jan Goldstein (eds.), *Readings in Western Civilization*, p. 153.
43. Friedrich H. Tenbruck, 'Max Weber and Edward Meyer', in Wolfgang J. Mommsen and Jürgen Osterhammel (eds.), *Max Weber and His Contemporaries* (London: Allen and Unwin, 1987), pp. 234–67.
44. Roger Chickering, 'Dietrich Schäfer and Max Weber', in Mommsen and Osterhammel (eds.), *Max Weber and His Contemporaries*, p. 341.
45. Weber, 'Politics as Vocation', p. 115.
46. Morgenthau, *The Impasse of American Foreign Policy* (Chicago: University of Chicago Press, 1962), pp. 152–3.
47. Morgenthau, *The Impasse of American Foreign Policy*, p. 167.
48. Morgenthau, *The Decline of Democratic Politics*, p. 130.
49. Morgenthau, *The Restoration of American Politics*, pp. 101–08; Morgenthau, *Truth and Power*, p. 104.
50. Morgenthau and David Hein, *Essays on Lincoln's Faith and Politics* (Lanham: University Press of America, 1983), pp. 17–24, 88, 30, 45, 53, 59, 82.

5

Hans J. Morgenthau Versus E. H. Carr: Conflicting Conceptions of Ethics in Realism

Seán Molloy

5.1. INTRODUCTION

It is commonplace to assert that realism is an amoral or immoral theory of international politics, that its focus on power is to the exclusion, or at best the marginalization, of ethical concerns.[1] The purpose of this chapter is to challenge this general criticism and to identify the ethical content in the works of two of the most foundational realist thinkers, E. H. Carr and Hans Morgenthau. The selection of Carr and Morgenthau is not arbitrary, for it is their work that marks the definitive entry of realism into the discourse of academic International Relations (IR)—the so-called realism of Thucydides, Machiavelli, Hobbes, and so forth is significant in itself, but it is anachronistic to label these authors as realist in the IR sense. It is Carr who makes the discipline defining conceptual division between the Utopian and the Realist and Morgenthau who expounds realism as a political theory of international relations. I argue that Carr and Morgenthau provide two competing perspectives on the possibility of ethical life in international relations. Carr can be seen as a pragmatist, convinced of the social construction of norms and ethics in international society. The relativism of Carr offended Morgenthau, who insisted on a transcendent perspective on matters of political morality, a perspective located outside of politics and rooted in a moral philosophy of the lesser evil.

5.2. REALISM: ETHICAL CRITIQUES

Realism's critics have in common (despite their own wide diversity) a tendency to treat realists as 'a group, reflecting a distinctive school or style of analysis'. This group is characterized by an adherence to the primacy of power, the egoism of human nature and the insecurity inherent in the international system, resulting in the familiar logic of the security dilemma.[2] It is this pursuit of power, egoism, and the determination to counter insecurity that precludes the consideration of ethics in international politics.[3] David Campbell in his analysis of the possibility of

justice within the international order identifies Kennan's statement that the interests of the national society have no moral quality as encapsulating 'concisely the
realist tradition's view that moral concerns are largely inappropriate to international affairs'. Yet as Campbell observes, Kennan's reification of *raison d'état* is itself
'insinuated' with moral considerations. Jack Donnelly recognizes the existence of
various 'hedges' in realism where the strict adherence to power politics is mitigated
by the presence of 'non-realist' elements. Realism is a continuum, he maintains,
from adherence to its 'core' principles up to a point where the non-realist elements
take over.[4] This identification of a realist continuum marks a progress of sorts
from Marshall Cohen's perhaps more typical assessment: 'The realists argue that
international relations must be viewed under the category of power and that the
conduct of nations is, and should be, guided and judged exclusively by the amoral
requirements of the national interest.' According to Charles Beitz, one of the main
principles of realism is 'that moral judgments have no place in discussions of
international affairs or foreign policy'.[5] Contemporary critics of realism hold that
it must be considered responsible for producing a 'moral cartography' that has
legitimized 'the evacuation of ethical concerns from international relations' and
for circumscribing the very discourse of international ethics. Even to the extent
that some theorists accept the existence of realist ethics, they insist that it is hostile
to the human interest.[6]

It is a part of IR folklore that realism is amoral or immoral, without any of its
critics properly elucidating the reasons why this is the case. The realists certainly
provided a critique of a particular form of moral thinking, but this does not
necessarily make them amoral, unless one insists on the infallibility of a single
ethical code, one that is liberal in origin and universal in scope. Realist ethics are in
fact built on a rejection of the notion of overarching moral codes, the observance
of which signifies 'good' behaviour and the contravention of which signifies bad
or evil behaviour. Realism instead asserts that political ethics should not be based
on the subordination of political life to absolute standards of ethical conduct
that are derived from an inappropriate context. This inversion of morality over
power, to a position of power over morality, does not necessitate an ethical void,
however, as realists have developed a variety of ways through which to reformulate
and modulate the relationship, not by the excision of ethical concerns, but rather
through the accommodation of political power and ethics.

5.3. CARR AND THE 'PROBLEM' OF MORALITY

Jonathan Haslam, Carr's former student and biographer, presents a Carr who, like
Machiavelli, attempted 'to treat politics as an ethically neutral science, not as a
branch of ethics'.[7] Haslam is, however, only partially correct in his appreciation
of Carr's concern with Machiavelli. As Haslam quotes Carr: the 'greatness of
Machiavelli is that he saw a part, though not *the whole truth of politics* with
unrivalled penetration'.[8] One may infer from the rest of the article that the part

of politics that Machiavelli did not see was the role played by morality. Carr's epitaph on Machiavelli is telling: 'His tragedy is that those who least need to learn from him make him their bible, and that those who need him most can seldom stomach a doctrine so pungent and so merciless.'[9] Carr views Machiavelli's work as a corrective, but regards his own writings as synthesizing the insights of Realism and Utopianism (albeit a synthesis that is clearly Realist in orientation).[10]

Carr presents the place of morality in international politics as 'the most obscure and difficult problem in the whole range of international studies'.[11] Carr icono-clastically dismisses the moral code of the philosopher as the most discussed guide but least practised form of moral activity in international politics. He argues instead that it is the ethical sentiments and actions of the 'ordinary man' wherein lies the true substance of ethical understanding and behaviour.[12] On the first page, Carr also introduces a distinction between personal and political morality (again, based on the perspective of 'the ordinary man').

Political morality is peculiar to the modern age in that the transition from the personal authority of the monarch to the virtual authority of the state entailed the development of a corporate, group identity. The modern state, formerly 'liberal and progressive . . . is now commonly denounced as reactionary and authoritarian', but nonetheless it is the moral subject of international politics. This personality and agency is 'a necessary fiction . . . an indispensable tool devised by the human mind for dealing with the structure of a developed society'. This fiction underpins the possibility of an international society and its ethical potential. However, one should not engage in the 'confused thinking' that equates individual and group morality: 'the obligation of the state cannot be identified with the obligation of any individual or individuals; and it is the obligations of states which are the subject of international morality.'[13] Carr is not arguing that morality should play no role in international politics, but rather that an appropriate morality is necessary. He recognizes that belief in the moral obligations of the abstractions 'Great Britain', 'France', and 'Germany' may be absurd, but it is the basis of the working international order in that these legal fictions form the foundations of an international society grounded in such concepts as recognition and sov-ereign equality. In short, he argues that states have obligations to each other proceeding from the recognition of statehood. Carr's argument is that a morality specific to these legal, corporate entities applies in international politics. The existence of this morality depends on the acceptance of individual statesmen of the idea of obligation. What Carr does not investigate are the implications for this 'hypothesis' if the statesmen in control of the various entities no longer subscribe to this notion of commitment to a wider international society. Carr blames the viciousness of contemporary international society on the influence of Darwinism. The rejection of the commitment to the web of obligations regulating international society could, however, be seen as in itself a violation of the 'virtual' ethics of that society, for it would challenge the very basis of international order. The ethics here may be grounded in convenient legal and political fictions, but they may be transgressed and the transgressions are regarded as unethical in turn.

Despite his earlier dismissal of their work, it is in his engagement with the philosophers of both Utopianism and Realism that Carr seeks to identify a political ethic of 'the ordinary man', although as he is at pains to stress '[n]either the realist view that no moral obligations are binding on states, nor the utopian view that states are subject to the same moral obligations as individuals, corresponds to the assumptions of the ordinary man'.[14] Although anxious to emphasize that neither Realist nor Utopian has the monopoly on the truth of matters in international politics, Carr's arguments proceed from the 'reality' of state conduct in marked contrast to the legalistic and moralistic statements of the Utopians.

The statesman has created a moral framework derived from the concept of obligation as the key factor in the preservation of civilization, itself a common good. This framework underpins the normative element of international society: 'A state which does not conform to certain standards of behaviour towards its own citizens and, more particularly, towards foreigners will be branded as "uncivilised".' This commitment to civilization is not a norm of overriding political significance, but it is an important norm and one that guides, if not trumps, state behaviour in the operation of international society, or the comity of nations. The violation of treaties and other anti-social behaviour in international politics is, according to Carr, rare and exceptional, 'requiring special justification. The general sense of obligation remains.'[15] From this obligation emerges the basis for morality in that the recognition of obligation to other members of the international society and to the maintenance of that society produces the institutions of diplomacy, alliances, formal treaties, the various strands of international law, and eventually international organizations.

This moral universe of obligation towards civilization and the observance of commitments to international society does not, however, proceed from the standards of individual morality, grounded as they are in the great religions or in modern liberal thought. Although the statesman and the ordinary man in the street could distinguish the difference between the types of observance and moralities at play, '[m]any utopian thinkers have been so puzzled by this phenomenon that they have refused to recognise it'.[16] The morality of statecraft is a special case of 'group morality' other examples of which include professional and commercial morality. Statecraft is a special case by 'virtue of its position as the supreme holder of political power'. Political power then is the basis for collective ethics.

The state may act altruistically, but according to Carr the defining characteristic of state morality is anchored in a different concept of duty to that which applies to the individual: 'the duty of the group person appears by common consent to be more limited by self-interest than the duty of the individual.'[17] It is not that there is no limit to the states self-interest in Carr's scheme—for example, when discussing immigration he states 'it may be its duty to admit as large a number as is compatible with the interests of its own people'—but rather that the kind of altruism that an individual can practise in giving away all his wealth cannot be expected of a group person such as a state. Self-interest in the group person therefore is more legitimate and different in kind than self-interest in the individual.

5.3.1. 'A State or a Limited Company Cannot be a Saint or a Mystic'

Realism inflects the ethics of political life in the calculation of interest. In relation to the altruistic virtues, 'a state should indulge in them in so far as this is not seriously incompatible with its more important interests'. Furthermore, the standards of behaviour are more lax at the international level as there is a prior and overriding commitment to the state and its interests over the interests of international society. The competition of ethical obligations leads 'the ordinary man' to expect 'certain kinds of behaviour which he would definitely regard as immoral in the individual'. Individual morality therefore is different from group morality: 'Acts which would be immoral in the individual may become virtue when performed on behalf of the group person.'[18] Egoism plays a part in the creation of the group person of the state and its conduct in international affairs as the 'individuals' concerned seek to amplify their strength. Loyalty to the state, the vehicle for the realization of this amplified strength and achievement of desires, 'becomes the cardinal virtue of the individual, and may require him to condone behaviour by the group person which he would condemn in himself'. Not only are individual and group morality qualitatively different but in certain circumstances they can conflict, introducing an ethical dilemma where a choice is necessary between two distinct ethical commitments. As Carr writes, there is a 'moral duty to promote the welfare, and further the interests, of the group as a whole [the duty to the state]; and this duty tends to eclipse duty to a wider community', that is, international society. Carr is not denying the role of morality and obligation, rather he is consciously placing the practice of international politics in the context of competing obligations. One may disagree with his formulation of the morality of state action within international society, but one cannot deny that it is a species of moral reasoning, with a considered moral viewpoint underpinning its logic and operation.

Carr recognized the emotive appeal and the intense loyalty that the state commands from its citizens as a basis for making choices, including moral choices about international politics. The state, as part of the society of states, also provides the foundation for a sense of 'the good' in international affairs in that the right to self-preservation becomes the moral basis of that society: 'The good of the state comes more easily to be regarded as a moral end in itself...The state thus comes to be regarded as having a right of self-preservation which overrides [other] moral obligation.'[19] This *über*-norm of self-preservation explains the apparent immorality of state behaviour. Carr seems to be arguing in a quasi-Humean fashion that loyalty to others increases in relation to proximity to the self, and diminishes after the last 'close' identification with the state. Carr follows Spinoza in arguing that 'states could not be blamed for breaking faith; for everyone knew that their states would do likewise if it suited their interest'; however, the breaking of faith is not the same as stating that there is no moral framework for action in international politics.[20] While Carr recognizes that this is a lower standard of morality, and says that this is to be expected given how states act and because there are no means of compelling them to do otherwise, it does not imply that states abnegate any and all social and ethical responsibilities. Carr presents a version of moral reasoning that starts from existing state practice, saying, in effect, that states act according to the norms implicit or embedded in the structure and processes of international society. One may argue that this is an immanent form of moral reasoning, that there is no 'outside', no Archimedean point, from which to offer judgement, only a morality that is contingent and historically fluid.

5.3.2. The Social Contra the Real: Carr Versus Bosanquet

Perhaps the key to understanding the ethical universe of Carr lies in his treatment of the Hegelian Bernard Bosanquet, who argued that the natural and real limits of the moral community are coterminal with the borders of the state. Carr's reply to Bosanquet's rejection of humanity as a really existing corporate being to whom an obligation (of whatever kind) is owed as such is telling:

The reply to this would appear to be that a corporate being is never 'real' except as a working hypothesis, and that whether a given corporate being is an object of devotion and a guide to moral duty is a question of fact which must be settled by observation and not by theory, and which may be answered differently at different times and places. It has already been shown that there is in fact a widespread assumption of the existence of a world-wide community of which states are the units and that the conception of the moral obligations of states is closely bound up with this assumption. There is a world community for the reason (and no other) that people talk, and within certain limits behave, as if there were a world community.[21]

This reply is significant in that it illustrates that for Carr, the political ethics of 'reality' are unfixed—that the obligations and duties of international politics are dependent upon the perspectives and sentiments of those charged with their conduct. It is the belief in the primacy of the obligation to the state, as well as the weaker obligation of the state to the international society, that is the basis for international morality. To paraphrase Alexander Wendt, ethics is what states make of it, were they so to wish it they could completely reorient the nature of the international society, for 'good' or 'ill'.[22] This is an example of Carr's commitment to pragmatism, a commitment which informs the whole range of projects undertaken in the *Twenty Years' Crisis*.[23]

That said, according to Carr, it would be a 'dangerous illusion' to attribute to this world community the kind of coherence and unity necessary to transcend the current incarnation of the international society. In particular, two obstacles prevent this transformation: the inequality of states and the preference of the parts (states) for their interests over the interests of the whole (international society). The problem of equality is that absolute equality is impossible due to differences in power. Proportional equality is also impossible because as Carr says in relation to any putative proportional equality of Guatemala and the United States, 'that such rights and privileges as Guatemala has are enjoyed only by the good-will of the United States'. The problem of equality is, in effect, a problem of power: 'The constant intrusion, or potential intrusion, of power renders almost meaningless any conception of equality between members of the international community'.[24] The morality at play here is not one of equals, but one of the powerful in relation to the weak.

The problem of the relationship between the part and the whole is more complex and sets up the last chapters of *The Twenty Years' Crisis*. It is, according to Carr, 'the fundamental dilemma of international morality', fundamental because it gets to the core of whether or not there is actually an international society. The promotion of the well-being of the whole over its parts is identified by Carr as one of the foundations not only of the morality of international society but that 'every code of morality, postulates some recognition that the good of the part may have to be sacrificed to the good of the whole'.[25] The preservation of international society (and its attendant normative framework) revolves around this recognition of the rights of lesser powers, as those in power must acknowledge the claims of those without power, and for the preservation of order by the appeasement of the less powerful. The power/morality relationship is best described in the following passage:

Any international moral order must rest on some hegemony of power. But this hegemony, like the supremacy of a ruling class within the state, is in itself a challenge to those who do not share it; and it must, if it is to survive, contain an element of give-and-take, of self-sacrifice on the part of those who have, which will render it tolerable to the other members of the world community. It is through this process of give-and-take, of willingness not to insist on all the prerogatives of power, that morality finds its surest foothold in international—and perhaps also in national—politics.[26]

In 'Moral Foundations of World Order', Carr makes more explicit his reading of the relationship between power and morality. Those who offer a choice between morality and power politics are, according to Carr, 'guilty of confusing an already complicated issue by an unwarrantable over-simplification'.[27] Carr locates the blame for the inability of those engaged in international politics to deal with 'naked clashes of power' in the compromise-led manner of domestic politics in the fact that 'no effective community yet exists to develop common loyalties and a common stock of ideas'. The absence of a community of common loyalties results in the 'appeal to morality [being] less likely to be listened to'. While 'exceedingly complex', however, a compromise is possible between power and morality at the international level. Carr insists that '[e]ven if we believe—as I think we must believe—in an absolute good that is independent of power, it is none the less difficult to pretend that human beings have more than a fitful and faltering knowledge of this absolute good'.[28] Carr here attempts to root his essentially pragmatic and relativist reading of ethics in an idea of absolute good that contradicts that relativism. This is of course problematic in that in the final analysis we can no longer regard Carr as a strict relativist in relation to morality as he insists on the existence of an absolute good, even if this absolute good is only to be invoked *in extremis*. The presence of this absolute good is practically irrelevant, however, as Carr admits later in his discussion: 'we are compelled to concede that the individual man's conception of the good is highly relative and is therefore always apt to be fluctuating, uncertain, and tainted'.[29] Carr accepts that there is an objective morality 'out there' but his moral theory of international relations is, in essence, relativist, in that this objective morality is impossible to recognize and perceptions of it shift through time. As Peter Wilson writes, 'Carr was not "running away from the notion of good" so much as pointing out that "good" was a good deal more complicated than many people made it out to be.'[30]

Carr's understanding of morality is based on the observation of moral practice—morality can only be understood through observation and discussion of its nature rather than cast in primarily deontological terms. Carr's insistence that it is moral certitude that poses the greatest threat to the establishment of 'acceptable world order' is an implicit defence of his relativistic pragmatism.[31] It is recognition of the need for incremental change, from an established position derived from consensus about the necessity and utility of a moral template already in (virtual/fictional) existence, which can provide the basis for moral improvement over time. The idea of progress in human affairs is central to Carr's vision of international affairs:

It has become fashionable among some writers to dwell with almost sadistic pleasure on the fact of original sin. This is the truth, but certainly not the whole truth, and perhaps not even the most important and relevant part of the truth. Let us at any rate remind ourselves that mankind is also capable of great achievements and has great achievements to its credit. We may be utopian if we expect to attain our goal. But we shall indubitably fail if we have no goal ahead by which to set our course.[32]

The most important task is to reduce the distance between the domestic and international standards of morality, particularly in relation to the issue of discrimination. Carr's formulation of this specific issue is important in terms of his general attitude towards norm creation: 'No effective world order can be built on a denial of moral principles already accepted by an overwhelmingly preponderant part of the civilized world.' The answer is to break down the distinction between the citizen and the outsider.[33] Yet while the individual becomes magnified in importance, for Carr the state's importance must be redressed: 'The proposition "one man, one vote" may be a sound working rule. The proposition "one state, one vote" makes nonsense.'[34]

Morality, Carr argued, cannot be empowered by formal bureaucracy, 'as the short experience of the United Nations organization plainly shows'. However, he was not prepared to jettison morality simply because the aping of domestic institutions and ideology is doomed to failure: 'But let us at least make sure that power does not carry off the prize uncontested and drag an obedient morality at its chariot wheels . . . Unless we can find some commonly accepted ground on which to meet and discuss differences in order to reach some synthesis between them, there can be no moral foundation for our world order.'[35] Discussion, agreement, and a commitment to community, freedom, and progress, however weak and unreliable, underpin the moral project of international society, in which the onus is on the rich and powerful states to create the conditions for peace. This can be achieved, for example, through a pragmatic, functionalist extension of orderly economic planning from the national to the international sphere, as explored in

Conditions of Peace (1942), *Future of Nations: Independence of Interdependence?* (1941), *Nationalism and After* (1945), and *The New Society* (1951).

The complex interrelationship of power, ideas, and an observable social reality in Carr's work provides the context in which the normative dimensions of his realism emerge and develop. Carr demonstrates the need for a prudent, redistributive even-handedness, in the sense that the great powers should recognize the claims of lesser powers for a place at the table of international power.

5.4. MORGENTHAU AND THE ETHICS OF EVIL

Despite their membership of a supposed realist school, Carr and Morgenthau have very different ideas about the nature of morality in international relations. The extent of this difference is manifest in Morgenthau's rebuke of Carr, published in *World Politics* in 1948. Carr's diagnosis of the 'decline' of political thought, described in terms of 'blindness', 'barrenness', and 'disease', according to Morgenthau, is surpassed only by Reinhold Niebuhr. The problem with Carr was that he did not confine himself to being a critic, but rather tried to offer an alternative to liberal Utopianism. In this context, Morgenthau concludes that 'the over-all impression of Mr. Carr's work is one of failure'.[36] This failure is rooted firmly in the 'relativistic, instrumentalist conception of morality' proposed by Carr. Morgenthau detects in Carr a desire to transcend the reality of power and maintains that 'all his subsequent thinking [post *Twenty Years' Crisis*] becomes the Odyssey of a mind which has discovered the phenomena of power and longs to transcend it'. The fundamental problem is that Carr, as a relativist (in Morgenthau's understanding of the term), has no transcendent ethical stance from which to examine the political. The importance of a transcendent standard of ethical behaviour is implied in his epithet on Carr (and Schmitt and Müller): 'it is a dangerous thing to be a Machiavelli, it is a disastrous thing to be a Machiavelli without *virtù*.' Without a transcendent point of view one is philosophically ill-equipped to 'appraise the phenomenon of power'.[37]

What Morgenthau proposes is a reformulation of morality in terms different from the dominant liberal and rationalist understandings of ethical behaviour.[38] Part of this project is the rediscovery of good and evil in contrast to the utilitarian ethics of 'how certain effects are co-ordinated with certain actions', that is, an existential, transcendent ethic as opposed to an empirical, utilitarian ethic typical of liberalism or the instrumental relativism of Carr. Whereas there is no fixed standard of morality from which to survey political life in Carr's analysis (and arguably Carr's is a variation on utilitarian ethics), only shifting, intimations of an absolute good, for Morgenthau there is a realisable point from which a moral code can be developed and which can form the foundations for moral judgement and speaking truth to power. The essay 'Love and Power' is perhaps the most revealing of Morgenthau's texts regarding the basis for a transcendent ethics, for although it is in the earlier *Scientific Man Versus Power Politics* (1946) that Morgenthau first expounds an ethical system for realism, it is in 'Love and Power' that he describes why such a system is necessary as a consequence of the emergence of the *animus dominandi* (the central concept of *Politics Among Nations*).[39] Morgenthau's treatment of love is complex: love and power play opposite roles as responses to the fundamental existential experience of isolation. Man is restricted in his choices in that he either embraces love or power. Love is, according to Morgenthau, 'in its purest form the rarest of experiences. It is given to few men to experience it at all, and those who experience it do so only in fleeting moments of exaltation.' The rarity of this pure form, and the corruption of most love by power, entails the 'inevitable frustration of love'.[40] Philia and Agape are insufficient and ephemeral, and cannot serve as the basis for life in that they are inevitably frustrated. The potential of eros to degenerate into a power–sex relationship is perhaps the most depressing perversion of the intentions of love in that the lovers become degraded by the politicization of the erotic impulse.[41]

With love frustrated and corrupted, power and the lust for power enter as substitutes to fill the existential void: 'What man cannot achieve for any length of time through love he tries to achieve through power: to fulfil himself, to make himself whole by overcoming his loneliness, his isolation.' Morgenthau's inversion of Rousseau, that everywhere man is born a slave but longs to be master, has its root in the perversion of love:

It is in the very nature of the power relationship that the position of the two actors within it is ambivalent. *A* seeks to exert power over *B*; *B* tries to resist that power and seeks to exert power over *A*, which *A* resists. Thus the actor in the political stage is always at the same time a prospective master over others and a prospective object of the power of others. While he seeks power over others, others seek power over him.[42]

The lust for power, the elevation of power over love, is nonetheless insufficient to fill the gap of loneliness as 'the acquisition of power only begets the desire for more'. The desire for more power, or the desire to discharge power, in addition to the inherent selfishness of Man, leads to the 'ubiquity of evil' in life and politics ('the paradigm and prototype of all possible corruption').[43] Universal love is an impossibility, the quest for universal power doomed, isolation an existential inevitability and all political life compromised by the corruption of selfishness and lust for power, while every political act is at least in part an injustice as the statesman is inevitably forced to do some party an injustice by his choices. This unpromising wasteland is the foundation for the transcendent point of view that Morgenthau considers essential for the ethical appraisal of political life. In answer to the question 'how must moral man act in the political sphere?', Morgenthau expresses the core of his approach: '[T]he best he can do is to minimize the intrinsic immorality of the political act. He must choose from among the political actions at his disposal the one which is likely to do the least violence to the commands of Christian ethics. The moral strategy of politics is, then, to try to choose the lesser evil.'[44]

The first task for Morgenthau is to reassert the unity of moral evaluation and to jettison the dual-morality perspective as employed by Carr. Distinguishing between the acts of states and individuals is, according to Morgenthau, 'a formidable perversion of the moral sense itself, an acquiescence in evil'. The liberals can only offer a 'narrow and distorted formulation' of the problem of dealing with the ethics of politics, while their answer to the problem is 'sentimental and irrelevant'. The irrelevance of liberal thought to the ethics of politics is, for Morgenthau, largely due to the epistemological shortcomings of rationalism, which had become increasingly anachronistic in the face of the problems of the mid-twentieth century.[45] Not all political philosophy shares this fate, however, with Plato and Aristotle being singled out as 'at least partly' capable of representing 'eternal verities... able to guide the thought and action of our time as well as of any other'. Morgenthau's perennial endeavour was to seek the 'eternal verities' in order to rescue politics and ethics from the perceived dead ends of rationalism and relativism.[46]

Finding the moral 'truth' of politics is related to Morgenthau's development of a particular philosophy of history, one in which 'autonomous forces' have the effect of engendering 'historic necessity in their own right and not as mere deviation from reason'. Against what we might call the 'constructivism' of Carr, Morgenthau presents a universe where ethics is predicated on necessity, and also in which a permanent ethics of necessity is possible and practicable, deliberately contrasted against Thrasymachus's outright moral scepticism and Machiavelli's belief in the impermanent convergence of politics and morality.[47]

It is important to recognize that the ubiquity of evil does not necessitate the abandonment of ethics, but that it produces the conditions for a universal ethic of its own, the ethics of the lesser evil. Political ethics is the 'ethics of doing evil' yet the quantity and quality of the evil involved in the decision to act (or not to act) are unequal. The individual or the state has the capacity to choose that action which causes the least harm and moral behaviour stems from the 'endeavor to choose, since evil there must be, among several possible actions the one that is least evil'. This is the political ethics of despair, but also of moral courage: 'To choose among several expedient actions the least evil one is moral judgment. In the combination of political wisdom, moral courage, and moral judgment man reconciles his political nature with his moral destiny.'[48] This reconciliation of political life and moral life is best achieved through what may be termed a tragic sensibility and the 'knowing insecurity of the wisdom of man'.[49] The later Morgenthau embraced this 'knowing insecurity' to the extent that he was willing to recognize two species of relativism, historical and cultural, while still insisting on an objective morality. All different moral codes, argues Morgenthau, filter an objective moral code ('something objective that is there to be discovered. It is not a product of history'). When questioned about the lack of applicability of this universal code, Morgenthau replied: 'I think the normative function of the moral code remains intact. Only it is put in a situation in which the compulsive force, the normative force of the code, is qualified by potential considerations. I mean what we call circumstantial ethics.' The nature of this code is minimal, being simply, 'certain basic moral principles applicable to all human beings'. When pressed on the non-observance of the moral code Morgenthau conceded: 'this is correct in the pragmatic situation, but it does not necessarily affect general principles.' As he later clarifies, '[i]n other words, there exists a moral order in the universe which God directs, the content of which we can guess. We are never sure that we guess correctly; or that in the end it will come out as God wants it to come out.'[50]

5.4.1. Virtues in the Ethics of Evil: Prudence and the National Interest

The existence and value of political virtues in Morgenthau's work is demonstrated in contrast with secular or Christian values of universal love, best exemplified in Morgenthau's opinion by Kant's concept of universal justice. Morgenthau's basic position is that 'even assuming the reality of justice, man is incapable of realizing it'. Morgenthau argues that 'our knowledge of what justice demands is predicated upon our knowledge of what the world is like and what it is for, of a hierarchy of values reflecting the objective order of the world. Of such knowledge, only theology can be certain, and secular philosophies can but pretend to have it'. The problem is that justice is, in essence, a relative virtue: 'Empirically we find then as many conceptions of justice as there are vantage points, and the absolute majesty of justice dissolves into the relativity of so many interests and points of view.'[51] Yet as we saw in his criticisms of Carr, Morgenthau does not allow for the possibility of a relativist ethics.

If relativism is an inadequate basis for ethics, then the Golden Rule and other attempts to create an ethical framework based on absolute and universal values for political action are, according to Morgenthau, 'appropriate only in an already perfect moral world where nobody wants what could infringe upon anybody else's wants'.[52] In an imperfect world, characterized by the ubiquity of evil, what is necessary is the discovery and application of imperfect values rooted in political existence and the ethics of the lesser evil. This would form the appropriate normative context for the ethical conduct of politics in so far as this is possible. This judgement of political morality is, however, characterized by 'essential ambivalence'.[53] In effect, Morgenthau rejects the Kantian metaphysics of the Golden Rule and embraces instead the Aristotelian ethics of the Golden Mean, a mean between Thrasymachus and the Utopians.[54] Morgenthau stresses that this Golden Mean is also dependent on the 'determination ... upon the pre-existence of a moral order which assigns a specific place to a particular action in the total spectrum of human actions'.[55] This Aristotelian approach, however, does not proceed from a universal determination of what is ethical applied to the political, but rather that the demands of political practice determine what is ethical. While the greater evil of Man's lust for power cannot be avoided or remedied, 'specific evils' are susceptible to amelioration through the operation of 'historical forces' supported by conscious human effort.[56] This conscious human effort is informed by the existence of certain explicitly political virtues, namely, 'prudence' and 'moderation'—both rooted in an *über*-virtue of self-interest. Where justice attempts to obscure the element of self-interest in its appeal to universalism, the political virtues embrace it as the foundation of their appeals to universality.

For Morgenthau, the self-interest of the state is a positive value and an admirable aim, if not the basis for moral statecraft, in that the statesman has a duty to preserve the well-being of those he represents. Defining that self-interest in the context of an existing international society, and determining the content of a theory of moral behaviour, is consequent upon recognizing the priority of the interest of the state, while always acknowledging the necessity of the lesser evil as opposed to the technical standard of Thrasymachus or the shifting morality of Machiavelli (or Carr).

Moral behaviour in international relations proceeds from a sense of proportion. Thus it is that Morgenthau, agreeing with the 'Greek tragedians and biblical prophets', identifies hubris as a primary example of a political vice and moral danger against which leaders should be warned.[57] Without the correct perspective, or at least an informed opinion, the pathology of power leads to the hubristic identification of power and virtue (the Thrasymachian perspective), and to 'moral delusions' and 'intellectual errors' that direct nations to disaster. Prudence and moderation are the political virtues of perspective and proportion respectively.[58]

As Morgenthau wrote in 1960, '[n]o one can be certain before the event which choice is morally right and politically sound', and the only, and admittedly imperfect means by which to even approximate the correct moral action is to follow the dictates of prudence, which Morgenthau defines as the ability to make morally responsible decisions in international politics.[59] One could argue that this is circular logic, that that which is moral is prudent, which is in turn moral. It is perhaps better to conceive of prudence as a species of reasoning designed to effect the lesser evil. It is the means by which moral aspirations can be filtered through the particular circumstances of political life. The example Morgenthau uses is that of liberty: the individual may choose to sacrifice himself to such a notion, but a state may not, due to the competing and superior moral principle of national survival. Thus although liberty is a universal moral value, the prudent moral choice in this instance is to choose survival over a commitment to an abstraction (albeit an important one) like the imperative to protect or spread liberty in other nations. The centrality of prudence to the existence and operation of a distinct political morality is vital:

There can be no political morality without prudence; that is, without consideration of the political consequences of seemingly moral action. Realism, then, considers prudence— the weighing of the consequences of alternative political associations—to be the supreme virtue in politics. Ethics in the abstract judges action by its conformity with the moral law; political ethics judges action by its political consequences.[60]

Prudence in itself is insufficient to ground ethics in politics. What is necessary is a moral purpose, of necessity a minimal moral purpose given the nature of the international society, which Morgenthau finds in the concept of the 'national interest'. If prudence is the cardinal political–ethical virtue, the national interest is its imperative.

The national interest is a special case of the second of Morgenthau's six principles. The second principle revolves around the concept of interest in general, that is, that the 'main signpost that helps political realism to find its way through the landscape of international politics is the concept of interest defined in terms of power'. Morgenthau's assumption is that 'statesmen think and act in terms of interest defined as power, and history bears that assumption out'.[61] This idea of the national interest is the fundamental basis for an international community. It is a role that Morgenthau invests with particular significance describing it in terms of its 'moral dignity'. It also provides the basis for a genuine understanding of the nature of moral choices at the level of the international:

> The equation of political moralising with morality and of political realism with immorality is itself untenable. The choice is not between moral principles and the national interest, devoid of moral dignity, but between one set of moral principles divorced from political reality, and another set of moral principles derived from political reality.[62]

The 'moralistic detractors' who refuse to see the ethical necessity of the national interest are guilty of 'both intellectual error and moral perversion' due to their insistence on 'a standard of action alien to the nature of the action itself'. The perversion is threefold: (1) the inappropriate nature of the ethical evaluation, (2) the costs of realizing an 'idealist' foreign policy would destroy the very values that prompt intervention, and (3) idealism denies any validity to any moral framework other than itself, 'placing the stigma of immorality upon the theory and practice of power politics'.[63] A commitment to the lesser evil in the service of the national interest has the advantage of being realizable and of being consistent with the norms of existing international society. The national interest can, in short, serve as the basis for the universal recognition of particular interests, and therefore, of their accommodation. Morgenthau is here endorsing a type of 'situational ethics' in which the strict application of Christian ethics (a saintly ethic) is replaced by an alternative ethic in which the question is not how do I act to achieve salvation? In situational ethics, according to Morgenthau, 'you have to ask yourself, "What is possible for the average man who is not a saint, who doesn't aspire to sainthood, under the concrete conditions under which he lives".[64]

5.4.2. Civilization as the Locus of Political Ethics

International community can be seen as predicated on the concrete plurality of conflicting and complementary interests. The lust for power is an ever present reality in this community of interests, as various (though not necessarily all) parties clash in their attempts to secure or retain power. This we may term, following the first part of Morgenthau's subtitle to *Politics Among Nations*, 'the struggle for power'. It is clear how the 'struggle for power' fits into the realist political theory of international relations; what has been forgotten or elided is the second part of the subtitle, 'the struggle for peace'. Peace also has a major role to play in realist theory as it is through peace that the 'rational' community of interests can best be served. This preference is a result of the convergence of the demands of morality and politics in the 'Nuclear Age' when, given the risks of escalation, war is no longer usable as an instrument of policy.[65]

The social expression of the ethics of the lesser evil is the fragile concept of civilization, itself a product of the revolt against power. Civilization may be understood as the product of the community of interests. Alliances, trading blocs, even international law and the norms of statecraft and diplomacy are rooted in a desire to control the effects of the lust for power and the preservation of communal order in the face of various attempts to replace the society of states by hegemony, or the effects of war on the state system. The initial impetus of this society of interests is, of course, self-interest, but norms and laws increase in power over time with moral rules becoming embedded not only in the formal structures of international relations but also in the activities of international relations.[66] Like Carr, Morgenthau states that there is a disparity between the discourse of international morality and the reality of international morality, but there is without doubt an important moral component to the practice of statecraft:

They [statesmen] refuse to consider certain ends and to use certain means, either altogether or under certain conditions, not because in the light of expediency they appear impractical or unwise but because certain moral rules interpose an absolute barrier. Moral rules do not permit certain policies to be considered at all from the point of view of expediency. Certain things are not being done on moral grounds, even though it would be expedient to do them. Such ethical inhibitions operate in our time on different levels with different effectiveness.[67]

One might refer to Morgenthau's ethics as a theory of the limits of power politics as opposed to a theory of pure power politics. On the one hand, there is the idea of expedience, in which the practice of power is determined solely according to a technical rationale that permits no moral or ethical input—the realm of Rome's total destruction of Carthage or the Nazis use of 'firing squads and extermination camps'. On the other hand, there is an ethical rationale for the use of power in international politics in which power is conceived not in terms of expediency, but rather in terms of limitation, which 'derives from an absolute moral principle, which must be obeyed regardless of considerations of national advantage'.[68] Even the national interest must recognize higher moral obligations once the purely technical standard is abandoned, leading to the sacrifice of the national interest when 'its consistent pursuit would necessitate the violation of an ethical principle, such as the prohibition of mass killing in times of peace'.[69] International relations then skirts between two standards, an ethical standard and an unethical, technical standard. The emergence of the two standards is related to the *animus dominandi* that undergirds much of Morgenthau's realism. Hobbes's war of all against all does not characterize the international system because, 'the very threat of a world where power reigns not only supreme, but without rival, engenders that revolt against power which is as universal as the aspiration for power itself'. Over time, argues Morgenthau, the ethical standard, informed by a 'moral conscience' has come to the fore, best exemplified by 'the attempts to bring the practice of states into harmony with moral principles through international agreements'.[70] This moral quality of international politics may be ignored or violated, but it is there nonetheless as a permanent and vital aspect of international life.

The greatest threat to the moral quality of international politics comes not from the practice of power, but rather the development of modernity itself, and in particular modern warfare which in its commitment to and capability for destruction and ideological fanaticism 'has been too strong for the moral convictions of the modern world to resist'.[71] The conduct of war is symptomatic of a wider moral malaise in the international system for Morgenthau, who posits a crucial difference between the 'ethical system' of early modernity, informed by agreement about aristocratic mores and norms, and the deterioration that results from a substitution of democratic for aristocratic ideals, resulting in the replacement of a universal, aristocratic perspective by particular, conflicting, nationalistic perspectives on the conduct of international politics.[72] The prospect of nuclear holocaust was such that it provokes a refiguring of the very existence of Man, 'throwing life back upon itself'.[73] All that is left in the shadow of the Bomb is a relentless self-indulgence and narcissism.[74] The crisis of modernity in moral terms can only be understood in the context of a declining moral framework—if anything in his works Morgenthau is lamenting the deterioration of a moral standard in international politics rather than advocating an immoral or amoral approach.

5.5. CONCLUSION

In his controversy over the editing of his work with Norman Podhoretz, Morgenthau complained of 'that degeneration in our culture which, by losing respect for individual language, has lost respect for individual thought as well'. Morgenthau further complains: 'Standardized language is appropriate to standardized thought'.[75] In many respects, Morgenthau and Carr are posthumous victims of a thorough-going standardization of language in IR, in which their complex visions of the ethical–political potentialities of international politics have been sacrificed in the name of a paradigmatic purity that insists on their status as moustache-twirling villains tying the prone body of ethics to the rail tracks of IR theory.[76] The individuality of the creative efforts of realism must be reasserted, for in Morgenthau's formulation, the theorist's 'language is not just a carrier on which his thoughts as well as other thoughts can be transported or for which another could be substituted performing the same mechanical function of transportation'. Lumping realists together into a school based of straw-man propositions robs them of their 'intellectual and moral personality'.[77]

Rather than presenting an unethical or amoral theory of politics wherein normative concerns are dictated according to a solely instrumental, technical logic of pure power, realism provides at least two ethically informed perspectives on how actors should behave in international relations. The first of those examined here was that of E. H. Carr who presents a relativistic account of a shifting, unfixed ethics grounded in convenient fictions and obligations to a wider community. In normative terms, while Carr recognizes an overriding commitment of each individual state to pursue its own interests, there is nonetheless in his analysis a commitment to the Other, which while not being entirely altruistic, forms the basis for a redistributive and even-handed international society. Carr's political morality does not proceed from an identification of Man as intrinsically good, or for that matter, intrinsically evil; rather he saw Man as capable of both good and evil.[78] To behave morally in international politics is to recognize the legitimacy of the claims of others. Actions that run contrary to this even handedness, and a political culture that supports such bias is, according to Carr, to be regretted as a case of ethical blindness and political short-sightedness which he attributes to a failure of modern politics. For Carr, a Darwinian modernity had lost a sense of moderation and the correct limits of political activity. As political life had been deformed so also it could be reformed by synthesizing the insights of utopian and realist thought, and drastic reform of the actors, processes, and structures of international relations.

For Morgenthau, modernity is characterized by the moral and political short-comings of international politics. He advocated a transcendent as opposed to a relativistic standard of international ethics. Politics for Morgenthau, like Carr, remains fixed in a dialectic, but his is the existential dialectics of love and power, not the intellectual dialectic of Utopianism and Realism. This existential dialectic, however, is not without its ethical requirements rooted not in a conception of self-interest as brutal *machtpolitik* but rather self-interest being served by the communion of interests through the observance of international law, norms, and mores of statecraft.

In terms of normative prescriptions, the two approaches are fairly similar. The actor should observe their own interest, but also recognize that their interests are served by bearing in mind the needs of a wider community.[79] International law and other conventions may be convenient fictions, but they serve the interests of the individual and the group and as such are of practical and social benefit and therefore deserve investment. Morality may be plastic in the case of Carr, or existential in the case of Morgenthau, but it plays an important part in the operation of world politics—in neither case can the realist traditions that they represent be described as amoral. The texts of Carr and Morgenthau bear witness to the context in which they were written. They are not, however, mere curiosities of a bygone age. The distortions of realism in the textbooks and 'debates' in IR have led to a diminution of realism's potential as a moral theory and the contribution it can make to issues in international ethics. This neglect of the moral dimensions of realism must be redressed and realism returned to the fore of normative international theory.

NOTES

1. The terms 'ethics' and 'morality' are used synonymously throughout the text as was common among the two authors under consideration.
2. Jack Donnelly, 'Twentieth Century Realism', in David Mapel and Terry Nardin (eds.), *Traditions of International Ethics* (Cambridge: Cambridge University Press, 1993), pp. 85–7.

3. See, for example, Mervyn Frost, *Towards a Normative Theory of International Relations* (Cambridge: Cambridge University Press, 1986), p. 66.
4. Campbell, 'Justice and International Order: The Case of Bosnia and Kosovo', in Jean Marc Coicaud and Daniel Warner (eds.), *Ethics and International Affairs: Extent and Limits* (New York: UN University Press, 2001), pp. 105, 107; and Donnelly, 'Twentieth Century Realism', p. 90.
5. Cohen, 'Moral Skepticism and International Relations', in Charles Beitz, Marshall Cohen, and A. John Simmons (eds.), *International Ethics* (Princeton: Princeton University Press, 1985), p. 4; Beitz, *Political Theory and International Relations* (Princeton, N.J.: Princeton University Press, 1979), p. 15.
6. Ken Booth, 'Critical Explorations', in Booth (ed.), *Critical Security Studies and World Politics* (Boulder: Lynne Rienner, 2005), pp. 7–8.
7. Carr, 'Is Machiavelli a Modern?' *Spectator*, 28 June 1940, quoted in Haslam, *No Virtue Like Necessity: Realist Thought in International Relations Since Machiavelli* (New Haven: Yale University Press, 2002), p. 189.
8. Carr, 'Is Machiavelli a Modern?' p. 189. Italics added.
9. Carr, 'Is Machiavelli a Modern?' Carr also refers to Machiavelli as 'shocking and provocative', *Spectator*, 28 June 1940, p. 868.
10. On the various debates about whether Carr is or is not a realist, see Seán Molloy, *The Hidden History of Realism: A Genealogy of Power Politics* (London: Palgrave Macmillan, 2006), ch. 4.
11. Carr, *The Twenty Years' Crisis, 1919–1939: An Introduction to the Study of International Relations*, 2nd edn. (London: Macmillan, 1946/1969), p. 146. For a more detailed discussion of the dialectical play of Utopian and Realist thought, see Molloy, *The Hidden History of Realism*, ch. 3. The purpose of this chapter is not the engagement of Carr with the Utopians and Realists (except where this is unavoidable) but rather the particular statements Carr made consequent to his synthesis of the two positions.
12. Carr is being mendacious here, for his conception of the 'ordinary man' is heavily influenced by those philosophers that he elsewhere dismisses. In fact, Carr spends the rest of the chapter engaging with the derided philosophers.
13. Carr, *The Twenty Years' Crisis*, pp. 148–9, 151.
14. Carr, *The Twenty Years' Crisis*, p. 154.
15. Carr, *The Twenty Years' Crisis*, pp. 154, 156.
16. Carr, *The Twenty Years' Crisis*, p. 156. Dewey and Zimmern according to Carr at least 'confessed their bewilderment'.
17. Carr, *The Twenty Years' Crisis*, p. 158.
18. Carr, *The Twenty Years' Crisis*, p. 159.
19. Carr, *The Twenty Years' Crisis*, p. 160. Presumably Carr means the moral obligations of individual morality or the moral obligations due to other states within international society. On the issue of Carr and the state, see Seán Molloy 'Realism: A Problematic Paradigm', *Security Dialogue*, 34 (2003), pp. 10–11; and Molloy *The Hidden History of Realism*, pp. 58–64 and p. 140.
20. Carr, *The Twenty Years' Crisis*, p. 161.
21. Carr, *The Twenty Years' Crisis*, p. 162.
22. Wendt, 'Anarchy is What States Make of It: The Social Construction of Power Politics', *International Organization*, 42 (1992), pp. 391–425.
23. Carr, *The Twenty Years' Crisis*, ch. 1.
24. Carr, *The Twenty Years' Crisis*, p. 166.

25. Carr, *The Twenty Years' Crisis*, p. 167. Carr later repudiated the whole notion of international society and IR as a discipline: 'I suspect that we tried to conjure into existence an international society and a science of international relations. We failed. No international society exists ... No science of international relations exists.' Letter to Stanley Hoffman, 30 September, 1977, quoted in Jonathan Haslam, *Vices of Integrity: E.H. Carr, 1992–1982* (London: Verso, 2000), p. 252.
26. Carr, *The Twenty Years' Crisis*, p. 168.
27. Carr, 'Moral Foundations for World Order', in E. L. Woodward et al., *Foundations for World Order* (University of Denver: Social Science Foundation, 1949), p. 62.
28. Carr, 'Moral Foundations for World Order', pp. 63, 66. Carr can be occasionally inconsistent or positively mystical on these matters: in this case an absolute morality lurking around the corner, so also in his essay on Mannheim there is an ultimate rationality to be appealed to *in extremis*. Carr, 'Karl Mannheim', in *From Napoleon to Stalin and Other Essays* (Basingstoke: Macmillan, 1980), p. 182.
29. Carr, 'Moral Foundations for World Order', p. 67. 'Tainted' is used repeatedly throughout the essay in order to express the inability of 'Man' to extricate himself from the limits of experience and the prevalence of power.
30. Peter Wilson, 'Carr and his Early Critics: Responses to *The Twenty Years' Crisis, 1939–1946*', in Michael Cox (ed.), *E.H. Carr: A Critical Appraisal* (Basingstoke: Macmillan, 2000), p. 187.
31. Carr's relativism continues to be the source of much criticism, with early critics such as Susan Stebbing and later critics such as Robert Kaufman united in their condemnation. Stebbing, *Ideals and Illusions* (London: Watts & Co., 1941.), pp. 6–15; and Kaufman, 'The Case for Principled, Prudential, Democratic Realism', in Benjamin Frankel (ed.), *Roots of Realism* (London: Frank Cass, 1996), pp. 318–25.
32. E. H. Carr, *The New Society* (London: Macmillan, 1951), pp. 111–2.
33. Carr, 'Moral Foundations for World Order', p. 71. 'Effective' here is presented in contrast to institutional reform.
34. Carr, 'Moral Foundations for World Order', pp. 72–3.
35. Carr, 'Moral Foundations for World Order', p. 74. Elsewhere, Carr makes the case in more pronounced terms declaring states to be anomalies and anachronistic and that international relations should be predicated upon 'the value of individual human beings, irrespective of national affinities or allegiance and in a common and mutual obligation to promote their well-being'. Carr, *Nationalism and After* (London: Macmillan, 1945), p. 44.
36. Morgenthau, 'The Political Science of E.H. Carr', *World Politics*, 1 (Oct., 1948), p. 133.
37. Morgenthau, 'The Political Science of E.H. Carr', pp. 129, 134. Murray identifies both Morgenthau and Niebuhr as transcendent realists and Kennan as a religious realist (*Reconstructing Realism*, p. 31). According to Haslam, the early Morgenthau was more willing to accept a relativist basis for shifting norms: *No Virtue Like Necessity*, p. 192. The presence of a transcendent perspective also qualifies the claims of Michael Williams that Morgenthau is engaged in the development of a Weberian 'ethics of responsibility': *The Realist Tradition and the Limits of International Relations* (Cambridge: Cambridge University Press, 2005). Morgenthau's consistent anti-Machiavellianism also calls into question Beitz's identification of a moral scepticism in Realist thought from Machiavelli via Hobbes to Morgenthau (Beitz, *Political Theory and International Relations*, ch. 1). On Morgenthau and transcendence, see also Vibeke Schou Tjalve's Chapter 10 in this volume.

38. This commitment to theorizing moral aspects of politics extended from the earliest to the latest phases of Morgenthau's career—albeit with significant revisions. See William Scheuerman's Chapter 3 in this volume for a consideration of Morgenthau's pre-war writings.

39. The *animus dominandi* is in effect the lust for power. The foundation of Morgenthau's philosophy of power is that all men seek power and to subject other men to their power.

40. Morgenthau, 'Love and Power', *Commentary*, Vol. 33, No. 3, p. 248.

41. '[T]he lust for power is, as it were, the twin of despairing love.' Morgenthau, 'Love and Power', p. 249.

42. Morgenthau, 'Love and Power', p. 249.

43. Morgenthau, 'Love and Power', p. 250; and Morgenthau, 'The Evil of Politics and the Ethics of Evil', *Ethics*, 56 (October 1945), p. 14. See Richard Ned Lebow, *The Tragic Vision of Politics. Ethics, Interests and Orders* (Cambridge: Cambridge University Press, 2003), p. 237; and Murray, *Reconstructing Realism*, p. 126.

44. Morgenthau, 'The Demands of Prudence' in his *Politics in the Twentieth Century Vol.3: The Restoration of American Politics* (Chicago: University of Chicago Press, 1962), p. 16. There are obvious parallels here to Niebuhr, as many commentators have observed. See also Benjamin Wong, 'Hans Morgenthau's Anti-Machiavellian Machiavellianism', *Millennium*, 29 (2000), pp. 391, 402ff. See Benjamin Mollov's analysis of both the Christian and especially the Judaic element of Morgenthau's commitment to moral critique as speaking truth to power: 'Jewry's Prophetic Challenge to Soviet and Other Totalitarian Regimes According to Hans Morgenthau', *Journal of Church and State*, 39 (1997), pp. 561–75.

45. Morgenthau, 'Evil of Politics', pp. 16–17.

46. Morgenthau, *Scientific Man Versus Power Politics* (Chicago: Chicago University Press, 1946), pp. 4, 9.

47. Morgenthau, *Scientific Man Versus Power Politics*, pp. 38–9. For Thrasymachus's various statements (and ultimate repudiation) of power's role in determining justice, see Plato, *The Republic*, Book IV.

48. Morgenthau, 'Evil of Politics', pp. 17–18. Compare with the Aristotle's formulation of the lesser evil as a course between extremes in the *Nicomachean Ethics*: 'For since one extreme is more in error, the other less, and since it is hard to hit the intermediate extremely accurately, the second best tack, as they say, is to take the lesser of the evils.' Aristotle, *Nicomachean Ethics*, 1109b, 2.33.

49. Morgenthau, *Scientific Man Versus Power Politics*, pp. 204–23.

50. Morgenthau, *Human Rights and Foreign Policy* (New York: Council on Religion and International Affairs, 1979), pp. 17, 25, 36.

51. Morgenthau, 'On Trying to be Just', *Commentary*, 35 (May 1963), pp. 421–2. For a reading of Morgenthau that stresses the possibility of justice, see Lebow, *The Tragic Vision*.

52. Morgenthau, 'Justice and Power', *Social Research*, 41 (Spring 1974), p. 168. This attitude towards deontological prescription, whether Christian or liberal, leads me to question the attribution of a dominant Judaeo-Christian ethic in Morgenthau's work beyond an identification of the power of Augustine's political thought and the existence of God. See Murray, *Reconstructing Realism*, p. 133; and Roger Epp, *The 'Augustinian Moment' in International Politics: Niebuhr, Butterfield, Wight and the Reclaiming of a Tradition* (Aberystwyth, 1991).

53. Anthony F. Lang, Jr. (ed.), *Political Theory and International Affairs: Hans J. Morgenthau on Aristotle's The Politics* (London: Praeger, 2004), p. 100.

54. Roger Spegele has noted the potential of attenuating what he calls neo-Kantian non-cognitivism with the Aristotelian tradition of ethics, culminating in what he terms Evaluative Political Realism: Spegele, *Political Realism in International Theory* (Cambridge: Cambridge University Press, 1996), p. 195.

55. Morgenthau, 'Justice and Power', p. 168. Aristotle's concept of virtue as a mean is defined in *Nichomachean Ethics*, 1107a, 2.23, p. 44.

56. Morgenthau, 'The Evil of Power', *Review of Metaphysics*, 3 (1949/1950), p. 516. Greg Russell deals with evil in a general sense, primarily in relation to twentieth century political theorists such as Voegelin and Arendt in 'Morgenthau's Political Realism and the Ethics of Evil', in W. David Clinton (ed.) *The Realist Tradition and Contemporary International Relations* (Baton Rouge: Louisiana State University Press, 2007).

57. Morgenthau, 'The Moral Dilemma of Political Action', *The Decline of Democratic Politics* (Chicago: University of Chicago Press, 1962), p. 326.

58. On Thrasymachus, see Robert H. Jackson , *Classical and Modern Thought on International Relations: From Anarchy to Cosmopolis* (New York: Palgrave, 2005), ch. 2.

59. Morgenthau, 'Demands of Prudence', p. 16. See also Murray, *Reconstructing Realism*, p. 118.

60. Morgenthau, *Politics Among Nations*, 5th edn. (New York: Knopf, 1978), pp. 10–11. William Bain refers to this process as 'judgement': 'Deconfusing Morgenthau: Moral Inquiry and Classical Realism', *Review of International Studies*, 26 (2000), pp. 445–64.

61. Morgenthau, *Politics Among Nations*, p. 5.

62. Morgenthau, *In Defense of the National Interest* (New York: Knopf, 1951), p. 33.

63. Morgenthau, *In Defense of the National Interest*, pp. 33–4.

64. Morgenthau, *Political Theory and International Affairs*, p. 95.

65. Morgenthau, 'Atomic Force and Foreign Policy', *Commentary*, 23 (1957), p. 502. See here Campbell Craig, *Glimmer of a New Leviathan: Total War in the Realism of Niebuhr, Morgenthau and Waltz* (New York: Columbia University Press, 2003).

66. Lebow, *Tragic Vision*, p. 239.

67. Morgenthau, *Politics Among Nations*, p. 237. Ethical standards of statecraft have, according to Morgenthau, improved over time, from the early days of poisoning and assassination typical of Italy in the fifteenth and sixteenth century to a more civilized regime where '[s]uch methods to attain political ends are no longer widely practiced today' (p. 238).

68. Morgenthau, *Politics Among Nations*, p. 240.

69. Morgenthau, 'The Twilight of International Morality', *Ethics*, 58 (1948), p. 82.

70. Morgenthau, *Politics Among Nations*, pp. 231, 243.

71. Morgenthau, *Politics Among Nations*, p. 245.

72. Morgenthau, 'The Twilight of International Morality', p. 96.

73. Morgenthau, 'Death in the Nuclear Age', *Commentary*, 32 (September 1961), p. 233.

74. Joel Rosenthal, *Righteous Realists* (Baton Rouge, LA: University of Louisiana Press, 1991), p. 162

75. Morgenthau, 'The Writer's Duty and his Predicament', *Hudson Review*, 18 (Summer 1965), p. 272.

76. Morgenthau was incensed by this portrayal: see his preface to the second edition of *Politics Among Nations* (reproduced in the Fifth Edition): *Politics Among Nations*, 5th edn., p. xiv. See also Haslam, *No Virtue Like Necessity*, pp. 199–200. Peter Wilson

argues that Carr incorporated elements of various moral and ethical criticisms into works such as *Conditions of Peace*: Wilson, 'The Myth of the First Great Debate', *Review of International Studies*, 24 (1998), p. 7.

77. Morgenthau, 'The Writer's Duty and his Predicament', p. 272.
78. Carr, *New Society*, p. 8: 'It would not occur to me to deny that human beings are often very wicked. Evil as well as good is of the stuff of almost everything men do.'
79. Contrary to critics such as Jim George, realism thus proceeds from but is not limited to egotism as the basis of its ethics. George, 'Realist "Ethics", International Relations, and Post-Modernism: Thinking Beyond the Egoism-Anarchy Thematic', *Millennium*, 24 (1995), pp. 195–223. See Bain, *op. cit.*, for a refutation of George's position on Morgenthau in particular.

6

The Ethic of Reality in Hannah Arendt

Patricia Owens

> It is in the very nature of every new beginning that it breaks into the world
> as an 'infinite improbability,' and yet it is precisely this infinitely improbable
> which actually constitutes the very texture of everything we call real.
>
> Hannah Arendt, *Between Past and Future*

6.1. INTRODUCTION

To the extent that realist traditions of political thought are concerned with politics
as a form of rulership whose essence is violence and domination, it is difficult to
imagine a thinker as un-realist as Hannah Arendt (1906–75). If modern realism
is a footnote to Thomas Hobbes and realist ethics is a footnote to Max Weber,
then its students will have little time for Arendt's political theory. But realism
can be parsed differently. The idea that there is an inevitable and intrinsic ethical
deficit in realist political thought has long been a staple in critical and normative
international theory. Yet we have become increasingly aware that the peculiar
way in which the discipline of International Relations has constructed realism
obscures its rich political—and ethical—insights. Arendt's relationship to realist
traditions is complicated. Her work defies easy classification and those who care
for her legacy do not seek to contain her diverse writings within any conventional
schools of thought. Hannah Arendt is no straightforward realist. However, in her
writing we do find a form of 'realism' in which attentiveness to reality itself and the
cultivation of a character trait in which to face and enlarge one's sense of reality
are ends in themselves with serious ethical implications.

Witness to the worst atrocities of the twentieth century, Arendt condemned
the naivety of interwar liberals and was a critic of the same liberal idealists that
so provoked the wrath of post-war realist international thought. She considered
idealism (the notion that anything was possible) as central to totalitarianism's
hubristic 'contempt for reality' and she expressed little sympathy for grandiose and
ideologically motivated programmes for political change.[1] Such agendas revealed
no deeper political meaning. They were anti-political, representing a 'conspicuous
distain of the whole texture of reality'.[2] What does Arendt mean by this 'texture of

reality'? How, and under what conditions, may we best comprehend it? Daniel Deudney has recently shown that realism and international theory more generally have 'unknowingly' been 'speaking republicanism'.[3] Hannah Arendt uniquely offers this tradition a more sophisticated account of the necessity of a strong *public* culture for our sense of the real.[4] She did not develop a systematic *theory* of reality. Rather she argued that there is a direct relationship between the political, public realm, the necessary condition of all politics, which is plurality, and our ability to comprehend what is real. This is not a question of reality versus ethics. Arendt offers an ethic of reality. Indeed, she points us in the direction of ethical grounds for action in a world in which reality is in danger of being eclipsed. She offers a tough-minded and 'attentive facing up to, and resisting of, reality—whatever that may be'.[5]

Section 6.2 of this chapter sets out Arendt's engagement with, but distance from, realist understandings of politics, power, and ethics. The fundamental divergence between Arendt and Weber's idea of the 'ethic of responsibility' hinges on her rejection of the categories of means and ends in the political, public sphere and her entirely different understanding of the meanings of politics, power, and violence. Section 6.3 shows how, by Arendt's account, the public world is constituted by a not fully tangible but nonetheless real intersubjectivity that emerges between individuals as they speak and act in the public realm. As she put it, 'our feeling for reality depends utterly upon appearance and therefore upon the existence of a public realm into which things can appear'.[6] Section 6.4 moves from one of Arendt's case studies in the *avoidance* of reality, the Nazi war criminal Adolf Eichmann, to her distinctive grounds for action against what she took to be the greatest mortal sin of politics, genocide, or wars of annihilation. However, the grounds for action are not found in the moral imperative to end massive human suffering as such. The effort to destroy a particular group cannot be countenanced because it is a threat to the reality of the public, political world which requires a plurality of peoples.

6.2. BEYOND THE ETHIC OF RESPONSIBILITY

Hannah Arendt directly engaged with, or can be read alongside, the major figures in the realist canon. She wrote on Thucydides, Hobbes, Machiavelli, and Rousseau. She held that the causes of war derived from the 'well-known realities of power politics—such as conquest and expansion, defense of vested interests and preservation of power or conservation of a power equilibrium'.[7] However, as we will later observe, she strongly diverged from the assumptions and methods of neo-realist policy science. Arendt was also more explicitly attentive to the imperial character of the interstate system than most realist international theory; 'neither the racism of modern nationalism nor the power-craziness of the modern state', she wrote, 'can be explained without a proper understanding of the structure of imperialism'.[8] In contrast to the conventional International Relations (IR) reading of Thomas Hobbes from inside out, from the domestic to the international, Arendt argued that the 'magnificence of Hobbes's logic' was truly revealed with nineteenth-century imperialism.[9] More importantly for our purposes, Hobbes represented for Arendt the pre-eminent modern theorist of rulership, of politics as the accumulation of power *over* others, a view with enormous ethical and political repercussions.

Power in the realist tradition is usually seen as something that is possessed, an instrument of rule that produces a hierarchical, indeed coercive, relationship between rulers and ruled. This relationship has been considered the essence of politics in virtually all traditions and is closely related to the idea that domination and ruling are the most basic categories of politics, and violence is the essence of power. Those who have power command and those who do not obey; even in a democracy, the rotation of rulers is still a system of rule. The social contract in Hobbes's imaginary state of nature justified a relationship of rulership that was already being exercised by the King in the interests of protecting life. 'Security remained the decisive criterion', Arendt interpreted, 'but not the individual's security against violent "death", as in Hobbes...but a security which should permit an undisturbed development of the life process of society as a whole.'[10] The modern nation state became not only the possessor of 'legitimate' force but also the expected protector of 'life' within the state. Arendt was among the first to warn of the dangers of placing the protection and the servicing of the life process at the centre of politics. Coinciding with the liberal idea that 'life is the highest good', the principle function of modern politics became the cultivation and sustenance of 'life itself', a concern with 'the naked existence of us all'.[11]

Arendt, like all realists, believed in the centrality and autonomy of politics. She feared that the political way of life was under threat from some of the major features of modernity, including the view that political conflict and the political realm itself could be reduced to a scientific problem with a technical solution. On this she displayed affinities with Weber.[12] Her criticisms of modern liberal politics and society—its repudiation of politics—are rooted in many of the same assumptions that drove other German émigrés who came to the United States during World War II and helped re-found the 'realist' discipline of International Relations. Hannah Arendt, like Hans J. Morgenthau, was persuaded that republican institutions and public-spirited citizens were the best defence against totalitarianism and the lesser but no less real (or unconnected) hold of politics as the technical administration of political affairs, of political action as narrow 'social' behaviour.[13]

And yet Arendt's thought is almost totally at odds with the dominant realist conceptualizations of political ethics and action. As Margaret Canovan has put it, Arendt 'defied the German tradition of "realism" by maintaining that it is action-as-speech rather than government that constitutes true politics; that agreement and consent, not domination, found republics, and that acting in concert, not violence, creates power'.[14] The particular features of Arendt's theory of politics—and understanding of reality—are addressed momentarily. Here the point to note is that political realism conceives politics instrumentally; to be political is to responsibly use violence when necessary to achieve determined ends. Weber's sobering judgement about the ethical implications of this is that the choice of end is ultimately arbitrary, but to have one's hand on the 'wheel of history' one must choose.[15] This 'ethic of responsibility' holds that the political actor must accept the reality of dirty hands; to be political is sometimes to do evil.[16] But the lesser evil must always be chosen and it should never be accompanied by self-aggrandizement or appeals to high-minded principles.

Arendt's divergence from the 'ethic of responsibility' had nothing to do with any support for what Weber deemed to be the main alternative, an ethic of 'ultimate ends', to act on a principled faith no matter the result. Arendt too, and like Morgenthau, believed that moralism in political and international affairs could only lead to disillusionment and the further intensification and brutalization of politics and war. She shared with Carl Schmitt the view that by fighting a war on behalf of civilization, some other ultimate end, or in her words, 'by applying the absolute— justice, for example, or the "ideal" in general . . . to an *end*, one first makes unjust, bestial actions possible, because the "ideal" . . . no longer exists as a yardstick, but has become an achievable, producible end within the world'.[17] The danger of thinking about politics this way is that the end can be quickly overwhelmed by violent means. The moral and political results are disastrous: effective action is equated with violence. As Arendt put it, 'in the context of expedient action, where nothing counts except the achievement of postulated and fixed ends, brute force will always play a major role.'[18]

We see this clearly in Machiavelli's understanding of political founding. Arendt praised Machiavelli for his appreciation of the 'splendor of the public realm'.[19] In fact, she rarely criticized him. But in linking violence to the greatness of political founding Arendt believed he undertook a heroic but nonetheless misguided effort 'to save violence from disgrace'.[20] Machiavelli's so-called realist contention that politics and violence were two sides of the same coin expressed *not* his 'so-called realistic insight into human nature'. Rather it represented nothing more, Arendt wrote, than 'his futile hope that he could find some quality in certain men to match the qualities we associate with the divine'.[21] The 'Machiavellian' justification of violence derived from the revolutionary effort to find a republic in the absence of traditional morality or appeals to God. It came from his search for a 'new absolute' (violence) upon which to ground politics. For the violence involved in founding and maintaining the republic seemed inherently plausible: 'You cannot make a table without killing trees, you cannot make an omelette without breaking eggs, you cannot make a republic without killing people.'[22]

In short, the fundamental divergence between Arendt and all that is implied in an ethic of responsibility is that efforts to relate means and ends in the specifically political sphere fail to properly understand 'what politics is about'—the plurality of men and women coming together to talk and initiate action in concert. She also objected to thinking in terms of the 'lesser evil' for political reasons: 'the weakness of the argument has always been that those who choose the lesser evil forget very quickly that they chose evil . . . Moreover . . . it is obvious that the argument of "the lesser evil"...is one of the mechanisms built into the machinery of terror and criminality' in totalitarian regimes.[23]

To reject the commonplace categories of means and ends when discussing politics is certainly an unusual step. But in the political sphere, Arendt argued, it is always the means that count most. 'Every good action for the sake of a bad end', she wrote, 'actually adds to the world a portion of goodness; every bad action for the sake of a good end actually adds to the world a portion of badness.'[24] Violence could be justified and was rational only for short-term ends, but she did not write about this in terms of being the lesser of evils; and she wholly rejected any criteria for weighing up the lives of the dead. 'This sounds to me like the last version of human sacrifices: pick seven virgins, sacrifice them to placate the wrath of gods. Well, this is not my religious belief.'[25]

Rather, Arendt's political morality (if that is what we may call it), especially her criticisms of goodness in politics, overlap with elements of the realist-republican tradition. Machiavelli's writing was central to Arendt's ideas about the autonomy of politics with its distinct motives and principles for action. As already noted, political speech and action could not easily be measured in terms of conventional moral standards. She praised Machiavelli's claim that 'I love my native city more than my own soul'. It was the city itself not the people in the city that was the object of his affection. This 'was no cliché', Arendt believed, and it was not a statement about the virtues of patriotism. It was a radical claim and against the grain of his time in protecting the political realm from the effects of Christianity. At issue, Arendt wrote, was 'whether one was capable of loving the world more than one's own self. And this decision indeed has always been the crucial decision for all who devoted their lives to politics.'[26]

Machiavelli understood the kind of politics necessary for secularism in which the norms and rules of the political realm are separate from the doctrines of the Church. When Machiavelli 'insisted that people...learn "how not to be good,"' Arendt noted, this was not a call to become evil.[27] It was an observation that what it took to be good in the Christian sense of the term is unworldly and fundamentally opposed to the proper character of the political.[28] For Machiavelli, it mattered only that the political actor appeared good to others; only God, who was 'beyond the realm of appearance', could judge the goodness of a human heart. There was a necessary gap between how the actor appeared to others and to any 'transcendent Being'. Machiavelli taught, in Arendt's words, "'Appear as you may wish to be", by which he meant: "Never mind how you [really] are [on the inside], this is of no relevance in the world and in politics, where only appearances, not 'true' being, count; if you can manage to appear to others as you would wish to be, that is all that can possibly be required."[29]

The criticism of Christian un-worldliness is related to Arendt's concern about its impact on our ability to register reality. Christian political ethics are motivated, at base, by an effort to fill with good deeds a gap in the sinful self. It is ultimately about the self and not the world or worldly greatness. In Christian thought, it is not the human world that may 'shine...as real as a stone or a house' and be immortalized. The only immortal thing 'is the single living individual' in the image of Christ.[30] 'The decisive difference between the "infinite improbabilities" on which the reality of our earthly life rests and the miraculous character inherent in those events which establish historical reality', Arendt noted, 'is that, in the realm of human affairs, we know the author of the "miracles". It is men who perform them—men who because they have received the twofold gift of freedom and action can establish a reality of their own.'[31] Throughout Arendt's work we see why Christian ethics are an anathema to the worldliness of politics, the only realm from which an ethic of reality can be derived.

6.3. POLITICS AND WORLDLY REALITY

Power is not a possession and politics is fundamentally not about rulership. To understand how this is so—and how what we are calling Arendt's ethic of reality emerges from it—we must be clear about how she understood politics and how she distinguished power from violence. She unfailingly maintained that the concepts of power and violence refer to basically different things. Power springs up between people as they act together; it belongs to the group and disappears when the group disperses. It is a collective capacity. Until this coming together, it is only a potential. Power, therefore, cannot be a possession, a thing to be held in ones hand like a gun. It is an end in itself. Violence, on the other hand, is essentially an instrument that can be possessed. And as such it is a means to an end. Violence is the use of implements to multiply strength and command others to obey.

The distance from Weber is clear. The most articulate proponent of political realism's ethic of responsibility began by defining the state in terms of its monopoly on the legitimate use of violence. But for Arendt, violence could not be the *essence* of the political realm itself. 'Everything', she argued, 'depends on the power behind the violence.'[32] Power can be channelled by the state apparatus. Indeed, this is the necessary precondition for the accumulation of the means of violence by the administrative state. It is true that when power and violence are combined, Arendt noted, 'the result is a monstrous increase in potential force'. It is for this reason that under modern conditions power and force appear to be the same and why violence and power, which is 'derived from the power of an organized space', are combined in modern states.[33] But this combination is historically contingent rather than intrinsic and necessary. It tells us very little about the nature of politics itself.

The basic meaning of politics, if it is to have a meaning distinct from other human activities, is the freedom to act in concert with plural equals. When Arendt referred to politics as such or the public realm 'properly understood', she was not referring to politics in the everyday sense of government and party politics. As others have argued, the 'definition of the political can be obtained only by discovering and defining the specifically political categories ... to which all action with a specifically political meaning can be traced'.[34] This is also true for Arendt, though she usually spoke in the lexicon of the 'public realm' and 'politics, properly speaking', rather than 'the political'. She understood politics as having its own meaning, distinctions, and separate logic. 'For political thought', she wrote, 'can only follow the articulations of the political phenomena themselves, it remains bound to what appears in the domain of human affairs; and these appearances, in contradistinction to physical matters, need speech and articulation.'[35] The meaning of politics is the freedom to appear among a plurality of equals and to engage in speech and persuasion. Political power is constituted *in-between* people, the 'realm of appearances', not 'things' to be shaped, or owned.

Like Machiavelli, Arendt conceived of the political realm as an artificial space of appearance where only words and actions can be judged because only they can appear in the 'world'. (Arendt rejected the distinction between essence and existence, reality and appearance. In public, to appear is to be. As she put it in *The Life of the Mind*, 'All that existentially concerns you while living in the world of appearances is the "impressions" by which you are affected. Whether what affects you exists or is mere illusion depends on your decision whether or not you will recognize it as real.'[36]) The 'world' in Arendt's lexicon refers to the common space which is available for politics. It is the tangible (because visible) worldly reality made of institutions, constitutions, and buildings. But the political world is also constituted by the less tangible, yet as she put it, 'no less real' 'subjective in-between', 'the "web" of human relationships' which emerges out of action and speech. In the political realm, nothing passes 'back and forth except speech, which is devoid of tangible means'.[37] This form of public speech, action, and appearance is necessary for an adequate comprehension of the reality of the world itself and of others; 'our apprehension of reality is dependent upon our sharing the world with our fellow-men.'[38] The acquisition of this sense of the real, a reality that can only be disclosed in the process of public speech and action, is a precondition for the illumination of the common world. As Arendt put it, 'the reality of the world is guaranteed by the presence of others, by its appearing to all . . . ; and whatever lacks this appearance comes and passes away like a dream, intimately and exclusively our own but without reality.'[39]

There is an intrinsic relationship between attentiveness to reality and the political condition of plurality, 'the fact men, not Man, live on the earth and inhabit the world'.[40] Whatever 'reality' is, for Arendt a robust sense of it is only possible with a strong public culture where diverse and conflicting perspectives are heard. The plurality of voices is constitutive of worldly reality, the 'in-between which consists of deeds and words and owes its origin exclusively to men's acting and speaking directly *to* one another'. To speak and act in the public world involves the disclosure of individuals 'as subjects, as distinct and unique persons'. This is 'who' somebody is; their unique identity is constantly created and recreated and revealed in their actions and speech. It is the 'specific uniqueness' of every single individual. In the process of speaking and acting in public, men and women can reveal something about themselves that even they would not otherwise have known. Indeed, without this space of appearance, the shared self-disclosure, 'and without trusting in action and speech as a mode of being together, neither the reality of one's self, of one's own identity, nor the reality of the surrounding world can be established beyond doubt'. It is therefore 'simply unrealistic', Arendt wrote, to ignore or even 'dispense with this disclosure...[or to] deny...that [it] is real and has consequences of its own'.[41]

Central to Arendt's argument is that political discourse is only conducted in a manner that is tantamount to living in the real world when there are perspectives; 'the reality of the public realm lies on the simultaneous presence of innumerable perspectives and aspects in which the common world presents itself and for which no common measurement or denominator can ever be devised'.[42] Our sense of reality could only be partial, narrow, and shallow in the absence of this strong public realm. This also means that political freedom is not a question of will: do we or do not we have free will? Politics itself is about the performance of freedom in action. Politics and freedom, public freedom, are fundamentally ends in themselves. Freedom is action with others 'to call something into being which did not exist before'.[43] It is the very meaning of politics. Here, as Arendt put it, 'freedom is not a concept, but a living political reality'.[44] The question is: do we or do not we possess a sufficient sense of common worldly reality?

The historiographical counterpart to Arendt's political ethic of reality is a form of history-telling in which the world comes into its full reality when the 'thing or event' in 'all its aspects...has been acknowledged and articulated from every possible stand-point within the human world'.[45] Arendt's method and purpose here has rightly been compared with Thucydides, including by Hans Morgenthau. Indeed, Arendt has been described as more Thucydides's heir than any of the realists of conventional international thought.[46] His description of the brutal lessons the Athenians sought to impose on the islanders of Melos is cited by many realists as evidence of the timeless and often brutal power struggle between groups. In contrast, Arendt presents Thucydides as suggesting something other. The real meaning of an event such as war and of apparently 'haphazard single actions' becomes clear only once we are able to relate what has happened as part of a story, revealed in the reflections of the political actors and the opinion of the judging spectators.[47] Through the 'active nonparticipation' in historical events, the historian's judgement becomes part of the story, which also shapes history. Truth for Thucydides was determined by the plurality of judging spectators, the eyewitnesses to great events, with each one different and viewing the events from their unique perspective.[48] His method was to reconstitute the concrete political dilemmas faced by the actors themselves in a manner that leaves the interpretation of those choices and events to the reader.

In interpreting the foundation of 'realist' historiography in this way, Arendt's point concerned the wider political role of historical representation. She took from Heraclitus's famous statement that war is 'the father of all things', for example, not that war is the origin of all politics. Rather, she argued that the method of making apparent the many-sidedness of things and the necessary diversity of perspectives makes its 'real appearance only in struggle'. Her other example was the historical and poetic tale of the Trojan War. This legendary conflict between the Greeks and the Trojans was a historical-political event 'forced...to appear...in both of its originally opposing aspects'. Homer believed that the many-sidedness of things was 'inherent in man-to-man combat'. Elements of Homer's epic tale are suggestive of 'what politics actually means and what place it should have in history'.[49] It is nothing short of the historical counterpart to Arendt's ontological basis of all politics, plurality. This form of historical narration also has a political function. The role of the story-teller is to reconcile us with reality, 'to teach acceptance of things as they are'.[50]

6.4. THINKING TOWARDS AN ETHIC OF REALITY

In the scholarship on Hannah Arendt, it is a commonplace to note that she embarked on her last book, *The Life of the Mind*, because she wanted to work through (accept?) what she had encountered and written about during the trial of Nazi bureaucrat and war criminal Adolf Eichmann. Eichmann had organized the transportation of the Jews to the death camps during World War II. After the war, he fled to Argentina where he was captured in 1960 by the Israeli secret service, smuggled out of the country, put on trial in Jerusalem and hanged for his crimes. Arendt volunteered to attend and report on the proceedings for *The New Yorker* magazine. The essays were expanded and published in 1963 as *Eichmann in Jerusalem: A Report on the Banality of Evil*. This was undoubtedly Arendt's most controversial book. She was denounced by the organized Jewish community for complicating the innocence of its leadership; she had condemned early negotiations with the Nazis as '*Realpolitik* without Machiavellian overtones'.[51] She observed that Eichmann was a rather unremarkable functionary, not the sadistic monster many seemed to want him to be. His evil was not radical, but banal. 'He *merely*, to put the matter colloquially, *never realized what he was doing* . . . That such remoteness from reality and such thoughtlessness can wreak more havoc than all the evil instincts taken together . . . —that was, in fact, the lesson one could learn in Jerusalem.'[52]

Eichmann was Arendt's case study in the avoidance of reality. At issue was his thoughtlessness; his utter inability to think; his continual use of stock phrases and clichés to explain his motives and actions. All this was his protection 'against reality' and the magnitude of what he had done.[53] During and after the trial, we see Arendt's characteristic unsentimentality. She faced unpleasant facts head-on. Yet she did not 'dwell on the horrors' or spend much time on the victims; her writing style in the report is rather detached and ironic. She believed the purpose of the report was to convey to others what happened *in the trial* and to evaluate Eichmann's innocence or guilt. It was not to romanticize or even express much pity for his victims. We see her willingness to judge the meaning of the event for herself, but also a belief that no matter what reality is it can also be resisted. But in doing so, Arendt violated a number of conventions of Holocaust representation and tone.[54] One critic, Gershom Scholem, accused her of heartlessness and demonstrating a lack of *Ahabath Israel*, or love of the Jewish people.[55]

While Arendt was always clear that Jewish-ness was 'one of the indisputable factual data' of her life—to such an extent that she believed it was 'nothing but a grotesque and dangerous evasion of reality' for the Jews to violently resist Hitler as anything other than Jews—she totally refused to become politically swallowed up in any love for a people.[56] 'I do not "love the Jews,"' she replied to Scholem, 'nor do I "believe" in them; I merely belong to them as a matter of course, beyond dispute or argument.' Anything else was too narcissistic. 'I have never in my life "loved" any people or collective... I indeed love "only" my friends and the only kind of love I know of and believe in is the love of persons.'[57] Anything else was too vague and potentially dangerous. Arendt preferred love of the world.

Love of people and love of the world are not the same because the 'world and the people who inhabit it are not the same'. The world lies between people, and this in-between is literally the space for politics. The principal subject of Arendt's political ethics is the world and not those individuals who may live in it. 'Strictly speaking', she wrote, 'politics is not so much about human beings as it is about the world that comes into being between them and endured beyond them.'[58] Hence, reflecting on Socrates statement that '[i]t is better to be wronged that to do wrong', Arendt looked at it 'from the viewpoint of the world ... [and] we would have to say what counts is that a wrong has been committed; it is irrelevant who is better off, the wrongdoer or the wrong-sufferer. As citizens we must prevent wrong-doing since the world we all share, wrongdoer, wrong-sufferer, and spectator, is at stake; the City has been wronged'.[59] The greatest wrong in the political realm is the destruction of the necessary condition for all politics, the destruction of plurality.

We find that Arendt's antidote to the political problem of large-scale human suffering is a form of realism. Arendt was not a realist who would reject human suffering though she was certainly unsentimental about it, mistrustful of its 'anaesthetic' effect.[60] But this is not a cold-hearted realism or the amoral realism that is caricatured in international theory. Consider the case of genocide. In debates about the ethics of humanitarian intervention, a narrowly construed 'realism' is presented as the immoral position that favours order over justice, national interest and state sovereignty over human rights. Indeed, Douglas Klusmeyer has rightly pointed to a lack of engagement with genocide in the writing of post-war realists such as George Kennan and Morgenthau in contrast to Arendt's central focus on the Holocaust as the defining twentieth-century event. He describes this as Arendt's 'critical realism'.[61] The analysis offered here suggests that we may also derive from Arendt's ethic of reality distinctive grounds for action *against* genocide, what she called a 'war of annihilation'.

R. J. Vincent formulated his influential defence of 'humanitarian' military intervention in terms of two basic rights to life, security against violence and of subsistence. He took this to be a direct alternative to the principles underlying humanitarian military intervention he imaged Arendt might endorse. In Vincent's words, 'I embrace as a project for international society what Arendt called the "politically pernicious" doctrine derived from Marx that life is the highest good.' He then contrasts this with an imagined case for intervention drawn from Arendt. Because she praised the importance of democratic revolution, Vincent strangely claims she must therefore endorse military intervention to spread 'political liberty'. As a contrast to Arendt, Vincent argues that international society works 'as well as it does by seeking to contain revolutions within the frontiers of states . . . Liberty upheld with revolutionary enthusiasm should exhaust itself at the border'.[62] The idea that revolutionary enthusiasm should be borderless is nowhere expressed in Arendt's work. The reality is far from it.[63]

Like others, Arendt believed the crimes that had occurred in World War II were too immense to be satisfactorily dealt with in the setting of a national court. She argued for an international penal code that recognized Nazi crimes as not just a matter for the Jewish people to be settled in Jewish courts as the Eichmann case had been; 'the international order, and mankind in its entirety' was also 'grievously hurt and endangered' by the effort to wipe an entire people from the face of the earth.[64] But Arendt's point had nothing to do with the numbers of the dead or basic rights as such. Her condemnation of genocide, and by extension her criteria for action to stop it, was for the sake of the political reality that only a plurality of human perspectives may bring to the world.[65] Wars of annihilation are crimes against the very nature of humanity and not just a simple crime of war. The point about genocide is that 'an altogether different order is broken and an altogether different community is violated'. Aggressive warfare is an old and common practice. But a war to annihilate an entire people, though old and still too common, is different 'not only in degree of seriousness', Arendt believed, 'but in essence'.[66]

We have noted that the subject of Arendt's ethic of reality is the political world itself and not the individuals within it. Above all, Arendt was the defender of the reality of the public, political world. Rather harshly she noted that individuals are mortal, but what does not necessarily die is the political reality and historical understanding that a plurality of people creates. Indeed, to engage in political action is to participate in founding and sustaining the common, political world that lasts longer than a natural human life. This world, Arendt wrote, 'is what we enter when we are born and what we leave behind when we die'.[67] The fact of birth, of natality, means that each man and woman that is born has the ability to bring into being something new. The very fact of human mortality can itself be a motivation to political action just as it may be the motivation for the creation of a new human life. Men and women are mortal but the body politic is potentially immortal. 'If the world is to contain a public space', she wrote, 'it cannot be erected for one generation and planned for the living only; it must transcend the life-span of mortal men. Without this transcendence into a potential earthly immortality, no politics, strictly speaking, no common world and no public realm, is possible.'[68]

With genocide, we are not 'just' talking about large numbers of dead but something that is potentially immortal. The public, political world, the political constitution of a people, the outcome of a people's living together and debating their common affairs is also destroyed. 'If it is true', as Arendt wrote, 'that a thing *is* real . . . only if it can show itself and be perceived from all sides, then there must always be a plurality of individuals or peoples . . . to make reality even possible and to guarantee its continuation.' Wars of annihilation that aim to wipe out a particular group attack the basic fact of human plurality and breach the 'limits inherent in violent action'. As she put it,

...the world comes into being only if there are perspectives...If a people or a nation, or even just some specific human group, which offers a unique view of the world...is annihilated, it is not merely that a people or a nation or a given number of individuals perishes, but rather that a portion of our common world is destroyed, an aspect of the world that has revealed itself to us until now but can never reveal itself again. Annihilation is therefore not just tantamount to the end of the world; it also takes its annihilator with it.[69]

Genocide may begin with the burning of built space, of houses and hospitals, temples and mosques. But it breaches the limits on violence not because the human-made world is shattered. This can be rebuilt. With a war of annihilation, the 'historical and political reality housed in this world' is also wiped out.

6.5. CONCLUSION

One virtue of a realist sensibility is that one does not—or does not have to—seek to fit all important political events into some overarching historical process. Hannah Arendt identified a tradition of historiography in the writings of Homer and Thucydides in which the meaning of an event is different from its place in any historical process or causal chain. Much modern social science seeks to absorb events within ideal types so that they appear as the manifestation of some deeper structural cause or general framework of which the event is a mere example. Arendt, in contrast, was a theorist of the unprecedented, of political novelty. She warned against efforts at, in her words, 'deducing the unprecedented from precedents, or explaining phenomena by such analogies and generalities that the impact of reality and the shock of experience are no longer felt'.[70] Arendt railed against the effort of behaviourist social science to predict and control political action and was unimpressed by its methodological quarrels which, she believed, tended to overshadow far more important problems. All historical and political processes are 'created and constantly interrupted by human initiative', she wrote. 'Hence it is not in the least superstitious, it is even a counsel of realism, to look for the unforeseeable and unpredictable.'[71] Some things cannot be understood within normal frameworks of thought. Arendt gave the example of the 'skilfully manufactured unreality' of the Nazi concentration camps, which she took to be totally without parallel; 'we actually have nothing to fall back on in order to understand a phenomenon that nevertheless confronts us with its overpowering reality and breaks down all standards we know.'[72] As she observed in 1943, 'hell is no longer a religious belief or a fantasy, but something as real as houses and stones and trees.'[73]

Two of the most common criticisms of Hannah Arendt are that she unapologet-ically privileges action in public as the highest form of human activity and that she appears disinterested in ethics. The ever-present danger that politics could degenerate into the sponsorship of evil was a constant preoccupation of her work. But Arendt was not principally concerned with ethics conventionally understood. (She criticized pacifism not on moral grounds but because it was 'devoid of reality'.[74]) Her purpose was to theorize the conditions for a strong political realm, rather than create a 'better' world as such or provide grounding for moral action. The ethical implications that we might draw from Arendt's understanding of politics are important, but not the most important thing about Arendt. She urged us to think, not to moralize. The direct ethical implications of thinking—of asking the question of how things really are—are second order; 'thinking as such does society little good', she observed. 'It does not create values; it will not find out, once and for all, what "the good" is... And it has no political relevance unless special emergencies arise.'[75] The emergency she had in mind was totalitarianism. The question is of personal responsibility under dictatorship: when the public realm has been totally destroyed and we are deprived of the realty it uniquely affords.

Arendt privileged the public because, as she put it, to be 'deprived' of the space of appearance 'means to be deprived of reality, which, humanly and politically speaking, is the same as appearance'.[76] Our sense of the real is fundamentally rooted in the public world and what is made manifest in the 'space of appearance' that is the world. Much of Arendt's work can be read as seeking to understand how different ways of being—in the world of work, acting and speaking in public, private family existence, introspection, and the life of the mind—relate to and shape our sense of reality.[77] Attentiveness to what Arendt repeatedly referred to as 'reality and factuality' is properly attained when one is able to register things that are almost unbearable to comprehend. It is not always easy to distinguish 'nightmare' from 'the reality of... experience'.[78] Arendt's committed response was dedication to the reality that totalitarianism, as well as a number of lesser evils, has sought to destroy. 'The question', as she put it, 'is how much reality must be retained even in a world become inhuman if humanity is not to be reduced to an empty phrase or phantom.'[79]

NOTES

1. Arendt, *The Origins of Totalitarianism*, new edition with added prefaces (New York: Harcourt Brace, 1966), p. 458.

2. Arendt, *The Origins of Totalitarianism*, p. viii. For a discussion of Arendt, ideologies and neoconservatism, see Patricia Owens, 'Beyond Strauss, Lies, and the War in Iraq: Hannah Arendt's Critique of Neoconservatism', *Review of International Studies*, 33 (2007), pp. 265–83.

3. Deudney, *Bounding Power: Republican Security Theory From the Polis to the Global Village* (Princeton: Princeton University Press, 2007), p. 5.

4. Kimberley Curtis, *Our Sense of the Real: Aesthetic Experience and Arendtian Politics* (Ithaca: Cornell University Press, 1999).

5. Arendt, *The Origins of Totalitarianism*, p. viii. These and other themes are developed in greater detail in Patricia Owens, *Between War and Politics: International Relations and the Thought of Hannah Arendt* (Oxford: Oxford University Press, 2007).

6. Arendt, *The Human Condition* (Chicago: University of Chicago Press, 1958), p. 51.

7. Arendt, 'The Cold War and the West', *Partisan Review*, 29/1 (1962), p. 13.

8. Arendt, 'The Nation', *Review of Politics*, 8/1 (1946), p. 141.

9. Arendt, *The Origins of Totalitarianism*, p. 138.

10. Arendt, *Between Past and Future: Eight Exercises in Political Thought* (New York: Viking, 1968), p. 150.

11. Arendt, *The Promise of Politics* (New York: Schocken, 2005), p. 145.

12. Yet as Peter Baehr has written, 'few authors of the twentieth-century offered a more comprehensive alternative to Weber's political and sociological thought than Arendt did.' However, surprisingly, she seldom addressed his writings directly, only as 'part of a broader tradition'. There is strong evidence that she believed that to do so would compromise her close friendship with Karl Jaspers, her doctoral supervisor and mentor, who was a former student of Weber. Baehr, 'The Grammar of Prudence: Arendt, Jaspers, and the Appraisal of Max Weber', in Steven E. Ashheim (ed.), *Hannah Arendt in Jerusalem* (Berkeley: University of California Press, 2001), pp. 307, 323.

13. Arendt, *The Human Condition*; Morgenthau, *The Purpose of American Politics* (New York: Vintage, 1960). Michael C. Williams has shown the connection between Hans Morgenthau's realism and the 'Atlantic republication' tradition. Williams, *The Realist Tradition and the Limits of International Relations* (Cambridge: Cambridge University Press, 2005), p. 84.

14. Canovan, *Hannah Arendt: A Reinterpretation of Her Political Thought* (Cambridge: Cambridge University Press, 1992), p. 185.

15. Weber, 'Politics as a Vocation', in H. H. Gerth and C. Wright (eds.), *From Max Weber: Essays in Sociology* (Oxford: Oxford University Press, 1946), p. 115.

16. At the beginning of 1933, Arendt presciently wrote that, 'Germany means my mother tongue, philosophy, and literature. I can and must stand by all that. But I am obliged to keep my distance, I can be neither for nor against when I read Max Weber's wonderful sentence where he says that to put Germany back on her feet he would form an alliance with the devil himself'. See Arendt and Karl Jaspers, *Correspondence, 1926–1969* (New York: Harcourt Brace Jovanovich, 1992), p. 16.

17. Arendt, *The Promise of Politics*, p. 3.

18. Arendt, *The Promise of Politics*, p. 194.

19. Arendt, *On Revolution* (New York: Viking, 1970 [1963]), p. 29.

20. Arendt, *Between Past and Future*, p. 22.

21. Arendt, *On Revolution*, p. 32.

22. Arendt, *Between Past and Future*, p. 139.

23. Arendt, *Responsibility and Judgement* (New York: Schocken, 2003), p. 36.

24. Arendt, *Men in Dark Times* (New York: Harcourt, Brace, and World, 1968), p. 148.

25. Quoted in Elisabeth Young-Bruehl, *Hannah Arendt: For Love of the World* (New Haven: Yale University Press, 1982), p. 374.

26. Arendt, *On Revolution*, p. 290.

27. Arendt, *On Revolution*, p. 29.

28. Arendt, *Between Past and Future*, p. 137; *Men in Dark Times*, p. 236.

29. Arendt, *On Revolution*, p. 97.

30. Arendt, *Between Past and Future*, p. 52. 'World alienation, and not self-alienation as Marx thought, has been the hallmark of the modern age.' Arendt, *The Human Condition*, p. 254.
31. Arendt, *Between Past and Future*, p. 171.
32. Arendt, *Crises of the Republic* (New York: Harcourt Brace Jovanovich, 1972), p. 148.
33. Arendt, *The Promise of Politics*, p. 147.
34. Schmitt, *The Concept of the Political* (trans., intro., and notes by George Schwab) (Chicago: University of Chicago Press, 1996 [1932]), pp. 25, 26.
35. Arendt, *On Revolution*, p. 9.
36. Arendt, *The Life of the Mind: One-Volume Edition* (New York: Harcourt, Brace, Jovanovich, 1978), p. 155.
37. Arendt, *The Human Condition*, p. 183; Arendt, *The Promise of Politics*, p. 193.
38. Arendt, *Between Past and Future*, p. 254.
39. Arendt, *The Human Condition*, p. 199.
40. Arendt, *The Human Condition*, p. 7.
41. Arendt, *The Human Condition*, pp. 183, 208, 183.
42. Arendt, *The Human Condition*, p. 57.
43. Arendt, *Between Past and Future*, p. 151.
44. Arendt, *Men in Dark Times*, p. 82; Hanna Fenichel Pitkin, *The Attack of the Blob: Hannah Arendt's Concept of the Social* (Chicago: University of Chicago Press, 1998), p. 274.
45. Arendt, *The Promise of Politics*, p. 174.
46. Klusmeyer, 'Hannah Arendt's Critical *Realism*': Power, Justice and Responsibility in Anthony F. Lang Jr and John Williams (eds.), Hannah Arendt and International Relations: Reading Across the Lines (London: Palgrave, 2005), p. 126. See discussion in Young-Bruehl, *Why Arendt Matters* (New Haven: Yale University Press, 2006), p. 34.
47. Arendt, *Between Past and Future*, p. 85.
48. These 'great deeds and great words were, in their greatness, as real as a stone or a house ... Greatness was easily recognizable'. Arendt, *Between Past and Future*, p. 52.
49. Arendt, *The Promise of Politics*, pp. 175, 163.
50. Arendt, *Between Past and Future*, pp. 85, 262. As Mary Dietz has put it, 'the act of facing up to reality—of making the facticity of certain traumatic events palpable and real—is also an act of creating a luminous and healing illusion ..., as well as a kind of moving on.' Dietz, 'Arendt and the Holocaust', in Dana Villa (ed.), *The Cambridge Companion to Hannah Arendt* (Cambridge: Cambridge University Press, 2000), p. 92.
51. Arendt had criticized the 'readiness of the German Jewish community to negotiate with the Nazi authorities during the early stages of the regime' for example, by providing lists of names. She continued,

    Needless to say, these negotiations were separated by an abyss from the later collaboration of the *Judenräte*. No moral questions were involved yet, only a political decision whose 'realism' was debatable: 'concrete' help, thus the argument ran, was better than 'abstract' denunciations ... and its dangers came to light years later, after the outbreak of the war, when these daily contacts ... made it so much easier for the Jewish functionaries to cross the abyss between helping Jews to escape and helping the Nazis to deport them.

    Arendt, *Eichmann in Jerusalem: A Report on the Banality of Evil* (New York: Viking, 1968 [1963]), pp. 10, 11.

52. Arendt, *Eichmann in Jerusalem*, pp. 287–8. This insight would later lead Arendt to ask the following: 'Could the activity of thinking as such, the habit of examining whatever has come to pass or to attract attention, regardless of results or specific content, could this activity be among the conditions that make men abstain from evil-doing or even actually "condition" them against it?' Arendt, *The Life of the Mind*, Vol. 1, p. 5

53. Arendt, *Responsibility and Judgement*, p. 160.

54. Deborah Nelson 'Suffering and Thinking: The Scandal of Tone in *Eichmann in Jerusalem*', in Lauren Berlant (ed.), *Compassion: The Culture and Politics of an Emotion* (London: Routledge, 2004), p. 234.

55. Quoted in Arendt, *Jew as Pariah: Jewish Identity and Politics in the Modern Age* (New York: Grove Press, 1978), p. 241.

56. Arendt, *Men in Dark Times*, p. 18.

57. Arendt, *Jew as Pariah*, pp. 246, 247.

58. Arendt, *The Promise of Politics*, p. 175.

59. Arendt, *Responsibility and Judgement*, p. 182. For a useful discussion, see Rei Terada, 'Thinking for Oneself: Realism and Defiance in Arendt', *English Literary History*, 71 (2004), pp. 839–65.

60. Deborah Nelson, 'The Virtues of Heartlessness: Mary McCarthy, Hannah Arendt, and the Anesthetics of Empathy', *American Literary History*, 18 (2006), p. 88.

61. Klusmeyer, 'Hannah Arendt's Critical *Realism*', pp. 113–78.

62. Vincent, *Human Rights and International Relations* (Cambridge: Cambridge University Press, 1986), p. 126.

63. While Arendt acknowledged that 'the boundaries of the territory are never entirely reliable safeguards against action from without', she argued that boundaries (and laws) provided the main—and necessary—limits to political action. Arendt, *Human Condition*, p. 191.

64. Arendt, *Eichmann in Jerusalem*, p. 276.

65. For a different extension of Arendt's ideas on plurality to global politics, but which avoids the pitfalls of associating her too closely with any so-called English School approach, see Roland Axtmann, 'Globality, Plurality and Freedom: The Arendtian Perspective', *Review of International Studies*, 32/1 (2006), pp. 93–117.

66. Arendt, *Eichmann*, pp. 272, 267.

67. Arendt, *The Human Condition*, p. 55.

68. Arendt, *The Human Condition*, p. 55.

69. Arendt, *The Promise of Politics*, p. 175.

70. Arendt, *The Origins of Totalitarianism*, p. viii.

71. Arendt, *Between Past and Future*, p. 170.

72. Arendt, *The Origins of Totalitarianism*, pp. 445, 459. Michael Rothberg places Arendt on the side of the 'realists' in debates about the Holocaust. Realism here refers to 'both the epistemological claim that the Holocaust is knowable and a representational claim that this knowledge can be translated into a familiar mimetic universe...inscribing the events within continuous historical narratives'. *Traumatic Realism: The Demands of Holocaust Representation* (Minneapolis: University of Minnesota Press, 2000), pp. 3–4.

73. Arendt, *Jew as Pariah*, p. 56.

74. Arendt, *The Origins of Totalitarianism*, p. 442.

75. Arendt, *Life of the Mind*, p. 192.

76. Arendt, *The Human Condition*, p. 199.

77. It is noteworthy that a key figure in realist international theory is strongly criticized in these terms by Arendt. Rousseau's 'mania for introspection' casts him as deeply unreal. 'In the isolation achieved by introspection thinking becomes limitless because it is no longer molested by anything exterior ... Man's autonomy becomes hegemony over all possibilities; reality merely impinges and rebounds. Reality can offer nothing new; introspection has already anticipated everything.' Arendt, *Rahel Varnhagen: The Life of a Jewish Woman* (revised edition) (New York: Harcourt Brace, 1974 [1957]), p. 10.
78. Arendt, *The Origins of Totalitarianism*, p. 439.
79. Arendt, *Men in Dark Times*, p. 22.

7

Towards a More Reflective Political Realism

Roger Spegele

7.1. INTRODUCTION

This chapter is conceived as an intellectual adventure, a bumpy ride across the seemingly obscure terrain barely hinted at in the title. Its ostensible value lies in teasing out and evaluating different conceptions of theory, practice, and the relations they comport. Although the ride may have all the drawbacks of taking a roller coaster when one wanted a Ferris wheel, its intention is to shake up orthodox assumptions about the topics considered. In international political theory as currently conceived each contending discourse—positivism, postmodernism, international critical theory, feminist international relations—insists that it is the only valid conception of international relations, leading to inevitable despair at the self-evident unreasonableness of any such claim. This chapter may, at the end of the ride, have something of enduring value to offer in its examination of theory and practice for those scholars who are looking for a way out of the current stasis of international political theory.

It would be difficult to cavil at the idea that theory and practice provide not only fundamental concepts but also the very framework in which to examine international political theory. Consider, for example, the question of whether we intend to examine international relations from within a positivist, Marxist, or interpretive perspective. A positivist perspective will deploy an essentially instrumentalist understanding of theory and practice in which the former is regarded as providing efficient means to the latter, paradigmatically in the form of policy ends. A Marxist view, on the other hand, holds that the test of a theory's truth is whether the actions named in the theory take place, that is, whether there is a successful revolution. Here the relationship between theory and practice is regarded as essentially 'constitutive'. By contrast, an interpretive understanding of the relation between theory and practice holds that the former provides actors with good reasons for actions. Here the relation between theory and practice is seen as essentially purposeful. Reflection on this result shows the decisive sense in which the relation of theory and practice is bound up with metaphysics since the three perspectives just cited mark off, respectively, naturalistic, materialistic, and linguistic metaphysical frameworks. These, as they are, simplistic illustrative examples fail to make contact with the deeper issues which these seemingly anodyne terms involve.

This brings me to my principal arguments. First, I will argue against an under-standing, derived ultimately from Kant, which conceives the relation of theory and practice as essentially unmediated and counterpose to it an alternative that separates theory from practice and sustains the latter against the former.[1] Second, I will then describe Heidegger's contrasting Aristotelian conception of theory and practice and associated concepts and the difficulties Heidegger encountered in deploying them, difficulties that rendered their use, two concepts excepted, nugatory. Third, I will argue that Heidegger is largely correct in his view that neither the Kantian nor the Aristotelian conceptions of theory and practice are sustainable in the age of technological domination. Fourth, I will draw out certain implications of Heidegger's views as discerned here for a somewhat different, and more reflective version, of political realism, without implying that Heidegger was a realist.

Such a version of realism makes capacious space for poetry (in the larger sense), classical political thought, history, and commonsense. It is a form of political realism exemplified more tellingly by the writings of the pre-Socratics, Thucy-dides, Machiavelli, and Nietzsche rather than the works of Plato, Hobbes, Spinoza, and Hegel. It is anti-theoretical and anti-metaphysical and insists on the need to draw 'lessons' from history and the concrete doings of men and women rather than to construct 'models' of human behaviour from which inferences are drawn. This conclusion, if even roughly correct, should serve, notwithstanding certain obstacles, to put Heidegger on the radar screen of realist international political thinking.[2]

7.2. THEORY AND PRACTICE: FROM ACADEMIC THINKING TO HEIDEGGER

Although the relationship of theory to practice is one of the most significant theoretical subjects in international relations, rarely are the key terms analysed and given precise meanings. A case in point is a 1996 review article by William Wallace. Conceptualizing the role of theory in international relations as involving 'interaction between theoretical and empirical work, between concepts and evi-dence, is', we learn, 'at the heart of social science'.[3] This might appear anodyne enough until we start raising some pointed questions concerning what Wallace means by 'theoretical and empirical work', not to mention 'concepts and evidence'. He does not tell us. The resulting difficulty for understanding theory and practice has not gone unnoticed by commentators. As Steve Smith complains: 'Wallace fundamentally misrepresents the relationship between theory and practice.'[4]

Let us accept Smith's judgement. The next question is whether Smith has an alternative which he believes to be the true', 'correct' or 'warrentedly assertible' relationship of theory and practice. The answer is affirmative and may be found in an address in 2003 in which he provides us with what might be regarded as his account of this relationship.[5] Smith says he wishes to argue for a 'view of theory as constitutive of practice...I see the two activities as linked together.[6] But what does it mean to say that theory and practice are 'linked together'? Surely, one can only determine this by unpacking the terms 'linked together' which Smith, unfortunately, does not do. Where do we go from here?

Although Smith does not allude to Immanuel Kant, there are many Kantian elements in his address. Perhaps, then, we might get a better idea of Smith's intentions from looking to its evident source in Kant's renowned conception of theory and practice because, unlike Smith, he identifies not only *how* theory and practice are linked together but also *why*. In the *Critique of Practical Reason*, Kant argues that theoretical and practical reason are combined 'in one cognition'.[7] Other textual references to such 'a unity of reason' may be found throughout Kant's three major treatises. On the dominant interpretation Kant thought there were distinct advantages to subordinating the practical to the theoretical.[8] First, in giving priority to speculative over practical reason, the unity of reason guarantees that the practical cannot contradict any results of theoretical action. Second, when theoretical reason attempts to bring about the unity of theoretical and practical reason, there is the possibility of organizing empirical data into a systematic body of empirical knowledge. Third, the unity of reason enables a teleological principle to be used as a way to understand historical progress. And, fourth, priority of belief enables one to make sense of metaphysical postulates concerning the existence of God, immortality, and freedom. It is this last feature of Kant's view of theory and practice that requires marking since it plays a pivotal role in Heidegger's rejection of Kant's view of theory and practice. It is also important to note that Kant's primacy-of-belief view entails that Smith's idea of the constitutiveness of theory and practice gets no support from Kant nor, so far as one can tell, from any other major philosopher. At the very least, Smith needs to provide an account supporting his position.

On an alternative view derived ultimately from Aristotle, we can resist a counterproductive appeal to theorizing by adopting a straightforward practical standpoint of agency independent of any theoretical considerations. Separating theory from practice and making a case for the latter over the former is valuable for many reasons. For one thing, it links up with anti-foundationalist, anti-metaphysical philosophy in so far as it holds that we are practically free in a sense which requires no reference whatever to ontological or metaphysical claims. Second, it puts the focus of morality not on abstract speculative questions of a philosophical sort but on the practical questions of what to do. This should have appeal to those policymakers who take a fundamentally pragmatic stance but who nevertheless increasingly want to know, through all the 'noise' of strident contending voices, what the right thing to do really is.

The upshot of these considerations is to raise the following question: can we do better than Smith's constitutive conception of theory and practice? One might suppose, as early Heidegger did, that a revised Aristotelian conception of theory and practice is just what was needed as an alternative to Kant's metaphysically entrenched conception of theory and practice. And there is merit to this view. Nonetheless, as we shall see, Heidegger's attempted retrieval ran afoul of the world in the form of vastly increased technological domination. Before relating this philosophical story, however, we need a clearer idea of the Aristotelian conception of theory and practice, or, as I will often refer to them, to underline their Greek provenance, *theōria* and *praxis*. The key point to emphasize is that these key words are mediated by three others: *technē*, *poiēses*, and *phronēsis*. All five of these words need to be understood in terms of Heidegger's special perspective, keeping clearly in mind not only the difficulty Heidegger experienced in achieving his project of retrieval but also how he responded to it. To understand this, we need a rough and ready understanding of these five words as Heidegger conceived them.

Theōria: Contemplating or 'pure observation'. *Theōria* had primacy in Aristotelian thought owing to its status as pure contemplation even though its primacy did not entail that it could act on its own; rather, its activity had to be understood in relation to those mediating concepts against which *theōria* delimits itself in establishing the primacy, that is, *technē*, *praxis*, and *poiēses*. For Heidegger, *theōria*, under technological domination, becomes an instrument of *technē*'s domination, a far cry from the nearly divine activity Aristotle attributed to it.[9]

Praxis: For Aristotle *praxis* is an activity whose end is nothing other than the activity itself. The relation between *theōria* and *praxis* was not a simple opposition since Aristotle identifies the activity of theorizing to be a *praxis*, indeed the highest form of *praxis*.[10] In contrast to the tendency to transcendentalize *theōria*, Heidegger's project was to establish, as one might put it, the transcendence of *praxis*.

Technē: Like *phronēsis* a form of human doing. It aims at production and is thus a form of knowing that is dependent on its end or *telos*. For Heidegger, *technē* in ancient Greece was not simply an activity of making or producing; it was also a bringing-forth of what was present out of concealment. In the age of technological domination, however, it links up with *theōria* and the accompanying couplet, *theōria-technē* shifts away from bringing-forth to a different kind of revealing, namely, a challenging-forth which sets upon all other things to extract, store, and use them as the system requires.[11]

Poiēses: For Aristotle, *poiēses* is an activity that aims at an end distinct from the activity itself. *Poiēses* is not what the English word 'poetry' names; it is related instead to bringing-forth as a mode of revealing. This corresponds to the sort of revealing characteristic of ancient crafts as well as what occurs in nature. As such, it stands in marked contrast with *theōria-technē*'s mode of revealing, what Heidegger calls 'challenging-forth'. One of Heidegger's projects is to establish the validity of poetic truth and knowing. This may be one reason that, for Heidegger, *poiēses* has a central role to play as 'the saving power', that is, the force that could prevent planetary domination by the 'essence' of technology.

Phronēsis: Usually translated in English as 'prudence' or 'practical wisdom'. Like *technē* and *praxis*, *phronēsis* is a practical form of revealing. Aristotle identifies *phronēsis* as the capacity to catch sight of concrete situations in which we must act, of the here and now, of the momentary situation. It is a practical perception of a situation in all its particularity. For Heidegger, the activity of *phronēsis* allows us to see not only the 'now' of the situation, what is to be done, and how it is to be done but also the basis for the command for it to be done.[12]

Although these were the concepts that Heidegger intended to employ to construct a scientific ontology, he came to see that their capacity to capture the world swirling around him was increasingly problematic. Not only did this put paid to any scientific ontology, but it also required radical revision of the concepts themselves.

7.3. THE DIMINISHMENT OF *THEŌRIA, PRAXIS,* AND *PHRONĒSIS* AND THE RISE OF *TECHNĒ* AND *POIĒSES*

7.3.1. Early Heidegger on Theory and Practice

Early Heidegger saw as one of his key tasks the need to restate Aristotelian ideas in critical terms consistent with the presuppositions, assumptions, and cultural proclivities of our epoch, the epoch of technology or, as Heidegger more felicitously called it sometimes, 'The Age of the World Picture'.[13] On Heidegger's reading, Descartes's metaphysics inaugurated a distinctive epoch, one in which the paradigm of knowledge is found not so much in modern science but in what almost all conceptions of the relation between science and technology would call its handmaiden, that is, 'modern technology'. As Heidegger sees it, Descartes removed important barriers to a technical way of thinking, a kind of thinking that Descartes thought vastly superior to Greek thinking in terms of its capacity to improve the practical condition of mankind. Descartes's metaphysics involved constructing and systematizing to the limits of the possible.[14]

In 'The Age of the World Picture', speculation or theorizing had to become 'useful', subservient to 'practical' ends and geared to mastering nature. This idea is most famously formulated in the sixth and final part of Descartes's *Discourse on Method*. Here Descartes writes of the possibility of attaining knowledge that is most 'useful' in life, expressing the hope that 'a practical philosophy' could be discovered in terms of which 'we could know the power and action of fire, water, the stars, and the heavens, and all the other bodies in our environment...and thus make ourselves, as it were, the lords and masters of nature'.[15] The need for theoretical knowledge to be deployed in the service of *technē*, and equated with the 'practical', could not be more clearly stated. *Theōria* could no longer be conceived as an end in itself, a straightforward apprehending and observing of the kosmos and of nature, but had to become a means whereby human beings could 'make' themselves master of the universe—as though this very mastery could itself be produced or fabricated through the new knowledge acquired.

Heidegger enumerates certain suggestive consequences of the emergence of 'The Age of the World Picture' (or the 'Age of Technological Domination' as we shall call it) in his essay 'The Question Concerning Technology'.[16] Here Heidegger reads Descartes as the philosopher who sets in place the entire structure of Western metaphysics, whose most important feature is a structure that Heidegger calls 'Enframing' (*Gestell*). Enframing involves gathering 'things' from within a particular horizon of disclosure and shaping them into 'resources' available for immediate delivery and consumption. Even human beings become a mere resource. Enframing transforms everything into 'standing reserve' (*Berstand*) to be calculated, consumed, or stockpiled for any technological purpose whatsoever. The overarching metaphysical principle of Enframing shapes every feature of modern life—business, government, medicine, universities, language, and so forth; it 'threatens the human being with the possibility' that *technē*, as the sole essence in the Age of Technological Domination, would constitute the only form of revealing available to human beings, notwithstanding the impoverishment to human existence.[17] With the emergence of the metaphysical conception of Enframing, the Aristotelian conception of *theōria* and *praxis* is radically changed. Theory (no longer *theōria*) searches out the real and makes it secure as standing reserve, ready for use, willy nilly, by techno-science. On the other hand, *praxis* is replaced by Descartes's passions, sensations and appetites as described in *Les Passions de l'âme*.[18] For Descartes, our appetites motivate us to take action when they are perceived to harm or benefit us. In other words, self-interest takes over as the criterion of human action. Neither *theōria* nor *praxis* has a role to play in determining the play of harms and benefits.

The transformation of *theōria* is accompanied by the rise to dominance of *technē*. It belongs to a power granted to humans to foresee aspects of the world—within certain limits—and this helps them to regulate the appearance of things in advance, to impose a particular form on material things. Thus, when in modernity human beings free themselves to become the titular masters of the universe, it is not surprising that this human power over making entities appear should seek constantly to establish and confirm itself, to 'prove itself' so to speak. The constant drive to secure and extend outward in order to gain domination over whatever lies in its path is irrepressible. In the Age of Technological Domination, the couplet *theōria-technē* yields a qualitatively different kind of knowing from their separate ancient counterparts. For Aristotle, *theōria*, whether as pure contemplation or as the highest form of *praxis*, was an activity worthy of the gods, while *technē* was also deemed to be of the highest worth in so far as it entailed 'bringing-forth' from out of concealment. When they are notionally linked together in the Age of Technological Domination, however, their function is reduced to a 'challenging-forth' where elements, including human beings, are set upon and ordered to be stock in a vast technological paradigm. The destruction of the essence of modern technology's use of *theōria-technē* was one of Heidegger's central projects.

But what, then, happens to *praxis*, *phronēsis*, and *poiēses*, all of which, as ways of disclosing, Aristotle regarded as forms of knowledge? For Aristotle, all *praxis* points beyond itself toward something that transcends or exceeds it, but this ultimate end is, as it were, excentric to *praxis*, not actualized in any particular action as such. Indeed, *praxis* can be an end in itself only if it does not aim primarily at any particular end, but rather at the highest good as a whole for human beings. Although *praxis* is a 'means' toward this ultimate end, the end itself does not determine in advance what the appropriate action should be on any given occasion. The particular action chosen is mediated by deliberation, which weighs up the best action to take in light of the situation and in view of its knowledge of the ultimate good. But in the Age of the World Picture *praxis*, as an alternative form of technical revealing, is effectively obliterated. It is not even mentioned in Heidegger's 1953 essay 'The Question Concerning Technology'. Whether Heidegger believed that *theōria-technē* dissolved *praxis* altogether or thought its disappearance another consequence of the demise of metaphysics is not entirely clear.

A similar fate awaits *phronēsis*. In Aristotle *phronēsis* is held to be higher than *technē* because *technē* aims at an end and as such is always for the sake of something beyond itself, while the activity at which *phronēsis* aims constitutes an end in itself. In *phronēsis* knowledge is directed toward the *phronimos*, the person of practical wisdom. *Phronēsis* is a knowledge attuned to human beings in their singularity and communal being with one another. In so far as it concerns particular cases, involves judgement, deliberative choice, and thoughtfulness, *phronēsis* puts primary focus on the kind of wisdom that is acquired via profound experience with similar kinds of cases. However, *phronēsis* too is sucked into the Enframing system which may be one of the reasons Heidegger does not see it as an antidote to the domination of technology.

One might think that *poiēses* has the possibility of avoiding Enframing since it, as the revealing that has to do with the beautiful, is non-practical and non-theoretical. Heidegger suggests this himself near the end of 'The Question Concerning Technology' where he writes: 'Once there was a time when the bringing-forth of the true into the beautiful was called *technē*. And the *poiēses* of the fine arts was called *technē*. In Greece, at the outset of the destining of the West, the arts soared to the supreme height of the revealing granted them.'[19] Although *poiēses* is not sucked into Enframing, it risks becoming extrinsic to the current domination of technology altogether. Yet, as we shall see, Heidegger thinks that *poiesis*, in listening to the strains of tragic poets, could become the 'saving power' of the West.

Before considering this we need to see the bearing of Heidegger's arguments on what he calls the planetary destiny of the West, that is, on the future of international political theory. For Heidegger, the end of metaphysics and the planetary destiny bound up with it was clearly foreseen by Nietzsche as 'the consummation of the modern age'.[20] In Nietzsche's notion of the 'will to will'—the exaltation of the will to achieve mastery of whatever can be mastered—we have a compelling self-demand to calculate and arrange everything unhistorically and technologically. Heidegger holds that the will to will may not appear to be the 'anarchy of catastrophes that it really is'; nonetheless, it 'still must legitimate itself'. To do so, the will to will 'invents' talk of 'mission', a goal that comes about from "'fate", thus justifying the will to will'.[21] This is where politics enters the picture, that is, politics in the sense of planetary willing, politics as power, 'realist' politics. Although not endorsing this kind of politics, Heidegger certainly gave due weight to its descriptive and explanatory value. More importantly, Heidegger's later work could be interpreted as pointing the way to a non-humanist anti-metaphysical version of political realism. In taking on board Heidegger's valid critique of humanism as an ideology, reflective political realists may want, following Hans Morgenthau in this regard (see below), to engage with humanism's non-metaphysical, salutary, and morally viable principles.

It is easy to see, however, that there will not be a single mission developed to justify the will to will but rather multiple missions. In the face of this inevitable fact, a struggle would arise 'between those who are in power and those who want to come to power'; a world would come about in which the struggle for power is everywhere; power itself would be 'what is determinative'.[22] The struggle between those who are in power and those who want to take power is of 'necessity planetary and undecidable'.[23] Why undecidable? This is because for Heidegger the question concerning the relationship between being and beings became forgotten to such an extent that it now stands in decisive obscurity with respect to the unfolding of Western history and thought.[24] World wars, arms races, and man's reduction to 'the most important raw material' meant the 'abandonment of Being'.[25] In such a world, one can no longer judge the value of 'war' or 'peace' or even properly mark their distinctive differences. The picture Heidegger presents here is unrelievedly bleak in so far as it entails '[t]he desolation of the earth'.[26] Although Heidegger rejects Hegel's contention that all this suffering and pain might only be a blip on the radar screen of the history of metaphysics, he does hold out some prospect of an alternative form of revealing through thinking and *poiēses*. Let us first consider the 'saving power' of *poiēses*, and leave thinking to the following section.

7.3.2. Discovering Tragic Poetry

There are two factors that seem to have led Heidegger to turn to *poiēses* and tragedy as a way to constrain the essence of technology: his disastrous failure to convincingly articulate a paradigmatic Aristotelian understanding of *theōria* and *praxis* in his Rectoral Address, 'The Self-Assertion of the German University',[27] and an increased recognition of the dangers which an unconstrained *theōria-technē* would bring in its wake. Given that *praxis* and *phronēsis* are cast into oblivion by technological domination, Heidegger turns to *poiēses*—the relation between poetizing and thinking—to break the bonds connecting *theōria* and *technē* and the danger it brings. The danger is twofold. First, there is the danger that the technological understanding of being will gain such sway that human beings will be cut off from other ways of revealing, now and in the future. And second, there is the danger that in our intense focus on the practical features that technology embodies we will ignore its character as a mode of revealing. *Poiēses* might be able to reduce such dangers because it is a privileged site for the production and analysis of conceptions of reality, not as a structure given for all time, since there are no such structures, but rather as a place that will allow us to get closer to the meaning of being, to grasp it in a way that will alter the relations between human beings, conventions, and the space of community. Poetizing points the way to what a human being is, what a people is, and what a *polis* is because it reveals the kind of world in which these 'things' will appear. For Heidegger, then, *poiēses* becomes the vehicle for appealing to greater thoughtfulness about these matters than would be available in any *theōria-technē* modality. That greater thoughtfulness becomes possible as a result of revealing the poetic truth in Sophocles's *Antigone*.

In *the Introduction to Metaphysics* (1935), Heidegger analyses the choral ode from *Antigone* as a form of *theōria-technē* in which there is a passionate drive to know and to place oneself in a position of power in the world.[28] He introduces the ode in the context of his reflections on the history of Western philosophy as a sequence of variations on a single metaphysical theme, to wit the establishment of Reason as the consummative action of thought. He says that 'the real target' of his attack is the polarity of 'Being and thinking' which constitutes the 'fundamental orientation of the spirit of the West'.[29] For Heidegger, thinking and being, when properly conceived, are inextricably bound up with one another. Poetry allows us to discern being as a manner of revealing, a contingent one in constant struggle with forces swirling around us. In poetry the world is revealed as world and thus the mode of revealing that sways in the technological age may be seen as only one possible mode of revealing. Poetry opens up another in so far as it gives rise to a fuller awareness of the understanding of being in which human beings dwell. The poetic mode of revealing manifests itself most acutely in Greek tragedy and in particular in Sophocles's *Antigone*.

The 1935 portrayal of human beings as powerful, violent, cunning, and, above all, strange or uncanny is consistent with Heidegger's picture of *theōria-technē* holding sway within an historically ineluctable technological domination except in one respect: the human being cannot escape from the constant reverberation of increasing and decreasing power, of building and destroying, that ends inevitably in death. Unlike the self-flattering picture man has of himself from within the confines of technological domination, the choral ode underlines the tragedy of the double bind, that is, the desire involved in struggling towards singularity which, when it succeeds, is destroyed.

To bring out the extent of Heidegger's shift in ideas about the *polis* and the nature of human beings, we would do well to consider Heidegger's 1942 reading and interpretation of *Antigone*.[30] Here Heidegger retains the earlier *theōria-technē* reading of the chorale ode but shifts the focus to its first and last lines. Spoken by the elders of Thebes, the first line reads: 'Manifold is the uncanny, yet nothing more uncanny looms or stirs beyond the human being.' The key to understanding this line lies in grasping that although the uncanny is equated with 'the fearful, the powerful, [and] the inhabitual', the 'essence' of the uncanny lies in being 'unhomely', that is, unfit to belong to the *polis* unless strong exculpatory grounds can be adduced. This understanding of homely will turn out to be of considerable importance when Heidegger analyses the last line of the choral ode. But in any case we already perceive the intimation of tragedy at work. For what makes the condition of humans so tragic is, first, that their uncanniness involves inevitable danger and risk. There is, however, a second reason for portraying unhomeliness as tragic, namely, that in trying to be everywhere and do everything, people wind up doing nothing meaningful.

Heidegger tries to ameliorate the tragic condition by bringing together a 'poetic' account of humanity and an account of the *polis* as their essential dwelling. For Heidegger, Sophoclean tragedy shows that human beings are sometimes compelled to be excessive and to precipitate their own downfall by being thrust to the outer reaches of the *polis*. Still, the *polis* is the historical abode of human beings. The key point for our purposes is that in so far as human beings are understood as 'uncanny', prepared to risk everything, they cannot properly be conceived as a collection of objects in stock, as resources to be mobilized in the project of mastering the earth. They are not entities that can be grasped and controlled via calculation.

Now Heidegger realizes that his reading appears to go against the grain of the last line of the ode in which the Theban Elders appear to expel Antigone from their city and their 'hearth', a rejection which surely applies as well to unnamed others deemed 'unsuitable' for the hearth/*polis*. If the *polis* is, as Heidegger suggests, the original self-gathering that sustains diversity among its members, and if Antigone is the truth of Greek humanity, on what basis should she be denied access to it? By what authority do the Elders intend to exclude her (or anyone else similarly placed)? Since human beings, like Antigone, must be uncanny, we might ask of the Elders: 'Are not they too human beings?'[31] But, as Heidegger points out, homeliness is, after all, an important aspect of communal life. Confusion about the contradiction within the ode arises, according to Heidegger, because we attempt to understand it in terms of the kind of knowing that is appropriate to *technē*, that is, as a form of knowing in which everything must be 'enunciated'.

For Heidegger, the closing words of the ode suggest two ways of being unhomely, a proper and an improper way. Those who consciously flout the ways of the *polis* and show no concern for it should be expelled, but exceptional people such as Antigone, who unintentionally become 'unhomely' through their desire to be true to their own conception of being, may be exempt from expulsion. A determinate answer, Heidegger suggests, is simply not available, nor should it be. On the other hand, there is something that is not indeterminate, namely, poetic truth. Saying and showing 'the potential of human beings for being homely' in the required way is 'in the highest sense worthy of poetising'.[32] By the same token, since Antigone personifies becoming homely in being unhomely, she enacts the tragedy of being human. She also calls attention to the deeply political character of the tragic drama in as much as it concerns the issue of who should belong to the *polis* and who should be excluded, and on what basis.

As the last paragraph intimates there is for Heidegger more at issue here than the proper interpretation of Sophocles's poem, namely, whether there is a form of disclosing that escapes technological revealing and the challenging-forth bound up with it. Clearly Heidegger thinks so. Unlike the scientific cognition that reigns in the Age of Technological Domination, poetry is a way of accessing the original nature of truth while at the same time recognizing the unsaid. Poetry, at least serious poetry, cannot be thought apart from the happening of concealment and unconcealment and its connection with truth-telling which 'thrusts up the unfamiliar and extraordinary and at the same time thrusts down the ordinary and what we believe to be such'.[33] In this respect its form of knowledge outstrips what *theōria-technē* can make available. In poetry tragedy is revealed as near to being and in constant struggle with non-beings.[34] Poetry so understood can open a new strand within us, giving rise to a fuller understanding of being in whose nearness we dwell so that we can turn our attention to building communities where violence is, if not entirely eliminated, potentially kept in check.[35]

The question arises, however, concerning to what extent Heidegger believed that *poiēses* would be able to sustain an alternative way of revealing such that it could truly be regarded as the 'saving power' of the West. To consider this question, we need to turn to Heidegger's 'Letter on Humanism' which brings *theōria* and *praxis* back into a frame that includes both *poiēses* and *technē*.

7.4. THE 'LETTER ON HUMANISM': THE DEMISE OF *THEŌRIA* AND *PRAXIS* AND THE RISE OF 'THINKING'

Heidegger's renowned 'Letter on Humanism', the first edition of which was published in 1949, constitutes the linchpin that clamps together his reflections on how on the one side to be free from the more pernicious forms of technicity and the possibility of moving from a metaphysically compromised notion of humanism to a more noble conception of humanity.[36] Quite remarkably, he manages this while simultaneously hinting at a more reflective version of realism. For in the middle of the pin and helping to keep the two ends in place, Heidegger develops an understanding of 'thinking' to match his revived notion of *poiēses* while simultaneously registering the diminishment of *theōria* and *praxis*. At the end of the line the later Heidegger's project may be viewed as an effort to replace the Aristotelian vocabulary of *theōria*, *praxis*, and *phronēsis* with thinking and *poiēses* in the interest of finding an alternative to *theōria-technē*. Whether thinking and *poiēses* can succeed in their goal of *destruktion* of technology's essence is an open question, but it is a deeply important one for the theory of international relations in so far as it highlights which concepts should be privileged and with what consequences for the relation of human beings to planetary technological domination.[37]

The 'Letter on Humanism' is a response to a series of questions from Jean Beaufret who translated many of Heidegger's writings into French. The nub of these questions concerns whether humanism is sustainable in the face of the Holocaust and the other horrors of the Nazi era. Beaufret's questions assume that there are many negative consequences to non-humanistic practices in the realm of art, culture, and politics that should be avoided. But how is one to rectify what one might glibly describe as 'a shortfall' in humanism? Will university courses remedy the situation? Will street demonstrations enhance humanist thinking and practice? What about philosophy: is it 'the solution' or in some sense a part of the problem? The answer to this provocative question depends for Heidegger on how philosophy is characterized. If we characterize it in the traditional way as more or less equivalent to metaphysics, then for Heidegger it is indeed a major part of the problem. If, on the other hand, we see philosophy as liberated from metaphysics, then it is 'thinking' and as such part of the 'solution'. When thinking is so understood, it puts paid to an understanding of *theōria* in which it serves productionist metaphysics; thinking thereby may truly be said to 'open other vistas'.[38] I will argue first that for Heidegger 'philosophy-as-metaphysics' (or 'philosophy') issues in various kinds of humanism whose explicit and implicit goals have never been attained.[39] But although the aims of any humanism turn out to be dogmatic illusions, Heidegger does not foreclose on the possibility of a noble and quite 'idealistic' conception of humanity. Second, I will argue that because, according to Heidegger, philosophy is coming to an end, thinking, when joined to *poiēses*, holds out some prospect of achieving a higher humanity while simultaneously providing a viable alternative to *theōria-technē*.

Heidegger raises the question of whether it is worthwhile retaining 'humanism' as a word and this, he claims, hinges on whether we can determine in what the humanity of the human being consists. For Heidegger, the rubric of humanism is capacious: it includes five historical types. Heidegger alludes to Marx's 'social' version of humanism; Christianity's distinction between the humanity of man and God; the Roman Republic's *homo humanitas*; the *homo romanus* of the Renaissance; and Sartrean existentialism. What is wrong, on Heidegger's view, with these or any other form of humanism that may come into existence later? It is quite simply that they 'all agree' on the content of the human. Since all humanisms posit a fixed understanding of a very large array of issues across history and culture, they are implausible and, worse, dogmatic. Dogmatism arises because '[e]very humanism is either grounded in a metaphysics or is itself made to be the ground of one'.[40] By the same token every metaphysics in turn is 'humanistic'. So all encompassing is the dogmatism that '[i]n defining the humanity of the human being, humanism not only does not ask about the relation of being to the essence of human being', it 'even impedes the question by neither recognizing or understanding it'.[41] Hence, paradoxically, the more humanism is given free reign to define the human, the further away from achieving the human we will be.

For Heidegger, the Roman Republic developed the first definition of humanism, locating it in the concept of 'thinking animal'. Although this may seem innocuous enough, it has resulted in presupposing an obviousness concerning the question of what humanism consists in that is thoroughly unwarranted. Heidegger is quick to point out that though the definition is not *per se* false, 'it is conditioned by metaphysics'.[42] It asks about beings but not about being; it posits a certain conception of life and accepts the idea that human beings are just one being among others. Heidegger maintains that in doing this '[w]e will thereby always be able to state something correct about the human being'.[43] Nonetheless, the price is exorbitant since we effectively 'abandon the human being to the essential realm of *animalitas* even if we do not equate him with beasts'. On Heidegger's view, such 'positing is the manner of metaphysics'. In thinking of human beings as belonging to the animal species, we are diverted from thinking of them as belonging to the human.[44]

Despite all this it would not be correct, I believe, to say of Heidegger's 'Letter' that it articulates a comprehensive anti-humanism. For Heidegger, the real trouble with dogmatic humanism is that all previous manifestations of it, determined by metaphysics, have been compelled to say what human beings are by comparing them with non-human animals.[45] But this, Heidegger says, is the wrong approach. 'The human body', Heidegger says, 'is something essentially other than an animal organism.'[46] Heidegger thus holds that '[h]umanism is opposed because it does not set the *humanitas* of the human being high enough'.[47] The various 'ideologies' alluded to above issue in determinations of the human which 'still do not realize the proper dignity of the human being'.[48] Heidegger finds such consequences unpalatable which is presumably why he advocates abandoning the word 'humanism', hoping that doing so will engender meditative thinking and not provoke outcries of 'inhumanity' and 'barbaric brutality'.[49] Whether Heidegger's 'strategy' will achieve its objective is beyond the scope of this chapter. What is important here is that Heidegger is clearly not persuaded that even in the Age of Technological Domination we are compelled to think of human beings as resources as one would if productionist metaphysics reigned free. There still remains the possibility of thinking of human beings in a noble and 'idealistic' way. To shape our practices, however, philosophy must come to an end. But how is this to be accomplished?

In a certain sense, nothing needs to be done since as Heidegger argues in 'Letter' and in a number of other works including, in particular, *The End of Philosophy*, philosophy-as-metaphysics is reaching its *terminus ad quem*. Philosophy in this sense has its roots in Plato and Aristotle and was subsequently advanced by Descartes, Leibniz, and Kant among others. The *completion* of philosophy, however, first became an explicit theme in Hegel's 'metaphysics of absolute knowledge as the Spirit of the Will'.[50] It was with Nietzsche, though, that philosophy *itself* actually came to completion. What takes philosophy's place in this age—our age— is anthropology that, however, becomes 'prey to the derivatives of metaphysics, that is, of physics in the broadest sense, which includes the physics of life and man, biology and psychology. Having become anthropology, philosophy itself perishes.'[51] Yet, 'thinking is not also at an end, but in transition to another beginning'.[52] To be sure, when thinking fails to unwind in conformity with its essence, it is just like 'completed philosophy', that is, a vacuous enterprise, 'a classroom matter and later a cultural concern'.[53] Genuine thinking is not at all like that. Whereas the sciences are 'artificial', thinking circulates near 'the truth of being', which is, for Heidegger, the highest form of activity in the age of productionist metaphysics.

To metaphysical thinking Heidegger counterposes *recollective thinking*. Recollective thinking not only 'belongs to being', but it also 'listens to beings'.[54] Thinking so understood has the capacity to embrace 'its essence in a destinal manner' and in certain modalities is able to embrace a 'thing' or a 'person'.[55] Heidegger says that '[t]he thinking that is to come is no longer philosophy, because it thinks more originally than metaphysics'.[56] It is not only a worthy successor to philosophy but, more to the point, is also capable of moving us to think of the human being in thoroughgoing contradistinction to non-human animality. To be sure, these are only intimations of what thinking freed from technicity can achieve since a comprehensive account cannot be determined at this point. Any such rendering is attendant on reaching *the clearing* that will only arise when metaphysics is overcome. To 'overcome' does not mean to be done with something as if one could then set something aside once and for all and start all over again. Overcoming is rather a refusal to remain complacent about, and therefore determined by, traditional answers. This is one sense in which thinking 'opens other vistas'.

But now a key question: what will happen to the Aristotelian concepts which Heidegger's original project meant to retrieve? Heidegger does not provide us with a definitive answer to this question in 'Letter'. Nonetheless, he suggests that technological domination has reduced *theōria* and *praxis* to the vanishing point so that it would be appropriate to think of them respectively as theory and practice where these translated words have distinctly different meanings from their Greek originals. For example, in the *Nichomachean Ethics*, Aristotle conceived *theōria* and *praxis* to issue in prescriptions on how to live. Theory and practice, on the other hand, are far too deeply entrenched in productionist metaphysics to provide us with any guidance on such a profoundly important matter. Thinking is a third option. Freed from technicity, it is neither a throwback to the Greek understanding (which is impossible to live or experience again in any case) nor a fall into reductionist theory and practice. This is, I take it, why Heidegger says that thinking is 'neither theoretical nor practical. It comes to pass [*ereignet sich*] before this distinction.'[57] To be sure, thinking unfolds as 'a deed' and '[w]e measure deeds by the impressive and successful achievements of *praxis*'.[58] At the same time, thinking 'surpasses all *praxis*'.[59] Thinking also 'exceeds all contemplation' in the sense of Aristotle's *theōria*, 'because it cares for the light' that *theoria* presupposes so it can 'live and move'.[60] In the 'inconsequential accomplishment' of bringing 'the unspoken word of being to language', thinking evidently outstretches *theōria* and *praxis*. This is evidently why Heidegger can confidently say that 'thinking is neither theoretical nor practical, nor...the conjunction of these two forms of comportment'.[61] But this does not mean that thinking has nothing to do with 'theoretical and practical comportment', keeping in mind that 'comportment' is a term derived from *Being and Time* and perhaps intended to convey concernful, human-oriented meanings along the lines of 'suitable endeavour' rather than narrowly political or agonistic ones.

7.5. TOWARDS A MORE REFLECTIVE REALISM?

Suppose we accept the charge that Heidegger's positive claims are paradigmatically utopian, as I think we must. Is there nonetheless merit in Heidegger's conception of thinking and *poiēsis*? I believe there is and it rests on making a distinction of art between good and bad utopianism. If we define 'bad utopianism' as metaphysical thinking of *theōria* and *praxis* that issues in 'directives that are applied to our active lives', then no matter the 'ism' or ideology, we will be doing something harmful to human beings.[62] The ideal character of the goal will do nothing to stop the intrusion of productionist metaphysics and its pernicious consequences for our lives. 'Good utopianism', by contrast, makes no claim that worthy ideals in proposed beliefs can be, or even should be, achieved, given what we know about the world and the self-centredness of human psychology. Its value lies in stimulating reflections and helping us to meditate about a distant future where the world and human psychology will have radically changed. Good utopianism is 'good' not because it is derived from a conception of *theōria* and *praxis* which has taken on a prescriptive character but because its meditations will inform us of what is not really possible in any future we are likely to know about. Given this distinction of art between good and bad utopianism, Heidegger's strenuous effort to bring *poiēses* and thinking into unison is surely 'good utopianism'.

But this is not all; for, when good utopianism is put together with the three other major themes pursued in this essay—the destructiveness of technology, the ineliminability of tragedy, and the incapacity to reconcile theory and practice— we are well on our way to obtaining support for a traditional version of political realism. This might appear to stretch Heidegger's ideas beyond the reasonable until one recognizes that no attribution is being made that Heidegger held realist views. The claim is the different and more plausible one that the themes we have explored lend some weight to the viability of traditional political realism. This is the sort of realism whose origins are to be found in Thucydides and whose central ideas were brought forward into our own time via Machiavelli, Hegel, Nietzsche, Reinhold Neibuhr, and Hans J. Morgenthau, among many others. Since we lack the space to examine the relationship of all these thinkers to Heidegger's thought, we will adumbrate the connection between Heidegger and traditional political realism as understood by Morgenthau, keeping in mind that not only similarities but also differences can result in fresh tracks of genuine thought.

Morgenthau, like Heidegger, points out the pernicious effects not of science *per se* but of 'technology as applied science' which 'threatens to destroy man and his social and natural environment through war and', in any case, 'destroy[s] the social and natural environment that makes healthy and civilized life possible'.[63] More than this (and in a manner that echoes Heidegger), technology as applied science exhibits destructive consequences not only for the 'outside' of an individual's life but also for the 'inside'. This occurs through 'destruction of the realm of inner freedom'; the human being's autonomy and control of its conditions become severely narrowed when technology undermines 'the human being's control of his destiny and movements'.[64] Technology is not, as many people evidently think, a 'free good'. Even when the necessary discipline is exercised by and enforced by central authority, technology may be used to 'bring the system to a halt'. Paradoxically, however, it is only in negative uses of technology such as sabotage that the individual can 'assert himself as an individual. Otherwise, the individual is the hapless object of these technological developments and political possibilities'.[65] In such a condition—our condition—there is no such thing as a decision without loss. For Morgenthau, and Heidegger before him, science as such has no answer to the question of how to protect the world from destruction by the tools science creates.[66]

This is one situation that makes the world tragic but it is not the only one. For tragedy is pervasive in modern life. On this Morgenthau also agrees with Heidegger. In *Scientific Man vs. Power Politics* Morgenthau holds that politics (in the broadest possible sense) is necessarily tragic.[67] Politics requires the use of power and this makes politics evil. If we act for our fellow men we necessarily engage in immoral actions and if in some misguided high-mindedness we refuse to act we 'still sin'. For Morgenthau, '[n]o ivory tower is remote enough to offer protection against the guilt in which the actor and the bystander, the oppressor and the oppressed, the murderer and his victim are inextricably enmeshed.' Although the high-minded show disdain for politics 'as the domain of evil par excellence', they will still, as political agents, need to 'reconcile' themselves 'to the enduring presence of evil in all political action'.[68] To be sure, Morgenthau's explanation for tragedy is quite different *from* Heidegger's, but the similarities are not without interest to traditional political realists seeking support for new versions of their favoured view.

However, the main difference between Heidegger and Morgenthau lies in their respective conceptions of humanism. As we have seen above, Heidegger wishes to overcome metaphysics and humanism, both of which concentrate on the human condition, in order to develop an outlook on being which resists subordination to human reason. Heidegger thus urged 'an open resistance to "humanism"', and it was precisely in such resistance, or so Heidegger believed, that one would be able to transcend the age of technology and its anthropocentric understanding of being.[69]

It is exactly here that Morgenthau parts company with Heidegger, though he does not explicitly name Heidegger as a target. As a humanist, Morgenthau contends that 'the future of science is tied to the future of man and his ability to communicate what he knows'.[70] But that is not the only moral, for it turns on Morgenthau's reckoning that 'man's future depends ultimately upon himself. Although he cannot live without social ties to other men, he alone, in the solitude of his autonomous reflection, decides his future as man.'[71] Unlike Heidegger, Morgenthau denied the possibility of a new humanity; a new beginning is not a real possibility for humanity. Accepting limits on rationality, for Morgenthau, could reacquaint us with the tradition of humanism and the resistance it has always offered against the illegitimate claims of scientism, to which Heidegger was also strenuously opposed. But Morgenthau, unlike Heidegger, ascribes the dominance of methodical science and the scientism it produces to the *abandonment* of the humanist tradition rather than to its triumph.[72] Seen from this perspective, humanism appears to be an attractive option for reflective political realists. For Morgenthau, what constitutes knowledge in the humanist tradition may be discerned in the concept of *Bildung*—formation, culture, education. In human culture, *Bildung* means the uniquely human way of developing dispositions that already belong to the human but require constant cultivation. Without *Bildung* there is little prospect that humanity will come to know its limitations and develop the requisite humility for a reflectively realist conception of foreign policy, not at least in an age of self-compelling forms of technological domination. Or, so I believe.

7.6. CONCLUSION

Heidegger held that any effort to give the concepts of theory and practice permanent meanings was doomed to fail. This applied in full force to Kant's project of giving theory and practice definitions intended for use across and over time. As indicated above, Kant's idea of theory is bound up with claims about the existence of God, immortality, and freedom and these are paradigmatic metaphysical claims which Heidegger rejects as incapable of capturing the forces at work in the Age of Technological Domination. For Heidegger, concepts are neither fixed nor timeless; they are contingent and contextual. This explains not only why Heidegger came to regard any attempt, including his own earlier effort, to retrieve Aristotle's central 'philosophical' concepts to be fundamentally mistaken but also why he thought Kant's determination to fix the meanings of concepts and words was just as decisively an error. Words and concepts have to 'fit' history and context.

If our general argument to the effect that Heidegger came to recognize that his original project of retrieving Aristotle's central concepts of *theōria*, *praxis*, *poiēses*, *technē*, and *phronēsis* was hopelessly outmoded by virtue of increasing technological domination, then we face a dilemma. For, in the event, any effort such as Smith's to reconfigure theory and practice along Kantian lines would have to be regarded, whether acknowledged or not, as part of a productionist metaphysics and, as such, bound up with ideological humanism. However, in concluding this, we would not be validating Heidegger's non-metaphysical perspective, resting as it does on what appear to be certain far-fetched and obscure arguments on behalf of thinking as a global replacement for theory and practice. Nonetheless Heidegger's notion of 'thinking' has advantages both for what it is not and for what it might possibly do.

Understood as an engagement with 'theoretical and practical comportment', thinking is not connected up with 'deed' in the sense of prescribing an ethics, a political institution, or an action even in an indirect way. Thinking is of great importance, not least of all because it reminds us that being is the destiny of thinking and that that destiny is historical.[73] What one should do, Heidegger is suggesting, is not to be determined *a priori* but from within an historical context. Thinking is related to political activity but only in so far as it assists in developing an *ēthos* in which the worthiness of asking what one ought to do within a specific historical context becomes manifest.

Whether a new kind of thinking along these lines is possible is not at all obvious. Still, it must be remembered that thinking is not alone in conducting the struggle against the essence of technology. It is joined by *poiēses* which, as Heidegger says in 'The Question Concerning Technology', holds 'complete sway in the fine arts, in poetry, and in everything poetical that obtained *poiēses* as its proper name'.[74] In the 'Letter on Humanism' Heidegger holds that '[t]he tragedies of Sophocles...preserve the *ēthos* in their sayings more primordially than Aristotle's lectures on "ethics" '.[75] Still, the idea that thinking and *poiēses*, whatever their value, can limit technological domination may strike observers as fanciful in the extreme. On the surface, it does indeed strain our credulity to think that such phenomena as the unpredictable expansion of the Internet, the historic hypertrophy of military technology, and the terrifying danger of nuclear proliferation, not to mention unimaginable future technological horrors as yet uninvented, can be constrained by Heideggerean notions of thinking and *poiēses*. On a more sympathetic reading one might hope that an entirely new ethos is still possible, one in which 'the malice of rage' might be swept away and a 'general healing' hold sway in the communities of human beings. If all one achieves is pervasive, astute, and constant questioning, one would have gone far towards fulfilling the crux of Heidegger's goals. One need not wait for a brave new world to give content to aspirations for a better one than the one we live in now. This is neither idealism nor 'bad utopianism'; it is the rigorous hope of a compassionate realism.

NOTES

1. Immanuel Kant, 'On the Common Saying: "This May be True in Theory, but it does not Apply in Practice"', in Hans Reiss (ed.), *Political Writings* (Cambridge, MA: Cambridge University Press, 1991), pp. 61–92.
2. The obstacles referred to are twofold: textual and political. Concerning the former there is the intrinsic difficulty of Heidegger's thought, his frequent use of infelicitous neologisms, and translations into antiquated English. In so far as I am attempting here to encourage as many scholars of international political theory as possible to engage with Heidegger's work, I have used English translations and avoided, wherever possible, Heidegger's neologisms even at the risk of distortion of his views. If we cannot see the forest, it is unlikely we'll be able to identify the trees growing within. The second problem is political and requires a certain suspension of disbelief that Heidegger, surely one of the greatest philosophers of the twentieth century, could have been a member of the Nazi party. Heidegger's admission of 'stupidity', as he subsequently called it, will not suffice to exculpate him; however, there is little profit for serious thinking in a *reductio ad Hitlerium* that leaves us ignorant and vulnerable to misinformation. Also, I would like to acknowledge the brilliant work of Louiza Odysseos in helping those interested in international relations theory to see the bearing of Heidegger's writings on the subject. See her 'On the Way to Global Ethics? Cosmopolitianism, Ethical Selfhood and Otherness', *European Journal of Political Theory*, 2 (2003), pp. 183–207; and 'Radical Phenomenology, Ontology and International Political Theory', *Alternatives*, 27 (2002), pp. 373–405.
3. Wallace, 'Truth and Power, Monks and Technocrats: Theory and Practice in International Relations', *Review of International Studies*, 22 (1996), pp. 301–21.
4. Smith, 'Power and Truth: A Reply to William Wallace', *Review of International Studies*, 23 (1997), pp. 507–16. My subsequent criticism of Smith should in no way be taken

as an endorsement of Wallace. On the contrary, I agree with the main lines of Smith's critique.

5. Smith, 'International Relations and international relations: The Links Between Theory and Practice in World Politics', *Journal of International Relations and Development*, 6 (2003), pp. 233–39.

6. Smith, 'International Relations and international relations', p. 237.

7. Immanuel Kant, *Critique of Practical Reason*, trans. Lewis White Beck (Indianapolis: Bobbs-Merrill, 1956), section v, p. 121.

8. Pauline Kleingeld, 'Kant on the Unity of Theoretical and Practical Reason', *The Review of Metaphysics*, 52 (1998), p. 314.

9. Martin Heidegger, *The Question Concerning Technology and Other Essays* (New York: Harper Torchbooks, 1977).

10. Aristotle, *Nichomachean Ethics* (Cambridge, MA: Harvard University Press, 1926), Bks. VI and X.

11. Heidegger, *The Question Concerning Technology*, p. 14.

12. Heidegger, *Phänomenologische Interpretationen zu Aristotles. Einführung in die Phänomenologische Forshung, Vol. 61, Gesamtausgabe* (Frankfurt/Main: Vittorio Klosterman, 1975). English translation, 'Phenomenological Interpretations with Respect to Aristotle', *Man and World*, 25 (1992), pp. 355–93.

13. Heidegger, *The Question Concerning Technology*, pp. 115–54.

14. Heidegger, *The Question Concerning Technology*, p. 141.

15. Descartes, '*Discourse on Method* (1637)', in John Cottingham, Robert Stoothoff, and Dugald Murdoch (eds.), *The Philosophical Writings of Descartes* (Cambridge, MA: Cambridge University Press, 1985), I, pp. 142–3.

16. Heidegger, *The Question Concerning Technology*, pp. 3–35.

17. Heidegger, *The Question Concerning Technology*, p. 28.

18. Descartes, *Les Passions de l'âme* (Paris: M. Bobin, 1679).

19. Heidegger, *The Question Concerning Technology*, p. 34.

20. Heidegger, in David Farrell Krell (ed.), *Nietzsche* (San Francisco: Harper, 1991), iii–iv, p. 8.

21. Heidegger, *The End of Philosophy* (Chicago: The University of Chicago Press, 1973), p. 102.

22. Heidegger, *The End of Philosophy*, p. 102.

23. Heidegger, *The End of Philosophy*, p. 102.

24. In Heidegger's view, 'being' means different things in different contexts. For our purposes here, being for Heidegger refers to what grants beings their specificity and distinctness.

25. Heidegger, *The End of Philosophy*, pp. 103–4.

26. Heidegger, *The End of Philosophy*, p. 110.

27. Heidegger, *Die Selbsthehauptung der deutschen Universität* (Franfurt: Klostermann, 1983). Originally delivered in Germany in 1933. Translated by Karsten Harries under the title 'The Self-Assertion of the German University', *Review of Metaphysics*, 38 (1985), pp. 470–80.

28. Heidegger, *Introduction to Metaphysics* (New Haven: Yale: Nota Bene, 2000).

29. Heidegger, *Introduction to Metaphysics*, pp. 123–4.

30. Heidegger, *Holderlin's Hymn 'The Ester'* (Bloomington: Indiana University Press, 1996).

31. Heidegger, *Holderlin's Hymn*, p. 105.

32. Heidegger, *Holderlin's Hymn*, p. 121.

33. Heidegger, 'The Origin of the Work of Art' in his *Poetry, Language, Thought* (New York: Perennial Classics, 2001), p. 72.

34. It is worth noting that late Heidegger's favoured understanding of being is derived from Heraclitus and involves a struggle in which beings come to presence. It is of significance for international political theorists that the '[s]truggle first projects and develops the unheard, the hitherto unsaid, and un-thought. This struggle is then sustained by the creators, by the poets, thinkers, and statesmen'. *Introduction to Metaphysics*, p. 65.

35. Heidegger, *Holderlin's Hymn*, pp. 82–3.

36. Heidegger, in William McNeill (ed.), *Pathmarks* (Cambridge, MA: Cambridge University Press, 1998), pp. 239–76.

37. *Destruktion* is a technical term derived from Heidegger's *Sein und Zeit* and means more or less what Derrida and others mean by 'deconstruction'.

38. Heidegger, 'Letter', p. 265.

39. Since Heidegger does not always distinguish between philosophy-as-metaphysics and philosophy-as-thinking, I will henceforth use the term 'philosophy' to indicate philosophy-as-metaphysics and 'thinking' to indicate what will, according to Heidegger, replace it.

40. Heidegger, 'Letter', p. 245.

41. Heidegger, 'Letter', p. 245.

42. Heidegger, 'Letter', p. 246.

43. Heidegger, 'Letter', p. 246.

44. Heidegger, 'Letter', pp. 246–7.

45. Heidegger, 'Letter', p. 246.

46. Heidegger, 'Letter', p. 247.

47. Heidegger, 'Letter', p. 251.

48. Heidegger, 'Letter', p. 251.

49. Heidegger, 'Letter', p. 263.

50. Heidegger, *The End of Philosophy*, p. 89.

51. Heidegger, *The End of Philosophy*, p. 99. Cf. Heidegger, *The Question Concerning Technology*, p. 153.

52. Heidegger, *The End of Philosophy*, p. 96.

53. Heidegger, 'Letter', p. 242.

54. Heidegger, 'Letter', p. 241.

55. Heidegger, 'Letter', p. 241.

56. Heidegger, 'Letter', p. 241.

57. Heidegger, 'Letter', p. 272.

58. Heidegger, 'Letter', p. 275.

59. Heidegger, 'Letter', p. 275.

60. Heidegger, 'Letter', p. 274.

61. Heidegger, 'Letter', p. 275.

62. Heidegger, 'Letter', p. 270.

63. Morgenthau, *Science: Servant or Master? Perspectives in Humanism* (New York: New American Library, 1972), p. 3.

64. Morgenthau, *Science*, p. 3.

65. *Morgenthau, Science*, p. 4.

66. Morgenthau, *Science*, p. 72.

67. Morgenthau, *Scientific Man vs. Power Politics* (Chicago: University of Chicago Press, 1946).

68. Morgenthau, *Scientific Man vs. Power Politics*, pp. 201–2.

69. Heidegger, 'Letter', p. 263.

70. Morgenthau, *Science*, p. 71.

71. Morgenthau, *Science*, p. 72.

72. In this respect, he follows Hans-Georg Gadamer in *Truth and Method*. Although Gadamer does not cite Heidegger as his target (perhaps out of respect for his former teacher), it is clear that Heidegger is his principal target.

73. Heidegger, 'Letter', p. 275.

74. Heidegger, *The Question Concerning Technology*, p. 34.

75. Heidegger, 'Letter', p. 269.

8

Realism's 'Hidden Dialogue': Leo Strauss, War, and Politics

Nicholas Rengger

8.1. INTRODUCTION

Throughout the history of human political engagements, the relationship of those engagements to the use of force has been one of the central questions that has challenged and perplexed those who seek to understand the character of the political tie.[1] There have been those, perhaps most obviously Thucydides in the ancient world and Clausewitz in the modern, who have believed that the key to the character of politics can be found in the consideration of war; there have even been those—Carl Schmitt springs to mind in the modern context, and we shall have occasion to refer to him again later on—who suggest that the experience of politics is, in at least a certain sense, the experience of war writ large. And there have been many, Tertullian, Erasmus, and Tolstoy perhaps most prominent among them, who have believed that war is perhaps the greatest mistake of human beings under any circumstances whatever. But however it is seen, the relationship between war—understood here as simply the possibility of, or the actual use of, lethal force—and politics is a centrally contested one.

This chapter seeks to shed a little light on the character of this relationship in the context of the modern world. The main claim with which I shall be concerned is the claim that war has been, and crucially still is, an unalterable feature of the human condition; unwelcome, ghastly, tragic, perhaps—though there have been many who professed to find in it also, excitement, intoxication, and the noblest of human virtues—but in any case inevitable and that we need to understand international politics, and perhaps all politics, in the light of this fact. War, the Greek philosopher and aphorist Heraclitus told us, was the 'Father of all things', and as such it was treated as an Olympian—as untameable and as mysterious as that other great Olympian, Aphrodite. This view has been the commonest view throughout history (and not just in Europe) and it still has many adherents.

In the literature of political theory and international relations in the modern period, the chief tradition insisting that war is a permanent feature of the human political landscape—whatever form it might in fact take in any given period—and that we should understand all politics, and especially international politics, in the light of this fact has usually been termed 'political realism'.[2] Here the claim has been made, though of course in multiple ways and with varying degrees of inevitability, that war as such was a permanent feature of politics—even if any particular war could not be said to be inevitable—and that therefore any attempt to eliminate it or even to reduce its salience as the ultimate arbiter of politics was doomed to failure. The reasons given for this claim have varied; the *animus dominandi* inherent in human beings, the human capacity for evil, the behavioural tendencies of certain kinds of governments, the overall structure of the international system; all have their champions. What they agree about is that the kind of progressivism that argues for the elimination of war not only is illusory, in that it can never be achieved, but also dangerous in that it means that the best ways of actually preserving peace—paying attention to the reality of war and seeking to block or amend it where possible—are often overlooked in favour of ambitious but ultimately futile attempts to eliminate war *tout court*. The Roman tag *si vis pacem para bellum*, is to be preferred, on this reading, to lengthy exercises in legalistic rhetorical exhortation, such as the Kellogg-Briand Pact or the Charter of the United Nations.

Of course, realism comes in many forms. In the contemporary context, however, one might suggest that two broad versions of realism are most prominent.[3] The first, and perhaps the most influential (in the academy at least), is that version of realism chiefly derived from Kenneth Waltz and his intellectual progeny.[4] 'Neo-realism', as it is usually termed, famously makes all subservient to the structure of the international system—an anarchic structure—and thus emphasizes that the particular characteristics of the 'units' in the system (states) are irrelevant to their performance; all that matters is their material capabilities vis-à-vis each other. While there have been some amendments and variations on this theme—perhaps most interestingly those suggested by on the one hand Stephen Walt and on the other by John Mearsheimer[5]—this basic set of assumptions remains perhaps the dominant version of realism in the academy, especially in the United States.

A second version, however, is gathering strength. This version draws on what is usually termed 'classical realism', that is to say the works that are deemed to have inaugurated realism as a self-aware approach to politics and international relations earlier in the twentieth century; those by, for example, Reinhold Niebuhr and Hans Morgenthau. Here the emphasis is far less on the structure of the system, though they would concede that it certainly plays a role, but rather on the specific characteristics of human knowing and doing. This is sometimes characterized as a focus on 'human nature' but in fact it is often not a view of human *nature* but rather of distinctive human proclivities. As with neo-realism, there are differing versions on offer. In *The Tragic Vision of Politics* (2002), Richard Ned Lebow defends a particularly compelling version of a 'neoclassical' version of realism, one that draws explicitly on Morgenthau but also on Classical Greek thought that, according to Lebow, was always the soundest grounding for realist insights. But other versions, drawing more from the Christian realism of Niebuhr have been offered by, for example, Jean Bethke Elshtain.[6]

It is not my purpose here to argue the toss between these two versions of realism—though I will return to them in my closing remarks. Rather, I want to look at the central realist claim—the permanent possibility of war—as it has been approached from a very different angle of vision and ask how we might understand realism and its central concerns in the light of it. The perhaps unlikely source of this version of the realist case is the political thought of Leo Strauss. I shall suggest that Strauss argued a version of the realist thesis, but did so from a position that is very distinct from the way that the realist case is usually put—in either of the two versions discussed above—a distinctiveness manifested, moreover, precisely by Strauss's concern for what many of the *opponents* of the realist case concentrate on, the importance of the character of particular political regimes. There is for Strauss what we might term a 'hidden dialogue' between the character of political regimes and the reality of the political world, and it is this that accounts for the permanent possibility of war and conflict in world politics.[7] Strauss therefore agrees on the central realist insight, but for reasons very different from most conventional realists, of any stripe. I shall then offer some reasons for supposing that Strauss's way of putting the dilemma is, in fact, an especially pertinent one for realism, before concluding that in fact one cannot derive quite what Strauss thinks one can from his reading of it. This chapter closes with some remarks as to the implications of all this for realism as a tradition of thought about politics.

8.2. STRAUSS'S WRITING AND READING STRAUSS

Before I can do any of this, however, I need to say something about how I read Strauss. Because, of course, this is no simple matter. Strauss, as is well known, did not generally write about issues such as 'war and politics' at all; rather he wrote about what, on one celebrated occasion, he said he taught: 'old books'.[8] Strauss's real thoughts about politics—his political theory—must therefore be sought in his encounters with other theories; through his engagements with the many texts he addresses in his teaching and writing. Only by doing this can we build up a picture of why Strauss thinks such encounters are so important and how he believes that we have forgotten what is at stake in them, in the modern West. In distilling Strauss's understanding of war and politics, then, it is necessary also to say something about his understanding of the distinctive crisis of modernity and this depends upon his reading of the character of modernity expressed through its own self-understanding. We get to that, Strauss tells us, by reading the characteristic expressions of modernity—the books that made modernity and expressed that self-understanding—and we realize what is at stake when we compare that self-understanding with the version that those books sought to supersede and displace, essentially that of the ancients, contained, of course, in their 'old books'.[9]

This represents one of the iconic debates to which Strauss saw himself contributing: the so-called quarrel between the ancients and the moderns.[10] However, this is perhaps less than half the story. Strauss also saw himself as investigating a second great dilemma, perhaps even more profound than the first—he referred to it once as '*the* theme of my investigations'[11]—and to name it he borrowed a term from his early studies of Spinoza: he called it the 'theologico-political problem'. At the heart of this dilemma are two completely comprehensive and seemingly irreconcilable alternatives: revelation and reason, or as Strauss puts it, Jerusalem and Athens. Sometimes Strauss presents them as irreconcilable alternatives but at other times he seems to suggest that they are the twin sources of European thought, that it is the tension *between* them that becomes the centrepiece of Western ideas and that it is the forgetting of this tension—or the attempt to effectively eliminate it—that is the source of 'the crisis of our times'.[12]

Indeed, given this it is perhaps not too extreme to see Strauss's investigations into the latter problem as generating, at least in a sense, his investigations into the former problem. It is his growing realization that modernity has forgotten the 'theologico-political problem' and what it represents that leads him to develop his reading of the particular manner in which modernity tries to express its self-understanding. In particular, Strauss thinks, modernity has forgotten how to write because it has forgotten how to read; because it has forgotten the esoteric character of much ancient writing. Strauss's development of the claim that ancient writers sought to hide their true meaning has been, of course, one of the most highly controversial aspects of his thought and has attracted an enormous amount of critical brickbats.[13] It is, to be sure, susceptible to a number of possible readings some of which are plainly rather silly, and Strauss is not always his own best servant here. Yet a careful reading of Strauss on this topic shows that he is far from endorsing an extreme position.[14] For example, he does not suggest that authors who write esoterically have a 'hidden meaning' in the strong sense of that term, a 'secret teaching'—one of the most frequently levelled criticisms at Strauss himself. Rather Strauss is pointing to the awareness in the classical writers he most admires—and their medieval Jewish and Islamic followers and descendants[15]—of the corrosive aspects of philosophy and the need to protect the political regime against such corrosion—as well as making the obvious point that in order to protect themselves as well, writers often do not quite always say exactly what they mean openly.

The crux is the character of the corrosion that philosophy brings to the city. Strauss makes clear that for him the city is necessarily entwined with its gods; thus philosophy in its relentless questioning must question the nature (and indeed the existence) of the gods. In as much as it does this, it threatens the existence of the city itself. It is no accident, Strauss thinks, that one of the crimes that Socrates was charged with was impiety—denying the truths of the gods of the city—and it was because of this 'crime' that Plato's great achievement was to make the city safe for philosophy again by crafting, in dialogue form, both a defence of the philosophic life and an accommodation of it to the city. Stephen Smith points to how central such an understanding was for Strauss's own understanding of Judaism and how someone like him—a 'philosophical' and unbelieving Jew—should respond to it.[16]

This problem is, however, reborn in the modern period, according to Strauss, because of the growing tendency to *fail* to recognize the fragile character of the social bond and the corrosive influence true philosophy will have on it. Rather, moderns think that we should be honest about the implausibility of religion and banish it. It is, for example, precisely this problem that Spinoza faced and on Strauss's reading it is Spinoza's answer to this question—the answer to equate God with nature, thus paving the way for a completely materialist naturalism—that is the distinctively modern one.[17] And, specifically, it is rooted in the attempt to forget or ignore the 'theologico-political problem'. Thus, Strauss's reading of modernity is prefaced on his readings of the extent to which modern writers 'forget' the 'theologico-political problem' and how ancient writers dealt with it. Over time, Strauss moves the beginning of the distinctively modern approach to it back from Spinoza, first to Hobbes, then to Machiavelli, but his basic understanding of it does not change and, indeed, in many ways it still revolves around the central manner in which Spinoza frames the question.[18]

It is this, Strauss thinks, that has led to what he variously terms the 'crisis of our times' and the 'contemporary crisis of the west' and in his attempt to illuminate it, he must perforce show how the canonical texts of the modern West have led to this point, and how the texts they rejected—the ancient texts—do not and thus allow us to grasp the essence of the 'theologico-political problem' and to think about how we should address it. Note that Strauss does not suggest that they tell us how to resolve it; for, in a very important sense the problem is irresolvable. As Strauss's engagement with Jewish thought in general makes clear, he felt that Spinoza's mistake was in failing to realize the danger inherent in the attempt to rationally refute revelation, not in the attempt itself. As Smith puts it, 'Strauss's difference with Spinoza is not with what he said, but how he said it'.[19] Obviously, given my concerns here, the highways and byways of the particular interpretations Strauss offers of his chosen texts would take us too far from our main topic. However, it is worth emphasizing both the general interpretive strategy that guides my remarks in what follows, and lay out the view of Strauss's overall assumptions I favour. We shall return to some of these claims a little later on.

8.3. TWO HIDDEN DIALOGUES: SCHMITT AND STRAUSS AND WAR AND POLITICS

The noted Strauss scholar Heinrich Meier, as is well known, entitled his book on the relationship between Strauss and Carl Schmitt, the 'hidden dialogue'. I want to suggest that one can also detect a second 'hidden dialogue' within the first, one between war and politics or perhaps better between two ways of seeing the relationship of war to politics.

Schmitt, as is well known, saw politics as, in effect, the continuation of war by other means, thus reversing Clausewitz's famous dictum. In his early work *Political Romanticism*, Schmitt explicitly states that war will be a permanent possibility 'till the end of time' because war is based on what he terms 'metaphysical oppositions'.[20] These can be hidden, forgotten, or ignored; they cannot be eliminated, thus neither can war. It is precisely the attempt to eliminate them—or rather to legislate them out of existence—that Schmitt thinks is so problematic about liberalism and is the source of his excoriating hostility to liberal politics. This claim was central to virtually all of Schmitt's Weimar works, most especially, of course, *The Concept of the Political*.[21] But while Schmitt was correct to see this tendency in nineteenth- and twentieth-century liberal thought (and practice) he was wrong (I suggest) in two crucial respects about its implications. First, the rejection of *this* liberal assumption does not require rejecting liberal thought per se. Only if liberal thought *must* take the juridicalized form that seeks to abolish war would this part of Schmitt's analysis be true. As I will argue in more detail in a moment, this is simply an error on Schmitt's part. Liberal thought *was* largely seen in this way in the nineteenth and much of the twentieth century, true enough, but it is open to very different readings as well.

More relevant for our current purposes, however, is the second error Schmitt makes. It is this error that is the concern that Strauss picks up in his celebrated commentary on *The Concept of the Political*. Strauss sees very clearly the central point of Schmitt's essay. In his commentary, he notes that for Schmitt:

...war is not merely the most extreme political measure; war is the dire emergency not merely in an autonomous region—the region of the political—but for man simply, because war has and retains a relationship to the real possibility of physical killing: this orientation, which is constitutive for the political shows that the political is fundamental and not a relatively independent domain among others. The political is the authoritative.[22]

It is important to note here that Strauss nowhere dissents from Schmitt's view in terms of its details on this particular topic. Rather he argues, effectively, that Schmitt has failed to free himself fully from liberal assumptions and therefore does not see that his way of framing the political is still bound up with liberal claims. His closing paragraph in his commentary makes this plain:

Schmitt undertakes the critique of liberalism in a liberal world...his critique of liberalism occurs in the horizon of liberalism: his illiberal tendency is restrained by the still unvanquished systematics of liberal thought. The critique introduced by Schmitt against liberalism can therefore be completed only if one succeeds in gaining a horizon beyond liberalism. In such a horizon Hobbes completed the foundations of liberalism. A radical critique of liberalism is thus possible only on the basis of an adequate understanding of Hobbes.[23]

This, to all intents and purposes, was what Strauss then set out to do after his exchange with Schmitt. His *The Political Philosophy of Hobbes*, generally regarded—even by those who disagree with it and, more generally, with Strauss—as a groundbreaking study of Hobbes appeared three years after his commentary on Schmitt (in 1936).[24] And so it is reasonable to claim that by then Strauss saw himself as at least beginning to have 'a horizon beyond liberalism'. Where that horizon was eventually located, as we have seen, was in the understanding of a particular kind of writing (and reading) that the ancients possessed and that we have lost, because liberalism deliberately obscured it.

Meier points out also that Strauss also dissented from Schmitt's celebrated definition of the political in terms of the friend/enemy distinction. The political was central for Strauss, Meier says, yet the enemy and therefore enmity was not. Meier argues this is in part because for Schmitt enmity is the guarantor of seriousness in life; in religious terms it is the guarantor of faith. But Strauss is not operating on those assumptions, rather he is thinking (in his terms) philosophically, which challenges (without negating) faith.

For Strauss the recovery of the art of esoteric reading (and writing) is thus part of understanding the nature and significance of the theologicio-political problem, but modernity cannot grasp it for it is operating 'in the horizon of liberalism'. And from this, of course, Strauss deepens and develops his account of how and to what respect modernity has deepened its forgetfulness. This, in turn, gave rise to much of his most important political thought, including his account of the three waves of modernity thesis,[25] his understanding of the character and issues surrounding the American Founding (in *Natural Right and History*)[26] and his critique of Nietzsche, Weber, and most of all Heidegger.[27] In all of these works he seeks to explain how—to use his locution—we have dug a 'pit beneath the cave': as moderns we have so powerfully forgotten the real source of our problems that we cannot any longer see even the flickering images on the wall of the cave, save as a secondary set of reflections: *mimesis* gone mad.

If all this is true, however, how should we react? What can be done? Strauss's preferred stance, the stance that he believes we can and should adopt in these desperate modern times, is what Thomas Pangle has called 'Socratic Zetetic scepticism' and it is, perhaps, here that Strauss's real radicalism lies.[28] For Strauss, the fundamental Socratic question is how should we live and the fundamental Socratic assumption is that we know only that we know nothing. The Socratic stance must therefore be one of constant and never-ending questioning and it is this fact, because of its corrosive effect on society—any society—that forces philosophers—true philosophers—to write and speak esoterically. The political result of this, however, is that philosophers must become centrally aware of the *essential character* of political regimes; for to write or speak esoterically requires knowing at least what forms of *doxa* control and sway regime A as opposed to regime B. Without knowing this, philosophers will be unable to speak effectively and thus they will be unable either to protect the philosophical life or to shield society from the corrosive effects of philosophy.

But in the modern age, indeed to some extent in any age, this creates a major problem. Strauss agrees with his ancient sources that true political society is small, enclosed, and homogenous. It is only under these circumstances that knowledge of the political things—*ta politika*, as Aristotle called them—is truly possible and it is for this reason that Aristotle, here formalizing the view of earlier Greek writers, most especially Plato, suggests that only the *polis* can properly possess *ta politika*.[29] Thus it is only in the *polis* that the characteristics of any given *politeia*, or regime, can properly be manifested.[30]

The significance of this is simple enough. Once one moves beyond the *polis* (and depending on the size, even within some *poleis*) the 'political tie' replaces direct knowledge with indirect knowledge, real participation with (at best) simulated participation. And then there is a permanent tendency, Strauss thinks, for what he calls a 'cosmopolitan imperative' to emerge. Strauss puts it this way:

> Citizen morality [morality in the *polis*] suffers from an inevitable contradiction. It asserts that different rules of conduct apply in war than in peace, but it cannot help regarding at least some relevant rules, which are said to apply in peace only as universally valid. To avoid this self-contradiction the city must transform itself into a world state yet this is equally contradictory for no-one and no group could rule a world justly.[31]

They cannot, for Strauss, because justice is a matter of direct knowledge and participation that cannot occur even in much smaller political entities. This is the reason why, for Strauss, Plato's *Republic* (the word simply is, of course, *Politeia* in its Latin form), rather than being a sketch about how we should plan the ideal city is in fact a demonstration of why there cannot *be* an actually ideal city, only one 'built in speech'.[32]

It is in these arguments that we find the hidden dialogue between war and politics surfacing once more in Strauss's work. Rather than 'enmity' being the essence of the political, as with Schmitt, it is rather the complete impossibility of political justice that creates the permanent possibility of war. In the absence of justice, all cities will be riven with contradictions which might—though also might not—become violent. War between cities, *stasis* within them, is simply *the* condition of political life properly understood. It is this claim, Strauss famously and controversially argues, that Plato presses in the *Republic* and which is the hallmark of all ancient writing on politics. It is at the centre of Strauss's reading of Thucydides in *The City and Man* and of his treatment of the Aristophanic critique of Socrates,[33] and it is the centre also of his argument for the 'mixed regime' so beloved of ancient authors from Aristotle to Polybius since it is the best *practical* regime (and opposed to the best city itself, the *Kallipolis*, that—as in the *Republic*—can only be built in Speech).[34]

War then is a permanent possibility—the realists are right about that—but not for any of the usual reasons they give, but rather because of the character of human political society itself. The usual way the realist case is put, for Strauss, is an essentially modern one, and as such it fails to engage with either the quarrel between the ancients and the moderns or the theologico-political problem and thus reaches the right conclusion for the wrong reasons. Equally, the eighteenth-century progressives were right to concentrate on the character of the political regime but wrong to wed to that concern the messianic hopes that modernity had invested it with. What Strauss thought a concern for the regime *should* express is the sense of moderation and prudence that he argued characterized the defence of the mixed constitution in Antiquity and that one finds—according to him—in passages of ancient writers such as Aristotle in the *Nichomachean Ethics* and the *Politics* but perhaps even more centrally, in Thucydides (e.g. in the Mytilenean debate, where it is central to Diodotus's critique of Cleon).[35] But the 'horizon of liberalism' had effectively blotted out that possibility, replacing it instead with a progressively more radical series of demands for world transforming moments that would—and will—in any event, come to nothing. For Strauss, we are in politics doomed to remain forever between polis and cosmopolis: it is the refusal to face that and accept the logic of it that distances moderns—including Schmitt and the realists—from the ancients whose wisdom Strauss wishes to capture for us.

8.4. ZETETIC SCEPTICISM, REALISM, AND… SCEPTICISM?

So what are we to make of all this? I want to close this chapter with three general sets of reflections on Strauss's arguments in general and on their significance for realism in particular.

In the first place, those who are self-confessed realists would do well to consider his arguments. Strauss provides an interesting and important corrective to the more usual views on these topics that I sketched at the outset. His critique of Schmitt is revealing and his differences from realists like Morgenthau and Niebuhr profound, however much he might share aspects of their conclusions. At the same time, his distance from contemporary liberal and radical thought is great. Strauss is not a 'conservative' if by that one means agreeing with, for example, the idea of a cosmic order, or natural principles of hierarchy, or the centrality of tradition; the sorts of things that most self-conscious conservatives believe.[36] But he is clearly a sharp and profound critic of modern progressivism, as many realists would be also. He is also an interesting commentator on liberal democracy as a regime—a point that has often been missed in complaints about his alleged 'elitism' and hostility to democracy.[37] He is, as he says (many times) a 'friend of liberal democracy' and I don't think there is much evidence that—at least in his mature thought—he was not. But, as Stephen Smith has pointed out, being a *friend* of liberal democracy rather implies that he was not himself a liberal democrat and on my reading at least that is quite correct. For he is a friend to liberal democracy precisely in as much—and only in as much—as it can be accommodated to a kind of quasi-Aristotelian mixed constitution that is the surest defence, under modern conditions, of the proper relations between philosophy and politics. It is essentially that view that attracted Strauss—and many of his followers—to the US constitution since they think it precisely possible to see it in these terms or at least to adapt it so that it can be seen as such.[38]

This leads to a second observation. The emphasis on the 'regime' in both Schmitt and Strauss—and especially in Strauss—has a distinctly odd aspect. For them both, 'liberalism' as a 'regime' has a form that is entirely too programmatic. To begin with 'liberal democracies', as they have historically evolved, are themselves enormously diverse. Of course they have certain institutional similarities, which is why it is fair enough to call them by a common name, but it is equally certain that there are many differences. Focusing on the 'regime' is all very well, but it has its problems. For, at least in the manner in which Strauss (and, I think, Schmitt) understand it, it assumes that the regime is undivided; that any particular form of regime expresses something about its 'spirit'. Such a claim is visible as well in much more recent (and very un-Straussian) claims about the behavioural aspects of 'liberal states'. For there to be anything properly meaningful in the now almost unchallenged (at least in some quarters) liberal or demo-cratic peace thesis, for example, one would have to say that, when push comes to shove, it was the 'liberal' (or 'democratic') aspect of a political community that mattered most, that *the fact* of country A or B being liberal or democratic in terms of its regime would overcome national or ethnic partiality, religious sensibility (or lack of it) or the simple perspective of profit and loss.[39] Yet it seems unlikely that this would *necessarily* be the case; it would surely depend upon the context. In which case, one is looking for *the context in which* the existence of a democratic (or liberal) political culture will lead to a certain kind of political behaviour, and, indeed, some theorists of the democratic peace have done just this.

Yet not only do liberal democracies differ between themselves, it is reasonable to suppose further that even a specific form of government we might describe as a liberal (or representative) democracy will have many fault lines within it. Michael Oakeshott, for example, famously suggested that European political consciousness is a polarized consciousness and that the poles around which modern political thought have turned are, on the one hand those which see the character of politics as effectively an agreement on non-instrumental rules that allow for a potentially limitless diversity and, on the other, that which sees the character of politics as the crafting of a common enterprise.[40] Similar in form, though not at all in content, is Quentin Skinner's development of two equally differing accounts of what he calls 'our common life'; one which sees sovereignty as a possession of the people, the other of the state; one emphasizes the citizen, the other the sovereign.[41]

Why is this relevant? Simply because, of course—as Skinner and Oakeshott each in their different ways make clear—the behaviour of a 'liberal democracy' in war, as in much else, will depend on which of the 'poles' is dominant at any given time. In Oakeshott's argument, for example, his first account, which he calls 'civil association', is fundamentally anti-belligerent, his second, 'enterprise association', quite the contrary. Yet for Oakeshott, it is enterprise association that has chiefly become the favoured understanding of contemporary liberal democrats, since enterprise association has been largely shaped by and through the experience of war. Thus, far from an enterprise association which happens to be a democracy being necessarily pacific, it will be organized for war in terms of its politics, even when there is no prospect of it fighting any really threatening enemies.

One does not have to accept the whole of Oakeshott's case (nor Skinner's for that matter) to accept that what we today call 'liberal democratic states' are a very odd ragbag and that there is little reason to believe that the mere fact of them all possessing in some form and to some degree, liberal politics and democratic institutions generates any particular commonality of behaviour. But if that is the case, then the *strong* link between regime type and behaviour disappears. And if it does then not only do arguments like the liberal democratic peace thesis face insuperable problems, so does at least much of what Strauss wants to link it to as well.

Finally, perhaps most seriously of all, there are real problems with the manner in which Strauss sets up the whole problem in the first place. It is difficult to know where to start here, especially given constraints on space. I am tempted to say that Strauss himself never really gets 'beyond the horizon of liberalism' if only because it is wholly unclear what a 'horizon of liberalism' might be, given the above point. One can be attentive to the many insights Strauss offers and accept also that he provides another set of reasons why it is unlikely that politics can ever escape war entirely and thus why realist claims need to be taken seriously, if not always accepted. But it is not the case that one is required to accept any of Strauss's particular conceptions to accept this. In particular the 'theologico-political problem', as Strauss defines it, seems to me to be largely a non-problem. 'Reason' and 'revelation' simply do not clash in the manner in which Strauss suggests they do. There are perhaps a number of reasons for supposing this. In the first place, I would argue that they are modally distinct forms of knowledge and in that context cannot 'clash'; rather they simply exist in oblique relation with one another. Reason—in as much as Strauss sees this as the presupposition of philosophy—is, I would agree, merely endless questioning; 'questioning without presupposition or arrest'. But this does not necessarily challenge faith, as I would understand it, since 'faith' in this sense is a practical mode of being in the world not a mode of knowing, and thus they cannot 'clash' in the required sense at all.[42]

If this is plausible, then Strauss's argument about the manner of writing and all that flows from it ceases, however, to be *necessary* and becomes instead a choice. There may—on occasion—be reasons to adopt it but on many other occasions there will not be. And if so then the whole careful edifice that Strauss has constructed collapses like a very unsteady pack of cards. The most important problem in Strauss's thought—powerful, suggestive, and interesting though it unquestionably is—is related to this: he simply gives us no reason to follow him if the theologico-politico problem is not as serious as he supposes it is. But to make it so, he would have to show us why reason and revelation *must* occupy the same epistemological and ontological space—and thus why they *must* clash, as opposed to sometimes, and contingently, actually clashing—and this he never does!

The final comment, then, is that for all Strauss's acuteness as a scholar and insight as a thinker—and he is both acute and insightful—I am not persuaded that the way he seeks to establish the 'permanence of war' convinces any more than do the more familiar realist claims I mentioned at the outset. And that, on reflection, seems an appropriate point on which to close. For we cannot simply ignore the obvious fact that the resort to force is—as I think it is—a permanent possibility in politics and will remain so for as long as politics takes on anything like its present shape. The most influential tradition to assume that has been realism and in Strauss's work we have found another set of claims that can be read as supporting a broadly 'realist' world view. My suggestion, however, is that we see this itself as a choice not as a necessity. Realists of all stripes, Strauss included, want to make the claim that we could never escape the possibility of war and that therefore we were (or should be) constrained to accept the consequences. But those consequences are precisely what I have suggested we might choose to dispute. Not, indeed, that we can escape from the recalcitrance of the world, as many reformists and cosmopolitans would suggest we might. Not even, as the more perceptive of them might suppose, that we can transcend or transform that world in ways that make the permanent possibility of force and all it brings in its train less likely. Rather, that we understand it as a choice that we can make or not, depending on the context and on what we think is at stake. It may be that we choose to 'stand and fight'; it may be that we do not; or that *I* do not. That is our—and my—choice. We are not compelled to accept the realist prognosis even if we accept elements at least of its diagnosis. The claim that conventional realists make—and that Strauss (and Schmitt) make too—is that human beings are fundamentally creatures of appetite and fear and, no doubt, they are often right. But often is not the same as always. It is a small distinction, perhaps, but a crucial one. Once you admit it, one can face the reality of the intractability of the world without thinking one has to agree with the judgement of the world or, indeed, the standards of that world. Realism thinks one must. Strauss does too as he seems to think that philosophy must hide, lest it be destroyed by the world. Yet these claims are only true if one accepts that the world is monochrome. Moreover, and more importantly, one is not required to think as the world thinks.

The sceptic, as I understand him—and her—adopts precisely this view. The realist, and the Straussian, however differently, accepts the view of the world. My sceptic denies it; for the world's view is not certain, not a necessary reality; it is merely a choice. Perhaps the general choice, but still a choice.

Of course, 'that the world should wreak its vengeance upon those who deny its view is only to be expected, but the world's vengeance harms none but the children of the world; those who have cultivated a contempt for the world have discovered the means of banishing it'.[43] Exactly what such a banishment might consist of, and how that might impact upon political theory or international relations is a topic for another essay, but it is worthwhile to close by emphasizing simply that one can perhaps learn a good deal about the possibility of such a banishing by thinking hard about the thought of those who claim most strongly that the world cannot be banished. In this respect, attractive and appealing though many utopian ideas may seem, they embed the claims of the world more firmly in our consciousness and our polities precisely because they suppose there is a root of *escape* that does not fundamentally change the logic of the world. Realism, in all its serious forms, does not make that mistake and that is why those of us who would, indeed, challenge the logic of the world do well to study it. And even more useful, perhaps, is reflection upon the thought of someone as profound, as original and as unflinching as Leo Strauss. For perhaps there is yet a third 'hidden dialogue' for us to understand—that between the logic of the world and those of us who would challenge the logic of the world. Strauss, I suspect, would not want to challenge its logic, however much he thought that philosophy represents something altogether other; but we are not obliged to follow Strauss in this. Rather, we can be grateful that his scholarship can help us, perhaps, to begin to elaborate an alternative that he did not himself envisage.

NOTES

1. I should like to acknowledge here the benefit I have obtained from discussions about Strauss with many friends over several years. Particularly, I should like to thank, Peter Euben, Ian Hall, Stephen Halliwell, Renee Jeffery, Noel O'Sullivan, David Owen, Christopher Rowe, Quentin Skinner, Christopher Smith, Steven B. Smith, and Tracy Strong. I would also like to thank all participants at the Nordic Summer University in Copenhagen in March 2007 for their very helpful comments on an earlier draft of this essay, delivered as a keynote lecture to the conference.

2. Canonical statements of this would include Hans Morgenthau, *Scientific Man Versus Power Politics* (New York: Knopf, 1948); Walter Lippmann, *US Foreign Policy: Shield of the Republic* (Boston: Little Brown, 1943); Henry Kissinger, *A World Restored* (Boston: Houghton Mifflin, 1954); Kenneth Waltz, *Man, The State and War: A Theoretical Analysis* (New York: Columbia University Press, 1954); Kenneth Waltz, *A Theory of International Politics* (Reading M.A.: Addison-Wesley, 1979); Richard Ned Lebow, *The Tragic Vision of Politics: Ethics, Interests and Orders* (Cambridge: Cambridge University Press, 2003); and John Mearsheimer, *The Tragedy of Great Power Politics* (New York: Norton, 2001). I would also include, though will not really discuss here, Rheinold Niebuhr's version, 'Christian Realism'. A key text here would be Niebuhr, *The Children of Light and the Children of Darkness* (New York: Scribner's, 1944). Among a lot of very bad treatments of the topic, some very good general treatments of realism as a tradition of thought can be found in R. N. Berki, *On Political Realism* (London: Dent, 1992); Michael Joseph Smith, *Realist Thought from Weber to Kissinger* (Baton Rouge: Louisiana State University Press, 1986); Joel Rosenthal, *Righteous Realists: Responsible Power in the Nuclear Age* (Baton Rouge: Louisiana State University Press, 1992); Alastair Murray, *Reconsidering Realism: Between Power Politics and Cosmopolitan Ethics* (Edinburgh: Keele University Press, 1997); Michael Williams, *The Realist Tradition and the Limits of International Relations* (Cambridge: Cambridge University Press, 2005); and Campbell Craig, *Glimmer of a New Leviathan: Total War in the Realism of Niebuhr, Morgenthau and Waltz* (New York: Columbia University Press, 2003). This is merely scratching the surface, of course. For further references, see Duncan Bell's introduction to this volume.

3. I do not suggest there are no others.

4. The *locus classicus* is, of course, his *Theory of International Politics* (1979), though the argument is prefigured in outline, if not in detail, in his earlier (and to my mind much more interesting) *Man, the State and War* (1959).

5. For Walt's development of neo-realism, see his *The Origins of Alliances* (Ithaca: Cornell University Press, 1986). For Mearsheimer's still more influential development of 'offensive realism' (by contrast with Waltz's 'defensive' realism—the terms are Mearsheimer's), see his *The Tragedy of Great Power Politics*.

6. Elshtain refers to herself explicitly as a realist in her *Just War Against Terror: The Burden of American Power in a Violent World* (New York: Basic Books, 2003). See also Lebow's Chapter 2 in this volume.

7. I take this term, of course, from Heinrich Meier's celebrated discussion of the relationship between Strauss and Carl Schmitt. See Meier, *Carl Schmitt and Leo Strauss: The Hidden Dialogue*, trans J. Cropsey (Chicago: University of Chicago Press, 1995).
8. This remark is quoted in one of the best general studies of Strauss to have appeared: Steven B. Smith, *Reading Leo Strauss: Politics, Philosophy, Judaism* (Chicago: University of Chicago Press, 2006), p. 6.
9. For a thoughtful and interesting express comparison of Arendt and Strauss on one especially controversial contemporary question, see Patricia Owens, 'Beyond Strauss, Lies and the War in Iraq: Hannah Arendt's Critique of Neo-Conservatism', *The Review of International Studies*, 33 (2007), pp. 265–83.
10. Strauss borrowed the phrase from the essay of Benjamin Constant, of course. It has also been a central concern of many of those influenced by Strauss. Perhaps the most interesting reading indebted to Strauss (but also one profoundly different from his) is Stanley Rosen's. See especially *The Ancients and the Moderns: Rethinking Modernity* (New Haven: Yale University Press, 1989).
11. See Leo Strauss, 'Preface to "*Hobbes Politische Wissenshcaft*"', in Kenneth Hart Green (ed.), *Jewish Thought and the Crisis of Modernity* (Albany: SUNY Press, 1997). See also the discussion in Smith, *Reading Leo Strauss*, pp. 10–12 and 26–42; and Meier, *Carl Schmitt and Leo Strauss*.
12. The emergence of this question in Strauss's thought is clear from his early book *Die Religionskritik Spinozas als Grundlage seiner Bibelwissenshaft: Unterschungen zu Spinozas Theologisch-politischem Traktat* (Berlin, 1930). It is developed further in 'Jerusalem and Athens: Some Preliminary Reflections', originally published in 1967 and now included in Leo Strauss, *Studies in Platonic Political Philosophy* (Chicago: University of Chicago Press, 1983). Other places where Strauss specifically discusses this question are: 'The Mutual Influence of Theology and Philosophy', in *The Independent Journal of Philosophy*, 3 (1979); in his exchange with Alexandre Kojeve and Eric Voegelin on his book *On Tyranny*—see Victor Gourevitch and Michael Roth (eds.), *On Tyranny* (Chicago: University of Chicago Press, 2000); in his correspondence with Voegelin, on which see Peter Emberley and Barry Copper (eds.), *Faith and Political Philosophy: The Correspondence between Leo Strauss and Eric Voegelin 1934–64* (Pennsylvania: Penn State Press, 1993); and, finally, in various aspects of his wider writings. Good discussions can be found in the scholarly apparatus surrounding some of the above books, many of which contain independent essays on the topic and, perhaps most interestingly, in Heinrich Meier, *Leo Strauss and the Theological-Political Problem* (Cambridge: Cambridge University Press, 2006).
13. Most famously, perhaps, in Myles Burnyeat, 'Sphinx Without a Secret', *The New York Review of Books* (30 May 1985).
14. See especially Strauss, *Persecution and the Art of Writing* (Glencoe: The Free Press, 1952).
15. It is worth pointing out that much of Strauss's early work—after his doctorate on Jacobi, completed with Ernst Cassirer at Hamburg—was on medieval Jewish and Islamic thought and this remained a powerful concern. In the Introduction to *Persecution and the Art of Writing*, Strauss avers to this when he points to an earlier essay of his, 'Farabi's Plato' [*Louis Ginzburgh Jubilee Volume*, American Academy of Jewish Research (New York, 1945), pp. 357–93], as being the basis on which he constructs his account of 'secret writing'. See also the discussion in Meier, *Carl Schmitt and Leo Strauss*, p. 87.
16. Smith, *Reading Leo Strauss*, chs. 1 and 2.

17. It is also the case, as Smith argues convincingly (*Reading Leo Strauss*, ch. 1), that Strauss saw this as a fundamental Jewish problem as well.

18. Ironically, a number of contemporary historians who would certainly not see themselves as 'Straussians' argue a similar case, though they do not do so in the manner Strauss would, or with the same motives. See, for perhaps the most exhaustive (and exhausting) version, Jonathan Israel, *Radical Enlightenment: Philosophy and the Making of Modernity, 1650–1750* (Oxford: Oxford University Press, 2002).

19. Smith, *Reading Leo Strauss*, p. 83.

20. Carl Schmitt, *Politsche Romantik*, 2nd edn. (Berlin und Leipzig, 1925).

21. See Schmitt, *Der Begriff des Politischen. Text Von 1932 mit einem Vortwort und drei Collarien* (Berlin, 1963). For an English version taken from this text, see Schmit, *The Concept of the Political*, ed. George Schwab (Chicago: University of Chicago Press, 1992).

22. See Strauss, 'Notes on The Concept of the Political', included in Meier, *Carl Schmitt and Leo Strauss*.

23. Meier, *Carl Schmitt and Leo Strauss*, p. 119.

24. Leo Strauss, *The Political Philosophy of Hobbes: Its Basis and Its Genesis*, trans. Elsa M. Sinclair (Oxford: The Clarendon Press, 1936).

25. See, especially, 'Three Waves of Modernity', in Hilail Gilden (ed.), *An Introduction to Political Philosophy: Ten Essays by Leo Strauss* (Detroit: Wayne State University Press, 1989).

26. See Leo Strauss, *Natural Right and History* (Chicago: University of Chicago Press, 1953).

27. See the essays gathered in *Studies in Platonic Political Philosophy*.

28. Pangle is among the most interesting and important contemporary interpreters of Strauss as well as being a very interesting and stimulating thinker in his own right. The particular book from which the phrase is taken is *Leo Strauss: An Introduction to His Thought and Intellectual Legacy* (Baltimore: Johns Hopkins University Press, 2006).

29. Strauss's discussion of this is best developed in his chapter on Aristotle in *The City and Man* (Chicago: Rand McNally, 1964). It is only fair to say, of course, that it is very far from being an unchallenged reading. For a reading that would challenge it, see Bernard Yack, *The Problems of A Political Animal: Community, Justice and Conflict in Aristotelian Political Thought* (Berkeley: University of California Press, 1993).

30. Strauss's mature thinking on the polis and its relation to the 'theologico-political problem can be found in his late works, most especially *The Argument and Action of Plato's 'Laws'* (Chicago: University of Chicago Press, 1975).

31. This argument is contained in *Natural Right and History*. See also the discussion in Pangle, *Leo Strauss*, pp. 83–8.

32. Strauss's reading of the *Republic*, and indeed of Plato more generally, is, of course, among the most controversial aspects of a body of work hardly devoid of others. Classicists—a class that often includes those working in Ancient philosophy—are notoriously hostile to those who trample on their territory and Strauss's case must be especially irritating given his genuinely profound knowledge of the philosophical and philological issues at stake. Strauss never really debated his reading (though many of his partisans, of course have), though he made a partial exception with his friend Hans-Georg Gadamer—from whom he used to borrow philosophical books from the Marburg philosophy library, when Gadamer was the librarian. See Strauss *What is Political Philosophy* (Glencoe: The Free Press, 1959) and Gadamer's

rebuttal in Supplement one, *Truth and Method*, 2nd edn., trans Joel Weinsheimer and Donald Marshal (London: Sheed and Ward, 1989). For the story about Strauss borrowing books from the Marburg library in the 1920s see Jean Grondin, *Hans-Georg Gadamer: A Biography* (New Haven: Yale University Press, 2003), p. 173.

33. See especially *Socrates and Aristophanes* (New York: Basic Books, 1966).
34. Made in many places, but especially, I would say, in *Natural Right and History*, *The City and Man* and *The Argument and Action of Plato's Laws*.
35. He develops this view in the chapter on Thucydides in *The City and Man*. A more recent, extremely penetrating and much more elaborate reading along the same lines, explicitly indebted to Strauss, can be found in Clifford Orwin, *The Humanity of Thucydides* (Princeton: Princeton University Press, 1994).
36. For a discussion of this, see Nicholas Rengger and Ian Hall, 'The Right that Failed: The Dilemma's of Conservative Thought and the Ambiguities of Conservative Practice in International Affairs', *International Affairs*, 81 (2005), pp. 69–82.
37. Robert Pippin has made a similar point in 'The Modern World of Leo Strauss', in his *Idealism as Modernism: Hegelian Variations* (Cambridge: Cambridge University Press, 1997), pp. 209–33.
38. The literature here is a veritable *sine qua non* of Straussian scholarship. Aside from Strauss himself, in *Natural Right and History*, one would have to add, as the apex of the triangle, Thomas Pangle, *The Spirit of Modern Republicanism: The Moral Vision of the American Founders and the Philosophy of Locke* (Chicago: University of Chicago Press, 1988); Harvey Mansfield, *Taming the Prince: The Ambivalence of Modern Executive Power* (Baltimore: Johns Hopkins University Press, 1989); and Mansfield, *America's Constitutional Soul* (Baltimore: Johns Hopkins University Press, 1991). But there is a great deal of other scholarship that seeks to establish a similar point.
39. Simply put, the democratic peace thesis holds that liberal democracies do not make war on other liberal democracies.
40. An argument pursued in different ways throughout his later work, but most efficaciously, I think, in the second and third essays of Oakeshott, *On Human Conduct* (Oxford: The Clarendon Press, 1975).
41. Implied, of course, in his *The Foundations of Modern Political Thought* (Cambridge: Cambridge University Press, 1978) but developed much more explicitly in his three volume *Visions of Politics* (Cambridge: Cambridge University Press, 2003). Note, for interest, Oakeshott's critique of Skinner in his review of *The Foundations* in the *Historical Journal*, 23 (1980), pp. 449–53.
42. Clearly, this is an argument I borrow from Oakeshott. I cannot develop it, or defend it to the extent it requires, of course, here; and I would put it in somewhat different terms than Oakeshott himself did. For different versions of Oakeshott's own explorations of it see *Experience and Its Modes* (Cambridge: Cambridge University Press, 1933), the essay 'The Voice of Poetry in the Conversation of Mankind' included in *Rationalism in Politics* (London: Methuen, 1962) and the first essay of *On Human Conduct*.
43. 'Michael Oakeshott', in Timothy Fuller (ed.), *Religion, Politics and the Moral Life* (New Haven: Yale University Press, 1996), pp. 37–8.

9

Pessimistic Realism and Realistic Pessimism

Joshua Foa Dienstag

9.1. INTRODUCTION

'Realism' and 'Pessimism' are two words that exist in a strangely symbiotic relation with one another on a scale of respectability that neither quite wants to admit.[1] 'Pessimism' is an expression often deployed to denigrate realism. It functions as a term of abuse to transform the clear-eyed into the sour-faced. Realists are always fighting off accusations of pessimism and insisting that, like the weatherman forecasting a hurricane, they merely fulfil their moral duty to offer an accurate account of a dire situation. Doubtless realists resent those who accuse them of pessimism. Yet perhaps they do not always mind the implied threat that the term carries, as if pessimism were the dangerous elder sibling that a realist might keep in reserve in case his or her predictions were insufficiently respected.

Likewise, when one wants to *complement* pessimism, one calls it 'realism' or perhaps 'simple realism' to save confusion with the international kind. It is a hard complement for the pessimist to refuse since pessimism, like every philosophy, strives to depict the world as realistically as possible. The pessimist, an outcast for so long, is grateful, at least, for being taken seriously. Yet he or she will perhaps also find something paternalistic or domesticating in this figure or speech. Why is it that pessimism cannot be taken on its own terms when those terms have so often proved correct?

In intellectual history, the relationship between pessimism and realism has a certain vital but intangible quality. On the one hand, those philosophers most commonly called pessimists (e.g. Schopenhauer, Nietzsche, Freud) have rarely had much to say about international affairs directly, but are thought to evince a generally tragic outlook on the world that might include the interstate domain as well as any other. Modern realists on the other hand are sometimes taken to have a rather abbreviated grounding in the canon of political theory, extending no further than superficial readings of Thucydides, Hobbes, and a few others and yet seem to share a sort of sensibility, if not a theory, with the pessimists. A natural solution presents itself: are not the modern realists the philosophical descendants of the pessimists, applying their insights into the international realm?[2] Perhaps they do so unwittingly? Or perhaps, indeed, the realists have actively sought to hide their family relations with the pessimists, in fear of being tarred by association? My aim in this chapter will be to establish that, although there is something to be said for this position, it is very far from complete and there is perhaps something more to be said against it. While a pessimistic theory of international affairs would undoubtedly share some elements with, at least, classical realism, there would be important points of difference as well. And while the policy implications of realism and pessimism may dovetail on certain points, there will be other places where they necessarily diverge.

9.2. A BRIEF SKETCH OF PESSIMISM

Pessimism, as I argue in more detail elsewhere, while descended in some sense from ancient philosophy both tragic and Stoic, is best understood as a modern discourse about politics.[3] Its modernity consists first of all in its reliance on a linear sense of time and history. Ancient cosmology was, for the most part, cyclical in nature. As a result, ancient political thought, again for the most part, did not think in terms of long-term trends but rather in terms of historical cycles. For a variety of (disputed) reasons, cyclicality gave way to linearity in the late medieval and early-modern era, both in cosmology and in political thought. As historical background, this much, I think, is undisputed. Indeed, it is widely acknowledged in the commonplace, repeated to the point of cliché by intellectual historians, that 'progress is a modern idea'. Less well-studied, however, are the non-progressive forms of theorizing that are also enabled by the transformation of historical and time-consciousness in the West. Pessimism is one of these.

The word 'pessimism' was first applied (by a critic) to Voltaire's satire *Candide*, which ridiculed the claim of Leibniz that ours was the best of all possible worlds. But pessimism got its first real theoretical statement in the work of Voltaire's rival Jean-Jacques Rousseau. Though Rousseau is sometimes depicted as a romantic, optimistic about the possibilities for rational human cooperation in the social sphere, a close reading of his work reveals that this is far from being the case. The happy condition of the natural savage is, for Rousseau, an unrecoverable starting point for the human species. It is a standpoint from which to condemn modernity, not a *telos* for political affairs. What his historical works, and especially the *Discourse on the Sciences and the Arts* and the *Discourse on Inequality*, reveal is a steady deterioration of the human condition, driven by forces that cannot be contained or controlled. The scheme of government offered in the *Social Contract* is meant to mitigate, not eliminate this problem—and even this scheme he acknowledges to be difficult to implement and quite impossible to maintain. While Rousseau's theory is sometimes called optimistic because of his belief in man's natural goodness, this can only be done by ignoring everything he says about human history and by confusing essence with outcome.

It is *time* and our awareness of it, for Rousseau, that denatures us and puts us on a path to moral depravity, political disorder, and personal unhappiness.

All living beings exist in time of course but what separates us from the stones, the plants, and even the animals, is our consciousness of time. The animal mind 'yields itself wholly to the sentiment of its present existence, with no idea of the future'.[4] Emergence into sentience means, above all else, being fully time-conscious, where time is understood in its modern, linear form. This claim is often repeated in the pessimistic tradition, by Schopenhauer, for example, who described animals as 'the present incarnate', but also by Nietzsche who famously contrasted human beings, with their sense of time and history to the cows in the field that are 'contained in the present'.[5] It is this focus on linear temporality, without the assumption of natural progress found in other modern theories, that is distinctive to pessimism.

For the pessimists, the time-bound character of life and consciousness has several related effects. First, and most importantly, it is the source of the impermanence of all things. No structure, natural or human, can be expected or designed to withstand the infinite variety of challenges that must appear over time. Hence, Rousseau writes, 'everything is in continual flux on earth. Nothing on it retains a constant and static form'.[6] Schopenhauer puts it thus: 'Time is that by virtue of which everything becomes nothingness in our hands and loses all real value'.[7] At the personal level, this means that all humans die and, what is more, as conscious beings, they are faced with foreknowledge of that death. Also, no person or object that gives us pleasure can endure unchanged; temporality means that nothing, however good, is permanent. Likewise in politics, no state, system or political structure, however powerful or well-adapted for its initial circumstances, lasts forever. Interests, sources of power, allegiances and even the fundamental organization of states and the state system have changed over time and will continue to do so, in ways that no one can predict.

These should, from a pessimistic perspective, be elemental pieces of political knowledge, as obvious to any observer as the prospect of his own eventual personal demise. But just as individuals can (and often do) blind themselves to their own fated end, so too can political theory obscure the fundamental flux of the political world and the fleetingness of existing arrangements. From this perspective, the political theory of Hobbes or Kant is optimistic (dangerously so), not because it has a 'positive' account of human nature, but because it does not acknowledge the destabilizing effects of temporality and time-consciousness. Instead such political theory attempts, at least at the domestic level, to produce a blue-print of the good society which, if implemented, will solve fundamental political problems once and for all. The contemporary incarnations of this optimism are found principally in the liberalism of Rawls, Habermas, and their followers who, while correcting or dissenting from the theory of Kant in many particulars, continue in this general project. Indeed, if anything, they are more insistent on the capacity of reason to restructure the world, or rather, on the amenability of that world to rationalist reconstruction.[8] But to the pessimist, the political world, like every other part of the world, is marked by change and disorder. Even the best blue-prints will confront circumstances they could not predict and eventually such circumstances will overwhelm them. For the pessimist, political theory should not be a matter of crafting blue-prints but rather of preparing individuals and political society to cope with the unexpected, to whatever extent that proves possible.

Temporal disorder means that there are no eternal conditions of nature or politics.[9] But this does not mean that there is no knowledge or insight into our circumstances. Conditions change and, as time-conscious creatures, we can appreciate these changes and study them. The historical pessimist, no less than the optimist, believes in the accumulation of experience. What separates them is their understanding of the effects of this accumulation. Pessimists do not deny, of course, that, by certain metrics, we can speak of progress in human affairs. No one doubts the increase in our technological powers, for example. Instead, pessimists ask whether these improvements have been linked with a set of costs that often go unperceived or underappreciated. Or they argue that the idea of a natural melioration of the human condition over time is, at best, unproven and, indeed, at odds with the evidence. In the context of international affairs, this amounts to a direct challenge to the Kantian idea of a pattern of knowledge-accumulation, embodied either in wiser electorates and state policies or more orderly international systems. It is a strange fact of intellectual history that many philosophers and historians have assumed that there exists a natural, exclusive connection between modern temporality and progress. Montaigne was already complaining about this tendency in the late sixteenth century when he wrote 'The philosophers...always have this dilemma in their mouths to console us for our mortal condition: "The soul is either mortal or immortal. If mortal it will be without pain; if immortal, it will go on improving." They never touch on the other branch: "What if it goes on getting worse?"'[10]

In sum, the practice of labelling political theories 'optimistic' or 'pessimistic' according to whether they possess accounts of human nature that are 'good' or 'bad' is, at the very least, a highly imprecise way of speaking. Beyond the fact that it is deeply mistaken to say, for example, that Hobbes accounts human beings as fundamentally violent or evil (dangerous, perhaps, but not *inherently* violent or evil),[11] this way of proceeding assumes that political theories always begin from accounts of human nature and that those accounts are always fixed. The real difference between Hobbes and Rousseau is not that the latter believes humans are naturally 'good' but rather that he does not believe human nature to be fixed at all in the manner that Hobbes does. Rousseau's theory is fundamentally historical in a way that Hobbes's is not.[12] Goodness may be our *original* condition to Rousseau but that is not sufficient ground for considering it our sole *natural* condition in light of our capacity for transformation and after centuries of change. It surely makes more sense to speak of political theories as optimistic and pessimistic in relation to where they end up, so to speak, rather than where they begin. Pessimistic political theory need not, and indeed for the most part does not, have a 'negative' account of human nature. Rather such political theory is concerned that there is no long-term process which improves the fundamental political outcomes for human beings and no sound procedure to create or sustain such a process. *It is not a theory of an evil beginning, but rather a theory that refuses to guarantee a happy ending.*

Likewise, we should take care before identifying pessimism too quickly and easily with a 'tragic' outlook, though here, certainly, the grounds for doing so are more tempting and Nietzsche, for one, certainly did claim a close relationship between the two.[13] Classical realists are often said to evince a tragic outlook, perhaps derived from Thucydides, wherein conflict and violence are unavoidable.[14] And if these terms are simply taken to indicate a world in which violence is prevalent, it is not a gross error to use them synonymously. But it is imprecise. The ontology that grounds the perspective of Thucydides and the authors of Greek tragic theatre is very different from that of, say, Hans Morgenthau and, in another way, different again from that of a truly pessimistic modern figure like Albert Camus. Both cyclicality and a strong sense of fatedness were elements of the ancient Greek world view that are not strongly replicated in modern realism and pessimism, however 'tragic' they may seem in other respects. Modern realists and pessimists may well have learned from the tragedians that our world is routinely one of suffering and conflict. (Of course, this being the case, they could also have just learned it *from the world*.) But the explanation of *why* this is the case does not really carry over from the latter to the former. While all of these views bear out a keen sensitivity to human suffering (something their critics often fail to notice), they describe the sources of that suffering in rather different terms (something their admirers often fail to notice). Optimistic or pessimistic, the modern world view is open-ended in a way that the ancient one is not. While it may well be our fate to live in a violent world, that is not a fate with the same sort of specificity as that of Oedipus who was cursed, from the day he was born, to kill his father, couple with his mother, and blind himself.[15] While pessimists believe that linear temporality structures our existence in ways we cannot control, a truly tragic world view projects a determinate plot that is even more dramatically constrained.

9.3. THE SOURCES OF INSTABILITY

From the sketch I have just given, it should be clear both where pessimism and realism overlap and where they do not. Both realists and pessimists conceptualize the international political realm as something fundamentally turbulent. All sources of order are, to both, insufficient or temporary, though they may well function for some extended period in particular circumstances. This is not a minor consideration, since most Western political theory is generally predicated on either finding order in nature or manufacturing sources of order that could cure or tame whatever disorder happens to exist naturally in politics. So the emphasis on permanent turbulence is a significant departure from the mainstream (indeed this perhaps is one of the reasons for realism's original alienation from the field of 'political theory' into the then-novel subfield of 'international relations').

Nonetheless realists and pessimists understand the sources and nature of the disorder, which the realists typically term anarchy, in not quite the same way. We should be careful not to conflate a common *diagnosis of condition* for a common *etiology*.

It is a regular criticism of the modern realist conception of political anarchy (perhaps overblown but certainly with a kernel of truth to it) that it is fundamentally ahistorical and even atemporal. International disorder is conceived as spatial or geometric phenomena. If this is not true in all cases, it is true, I think, for some of the most important and increasingly so in the twentieth century. It is clearly the case for Hobbes, whose political ontology was derived chiefly from Galilean physics and Euclidean geometry, which contains only the barest Newtonian conception of time and certainly nothing that we would today call an historical sense. (This was, after all, Rousseau's chief complaint about Hobbes.) While few realists today are simply Hobbesians, it is not, I think, too much to claim that the spatial ontology of politics that Hobbes initiated has been perpetuated, even as its details have been modified, by such figures as Hans Morgenthau and Kenneth Waltz: 'Over the centuries', Waltz writes, 'states have changed in many ways, but the quality of international life has remained much the same.'[16] In claiming that the anarchy of the international realm is 'structural' realists have specifically sought to dissociate that conclusion from any historical circumstance so that any thesis deduced from that conclusion would be general in application. Anarchy is conceived as a trans-historical condition that could be altered only by a planetary Leviathan. In so far as realism appeals to history at all, it is only to *verify* this truth, a truth which history *per se* can play no part in *explaining*. The reasons anarchy obtains (if we can even speak of reasons here) are not in themselves historical.

The case of Hans Morgenthau, as recent scholarship has made clear, is surely more complicated. In particular, the text *Scientific Man vs. Power Politics* contains many themes that resonate with pessimism. The book is an unremitting attack on the 'rationalism' of much modern political thought, which Morgenthau links directly to a foolishly 'optimistic outlook'.[17] There is much here that, as others have argued, seems derived from Nietzsche and Weber and, indeed, consonant with Rousseau.[18] Not only was this critique of rationalism derived from European theory, but it was also being carried on simultaneously with Morgenthau by figures as intellectually diverse as Michael Oakeshott and Horkheimer and Adorno, not to mention Morgenthau's Chicago colleagues Leo Strauss and Hannah Arendt. All were sceptical of the Enlightenment promise of long-term progress in human affairs predicated on the inexorable development of reason.

Yet while Morgenthau was not (especially in *Scientific Man*) a social-science enthusiast, it should not be forgotten that his work, and especially *Politics Among Nations*, did a great deal to set American international relations scholarship on the path that it took in the second half of the twentieth century. True though it may be that Morgenthau was inspired both by classical historians like Thucydides and by modern theorists like Carl Schmitt who disdained the pretensions of rationalist social science, we should not forget that the first principle of realism, to Morgenthau, was the idea that 'politics, like society in general, is governed by objective laws'.[19] One of the chief 'laws' that *Politics Among Nations* sought to describe was that of the balance of power. The balance, Morgenthau argues, is a 'universal concept' akin to that of equilibrium in physics or biology (a comparison which surely led students of Morgenthau to look for other such concepts). International balancing, he writes, 'is only a particular manifestation of a general social principle'.[20] And the chapter which describes it (from the very first edition in 1948) goes on to illustrate the various types of balancing with the sort of geometric billiard-ball diagrams that were, in more nuanced form, to become staples of social-science reasoning in the ensuing decades.[21] Even the preface to *Scientific Man*, perhaps conscious of the extreme scepticism that seems visible at some points in the text, claims that 'This book... continues the search for the general causes of which particular events are but the outward manifestations.'[22] Though current scholarship may unearth an interesting story about his diverse intellectual roots, it is this project that became Morgenthau's effective intellectual legacy. And, given the depth of earlier scepticism, it *is* clearly *his* project—not one foisted upon him by an existing social-science establishment which he had earlier shown himself perfectly willing to disregard.

Although pessimism is equally committed to a view of politics as fundamentally chaotic, the idea that a political disorder can be analysed so as to reveal underlying fundamental laws (of balance or anything else) is deeply alien to its practitioners. The difference with realism here can perhaps be outlined by focusing on realists' continuing preference for the term 'anarchy' and the related disanalogy between the domestic and international situation that they purport to describe.[23] Anarchy literally is of course an absence of *arche*, that is, a foundation, but corresponding to an *arche* is an *archon*, a ruler. Anarchy is understood by reference to its opposite, the normal condition of domestic politics, a stable polity ruled by some authority on a foundation of law (however flawed). To understand the international situation as anarchic, then, is normally to oppose it to civil stability. The disordered space of international politics is contrasted with the ordered space of domestic politics. While in some sense the idea of domestic anarchy remains as a possibility (domestic leviathans, being mortal, may die), in another sense, it does not. For if the domestic order were to dissolve, the boundary between the domestic and the international would be effaced and international anarchy *per se* would dissolve as well since there would no longer be any political units to face one another in an international sphere. Without domestic order, there would only be the war of all against all, which in itself has no particularly *international* character. The realists' reliance on the term 'anarchy' reflects, in this sense, the conceptual reliance of their theory on a strong dissimilarity between domestic and international affairs and this, in turn, can be traced to the spatial understanding of politics (billiard-ball diagrams, to be credible, require the existence of billiard balls). But since pessimism understands the root of disorder to be temporal and not spatial, even the existence of a terrestrial leviathan would not disrupt pessimism's account of change and chaos. Nor can it understand 'balance' as a universal, natural solution to the problem of turbulence.

Not only, then, does realism not share an etiology of anarchy with pessimism, but also the existence of pessimism allows us to ask whether realism, in its modern structural form anyway, really has an etiology of anarchy at all. To the question of *why* the international sphere lacks an order, the realist can give no reply beyond the observation that it has always lacked one, or the observation that no single actor seems to have the necessary power to impose one. But these are negative conditions; they cannot have caused anything. The origin of anarchy is never explained; it is rather the residual or baseline condition that is said to exist when all supposed sources of order are debunked. But this approach only appears sensible in the context of a theory that is geometric to the point of ahistoricality—if there is no fundamental change over time then it is not the case that anarchy ever 'emerged' or 'appeared' and no explanation of its emergence or appearance is needed. Indeed, anarchy, on this conception, can be said to lack any positive ontological weight and to be merely a negative condition, amenable to description but not true explanation.

By contrast, tracing the source of disorder and flux to temporality, as the pessimists do, yields a different perspective. The pessimistic commitment (ontological not moral) to disorder is, we might say, even more thoroughgoing than the realist one. Conceiving of politics as a system of quasi-physical forces, the realist can imagine both forces brought into balance, however tenuously, and lesser forces subordinated to a superior force. But for the pessimist there is nothing to balance and the problem cannot be conceived of mathematically or geometrically. There are no stable arrangements of power for pessimism because there are no stable sources of power, no stable structures to channel it and new problems constantly presenting themselves to disrupt any given arrangement. Not only is the international system anarchical; but its structure, to the pessimist, is also historically contingent. A systematic description of its features may be correct at a particular time, but to *know* that such features will obtain in the future as well would require that they be immune from all historical processes, which is impossible. This does not mean, of course, that violence is constant or unalterable in its quantity, or that there is no knowledge worth having about its immediate sources. Like the realist who seeks an 'economy of violence'—Sheldon Wolin's apt phrase for Machiavelli's aim[24]—the pessimistic politician can (and should) seek local circumstances of peace and security. Likewise, the pessimistic theorist can (and should) seek to understand the particular causes of contemporary dangers. But the rules of thumb or systemic 'laws' that realism has tried to establish are themselves, to the pessimist, contingent historical patterns unlikely to survive the next maelstrom. Thus thick description of immediate circumstances is far more likely to yield practical advice than the attempt to map such circumstances onto a matrix of timeless 'laws'. Such advice may not travel far but, as we shall see, it is also an element of pessimism to recommend a focus on the present at the expense of the future.

Putting it another way, we could say that modern realism (even that of Morgenthau but more egregiously that of later generations), in describing a political anarchy, has predicated its explanation of this phenomenon on an ontological *arche* supposedly impervious to time and history. This pessimism cannot accept. However accurate certain systemic accounts of international affairs may prove in the medium-term, the disorder of international political affairs is greater even than that created by the lack of a central authority. The fundamental unpredictability and flux which characterizes human affairs is not differently distributed between domestic and international realms but affects both equally and constantly. The sources of stability that realism hopes to locate in a situation of formal anarchy (e.g. balancing, deterrence, coordination) can only, to the pessimist, represent lucky circumstances or post hoc description of diverse phenomena which do not actually share common features.

Having said all this, it should still be clear that pessimism, sharing with realism a scepticism about the power of reason in human affairs, will have far fewer quarrels with it than with liberalism and its relatives as a theory of international affairs.[25] For if pessimism is more sceptical about the sources of order than realism, it cannot help but be at an even greater distance from liberal theory which, in addition to positing further sources of order in international affairs, has a reading of history that is deeply at odds with that of pessimism. In elaborating this distance, the kinship of pessimism with at least the classical realism of Morgenthau is more on display. His scepticism may, to the pessimist, be insufficiently thoroughgoing, but at least it was aimed at the right target: those theorists who presume to identify an underlying rationality to human affairs which time, or the proper theory, will bring to the surface. Such rationality, the pessimists insist (perhaps more consistently than Morgenthau), does not exist.

From another perspective, and at first glance, the antagonism of pessimism and liberalism might seem strange, since they appear to share a broadly 'historical' approach to international affairs (however ahistorical liberalism sometimes appears at the domestic level as a theory of justice). But liberalism's account of the accumulation of knowledge is in fact the main target of pessimism's complaint about philosophy in general and modern political theory in particular. Pessimism also shares with realism, as well as much postmodernism, a scepticism that there are permanent and unchanging moral values that can guide or be imposed upon political decision-making, in the international sphere or any other. But just because this sort of moral scepticism is not particularly distinctive to pessimism, I do not want to focus too much on it here. Instead I want to concentrate on liberalism's optimistic reading of history and the alternative that pessimism offers.

As a theory of international affairs, liberalism, as revived by Michael Doyle and others, has at its root a progressive account of human history that derives from Kant.[26] Kant not only postulated that democracies would tend not to fight each other, but he also described the mechanism by which this would come about. Just as the savagery of the state of nature would eventually force individuals to the conclusion—which was a real intellectual advance—that a system of laws is preferable to a system of self-help, so, Kant argued, international violence would eventually produce a parallel conclusion among free peoples, so long as they were not prevented from learning it. Thus, it is not a conclusion that democratic societies instantly come to but rather 'a long internal process of careful work on the part of each commonwealth is necessary for the education of its citizens'.[27] While Kant's particular description of the mechanism involved may have been distinctive to him, the idea of a general intellectual progress of the species, of course, was not.

But while Kant may have taken this idea of an accumulation of knowledge in the citizenry to be a particular feature of Enlightenment philosophy, that was not the view of the pessimists who criticized it. To them, this idea of accumulation could be traced back to the original Socratic justification of philosophy in the first place. It was Socrates's optimistic theory, Nietzsche wrote, that 'celebrates a triumph with every conclusion' and 'ascribes to knowledge and insight the power of a panacea'.[28] The Enlightenment, in this view, had only revived the Socratic-Platonic claim that all happiness derived from virtue and virtue from knowledge. The distinctive element of the modern version of this claim was only the use of a Baconian model of science as the exemplary form of knowledge. On this account, the only true obstacles to peace and justice are intellectual ones; once these are surmounted, political structures follow as a matter of course.

Even before Kant had written, this was a view about which Rousseau had expressed a deep scepticism in the *Discourse on the Arts and Sciences* as well as the *Discourse on Inequality*. Rousseau had several sources of concern, but the central one is his claim that the development of our intelligence, precisely because it individualizes us, simultaneously isolates us from others mentally and thereby renders us less concerned with the welfare of others. 'It is reason that engenders vanity, and reflection that reinforces it; It is what turns man back upon himself; ... It is Philosophy that isolates him.'[29] Uneducated man, to Rousseau, was a simpleton. He saw no basis for differentiating himself from others and, indeed, in an undeveloped state, humans *were*, for Rousseau, more alike than they later became. The empathy that human beings naturally possess is not, to Rousseau, a positive quality in and of itself; rather, it is the result of being unable to fully distinguish oneself from others. Developing our powers of 'reflection' for Rousseau is exactly like standing in front of a reflecting mirror and with the same moral effect: 'his first look at himself aroused the first movement of pride in him.'[30] Hence he postulates a direct correlation between intellectual improvement and moral decline: 'our souls have become corrupted in proportion as our Sciences and our Arts have advanced toward perfection.'[31]

From this perspective, the sort of learning that Kant argued for was beside the point. While we might gain a firmer grip on the cost–benefit calculations involved in war, this could not be expected to compensate for our fundamental loss of sympathy for other people. The idea that we might become more peaceful as we become more educated was, to Rousseau, a fantasy based on the idea that conflict arises out of lack of information. Conflict, to Rousseau arises out of an antagonism which is not natural but, in fact fostered by our intellectual and social development. Primitive humans do not come into quarrel with one another, in the first place, because they have few or no possessions and hence nothing to fight over—but more importantly because they are simply not highly differentiated from one another and hence are less capable of disagreement or disidentification. The degree of difference between individuals, not to speak of cultures and nations, is dramatically heightened by the acquisition of knowledge, even including self-knowledge. If we learn the costs of war over time, it is only after learning itself has produced, in a much more primordial way, the *sources* of conflict in the first place.

To Rousseau, any fair reading of history provided ample confirmation of this thesis, and it could only be an optimistic faith which insisted, against all evidence, that history was taking some other direction. Whatever power philosophy or science gives us over the world, it does not include the power to reverse time, which is the one thing which would be needed if we were to reverse the pernicious effects of time itself. Later pessimists, especially Giacomo Leopardi and Sigmund Freud, developed this argument, along with the thought that intellectual development multiplies our desires even faster than it multiplies the means we possess to satisfy them.[32] In a related vein, others argued that, in parallel with our alienation from other people, our increasing technological mastery of the world is simultaneously creating an increasing distance from it that will permit us to manipulate it as an object, to the detriment of both it and us. This is what connects Rousseau to later pessimists such as Horkheimer and Adorno who, in *Dialectic of Enlightenment*, propose that our intellectual and scientific development (the existence of which they are happy to acknowledge) is inexorably tied to a deepening social and worldly antagonism that eventually becomes murderous.[33]

From the pessimistic perspective, the liberal argument that democratic societies (wherein the sovereign may actually bear the cost of war) will tend to peace over time only looks at one half of the equation. Like realists, liberals assume that the ultimate sources of conflict (whether deriving from psychology, interest, or structure) are fixed by nature. Hence, if some countervailing force grows over time, the likelihood of conflict will diminish. But to the pessimist, there is no guarantee in history that the sources of conflict will not *increase* over time and much evidence that, in fact, they do increase. Given the genocidal wars of the twentieth century, this argument seems even stronger now then when Rousseau first made it. As many studies have argued, not only have 'primordial' conflicts not been effaced by time and intellectual development but also rather a strong case can be made that relatively minor differences have become dangerous political cleavages just to the extent that they have been intellectualized.[34] If there is a pacific democracy effect in evidence in international affairs, its consequences are swamped by a modernity effect from which it cannot be separated.

Despite intellectual differences then, pessimism shares with realism a deep suspicion of liberal theories of progress that is grounded, for both theories, not particularly in their *moral* scepticism but in their scepticism about rationalism in politics generally. The idea that reason is the engine of a long-term melioration of the human condition is their common target. While reason may yield some understanding of the causes of our immediate problems, it is not, in and of itself, a guaranteed solution to those problems. Pessimism goes further than realism, perhaps, in insisting that intellectual development is in fact, if not the ultimate source of conflict, one of the primary factors in its intensification. From Rousseau's argument that the modern human had lost a natural empathy towards others to Horkheimer and Adorno's contention that a technologized state was bound to see its opponents as objects amenable to manipulation, pessimism has insisted that we must extend our suspicions of progress from the political sphere to the intellectual sphere as well. Pessimism shares with liberalism an interest in historical understanding and historical change but it does so without any particular faith in a necessary historical directionality.

9.4. IMPLICATIONS

From a practical standpoint, the implications of pessimism for international relations theory and foreign policy centre on this point and on the unpredictability of events. While realism theorizes a structurally anarchic situation, it simultaneously suggests that the elements that create such a situation are computable or mappable, so that stability and order can at least be furthered by a calculable coherence of forces. For the pessimist, by contrast, the unpredictability of events trumps any notion of a fundamental structure. The most important events (say, most recently, the fall of the Berlin Wall and the 9/11 attacks) cannot be predicted. Nor is this a matter that will be remedied by further developments within social science. While it is certainly true that, after the fact, retrospective reconstructions can point to chains of circumstance which a perceptive analyst might have noticed, the fact of the matter is that a broad survey of the literature of 1988 or 2000 will find absolutely no reference to the impending upheaval of the international system that ensued in each case. That is to say, *the most important events in the international system since the end of the Second World War went largely unpredicted and even unspeculated about as possibilities* within either the highly developed fields of social science which might have been expected to anticipate them or the broader sphere of intelligent opinion. All events have antecedents of course, but the complexity, diversity, and flux inherent in the time-bound world make it impossible for us to know in advance the forces or situations that will threaten us with harm. The change that time marks can also only confirm to us that the structures and forces that we perceive now will not endure forever and we must theorize in the absence of such intellectual security as the idea of 'permanent structures' or 'permanent forces' or 'permanent interests' provides.

This suggests that ambitious attempts to remake the world so that its arrangement of forces is permanently less threatening to our interests is a fool's errand. The sandcastle will always crumble faster than it can be built up. We can be misled about this by periods of relative structural stability, as well as by short-term success, but viewed over the long-term, no one set of forces or powers has remained determinative of the international system; nor has the transformation of determinative powers followed a detectable pattern. The source and number of threats are not predictable in advance and our attempts to eradicate them will only resemble a frustrating game of whack-a-mole. What is more, attempts to manipulate the system routinely generate perverse effects which end up multiplying the threats they were intended to diminish. The United States should not have required its recent experience in Iraq to perceive this.

Pessimism therefore requires that we should think differently about the nature of power. Instead of conceiving power as the potential to control a system of known parameters or as the actions we take against threats that we already perceive,[35] we should think of it more particularly in terms of the resources we can marshal quickly and effectively against threats we have not predicted. While one might characterize such a stance as defensive, I would rather suggest that it involves thinking less like a policeman and more like a fireman. A policeman thinks in terms of creating and maintaining order; a fireman thinks in terms of containing and controlling disaster. All fires have antecedent events, of course; but the work of the fireman is only incidentally concerned with controlling these. Such events are too many and too diverse to be effectively regulated (many fires may derive from smoking, for example, but only a infinitesimal fraction of cigarettes lead to fires). Rather the bulk of his or her work is in responding to events in the present, as they occur, and training means acquiring a flexible set of skills and tools to deal with unpredicted and unpredictable situations.

Optimism and police power go together; both assume that there is an order to world events that can be mastered or brought about and administered through reasoned analysis. If the United States has appeared to many as an overweening policeman, it has done so less on account of imperial ambition, as is regularly and carelessly charged, and more out of its optimistic outlook on world affairs which entails that such a police power is both possible and necessary. The historical optimism at the root of the current US administration's foreign policy has been stated many times, nowhere more clearly than in George Bush's second inaugural address. 'We go forward with complete confidence in the eventual triumph of freedom', he said, 'History . . . has a visible direction, set by liberty and the author of liberty.'[36]

It is precisely the 'confidence' that historical optimism engenders that is the danger here, whatever its theoretical sources. The reliance on 'history' to do the work of politics will necessarily leave the work undone. In the short term, of course, such confidence can contribute to disastrous miscalculations of force as has happened with US policy towards Iraq. But even setting such avoidable miscalculations aside, there is a related, more important danger.

Albert Camus warned against policies that sacrificed peace or decency in the present in the name of a future outcome that would somehow compensate for the immediate distress imposed. Once one begins to make such calculations, he warned, the malleability of the future (in our imaginations of it) means that they can quickly spiral out of control. Since speculative benefits are weighed against present suffering, any increase in the latter can easily be mentally compensated for by an imaginary expansion of the future benefits. But this leads only to reckonings that are more and more indifferent to immediate consequences: 'He who dedicates himself to . . . history dedicates himself to nothing, and, in turn, is nothing. But he who dedicates himself to the duration of his life, to the house he builds, to the dignity of mankind, dedicates himself to the earth . . . and sustains the world again and again.'[37]

This is hardly a call to inaction. Keeping long-term projections to a minimum does not lead to passivity; firemen always have plenty to do. Camus did not oppose fascism because he believed in the inevitable triumph of freedom; rather, he opposed it because it was the only decent thing to do. And yet Camus was a lonely figure in post-WWII French politics precisely because he refused to join in the historical projections of either the Soviet-bloc powers (and their French Communist allies) or the cold-war liberalism of the Western powers. His call to 'give all to the present' echoes Rousseau's observation of 200 years before: 'What madness for a fleeting being like man always to look far into a future which comes so rarely and to neglect the present of which he is so sure.'[38] Focusing on the present means making decisions based on their most immediate and tangible consequences and less on the long-term effects which we predict them to have. It certainly does not mean forgoing action entirely.

While a pessimistic approach to international relations may in some sense be defensive in principle, that is no reason to think that it must necessarily be passive or retiring. But it will be focused on the present and it will be anti-systematic. If it defends democracy, it will be because democracy is the most decent system we can imagine for ourselves or others now, not because it is a guarantee against future hostility. If it opposes genocide, it will be because we cannot imagine living with ourselves otherwise, not because we believe ourselves in possession of an indefeasible theory of rights which authorizes our own actions and the submission of others to them. Pessimism does not exactly change our interests, but it does change our view of them by suggesting that they, and the system in which they make sense, will not be permanent. Preparing for change, the unexpected, or the worst does not mean that we eliminate from our imagination an image of what a better world would be like and use it to guide our actions. It simply means that we eliminate the idea that history or our own reasoning has some natural power to bring such a world about. The less we expect from the world, the better prepared we will be to deal with the emergencies it presents us with.

9.5. CONCLUSION

In sum then, I think we might do well to re-evaluate the relation between realism and pessimism. Realism, in fact, is not pessimistic, or rather, it is not pessimistic enough. Though it shares with pessimism a concern for disorder and a tendency to doubt the progressive readings of history, it has continued to hold out the hope of a form of theoretical, if not practical, mastery of the situation of international affairs. And, in that sense, it may have contributed to ambitious attempts to remake the international order. But pessimism certainly shares with realism an aversion to the historical optimism that has often driven foreign policy to the point of dangerous self-delusion.

Pessimism is a theory whose commitment to anarchy is even more radical than that of realism; anarchy is for pessimism an ontological condition, and not merely a political one, that has its source in the temporality that all beings exist in but only human beings experience. Realism and pessimism are not two words for the same thing. They are related to one another, but that relation should not be understood as one of euphemism. Pessimism should not disguise itself as realism nor should realism be insulted by means of pessimism. Rather, pessimism invites realism to extend its scepticism even further, to the point where even its own laws of anarchy are brought into question. Then and only then will we have a realism that is appropriately—realistically—pessimistic. Or pessimistically realistic. Your choice.

NOTES

1. I want to especially thank Duncan Bell for his encouragement of this essay, his careful editing, and his suggestion of many important sources which have greatly assisted me in the development of my arguments.
2. Christoph Frei's intellectual biography of Hans Morgenthau seems to take this tack, with respect to Nietzsche, at least. See Christoph Frei, *Hans J. Morgenthau: An Intellectual Biography* (Baton Rouge: Louisiana State University Press, 2001). Morgenthau, of course, was thoroughly acquainted with both canonical and contemporary political theory, as other contributors to this volume have amply demonstrated.
3. For more detail than I can provide here, see my *Pessimism: Philosophy, Ethic, Spirit* (Princeton: Princeton University Press, 2006), ch. 1.
4. Jean-Jacques Rousseau, *Discourses and the Essay on the Origin of Languages* (New York: Harper and Row, 1986 [1754]), p. 151. This idea, though quite common, is far from universal; Aquinas, for example, insisted on the animal's capacity for hope and expectation.
5. Arthur Schopenhauer, 'On the Suffering of the World', *Essays and Aphorisms* (London: Penguin, 1970), p. 45; Friedrich Nietzsche, 'On the Uses and Disadvantages of History for Life', *Untimely Meditations* (Cambridge: Cambridge University Press, 1984), p. 61.
6. Jean-Jacques Rousseau, *Reveries of the Solitary Walker* (Hanover: University Press of New England, 2000), p. 46.
7. Schopenhauer, 'On the Suffering of the World', p. 51.
8. See, for example, Jürgen Habermas, *Moral Consciousness and Communicative Action* (Cambridge, MA: MIT Press, 1990); and John Rawls, 'Kantian Constructivism in Moral Theory', *The Journal of Philosophy*, 77 (1980), pp. 515–72.

9. The question of whether this statement is self-contradictory (i.e. whether 'no eternal conditions' is itself an eternal condition) is less important than it seems. Pessimists view their understanding of the world as inductively conceived; that is, 'no eternal conditions' means 'none discovered thus far after thousands of years of exhaustive search; it may please you therefore to theorize in their absence'.

10. Michel de Montaigne, 'Apology for Raymond Sebond', *The Complete Essays of Montaigne* (Stanford: Stanford University Press, 1958), p. 413.

11. On this point, see Richard Flathman, *Thomas Hobbes* (London: Sage, 1993); and Michael C. Williams, *The Realist Tradition and the Limits of International Relations* (Cambridge: Cambridge University Press, 2005), ch. 1.

12. Kenneth Waltz clearly sees this distinction between Hobbes and Rousseau but he still tends to use the term 'optimistic' and 'pessimistic' in the unhelpful ways described above. See his *Man, the State and War: A Theoretical Analysis* (New York: Columbia University Press, 1959), ch. 1, passim.

13. Friedrich Nietzsche, *The Birth of Tragedy* (New York: Random House, 1967), *passim*.

14. See Richard Ned Lebow, *The Tragic Vision of Politics: Ethics, Interests, and Orders* (Cambridge: Cambridge University Press, 2003), as well as his Chapter 2 in this volume.

15. Sophocles, 'Oedipus Rex', *The Three Theban Plays* (New York: Penguin Books, 1982).

16. Kenneth Waltz, *Theory of International Politics* (New York: McGraw-Hill, 1979), p. 110. This is not to deny that there may be other, important points on which modern realism differs from Hobbes or, indeed, that Hobbes in general may be poorly understood by both critics and defenders of modern realism. See Noel Malcolm, 'Hobbes's Theory of International Relations' in *Aspects of Hobbes* (Oxford: Oxford University Press, 2002). But I do not think that Malcolm in his spirited, largely justified defence of Hobbes's unperceived subtlety on the subject of international affairs fully considers the ways in which Hobbes's ontology has structured the understanding of many who came after him, including modern realists.

17. Hans Morgenthau, *Scientific Man vs. Power Politics* (Chicago: University of Chicago Press, 1946), p. 18.

18. See Williams, *The Realist Tradition and the Limits of International Relations*, ch. 3; and William E. Scheuerman's Chapter 3 in this volume.

19. Hans Morgenthau, *Politics Among Nations*, 2nd edn., revised and enlarged (New York: Knopf, 1956), p. 4. Of all Morgenthau's contemporaries, his position here seems closest to that of Leo Strauss who similarly disparaged modern social science while maintaining that there were nonetheless objective, natural truths to which a certain kind of philosophical enquiry could lead.

20. Morgenthau, *Politics Among Nations* (1956), pp. 155–6.

21. Hans Morgenthau, *Politics Among Nations* (New York: Knopf, 1948), p. 129ff.

22. Morgenthau, *Scientific Man vs. Power Politics*, p. v. As a description of the text, this sentence is misleading. The book is largely a polemic against the rationalist tradition in philosophy and especially international relations. It seems very likely that in the gap of time between the original lectures for *Scientific Man* (1940) and the writing of the preface (dated 1946 when he would have been working on *Politics Among Nations*), Morgenthau had modified his views and that this sentence represents an attempt to recharacterize his aims in the earlier work. While there are a number of scattered attempts in *Scientific Man* to reconcile the extreme scepticism expressed

towards science with the repeated claims about the fundamental truths about power politics, these are not very persuasive and by the time of *Politics Among Nations*, Morgenthau seems to have scaled back the scepticism to the point where he embraces social science in a limited way.

23. I do not mean, of course, that the use of the term anarchy *proves* anything *per se*; I focus on it here only to illustrate the difference between the two tendencies of thought that I am describing. Morgenthau is something of an exception here. He insists, on the one hand, that international and domestic politics are 'but two different manifestations of the same phenomenon'. But then justifies a separate treatment of international affairs on the vaguest of grounds: 'Its manifestations differ in the two spheres [why two?] because different moral, political, and social conditions prevail in each sphere.' Morgenthau, *Politics Among Nations*, 2nd edn., p. 35.

24. Sheldon Wolin, *Politics and Vision*, 2nd edn. (Princeton: Princeton University Press, 2004), ch. 7.

25. I do not here discuss Marxist theories of international relations, but I think much of pessimism's critique of liberalism would also apply to Marxism, with appropriate modifications.

26. Michael Doyle, 'Kant, Liberal Legacies and Foreign Affairs', in two parts, *Philosophy and Public Affairs*, 12/3 (1983), pp. 205–35 and 12/4 (1983), pp. 323–53. I cannot discuss the vast literature that has appeared at the instigation of these articles in the last twenty-five years in any detail. The term 'liberalism' in IR could now be said to do no more than to indicate a group of theories, with contradictory accounts of causation and explanation with a common origin but perhaps no common theoretical core. In making the sort of generalizations that a paper like this must, I can only beg the indulgence of specialists who will know the details of such debates better than myself. I realize that there may be versions of liberalism (and of realism) that escape the critique I offer here.

27. Immanuel Kant, 'Idea for a Universal History with a Cosmopolitan Purpose' [1784] in Kant, *Political Writings* (Cambridge: Cambridge University Press, 1991), p. 49. Kant's statement of this idea is generally acknowledged to be the most sophisticated, but it was obviously not the first since, as I discuss below, Rousseau was already attacking it in the 1750s, having in mind, perhaps, the arguments of Diderot and D'Alembert.

28. Nietzsche, *op. cit.*, pp. 91, 97.

29. Rousseau, *Discourses*, p. 162.

30. Rousseau, *Discourses*, p. 172.

31. Rousseau, *Discourses*, p. 7.

32. See Giacomo Leopardi, *The Moral Essays* (New York: Columbia University Press, 1983 [1827]); and Sigmund Freud, *Beyond the Pleasure Principle* (New York: W.W. Norton & Co., 1961 [1920]).

33. 'The fallen nature of modern man cannot be separated from social progress. On the one hand the growth of economic productivity furnishes the conditions for a world of greater justice; on the other hand it allows the technical apparatus and the social groups which administer it a disproportionate superiority to the rest of the population.... Men pay for the increase of their power with alienation from that over which they exercise their power.' Max Horkheimer and Theodor Adorno, *Dialectic of Enlightenment* (New York: Continuum, 1988 [1944]), p. 9.

34. See, for example, Mahmood Mamdani, *When Victims Become Killers: Colonialism, Nativism and Genocide in Rwanda* (Princeton: Princeton University Press, 2002). I do not mean, of course, that this is a settled question.
35. As Morgenthau does: 'By political power we refer to the mutual relations of control among the holders of public authority.' *Politics Among Nations,* 1st edn., p. 13.
36. Text available at: http://www.whitehouse.gov/inaugural/.
37. Albert Camus, *The Rebel* (New York: Vintage Books, 1991), pp. 301–2.
38. Camus, *The Rebel*, p. 304; and Rousseau, *Emile* (New York: Basic Books, 1979), p. 82.

10

Realism and the Politics of (Dis)Enchantment

Vibeke Schou Tjalve

10.1. INTRODUCTION

Our current political reality is, as Henry Luce prophesized, an American one: shaped by US capital, US principles, and US policies.[1] But it is also an era tempted by the very logics with which the American century promised to do away: repression, exclusion, and forced uniformity. Putting it somewhat polemically, secular enlightenment won the war against totalitarianism, yet emerged from that victory on ideological foundations stretched so thin, that it recurrently finds itself tempted by the strategies of cohesion propagated by the side that lost.[2] To some, this paradox is but the product of pure hypocrisy—a proof of Western arrogance and insincerity. Hence, the frequent accusation that means and ends collide in the liberal 'war on terror'; hence the routine claim that Western enlightenment is *itself* a form of fundamentalism. It is understandable and in some ways comforting that this is a common reaction to the often blatant contradictions of liberal foreign policy. Yet to engage with the discrepancies displayed in contemporary politics, a different response is called for. If the democratic world, in order to achieve itself, relies on Schmittean means and modes of thought, this is partly because liberal democracy stands in a more complex relationship to the logics of closure than the architects of the American century have been willing to accept or understand. To recognize that complexity is not to accept the Schmittean predicament. But to do battle with the politics of enmity, one must understand its attractions: the gaps it appears to close; the functions it seems to fulfil.

The purpose of this chapter is to address the embrace of polarization and antagonism in contemporary politics and to rethink how alternative modes of aligning identity and difference may be conjured up. To achieve this, I explore three interrelated propositions. First, I briefly suggest that we can see the contemporary world as largely defined by a deep sense of disenchantment. Against that background, I turn to the post-war period and its foundational struggle over how to forge a sceptical yet hopeful political theory, as a route by which to avoid disillusion. More specifically, the bulk of this chapter casts Reinhold Niebuhr (1892–1971) and Hans J. Morgenthau (1904–80) as realists who, despite conventional depictions as 'conservative through and through, with deep suspicion against public opinion and control of foreign policy', sought to balance cohesion and critique, by framing the political order in transcendent yet radically anti-essentialist terms.[3] It is from such transcendence, I conclude, that a genuine alternative to conservative and nationalist strategies of re-enchantment must come. Only if the Enlightenment project of subversion, emancipation, and critique disentangles itself from that of disenchantment, will a critical political agenda become a transformative one.[4]

10.2. THE POLITICS OF (DIS)ENCHANTMENT: 'DECONS' VERSUS 'NEOCONS'

As the twentieth century came to a close, Nicholas Rengger perceptively framed it as a battle between 'defenders of the faith' and 'disturbers of the peace': an intellectual contest between those who saw modern Enlightenment as resting on secure epistemological foundations, and those who considered it rather a project of epistemological self-dismantling.[5] A decade later, this apt categorization still applies, only the contest seems now to have moved into a further, more decadent phase. In the political arena, defenders of the faith have come into fashion, yet the faith they defend seems more of a means than an end in itself. From the emergence of various forms of populist nationalism in Europe, to the increased importance of a particular, and particularly (late)modern, religion on the American stage, one gets the impression that a new type of absolutism, concerned with the functions more than the content of 'tradition' has taken hold: that tradition, as the theorists of reflexive modernity remind us, acts differently once it becomes an actual and self-conscious *choice*.[6] Thus, the basic argument of this section is that despite the return of religious or nationalist modes of argumentation in contemporary Western politics, the logics of disenchantment are creeping in. Arguably, the defining poles in contemporary struggles over identity and difference share an implicit commitment to what is really a Nietzschean premise: that the deities of modern life are gods of our own making. What is at stake is simply a struggle over how to handle the fact. Do we embrace the void? Or do we try to cover it up? That question, and the academic, cultural, political, national, and religious games played out around it, thus adds up to what we may term the politics of *dis*-enchantment.

In its most sophisticated, theoretical form, one extreme of this political struggle is that of deconstructive political theory. While admittedly a philosophical discourse limited mainly to the academic humanities, the *ethos* of deconstructive thought pervades the attitudes of much of the contemporary political left. An heir to the anarchism of the 1960s New Left, this is fundamentally a celebration of disenchantment—of absence, disintegration, revolt. As mood rather than theory, it is an attitude of subversion, a revolt against power and authority, or resistance towards 'truth' and tradition. According to Todd Gitlin, an influential

left-wing cultural theorist, critical attitudes since Vietnam have concerned themselves almost entirely with negation—with 'playing defence'. 'It is as if', Gitlin
continues, 'history were a tank dispatched by the wrong army, and all that was
left to do was to block it. If we had a manual, it would be called, *What is Not to
be Done* . . . The left has gotten comfortable on the margins of political life, and for
intellectuals it has been no different.'[7] It is thus not surprising that the political
left has been increasingly uncomfortable with the vocabularies of nationalism,
patriotism, or faith, viewing rites and sites of collective myth as little but prisons,
and common aspirations as little but 'ideological discourse entwined in a meta-
narrative of truth-seeking masking privilege and power'.[8]

Nor is it surprising that a left that hands over the initiative to others has
been outfought by another type of disillusion, with a very different spin on
the attractions of disenchantment. Most obviously and self-consciously, this is
found in the policies of the so-called neoconservatives, with their sharp analysis
of political and moral relativism, and their shrewd attempts to avoid disorder
and decadence. It is also present, however, in the various venues of European
identity politics. Indeed, we may stretch the neoconservative label to cover the
nationalist and fundamentalist enterprises of the present as such, for what unites
these is exactly the fact that they advocate a *new* type of conservative ethos: a
conservatism on the offensive, a conservatism that does not so much defend as
invent, and a conservatism that does not pursue religious principles or national
legacies for their absolute moral value, but rather, for the social functions which
such principles may serve. The nationalist projects on the European right may not
be as conscious of their own attempt to orchestrate sentiment for the purpose of
certainty, hierarchy, and order. But pervading their policies, as much as in those of
the American neoconservatives, is a highly strategic approach to the role that re-
enchantment will play: a tendency to utilize political and religious vocabularies,
rather than to venerate these in their own right. Admittedly, not all political
projects on the right would claim with Irving Kristol—the most sophisticated
voice among American neoconservatives—that the 'pillars [of order] are religion,
nationalism and economic growth' and that they are the only powers to truly
'shape people's character and regulate their behavior'.[9] But the stretch is not so far
from explicitly utilizing 'faith' as a means to political order, to implicitly deploying
'the national' as a means of social cohesion.

Examining the features of political thought and practice today in other words,
one is left with the impression of an increasingly polarized field, consisting of
mutually reinforcing forms of disillusionment: a critical choir mainly occupied
with resisting the implicit pretensions of nationalism, patriotism, or religion, and
a conservative camp equally aware that the foundations of traditional certainties
are unraveled, but devoted to somehow denying, opposing, or concealing the fact.
It is not that all in the former camp are seditious Foucaultians, nor all in the latter
conniving or devious Straussians. Yet, an echo of disillusioned withdrawal does
sound in the critical attitudes of many on the Western political left though, and a
note of instrumentality rings in the voices of the right. What, in the long run, is
likely to result from such stalemate? If it is true, as Maurizio Viroli argues, 'that

political languages cannot be assessed in absolute terms but must be evaluated for what they can do against other languages that sustain different or alternative political projects', one cannot help but worry that the various forms of new conservative populism, with their promise of closure and certainty, provides what neither the project of traditional liberalism nor that of a subversive emancipation has been able to do: a policy of ends not just means, of purpose not just process.[10] Ultimately though, the neoconservative attempt to force a 'return' to traditional religious or national values also relies on a reductive political psychology. If the proponents of a fundamentalist populism reach for Plato on ethics, they turn to Schmitt for tactics: building identity and coherence out of inflexible constructions of 'friend' and 'enemy'.[11] That is a strategy that overlooks the complexity of human desires: our engagement with questions of meaning not merely as a 'yearning for order and stability' but also for self-expression, vitality, and difference.[12] It is also a gross misreading of what a genuine search for transcendent experience is about, confusing the complex urge for private and public vocabularies in which to express experiences of doubt and wonder, with a simple demand for the answers of orthodox 'doctrine'. The human search for interpretative frameworks within which to make sense of existence is a search for vocabularies that will pay justice to the human experience of confusion, dilemma, or contradiction—not reduce or deny this. The stock phrases of nationalist bombast, then, are *not* what a present exhausted of resources for thinking freshly is in need of. As such, the critical left is right to oppose it. If we are to escape the Schmittean impulse however, we cannot ignore its implicit diagnosis. Instead, we must try to provide a cure.

10.3. COMING TO TERMS WITH DESOLATION: THE REALIST RESCUE OF ENCHANTMENT

Ironically, one of the most pertinent ways to do that may be to recover an intellectual strand that developed in parallel to the neoconservative mood and which builds on many of the same philosophical trajectories: the classical realism of Reinhold Niebuhr and Hans J. Morgenthau. Despite its reputation as the province of mindlessly optimistic Lockean liberalism, American political thought is a highly rewarding place to look for advice on how to move beyond the blind beliefs of modernity, without embracing pure disenchantment. In particular, it is worth consulting the moment of sobriety which marked American academia in the decades following World War II, bringing into dialogue the bleaker voices of Western modernity: the governmentality of Machiavelli and Hobbes, the vitalism of Nietzsche and Schmitt, and the Calvinist constitutionalism of the American Founders. Haunted by the failure of reason, what emerged out of that conversation was a resolve to wrestle the project of the Enlightenment from its overly optimistic prophets, and to reorient it by elaborating a darker and more complex form of social and political anthropology. Could a more robust and realist defence of the liberal faith yet be forged?[13]

In contrast to conventional depictions of realism as an amoral—perhaps even *im*moral—'effort to eradicate normative imperatives' in international affairs,[14] recent scholarship suggests that it be read as an integral part of this project: an attempt to salvage the political ideals of modernity without buying in to its weary epistemological commitments. One of the first works to recognize that it was Nietzsche, not Descartes—and, I would add, Hamilton, not Jefferson—who blazed the path by which realist thinkers like Niebuhr and Morgenthau were to travel was Ulrik E. Petersen's essay on classical realism as an early variant of deconstructive sentiment, albeit one with a deeper grasp of the dilemmas involved in accepting a Nietzschean ontology than most contemporary 'postmodern' or post-structural thinkers. The *leit motif* of that study was first of all political, seeking to utilize post-war realism as a necessary corrective to contemporary deconstructive practices, whose 'rhetorical sleights of hand' has in Enemark's opinion resulted in little but 'statements of intent masquerading as solutions'. In response to the post-structural call for a radically emancipatory 'return of the political', which to Enemark's mind tends to gloss over or distort the danger of pure difference, Enemark adumbrated a Nietzschean realism to serve as a reminder of their 'intractable, and ... insoluble' character.[15] The main contours of those historiographical lineages seem now to have been established, but the implications of Enemark's political intervention are yet to be fully unpacked.[16] In particular, more remains to be said about the potential of realism for countering what both left and right in contemporary politics has gotten wrong about the relationship between identity and difference. In several ways, the situation in which Niebuhr and Morgenthau found themselves, and crafted their realism as a response to, was similar to that described above. Both believed that the ideological struggle which had culminated in world war, delivering decadent liberal relativism to the manipulations of authoritarian rule, was an early manifestation of Western modernity's inescapable fate lest it found firmer philosophical ground on which to stand. If nothing but a rationalization of rules and procedure, liberalism would continue to feed the forces of its own dismantling. And, in response to such frailty, political philosophies of a less benign temper would continue to attract attention as disenchanted relativism paved the way for theories of the exceptional and superior: in the absence of all other Gods, man tends to make himself deity.[17] To Niebuhr and Morgenthau then, the challenge became to escape the nihilism of disenchantment, bolstering democracy against its totalitarian foes, without sliding into either certitude or smug complacency. Was it possible to weave a plural, self-reflective, and self-critical body politic from the fabric of shared beliefs?

A theologian and a legal scholar, the paths to a possible answer followed by Niebuhr and Morgenthau were bound to stray in diverse directions, but their ambitions were shared: to renew the spiritual foundations of democratic politics, replacing radical doubt with genuine faith, not absolute certainty. The weakness of liberal democracy, both believed, lay in a liberal ethos whose relativist philosophy of means over ends—method over purpose—had robbed politics of a mobilizing vocabulary of substantive values. It was not liberalism's epistemological scepticism that was the problem: Niebuhr and Morgenthau too embraced relativism as a precondition for tolerance, if relativism meant the view that it 'is not possible to state a universally valid concept of justice from any particular sociological locus in history'.[18] This, however, was a radically different claim than the ontological assumption that 'justice does not exist and is a mere illusion'. Democracy, as Morgenthau explained, must assume 'the reality of justice' though 'we are not capable of realizing it. The two positions are by no means identical. They are no more identical than the atheist position denying the existence of God is identical with the view that man is incapable of knowing God, even if he does exist'.[19] At stake, in other words, was an issue of the political and moral effects of relativism. The epistemological sceptic, insisting on truth as real but transcendent may be both moved by and humbled before absolute principles—the ontological sceptic may not. As such, both Niebuhr and Morgenthau argued, the latter is prone either to slide into empty passivity or idolize pure and immanent vitality. Or, as Niebuhr put it: 'only where there is a true sense of transcendence can we find the resource to convict every historical achievement of incompleteness and to prevent the sanctification of the relative values of any age or any era.'[20]

In response to this danger, Niebuhr and Morgenthau sought to recover what we may term 'enchanted scepticism' and place it at the heart of their cure for democratic politics, seeking to replace the constructed artificialities of totalitarian thought with more authentic, inclusive, and open-ended forms of meaning and belief: to bring about a renewed transcendence without lapsing into renewed delusions of grandeur. Attempts to strike that balance are present in almost all of their writings, but perhaps most consciously and consistently in Morgenthau's *The Purpose of American Politics* (1960) and Niebuhr's *The Children of Light and Children of Darkness* (1944). These works provide both a diagnosis and a cure for the liberal predicament—particularly its modern American variant—by arguing that all attempts to salvage democracy must look beyond the question of legal and institutional design to more fundamental issues of civic consciousness and mobilization. Both assumed that democracy relies essentially on a particular kind of dedicated yet detached *subjectivity*, which in turn relies on the presence of transcendent public philosophies. And yet, they continued, this was exactly what liberal modernity had squandered, robbing public debate of those utopian imaginaries that remind us of our current imperfections and hence make for critique and contestation. Indeed, critique and contestation had come to appear as the very antithesis of democratic practice, as the embrace of immanence leads naturally to a defence of the status quo. Without the humbling effects of a shared transcendent purpose, the body politic was left with nothing to cherish but itself, ultimately stifling in the blank rejection of all critique as treason.[21]

To counter this ethos of conformity and invoke 'the vital questioning and initiative' of a plural public sphere, Niebuhr and Morgenthau thus turned to initiate a spiritual public rebirth, roughly consisting of three interrelated components: a recovery of transcendent purpose in civic discourse; a redefinition of patriotism as deliberative dissent against conformist consensus; and finally, a reconstitution of leadership as the potential stimulus of agonistic and dissenting debate rather than stifled and uniform compromise.[22] In the pursuit of these measures, Niebuhr and Morgenthau revealed intellectual debts not only to continental vitalism but also to the powerful, albeit largely marginalized American scepticism that J. G. A. Pocock has famously cast as 'Atlantic republicanism'.[23] What both esteemed in this distinctly American tradition—traced by Niebuhr to Lincoln, and by Morgenthau to such founding figures as Hamilton and Adams—was that far from 'retreating into utopianism or pessimism', it responded to challenge or crisis by 'attacking in the pragmatic spirit of social reform'.[24] Not, as Morgenthau put it, because any of these figures had fooled themselves that political strategies, governmental reforms, or spiritual realignments could ever 'exercise the fact of power from society'— familiar with the wisdom of 'Calvin and Hobbes', all had hoped merely to 'minimize the relations of power and mitigate their burden'.[25] But instead of meeting crisis with a defence of the status quo, or difference with a defence of conformity, the republican temper suggested a 'continued American revolution, by attacking *within* American society, deviations from the American purpose'.[26] Niebuhr and Morgenthau thus argued that the transcendent ideals of politics were neither realizable in the sense imagined by the advocates of certainty nor irrelevant in the sense claimed by the advocates of doubt. Rather, that they acted as imaginaries able to stir an eternal political struggle. As a result, they continually critiqued what they saw as suppressive notions of patriotism in contemporary politics, invoking the argument of Washington or Lincoln that 'a dissenting minority', far from disloyal to the principles of democratic politics, 'performs a vital function for the political and moral *welfare* of the Republic'.[27]

On this primary assumption—that a government which transforms legitimate dissent into questions of loyalty forfeits its right to allegiance—Niebuhr and Morgenthau base the third and final component of their attempt to salvage liberal democracy: an insistence on the re-politization of leadership.[28] Undoubtedly, their fascination with statesmanship and duty is at times archaic, and not without pitfalls. Yet tied up with a critique of the homogenizing and totalizing forces in modern democracy, the endorsement of stronger political leadership was to them primarily a means to energize pluralism by giving a more explicit and deliberate profile to the policies of government. Immanentism, they claimed, with its teleological reading of history as the realization of pre-given and absolute truth, had caused politics to loose 'its fanatical bipartisanship and bitter animosities' and invoked instead 'the warming benevolence of a President who appears to be above politics' and which 'envelops the nation as in a *union sacrée*'. As a result, leadership had come to be viewed as the omnipotent and neutral representation of an alleged collective interest, making public critique seem like 'sacrilege against the spirit of the nation, incarnate as in the person of the President'.[29] To oppose such closure, both Niebuhr and Morgenthau claimed that the national interest and public purpose had to be treated not as 'a static thing to be ascertained and quantified by polls as legal precedents are by the science of law', but rather, as a 'dynamic thing to be created and continuously recreated'.[30] This by no means implied manipulation—only in 'non-democratic societies', as Morgenthau argued, is 'consent...created by the government's monopolistic manipulation of the mass media of communication'. Rather, the purpose of leadership was for them to provoke a 'free interplay of plural opinions and interests' and a multitude 'out of which the consensus of the majority' may legitimately emerge; to reopen 'the dialogue between the government and the people thereby restoring to the democratic process at least a measure of vitality'.[31]

In sum then, Niebuhr and Morgenthau's response to what they saw as the dangers of liberal disenchantment was a strategy of political mobilization: an attempt to evoke a public philosophy able to speak the language of purpose and power, to construe a civic subjectivity based on faith in and humility before shared moral principles, and to initiate a culture of political leadership equipped to spur and to stir. Given our current predicament, could such measures be of relevance for the present as well?

10.4. BEYOND THE FALSE DILEMMAS OF 'NO RELIGION' OR 'NOBLE LIES'

To answer that question, realism must be confronted more directly with the identity politics of today. Does the realist call for critique and transformation escape the problems of autonomy and fragmentation that the 'no religion' policies of a deconstructivist ethos face? And if so, does its insistence on the need for a transcendent framework to fence in fragmentation not merely erect those 'noble lies' which the neoconservative agenda calls out for? Arguably, the distinctiveness of Niebuhr and Morgenthau's cure, and hence its relevance for contemporary challenges, is visible only if we approach it as a sociology of citizenship, rather than merely a theory of institutions. Like all realists, Niebuhr and Morgenthau were concerned with the question of power in democracy, and, crucially, how to constrain it. Yet addressing the issue at a much deeper level than that of legal arrangements, the division of power relied in their opinion ultimately on the kinds of subjectivity expressed by the public; on the teachings of Tocqueville, not Montesquieu. Only Tocqueville asked about consequences: what kind of individual will democracy produce? Turning that query on its head, Niebuhr and Morgenthau ask us to consider what kind of individual will produce democracy: what kind of soul, what kind of ethos, if a truly politicized and vibrant republic is to be achieved?

To some extent, the pursuit of a particular kind of citizen is at the heart of both subversive and conservative agendas too: subversive strategies pursuing a civic posture of resistance, conservative policies a posture of submission. But neither deconstructive nor neoconservative strategies are sufficiently attentive to the question of civic subjectivity because they do not fully address the issue of actual production: how, over time, are the postures pursued to be energized, mobilized, and sustained? Indeed, lacking a concept of human motivation—a concept made impossible by the radically anti-essentialist foundations of both approaches— neither deconstructivsm nor neoconservatism put forward a strategy of process: they may stipulate the characteristics of the kinds of personality they wish to construe, but cutting themselves off from deeper assumptions about human motivations or psychology, they effectively cut themselves off from formulating a theory of how to (re)produce this over time. What will lastingly and perpetually cultivate and sustain subjectivity in systems that aspire either to absolute openness or closure? What, in the disenchanted system of near atomization and disintegration, will energize subversion? Or, if the public philosophy teaches only stasis and conformity, how will it hold onto a citizenry whose human condition is bound to search for perspectives—political, spiritual, religious—through which to deal with difference and change?

It is important to stress that the brand of realism endorsed finds much in a subversive ethics with which to agree. To the epistemological sceptic, deeply committed to countering national self-aggrandizement or ideological idolatry, resistance is the main political posture to be valued. But what, the realist asks, will nurture resistance in a world devoid of collective meaning? If we insist on freedom simply as a function of disenchantment—a 'protest', as Jacques Derrida terms it, 'against citizenship ... against membership of a political configuration as such'—then what will commit the citizen to action?[32] If we assume, as Ernesto Laclau does, that 'the greater the structural indeterminacy, the freer a society will be', how is politics, understood as the struggle over ideas, to find substantial issues over which to struggle at all?[33] These are questions that deconstructivism—hesitant to speculate or speak about human nature or needs—is incapable of answering, and which many on a political left, sceptical of the narratives of community, nation, or church, cannot adequately respond to. Taking heed of Niebuhr and Morgenthau's advice, it is hard not to doubt the efficiency of an ethics which rejects all attempts to define what is politically worth striving for in substantive terms, because what, in the absence of shared concepts of lasting or substantial worth, will inspire action or fortify contestation?[34] Certainly, difference depends on perpetual protests against definitions which seek to coerce either community or history into a dogmatic mould. To the extent that such protest is indeed to be perpetual however—to the extent that struggle is to be fed and revitalized—difference also relies on some measure of substance, enchantment, and affect.

In recognition of this schism, realism—while advocating an ethics of subversion not unlike that of deconstructivism—posits an unusually complex understanding of the relationship between personal meaning, public narrative, and active citizenry. This is not to suggest that realism is simply a form of communitarianism. There is a marked difference between the realist employment of communal narrative as a vehicle for individual vitality, and a communitarian position which views commonality as democracy's 'ideal condition' or insists that 'political debate ought to be conducted with agreement as a regulative ideal'.[35] Even more crucially, it is pivotal to distinguish between a genuinely enchanted realist vision of community and the purely strategic certitudes pushed by the neoconservatives. Realism seeks to re-enchant modern politics for the purpose of pluralism; neoconservative agendas for that of concord. Inherent to the neoconservative search for a re-enchanted public sphere is a basic assumption about political stability as dependent upon communal unity, an assumption that means that civic critique is regarded as a dangerous attempt to catalyse social fragmentation by 'inflaming passions'.[36] But 'bipartisanship', as Morgenthau elucidates the realist position, 'never did imply ... that the opposition should forego what is not only its privilege but also its mission, whose fulfilment is indispensable for the proper functioning of the democratic process: to submit alternative policies for the administration to adopt or else for the people to support by changing the administration'.[37] To endorse a recovery of narratives of community from a realist angle, then, is part of an attempt to inspire the creation of alternatives and hence to secure rather than contract a space for plurality.

The distinctive version of realism which Niebuhr and Morgenthau developed, in other words, instigates a radical break with founding dichotomies of the particular and the universal, arguing that practices of *identification* may serve to catapult processes of critique, dissent, and hence *differentiation*. That is a move that also sets them apart from most other realists, often sceptical of allowing diversity into the body politic. It would be misleading to deny that Niebuhr and Morgenthau share some conventional assumptions with this 'liberalism of fear'.[38] Both drew extensively on its arguments and priorities, uncomfortable with the ambitious moral vocabularies at play in modern politics. But if sympathetic to the Hobbesian idea that political power is best restrained where allegiance to authority is based on sober recognition for what it is—power, and as such, lethal—rather than seductive ideas of collective destiny, they had serious doubts about the checks and balances of a fully disenchanted republic. They agreed that fear is a strong motivation for political submission, and that at times it can even serve as the basis for political humility and tolerance. But it cannot inspire positive, creative, or constructive political agendas, and hence political participation. More ambitiously, and perhaps even less in tune with a somber Hobbesianism, there is an aspiration for more than mere survival in Niebuhr and Morgenthau's attitude: an often explicit claim that though moral categories will tend to be exploited, they remain the defining trait of human civilization and the vehicle of justice understood as critique of the status quo.

This point has implications for how to think of the role of utopias in politics. A realism along the lines sketched here would have to agree with Simon Critchley's deconstructivist remark that immanentism—understood as the belief in the realizability of utopias—'is the greatest danger in politics'.[39] This is exactly what Niebuhr means when he challenges all those who advocate absolute ideals in politics and 'falsely regard them as realizable rather than as transcendent principles'.[40] Yet if we accept that the inspiration to develop alternatives to the status quo, and the motivation to advance and pursue these, rely on some degree on involvement with the world—on an element of meaningfulness—it becomes clear that a measure of fixation or 'immantism' is not merely unavoidable, but even desirable. As a critique of the extensive closures of the neoconservative sort, Critchley is right that 'no political form can or should attempt to embody justice'. But to claim that justice 'must always lie outside the public realm, guiding, criticizing and deconstructing that realm, but never being instantiated within it'[41] is to miss out on what engages human beings in the struggle for justice to begin with. The point is particularly clear in Niebuhr's and Morgenthau's discussions of religion in politics, and their repeated insistence on various forms of faith as a source of imagination, transformation, and inclusion.[42] 'Man's vitality', as Niebuhr put it, 'is an expression of his quest for meaning which negates the "secularism" of modern democratic idealism and refutes the erroneous belief that man would be more creative in society and history, if he would confine himself within its limits.'[43] What he meant to imply with that verdict, and what is perhaps the most important aspect of his appropriation of 'enchantment' for political purposes today, was that faith—and the cultural, political, and religious utopias it generates—may play a positive politicizing function in democracy. Obviously, the core virtue of transcendent ideals in politics is their function as a source of charity, humility, and forgiveness. But this kind of argument also entails that such ideals are simultaneously productive of—and a precondition for—more assertive attitudes of imagination and creation.[44] In this sense, realism, far from the enemy of utopian thought, is its advocate, arguing that without an enchanted vision, there can be no drive, no struggle, no *life* in politics. Or, as Niebuhr put the point: 'mere emphasis upon religious humility may empty the political struggle of seriousness, persuading men that all causes are equally true or false.'[45]

Admittedly, this is a concern that advocates of the subversive agenda have now themselves begun to acknowledge. William Connolly, in his recent work on the flaws of a fully fledged secularism, helps highlight the mutually constitutive relationship between collective vision and political action when he explains that:

> ... generic cynicism is at risk of becoming the defining mark of the sophisticated left. Any expression of attachment to the world is thus chastised by being treated as incompatible with a commitment to social justice. But attachment to the world, it seems to me, provides an invaluable source for participation in the politics of social justice ... It may be wise then, to cultivate little spaces of enchantment, both individually and collectively, partly for your own sake and partly to lend energy to political struggles against unnecessary suffering.[46]

Connolly's observation is timely and may be indicative of a more general shift.[47] On the academic as well as the political left, there seems to be an increased awareness of the need for a competitive rhetorical armor—a development expressed in the growing concern with the darker sides of secularism in both post-structural literature, political debate, and the public media. However, while aspiring to 'cultivate a public ethos of engagement in which a wider variety of perspectives than hereto acknowledged inform and restrain one another' as Connolly suggests, it is difficult not to feel a lingering concern that the critical left, pervaded by resistance to the ethos of subversion, currently lacks the narrative and philosophical resources to bring such revived engagement about. The political left may want to escape the cynicism of complete disenchantment, but it will not find much useful advice from deconstructivists, who having rejected all notions of human 'nature' or 'psychology', are ill-suited to answer, let alone appreciate, the motivational and spiritual dimensions of politics.[48]

If theoretical resources that balance epistemological scepticism, critical political potential, and yet narrative or mobilizing power are to be found in contemporary political theory, the one voice which really stands out would seem to be that of

Richard Rorty. Rorty's pragmatist endorsement of an anti-essentialist, yet substantially committed, willful, and hopeful 'ironism' shares many concerns with realist thought, most notably the stress on rhetorics, narrative, and mobilization.[49] Rorty believes that a politics of the left must always exercise 'irony', but that to do so, it must simultaneously convince, persuade, and *move*. For this purpose, he suggests a strategy of sentimental storytelling, emphasizing that to be effective, political messages must be affective. Yet the depth of the realist search for a spiritual dimension to politics goes well beyond a mere concern with instrumental 'rhetoric'. To the pragmatist, our personal and political transgressions may be corrected with the mere exertion of 'irony', and if irony be understood as what John Diggins terms 'the minds way of dealing with the wounds of the heart', perhaps the realist would agree.[50] But there is no place for a 'heart' in the pragmatic vocabulary, and hence no depth to the kind of power, grief, or tragedy it mourns. According to Rorty, 'irony' does not grow from a sense of tragedy, but rather from light-headed and playful encounters with contingency teaching us not 'to take ourselves too seriously'.[51] Pragmatism considers irony the entertaining activity of endlessly spinning the hermeneutic wheel of human interpretation. Realism views it as a searching struggle to come to terms with power, evil, and pride.

More than mere 'tolerance', what grows from this deeper recognition of human limitations is a sense of humility that aspires to move forward, as Abraham Lincoln proposed, 'with malice toward none, with charity for all'.[52] In contrast to the deconstructive or pragmatist belief that a radically disenchanted view of justice is a precondition for democratic principles of difference and dissent, realism insists that a sense of faith, understood as the spiritual recognition of transcendent principles and our incapacity to fully understand or realize these, is necessary for a truly charitable and forgiving democratic dialogue. Unquestionably, perverted forms of religious belief merely aggravate human antagonism. But if the experience of fallibility is transformed into some sense of finitude before transcendent principles, this may serve to dampen conflict and to transform the relativism that lurks in the recognition of contingency, into lessons of self-restraint and forbearance.[53] Realism thus opens the door for a perspective which considers awareness of the complete transcendence of God's law a potentially moderating force in politics, as it reminds us both of our finitude and of our tendency to deny it. Genuine forms of faith in other words, might actually work 'to limit the often fanatical ambitions of man and to foster a sense of compromise and conciliation'.[54]

At the deepest level then, what the kind of realism advanced by Niebuhr and Morgenthau suggests for our contemporary predicament is not only that we rethink the role of communal narrative in advancing a radically pluralist and emancipatory agenda but also, even more controversially, that we redefine the relationship between faith and politics. Responding to the rise of various forms of religious neo-orthodoxy, contemporary observers are increasingly inclined to pit 'God' against democratic government, viewing moral conviction and political tolerance as inherently opposite postures.[55] Given the fundamentalist face which much contemporary religion puts up, this is hardly an unreasonable verdict, nor one which realists oppose: Niebuhr and Morgenthau too found zealous conviction the enemy of tolerant politics. Both held modern forms of faith responsible for much of the absolutism which had brought the twentieth century to the brink of destruction, and both found it 'open to serious doubt' whether 'religious ages are monopolistically or even especially productive of the values of civilization, as commonly understood'.[56] If they shared our current diagnosis of organized religion however, they would not have agreed with contemporary cures: that religious certitudes may be countered by the mere defence of *ir*religion. 'Most of the failures of the modern age', Morgenthau argued in this vein, 'stem from one single source: the lack of religiosity. Modern man has become a self-sufficient entity who knows what he sees and can do what he wills.' His point was not that we should—or can—reverse the process of secularization. It was to 'warn modern man against the irreligious self-glorification, which is in a sense his self-mutilation'.[57]

Is there something to be said for the claim that only if we maintain some form of eschatological proviso will we be able to remind ourselves that no human project is of absolute value?[58] It goes without saying that a mere 'return' to religion would, as David Harlan puts it, be 'little more than a regression into the womb of irresponsibility'. But responsibility, as Harlan also suggests, may well dictate a serious search for secular substitutes of its virtues: 'its realism, its recognition of human weakness and finitude . . . its acceptance of anguish and doubt' and its 'determination to confront our isolation and solitude without giving in to despair'.[59] The rush to make God an ally is indeed an imminent threat to contemporary democracy. But may the language of genuine transcendence still prove its most powerful shield?

10.5. CONCLUSION: TOWARDS A REALIST STRATEGY OF REPUBLICAN PEACE?

This chapter began with a claim that we live in a Schmittean world: a present prone to counter fragmentation with aggressive revivals of religious or nationalist absolutism.[60] Against such a background, it is understandable why nation and church have come to appear as the enemy of tolerance or inclusion, yet the case for realism made here suggests a different conclusion: that perhaps it is from *within* the language of faith or community that resistance must be sought. This is a crucial point, which connects to the realist view of how the national and the international connect. Above all, I want to conclude, the realism of Niebuhr and Morgenthau was a theory of the *linkages* between domestic and foreign policy: a strategy of 'Republican Peace' parallel to, but also corrective of, the liberal assumption that democracies are less prone to go to war.

Admittedly, to claim that realism may be read as a normative commitment to republican modes of civic resistance is not the textbook story. Indeed, it is exactly the *lack* of concern with what goes on inside the state that critics portray as realism's most fatal failure: in the words of Bruce Russett, it would cause the 'very edifice of realism to collapse if attributes of states political systems are shown to have a major influence on which states do or do not fight each other'.[61] It is true that realism refuses to discriminate between political societies as either virtuous or evil: to think oneself virtuous is exactly where evil begins. But while it does not 'expect even the wisest of nations to escape every peril of moral and spiritual complacency, for nations have always been constitutionally self-righteous', it does trust certain forms of political community to be more self-conscious of that complacency, and more prone to cultivate dynamics which will counter or restrain it.[62] To a certain extent then, the realism of Niebuhr and Morgenthau identifies a connection not unlike that of the Democratic Peace theory: that the features of a nation's political culture make a difference to the attitudes expressed in its foreign policy.[63] This, however, is where agreement ends, for while the Democratic Peace theorists assert peace as an inherent or automatic function of the political perfection of democracy, Niebuhr and Morgenthau believe it a function rather of acknowledging our inherent *im*perfection, and of pursuing the measures—debate, dissent, opposition—needed to remind us of that finitude. A republican polity will not be immune to the lures of pride or pretension. But it will, as Niebuhr argued, 'make a difference whether the culture in which the policies of nations are formed' contains 'a dimension . . . from the standpoint of which the element of vanity in all human ambitions and achievements is discerned'.[64]

Evoking that standpoint is not without peril, as the recovery of transcendence may well unleash affect in ways that make policy a 'prisoner of passions it has itself aroused'.[65] It is thus pivotal that we practically and perpetually debate the value, scope, and limits of constructing 'patriotic' or more broadly 'spiritual' subjectivities in an era where other and less hesitant forces would want to make popular 'faith' a vehicle of narrow political interest. A realist patriotism, as Jean Bethke Elstain puts it, must be a chastened one.[66] What is notable in Niebuhr and Morgenthau's advice on that challenge is their insistence that striking a balance need not mean making a trade-off: that commitment may in fact be a *precondition* for detachment. In both their writings, the stress on certain political principles or purposes as *transcendent* is meant to keep the democratic dialogue open—a means to remind us that the ultimate meaning of moral categories escape us, and to use this reminder of the insurmountable distance between promise and fact as a constant fertilizer of open and plural debate. In this sense, theirs was a patriotism that set out to stir and not close imagination, blending liberal and conservative impulses to cultivate a public ethos of enchanted dissent.

The final question, however, is whether such a form of patriotism is likely to prevail. It is pivotal to tackle the hard question of why, when the realist critique of an overly aggressive and triumphalist foreign policy seems now to appeal to broader audiences on both the left and the right, it is nationalist complacency and not realist humility that seems to win out. Is there an inherent tension between what appeals intellectually, and what works politically—and one which the realist analysis of the political need for mobilization only too readily understands? In the very short run, the answer would seem to be yes. While suspicious of the deconstructive reluctance to engage with questions of substantial purpose, realism too must find itself the weaker party in competing with a 'noble lie', insisting that no genuine sense of transcendence may be cynically and centrally construed. As was the fate of fascism and Nazism though, contemporary certitudes are bound to fail in adequately coming to terms with ambiguity: only authentic forms of meaningfulness which will deepen and describe rather than gloss over, or protest against, human finitude are likely to perform that task. These take time to grow however, and while certainly open to political cultivation do not lend themselves to simple manufacturing. 'May civilization recover its... faith by an act of will?' Morgenthau once asked in a review essay on Arnold Toynbee. If that question is as timely as ever, so is the patience advised in his final reply:

Neither a teacher nor a whole civilization can create sentiments of collective meaning out of the fragments of religions, whose decline has made the restoration of religiosity necessary in the first place. What religions will grow from this new religiosity man must leave to faith. He must be content to be ready, and to make others ready, to see the signs and to read them aright when they appear.[67]

NOTES

1. Henry Luce, 'The American Century', *Life*, 10 (1941).
2. For an analysis of Carl Schmitt's thoughts on the link between national homogeneity, international antagonism, and political order, see William E. Scheuerman, *Carl Schmitt: The End of Law* (Maryland: Rowman & Littlefield, 1999).
3. Martti Koskenniemi, *The Gentle Civilizer of Nations: The Rise and Fall of International Law 1870–1960* (Cambridge: Cambridge University Press, 2001), p. 440.
4. On this point, see also William Scheuerman's contribution to the present volume.
5. Rengger, *Political Theory, Modernity and Postmodernity: Beyond Enlightenment and Critique* (Oxford: Blackwell, 1995), pp. 77–127. It should be noted that Rengger applied these two labels in a more limited fashion than I do: to describe the 'moods' of late twentieth-century Western political theory.
6. Anthony Giddens, Ulrich Beck, and Scott Lasch, *Reflexive Modernization: Politics, Tradition and Aesthetics in the Modern Social Order* (Cambridge: Polity Press, 1994).
7. Gitlin, *The Intellectuals and the Flag* (New York: Columbia University Press, 2006), p. 2. For a historical analysis of the de-politicization of the left, see John Patrick Diggins, *The American Left in the Twentieth Century* (New York: Hartcourt, 1973).
8. Katznelson, *Desolation and Enlightenment: Political Knowledge after Total War, Totalitarianism, and the Holocaust* (New York: Columbia University Press, 2003), pp. 156–7.
9. Kristol, 'The Coming Conservative Century' in his *Neo-conservatism: Selected Essays 1949–1995* (New York: Free Press, 1995), p. 365.
10. Viroli, *For Love of Country* (New York: Oxford University Press, 1995), pp. 14–15.
11. For interpretations of the link between the contemporary politics of emergency and Schmittean identity politics, see Shadia Drury, *Leo Strauss and The American Right* (Albany: SUNY, 1993); and El-Din Aysha, 'Huntington's Shift To the Declinist Camp: Conservative Declinism and the "Historical Function" of the Clash of Civilizations', *International Relations*, 7 (2003), pp. 29–452.

12. Kristol, 'Some Reflections on Capitalism and "The Free Society" [1970]', in Mark Gerson (ed.), *The Essential Neo-Conservative Reader* (Reading: Addison-Wesley, 1996), p. 115.

13. On post–World War II American political theory, see Katznelson, *Desolation and Enlightenment*. See also John Patrick Diggins, 'Knowledge and Sorrow: Louis Hartz's Quarrel with American History', *Political Theory*, 16 (1988), pp. 355–76.

14. Andrew Linklater, *The Transformation of Political Community* (Cambridge: Polity Press, 1998), p. 15.

15. Petersen, 'Breathing Nietzsche's Air: New Reflections on Morgenthau's Concepts of Power and Human Nature', *Alternatives*, 24 (1999), p. 111.

16. See for instance Christoph Frei, *Hans J. Morgenthau: An Intellectual Biography* (Baton Rouge: Louisiana State University Press, 2001); Koskenniemi, *The Gentle Civilizer of Nations*; Scheuerman, *Carl Schmitt*; and Michael C. Williams, *The Realist Tradition and the Limits of International Relations* (Cambridge: Cambridge University Press, 2005), as well as Chapters 4, 5, and 3 by Turner, Molloy, and Scheuerman, respectively, in this volume.

17. Or, as Niebuhr's brother Richard put it, 'The essence of irreligion...is the sense of self-sufficient finitude'. Richard Niebuhr, quoted in Charles C. Brown, *Niebuhr and His Age: Reinhold Niebuhr's Prophetic Role and Legacy* (Harrisburg, Pennsylvania: Trinity Press International, 2002), p. 51.

18. Niebuhr, *The Children of Light and the Children of Darkness* (London: Nisbet & Co. Ltd., 1944), p. 49.

19. Morgenthau, 'On Trying to Be Just', in *Truth and Power: Essays of a Decade 1960–70* (New York: Praeger, 1970), pp. 62, 63.

20. Niebuhr, 'Optimism, Pessimism, and Religious Faith [1940]', in Robert McAfee Brown (ed.), *The Essential Reinhold Niebuhr: Selected Essays and Addresses* (New Haven: Yale University Press, 1986), pp. 15–16.

21. Hans J. Morgenthau, 'The Decline of the Democratic Process (1956)', in Morgenthau (ed.), *Politics in the Twentieth Century I* (Chicago: University of Chicago Press, 1962).

22. Hans J. Morgenthau, 'Freedom (1957)', in Morgenthau, *Politics in the Twentieth Century III* (Chicago: University of Chicago Press, 1962), p. 77.

23. Pocock, The *Machiavellian Moment: Florentine Political Thought and the Atlantic Republican Tradition* (Princeton: Princeton University Press, 1975).

24. Hans J. Morgenthau, *The Purpose of American Politics* (Washington: University Press of America, 1982 [1960]), p. 65.

25. Morgenthau, *The Purpose of American Politics*, p. 66.

26. Morgenthau, *The Purpose of American Politics*, p. 65. Italics added.

27. Morgenthau, 'The Right to Dissent' in *Truth and Power*, p. 44. Italics added.

28. For an analysis of how and when public dissent may be justified, see Hans J. Morgenthau, 'The Corruption of Patriotism (1955)', in Morgenthau (ed.), *Politics in the Twentieth Century I*, p. 407. For a discussion of his views on leadership, see also Turner's Chapter 4 in this volume.

29. Morgenthau, 'The Decline of the Democratic Process', p. 381.

30. Morgenthau, 'The Subversion of Foreign Policy (1956)', in Morgenthau (ed.), *Politics in the Twentieth Century I*, p. 418.

31. Morgenthau, 'Freedom', p. 98.

32. Derrida, quoted in David Campbell, 'Why Fight: Humanitarianism, Principles and Post-Structuralism', *Millennium*, 27 (1998), p. 503.

33. Laclau, *New Reflections on the Revolutions of Our Times* (London: Verso, 1990), p. 44.

34. For a succinct examination of the deconstructive ideal, see Kari Palonen, 'The History of Concepts as a Style of Political Theorizing: Quentin Skinner's and Reinhart Koselleck's Subversion of Normative Theory', *European Journal of Political Theory*, 1 (2002), pp. 91–106.

35. David Miller, 'Bounded Citizenship', in Kimberly Hutchings and Roland Dannreuther (eds.), *Cosmopolitan Citizenship* (London: MacMillan, 1999), p. 63.

36. Irving Kristol, 'American Intellectuals and Foreign Policy (1967)', in Kristol (ed.), *Neo-Conservatism: The Autobiography of an Idea* (New York: The Free Press, 1995), pp. 76–7.

37. Morgenthau, *The Decline of the Democratic Process*, p. 382.

38. Judith N. Shklar, *Political Thought and Political Thinkers* (Chicago: University of Chicago Press, 1998).

39. Critchley, 'Deconstruction and Pragmatism: Is Derrida a Private Ironist or Public Liberal', in Chantal Mouffe (ed.), *Deconstruction & Pragmatism* (London: Routledge, 1996), p. 36.

40. Niebuhr, *The Nature and Destiny of Man: A Christian Interpretation II* (London: Nisbet, 1943), p. 264.

41. Critchley, 'Deconstruction and Pragmatism', p. 36.

42. For interesting points on the realist use of religion in democracy, see June Bingham, *Courage to Change: An Introduction to the Life and Thought of Reinhold Niebuhr* (New York: Charles Scribner's Sons, 1972); Mary Doak, 'Hope, Eschatology, and Public Life: The Contributions of Rauschenbusch, Mathews, and Niebuhr to Reopening the American Imagination', *American Journal of Theology & Philosophy*, 23 (2002), pp. 409–23; Martin E. Marty, 'Reinhold Niebuhr: Public Theology and the American Experience', *The Journal of Religion*, 54 (1974), pp. 332–59; and Roger L. Shinn, 'Realism, Radicalism, and Eschatology in Reinhold Niebuhr: A Reassessment', *The Journal of Religion*, 54 (1974), pp. 409–23.

43. Niebuhr, *The Childen of Light and the Children of Darkness*, pp. 39–40.

44. Reinhold Niebuhr, 'Religious Politics (1951)', in Charles C. Brown (ed.), *A Niebuhr Reader: Selected Essays, Articles, and Book Reviews* (Philadelphia: Trinity Press International, 1992), p. 50.

45. Niebuhr, 'Christian Faith and Political Controversy (1952)', in Brown (ed.), *A Niebuhr Reader*, p. 48.

46. Connolly, *Why I Am Not a Secularist* (Minneapolis: Minnesota University Press, 1999), pp. 16–17.

47. Chantal Mouffe has also moved in this direction: *The Democratic Paradox* (London: Verso, 2000). Similarly, Cornelius Castoriadis calls for a new type of imaginary that would define goals that people considered worth striving for: Castoriadis, *The Rise of Insignificance* (Athens: Ypsilon Books, 2000).

48. Connolly, *Why I Am Not a Secularist*, p. 5.

49. Rorty, *Contingency, Irony, and Solidarity* (Cambridge: Cambridge University Press, 1989). For an appropriation of Rortian pragmatism in international relations, see Molly Cochran, *Normative Theory in International Relations: A Pragmatic Approach* (Cambridge: Cambridge University Press, 1999).

50. Diggins, 'Knowledge and Sorrow', p. 356.

51. Rorty, *Contingency, Irony, and Solidarity*, p. 74.

52. Abraham Lincoln, 'Second Inaugural Address [1865]', in John Gabriel Hunt (ed.), *The Essential Abraham Lincoln* (New York: Gramercy Books, 1993). Both Niebuhr and Morgenthau saw Lincoln as the incarnation of an ideal form of secular religiosity.

53. On this point, see particularly Reinhold Niebuhr, 'In the Battle and Above It [1942]', in Brown (ed.), *A Niebuhr Reader*, pp. 61–2.
54. Mark L. Haas, 'Reinhold Niebuhr's Christian Pragmatism: A Principled Alternative to Consequentialism', *The Review of Politics*, 61 (1999), p. 612.
55. See, for example, Timothy Samuel Shah and Monica Duffy Toft, 'Why God is Winning', *Foreign Policy* (July/August 2006), pp. 39–43.
56. Hans J. Morgenthau, 'The Rediscovery of Imagination: Arnold Toynbee', *Politics in the Twentieth Century III*, p. 61.
57. Morgenthau, 'The Rediscovery of Imagination', p. 60.
58. Doak, 'Hope, Eschatology, and Public Life', p. 125.
59. David Harlan, *The Degradation of American History* (Chicago: University of Chicago Press, 1997). p. 42.
60. Hence the claim by George W. Bush, that the 9/11 attacks represented not only a tragedy but also a 'unique opportunity' for America to recover 'our mission and our moment'. Bush, *State of the Union Address*, delivered on 29 February 2002.
61. Russett, 'And Yet it Moves', *International Security*, 19 (1995), p. 164. Michael Loriaux is slightly less categorical in his claim that realists tend to express a 'certain hesitation to discriminate between political societies according to the supposed merits of their domestic constitutional structures and values'. Michael Loriaux, 'The Realists and Saint Augustine: Skepticism, Psychology, and Moral Action in International Relations Thought', *International Studies Quarterly*, 36 (1992), p. 407.
62. Reinhold Niebuhr, *The Irony of American History* (New York: Charles Scribner, 1962), p. 150.
63. The Democratic Peace debates were triggered by Michael W. Doyle, 'Kant, Liberal Legacies and Foreign Affairs', *Philosophy and Public Affairs*, 12 (1983), pp. 205–35. For a recent restatement, see Bruce Russett and John R. Oneal, *Triangulating Peace: Democracy, Interdependence, and International Organizations* (New York: Norton, 2001).
64. Niebuhr, *The Irony of American History*, p. 150.
65. Richard Ned Lebow, *The Tragic Vision of Politics: Ethics, Interests and Orders* (Cambridge: Cambridge University Press, 2003), p. 242.
66. Elstain, 'Is there a Feminist Tradition on War and Peace?', in Terry Nardin (ed.), *The Ethics of War and Peace: Religious and Secular Perspectives* (Princeton: Princeton University Press, 1996), pp. 225–6.
67. Morgenthau, 'The Rediscovery of Imagination', p. 61. On this theme, see also Morgenthau, 'Thought and Action in Politics', *Social Research*, 35 (1971), p. 19.

11

Political Theory and the Realistic Spirit

Ze'ev Emmerich

I open books on right and on ethics, I listen to the scholars and jurisconsults and, moved by their ingratiating discourses, I deplore the miseries of nature, I admire the peace and justice established by civil order, I bless the wisdom of public institutions, and console myself for being a man by seeing that I am a citizen. Fully instructed about my duties and happiness, I close the book, leave the class-room, and look around me; I see unfortunate peoples groaning under an iron yoke, mankind crushed by a handful of oppressors, starving masses overwhelmed by pain and hunger, whose blood and tears the rich drink in peace, and everywhere the strong armed against the weak with the frightful power of the laws.[1]

11.1. INTRODUCTION

Philosophers have quarrelled for centuries about the relationship between thought and reality. At the centre of their concern has been the question of whether it is possible to say anything of cognitive value about 'reality in itself'. In contemporary philosophical debates, this problem is couched as in principle a question about whether talk of reality as it is outside any of its representations makes sense. The term 'philosophical realism' has traditionally been used to describe those doctrines that have given a positive answer to this question. However, the term 'realism' and its derivatives have other uses, one of which is related to a theory, a set of beliefs, desires or expectations being realistic. An example would be when we '...tell someone to "be realistic", when he is maintaining something in the teeth of the facts, or even refuses to look at them. Or again if he knows what the facts ought to be, either from a theory or wishful thinking, and will not take the world to be something capable of shaking his beliefs.'[2] On these occasions we make a distinction between realistic and unrealistic individuals or groups on the basis of their willingness to take account of what Cora Diamond calls 'surface phenomena', namely, those facts of life about the existence and significance of which people agree in a mundane rather than philosophical sense. This form of realism has been labelled by Diamond 'The Realistic Spirit'.

In this chapter, I seek to defend the importance of this sense of realism, and to offer a way of thinking about the character of political theory that is consistent with it. Realism will be identified negatively, in so far as a theory or a doctrine will be taken to be un-realistic if it is possible to identify in it an omission of a significant aspect of or a fact about political life. Realism here denotes a procedure for the evaluation of doctrines, rather than an alternative of a precise kind, and its aim is to examine the degree to which certain conceptions of politics correspond to politics as we know it. On this view, theories can be more or less realistic in their treatment of specific aspects of political life. They may be wholly realistic in their treatment of and sensitivity towards one aspect of politics, while at the same time entirely un-realistic in relation to other such aspects. As a rule of thumb, it would be overly optimistic to expect a theory to be entirely realistic—to expect that it would be *all* inclusive as well as equally sensitive towards *all* surface phenomena. Such an expectation would be premised upon unwarrantedly optimistic beliefs about human cognitive powers. Accounting for all past, present, and future phenomena would require something like cognitive omnipotence coupled with a high degree of clairvoyance, both of which are clearly out of reach for humans as we know them. Realism, in other words, denotes an attitude characterized by sensitivity to the details of 'surface phenomena' coupled with a propensity to accept the limits of theorization, in our case, the limits of theorizing about politics.

This chapter criticizes the dominant strands of contemporary political theory as preserving a traditional propensity to think about politics as essentially a domestic matter.[3] Roughly speaking, authors within the genre have been interested primarily in questions concerning the appropriate structure of 'political associations' (e.g. the *polis* in antiquity, or the state today). International concerns have been taken by them to be derivatives of (or secondary to) domestic ones. Being captivated by a picture according to which politics is understood primarily in terms of the norms that govern or ought to govern political associations, many contemporary authors either look for similarities between the domestic and the international arenas, or amplify the differences between the two. Since neither of them corresponds to the facts—or the surface phenomena—of contemporary politics as we know it, neither of these strategies is realistic.

The discussion begins with a general characterization of the internal logic (or the internal rationale) of political theory. Debates among political theorists will be characterized as essentially disputes concerning the correct understanding of, and the right attitude towards, 'humans as historical beings': between those who base their views on abstract conceptions of humans (John Rawls, Jürgen Habermas) and those who attempt to increase our awareness of the irreducibility of the historical dimension in our understanding of humans (Alasdair MacIntyre, Charles Taylor, and Richard Rorty). The protagonists of these two positions will be labelled 'abstractionists' and 'contextualists', respectively. The final sections examine avenues of thought that conceive the relations between the domestic and the foreign/international as mutually shaping and reinforcing each other. Put slightly differently, the last section attempts to point at a possible 'realist' route for thinking about politics which, while accepting many of the contentions made by the contextualists, also endeavours to ease the grips of prioritizing internal affairs over international ones. In particular, I argue that we need to reconsider the centrality of 'human sentiments' in the shaping of domestic and international matters.

More precisely, this chapter seeks to make the following related arguments. First, in keeping with the realistic spirit political theory has to offer a better account of human 'moral psychology', focusing on the interplay between sentiments and reason and its impact on human affairs. Second, any such account needs to avoid treating human sentiments and human reason as two entirely autonomous human endowments, for they are integrally intertwined. Moreover, third, both the content of and the interplay between reason and sentiment are intricately related to the specific historical circumstances within which they appear. For this reason, attempts to discuss and evaluate the political significance of human sentiments and human rationality *in abstractis*—outside the historical context to which they supposed to apply—are of limited value. Finally, the emergence of commerce and the rise of commercial societies are arguably the most significant historical developments which mark the difference between the ancient and the modern world. What is needed, therefore, is an account of the particular interplay between human rationality and sentiments in a commercial world-order.

11.2. TWO COMPONENTS OF POLITICAL THEORY

In *The Social Contract*, Rousseau explains his project in the following way:

I want to inquire whether in the civil order there can be some legitimate and sure rule of administration, taking men as they are, and the laws as they can be: In this inquiry I shall try always to combine what right permits with what interest prescribes, so that justice and utility may not disjoin.[4]

The political theorist, according to such a view, is concerned with answering the question of how to achieve legitimate 'civil order' and 'rule of administration'. This, Rousseau tells us, is best done by (a) identifying 'men as they are' and on the basis of that (b) determining 'the laws as they could be'. These two avowed components—the theory's 'conception of human nature' and its 'conception of the law' (or laws)—can be seen as characteristic of political theory as it has been traditionally construed.

In his insistence that legislation has to be based on manifested characteristics of human beings, Rousseau is clearly a realist. Realism of this kind is not however necessarily premised on a view of human nature as having some fixed attributes. Rather, as Rousseau saw it, humans' sense of themselves and their attitudes towards other fellow humans are subject to change. It follows from this that any serious political theory has to take *human beings as they have been historically formed* extremely seriously. This point is of utmost significance for both political theory and normative IR. Nevertheless, it incorporates the following dilemma: if one begins by understanding the task of the political theorist primarily as settling questions concerning the internal rationale of political associations, one is most naturally disposed to think about international relations in the following way—while political theory has the perceived advantage of conceiving laws which should/ought to govern this or that specific political association, it is far from clear what the status of the law is in the international arena.

11.2.1. The Laws as they Could be—the Legacy of Rawls (I)

While few share Rousseau's pessimism concerning the prospects of establishing legitimate order in the domestic as well as the international contexts, much of the contemporary literature on these matters still grapples with this dilemma. This is most manifestly evident in the writing of John Rawls. Initially construed as universal in its application, Rawls's *A Theory of Justice* generated a heated debate. As a response to his critics, in *Political Liberalism* Rawls was willing to temper his universalist zeal. Admitting a certain level of parochialism, he labelled his theory a 'liberal utopia'. Finally, in his last major contribution, *The Law of Peoples,* he turned his attention to the international domain, asking which foreign societies to tolerate and which to regard as unworthy of tolerance.[5] What we see, then, is a shift in his account of justice. Justice was first identified in terms of universal principles which might guide the laws and institutional framework of society— roughly corresponding to what Rousseau identifies as issues concerning 'civil order' and 'legitimate rule of administration'. This, in turn, was gradually changed into taking liberal (admittedly imperfect) societies as in principle (even if not in fact) just societies, which may tolerate peculiar but altogether 'decent societies', but (God forbid) not the 'unreasonable societies' that are governed by what he calls 'outlaw states'. We may say that the concept of the law in *The Law of Peoples* has changed its meaning and turned into a device for comparing the relative worth of societies, rather than a vehicle or a medium through which legitimate civil order is achieved.

Whether or not such a move is theoretically permissible has been the subject of heated debate. However, due to the tendency of especially Anglo-American political theory to couch politics in terms borrowed from a particular branch of moral theory, as evidenced by the field being dominated by the elaboration of competing 'theories of justice', the dilemma is perceived as a question concerning the scope and distribution of moral obligations, duties, or rights. At the centre of such debates is the question of whether in view of our belonging to a specific political association, the state, it is justifiable to defend a differential set of moral commitments—an extensive set of commitments to one's fellow citizens coupled with a much more thinly construed set of commitments to human beings as such.

Defenders of Rawls put forward what is *prima facie* a realistic normative justi- fication of differential moral commitments. They urge us to believe that beyond some minimal 'humanitarian concern' for the rest of humanity, the justification

of more extensive forms of justice is premised upon there being a political association. From a political point of view, they pronounce, principles of egalitarian or
distributive justice are best understood as 'associative obligations'. On this view,
our obligations are dependent upon the particular character of our relations to
one another—a character that is primarily shaped by the kinds of projects and
schemes we find ourselves in. Political justice accordingly denotes a set of special
obligations that reflect the 'reactive attitudes' or expectations of those who are
the members of (or those who are subjected to) political institutions. Proponents
of differential justice focus on, especially, the particular character of the relations
among citizens, the expectations they have from one another, as well as the specific
relations between the citizenry and the state. The special obligations that ought
to govern the relations among citizens, they explain, reflect the fact that the
interactions among citizens are different in kind from affairs between individuals
who are otherwise not members of the same political association. Thus, the 'call of
justice' as it applies to fellow citizens is different in kind from its call in relations to
members of other political associations. Following this line of thought, they claim
that members of liberal societies may or may not tolerate other societies. But,
apart from extreme cases of injustice, they are under *no* obligation to interfere in
the affairs of such societies in order to remedy even severe forms of inequality or
any other types of social ill.

This line of thought is premised upon a kind of causal argument about
the effects people's social life—especially, the institutional framework of their
societies—has on their moral outlook, expectations, and responsibilities. In this
sense, advocates of differential justice are realists of sort. But, to the extent that
they wish to preserve this realistic element of their own account, they need to
extend their causal analysis beyond the remits of making simplistic, overarching,
claims about the significance of social and political institutions in the shaping of
people's moral and political responsibility. Quite simply, all sorts of norms govern
human affairs. We may want to make distinctions between the norms that govern,
say, moral, political, economic, and amorous affairs. However,

(i). Political theorists should resist the temptation of conceiving these norms
and the spheres of life to which they belong as entirely (if at all)
autonomous domains.

(ii). They should resist the temptation of thinking about the norms we identify
or justify as exhaustive even in relation to the domains to which they are
supposed to apply. There is considerable confusion in the literature on
these matters. In particular, proponents of the differential conception of
justice tend to ignore—or fail to take sufficient account of—the causal
implications of their own view. They seem to overlook especially the fact
that:

(iii). Moral and political reasoning and action do not stop at the boundaries of
this or that particular institution. For this reason, the identification of special obligations which apply exclusively to members of this or that political
association has the further effect of establishing, perhaps even justifying,
alternative norms of conduct towards and among non-members.

Within the realm of human affairs, that is, there is no normative vacuum. For this reason, it is not sufficient to indicate or justify which clusters of norms govern human affairs in different spheres of life. What is needed is a thorough examination of the effects these norms have on each other. Thus, those who are willing to defend a conception of differential justice on the basis of essentially national boundaries would have to extend their investigation towards those types of governing rationale or regulative norms that typify interactions among individuals, groups, and institutions which transcend these boundaries. Put slightly differently, political theorists may want to account for the law within the confines of any specific political association in terms of the moral norms and the strictures of justice. But it does not follow from this that beyond the confines of political associations no law—that is, no norm-governed activity or rationale—exists. This simple truth was known to Rousseau and his contemporaries. It is probably equally admitted by political theorists nowadays. However the difference between then and now is that authors in the eighteenth century were less reluctant to specify which norms govern, say, relations among states, or for that matter, economic transactions, as part of their normative political theory. More importantly, they were willing to put forward arguments concerning the intersections and causal relations between these human interactions in different domains, including the norms that govern them, in ways which the dominant strands of contemporary literature tend to avoid.

Thus, for instance, Thomas Nagel, a leading advocate of differential justice, concludes his analysis of current affairs by stating the following:

> The path from anarchy to justice must go through injustice. It is often unclear whether, for a given problem, international anarchy is preferable to international injustice. But if we accept the political conception, the global scope of justice will expand only through developments that first increase the injustice of the world by introducing effective, but illegitimate institutions to which standards of justice apply, standards by which we may hope they will eventually be transformed. An example, perhaps, of the cunning of history.[6]

Bold as it may appear, this argument is confusing. First, analytically, since from a political conception, justice is essentially a virtue of political associations, and since co-members are under no special 'obligation' in relation to non-members, issues of political justice or injustice do not arise in the international domain. Stating that 'The path from anarchy to justice must go through injustice' is therefore either meaningless or false. Once the call of justice has been numbed, arguments can no longer be made in its name. But, second, it could be argued that the status of these claims, while analytically loose, is in principle synthetic, namely, that any historically informed conception of politics should admit that the establishment of political associations of whatever scale involves violent acts, atrocities, and other forms of misconduct. But here is the crux: viewed in this way, these statements can be read as unintentionally establishing the grounds for, even if not as directly recommending, a radical conception of political justice. If it is the case that injustice is a synthetic pre-condition of justice, says the Jacobin, why not incur a healthy dose of it in the name of a better future for humankind?

The political conception of justice, Nagel argues, has a long and respectable pedigree, one which was held by authors of very different moral and political convictions such as Hobbes and Kant. It is also one which, according to him, reflects the moral convictions of 'most people in the privileged nations of the world, so that' realistically, regardless of whether the political conception is 'true or false, it will have a significant role in determining what happens'.[7] The political conception, that is, is primarily a reflection of the sentiments of a particular group of people, whose circumstances are highly specific. Privileged and powerful, they would most definitely have a say in the shaping of future circumstances, in both the national and international domains. But the problem of justice, thus conceived, is not so much an issue related to analytical distinctions concerning what is just and unjust. Rather, it is the question of why the privileged and mighty exhibit a propensity to adopt the political conception over its alternatives. An answer to that would have to be historical in its orientation. But the history in question would be the history of human sentiments, roughly following Rousseau's first recommendation to investigate 'humans as they are'. This issue will be the focus of the remainder of this chapter.

11.2.2. Humans as they are—the Legacy of Rawls (II)

Instead of asking 'What is Rawls's conception of the law?' we could begin by asking 'What is his conception of human nature?' Much has been written about this matter. His critics have suggested two kinds of readings. The first, championed by Michael Sandel, portrays Rawls as offering us an 'unencumbered self'; a construction of a self innocent of any attachment to concrete historical (cultural as well as material) circumstances.[8] The second, championed by Onora O'Neill, accuses Rawls of constructing an 'idealized self'.[9] Interestingly, Sandel's communitarian critique coalesces with that of Kantians such as O'Neill. Both accuse Rawls of offering an unrealistic conception of humans. His, we may say, is a conception of humans that does not follow the Rousseauvian dictum—namely, that of taking people as they are. On the basis of that, both question Rawls's entire conception of justice and especially his conception of rights.

The irony is that while O'Neill and Sandel accuse Rawls's of being unrealistic in one domain, that is, in his depiction of what is true of humans as they are, it might be argued that his theory, especially his views on international matters, resembles the views expressed by American policymakers. Raymond Geuss notes that while 'Rawls's later work moves away from the Never-neverland of [his] early model with its glorification of the ignorance of agents in the original position', the conceptual apparatus and modes of reasoning expressed in *The Law of Peoples* exhibits an uncanny resemblance to US foreign policy. This is especially true of Rawls's characterization of 'Outlaw States':

'Outlaw state' is clearly Rawls' theoretical equivalent of a concept that has become one of the cornerstones of U.S. policy during the past 20 years, and has appeared in a variety of guises, from Reagan's proclamation that the Soviet Union was an 'evil empire' to the very emphatic use the term 'rogue state' by the current Bush administration.[10]

These are not necessarily incompatible interpretations of Rawls. In fact, it might be helpful to think of certain types of realist (or any other) positions concerning our attitudes towards others as based on a 'phantasm'—or an ideological bias— regarding who we are. Thus, if these lines of criticism are correct, it might be argued that Rawls's early domestic concerns are based on 'idealization' which impinges upon his later views: corresponding to no real human his theory has turned into adopting realism of a kind in the international arena. To be more specific, Rawls's *The Law of Peoples* is an expression of what many Americans, including many American academics, would consider to be a 'realistic utopia' which, as Rawls puts it, 'extends what are ordinarily thought to be the limits of practicable political possibility, and, in so doing, reconciles us to our political and social condition'.[11]

Some cosmopolitan attempts to rectify the Rawlsian approach have focused primarily on what seems to be a fact about the contemporary world, namely, that humans nowadays participate in 'cooperative schemes' on a trans-national or even global scale.[12] Consequently they argue that the scope of justice, even if we understand it essentially in terms of the political conception, ought to be global. What has been left largely unchallenged within this literature is Rawls's conception of human nature, the price of which is that their recommendations tend to be instrumental in kind. For each and every allegedly identified coopera- tive enterprise, the logic goes, a corresponding institution for the management of redistributive principles or laws should be erected. Proponents of such a view, to be sure, point to a significant aspect of modern life—the fact that interdependence among states is today qualitatively different in both its intensity and complexity from past forms of dependency. Clearly, this is a fact of utmost importance. However, without taking sufficient account of the impact such a rapid change has on humans' sense of themselves and others, their solutions tend to be too schematic.

Nagel and other defenders of a robust conception of differential justice chal- lenge Rawlsian cosmopolitanism on the ground that the mere existence of coop- erative schemes is not a sufficient condition for there being a political association. Cooperation alone cannot generate associative obligations. However, it remains an open question whether, beyond defending the status quo, these so-called asso- ciative obligations (rights, duties, and so on) have anything to do with morality, especially the kind of morality they seem to value.

Arguments in favour of any kind of differential justice are undoubtedly reflec- tions of a widespread sentiment among people. However, it seems that they reflect sentiments that are based on 'moral luck'.[13] While Nagel and other proponents of differential justice have sought to rectify the ills of 'bad luck' on the domestic level,[14] they put forward sophisticated arguments against extending the same kind of responsibilities beyond national boundaries. One's moral responsibilities, the argument goes, are dependent on the contingent circumstances of belonging to a certain political association or else the degree to which one happens to participate in cooperative schemes of various kinds. This line of thought has been criticized on the grounds that to the extent that our obligations are moral in character, they cannot be justified on the basis of arbitrary or contingent facts (place of birth, national boundaries, class, race, gender, and so on). Without rehearsing this line of criticism, it seems that a stronger—more politically oriented—argument against the differential conception of justice would take the following form: while it is true that people have no control over the circumstances of their birth, the ways in which these circumstances are conceptualized, especially the ways in which their moral and political significance is explained within each such conceptualization, although not entirely a matter of individual choice, are nevertheless a potential source for *contestation* and political struggle.

People would quite naturally wish to retain what they consider to be features of their good luck, but the challenge for any serious political theory is to include arguments about the predicament, including the moral convictions, of those who experience the unpleasant aspects of luck. For them, even more than for Machiavelli's Prince, the question 'Whether Fortuna can be tempted?' is of utmost importance. While we have no control over the circumstances of our birth, the advantages or disadvantages they confer on us are of less arbitrary origins than those which proponents of differential justice wish to admit or account for. Ignoring the historical origins of privilege, including the intellectual history of its justifications, would render these theories obsolete the moment luck turns its less accommodating face.

But there is more to accounting for 'moral luck' than tracing the origins of the current state of affairs or delineating the norms that govern affairs within and between societies with an uneven share of luck. The question of how to come to terms with and accommodate luck into our moral and political considerations is one of the most challenging components in the construction any normative theory. This is especially so given that we do not yet have a theory of moral sentiments that adequately addresses this problem. In order to be able to state more clearly which direction such a theory should take, an examination of other contemporary depictions of human nature is required.

11.2.3. Humans as they are—the Legacy of Habermas

The work of Jürgen Habermas has been enormously influential in political theory and normative IR. One way to understand the attraction of his *Theory of Communicative Action* is related to what *prima facie* is a less parochial, or a more robustly universalist approach.[15] This is not the place to examine his account in detail. However, in order to be able to characterize Habermas's conception of humans, a few comments concerning his general approach are needed.

Habermas develops and defends his theoretical position on two levels: analytical and historical. On his account the two complement and reinforce each other. In view of his quasi-Hegelian approach, a flaw in one of these dimensions has the consequence of jeopardizing the achievements in the other dimension, if not his entire comprehensive scheme. Each of these dimensions exhibits great difficulties. Analytically, his theory of communicative action is premised on the view that (a) the meaning of utterances is dependant on intersubjective consensus among participants. The 'intersubjectivist', according to Habermas:

> ...assumes that S successfully performs a given speech act if he reaches an understanding with the addressee about something in the world....It is in the achievement of mutual consensus with respect to a (potentially questionable) matter, and not the transfer of ideas, that serves here as a model of communication.[16]

Such a contention should strike us as unwarranted. Quite simply, it demands my agreement about the content of a remark issued by an interlocutor—say, her statement that I am an idiot—as a condition of the possibility for me to understand her insulting remark. The problem with such an account of meaning, hence also of communication, is that it puts the cart before the horse.[17] Thus, contrary to Habermas, in order to agree or disagree on anything, we must already understand what has been communicated to us.[18] The search for consensus is based on presupposing the possibility of a genuine understanding of the matters under discussion and not *vice versa*. Otherwise, either we think that consensus is an empty phrase, or (and this is important) consensus is better understood as reached by other means. On this last note, we may say that the history of reaching consensus—and, more generally, of consent—suggests that agreement is not necessarily the end-product of a (purely) cognitive (communicative or purely rational) enterprise. This might not be a pleasant conclusion. But, as far as historical awareness goes, a genealogy of our norms (moral as well as political) would, I believe, suggest quite a disconcerting picture: a picture of norms as products of coercion, manipulation, hegemonic power structures, authoritative personality, conformity, and so on.

But even if there is a way in which the above statement on its own can be defended, it seems that the theory of communicative action precludes the possibility of genuine understanding in any concrete historical setting. This is so, since according to the theory (b) each and every extant act of communication falls short of achieving the conditions of the 'ideal speech situation', a counterfactual communicative setting that is free of any form of coercion. As a consequence of that, one must wonder whether it is possible to hold the positions expressed in (a) and (b) together coherently. That is, one could not but wonder whether if (b) is true, talk of the consensus achieved in (a) makes any sense.

There is however another way to understand Habermas's theory. We could ask the following question: regardless of whether we find his theory of language convincing, what is Habermas's conception of humans? As already hinted above, the theory of communicative action is committed to an intersubjective conception of human nature. But the intersubjectivity it espouses is not simply the view of human beings as social beings whose sense of themselves is inherently dependent on their relations to others, but rather the more ambitious conception according to which intersubjectivity should be wholly understood in terms of communication. The justification of this last contention is based on a speculative historical account according to which language has turned into the only universally shared human practice.

In the past, Habermas avers, members of societies participated in a variety of shared practices. This state of affairs has been shattered by the process of modernization (or the project of Enlightenment, as he usually labels it). The accumulated effect of the so-called disenchantment of the world has been the destruction of all shared practices; sending all such practices, except language, off into oblivion. This world-historical development has left us with language (linguistic affairs; communication) *alone* as the residual kernel of all modes of being and sociability.

According to such a speculative approach, humans have always been communicative creatures. However, they were not fully aware of that. Fortunately, unenlightened modes of understanding and socialization have been destroyed by the Enlightenment, a process which has revealed communication (language; communicative action) to be our central mode of being, our true communicative nature. Yet, as Habermas maintains, the Enlightenment is an unfinished project. Once we understand the centrality of communication, what is left for us to do is to perfect our modes of communication; a process which, he claims, is closely related to perfecting the institutional design of our societies (including the law). No doubt, this is an admirable task. But it is questionable whether such speculative history, the conceptual apparatus it applies, and the claims it includes would stand rigorous examination.

In particular, one must wonder whether language is best described as a practice. The philosophical literature on the appropriate meaning of the term 'practice' is complicated and by no means conclusive.[19] But for our purposes it seems sufficient to say that since most, if not all, human practices include a linguistic component, it is not at all clear whether we can make a clear distinction between the practice of language and, say, the practice of law.[20] In other words, any description of the ways in which people have been practising the law has to include descriptions of linguistic affairs. Take these descriptions out, and it is not clear whether you are left with anything to describe. If we think of other practices, such as architecture, painting, or even playing the piano, in effect, we reach the same conclusion, namely, that the attempt to distinguish between the practice of language and other human practices is destined to fail. No less important is the fact that it would be largely impossible to state anything with any content about the so-called practice of language on its own, without reference to other practices. Therefore, even if the terminology of practices is helpful in other domains, it is clearly unhelpful, and to my mind entirely wrong, in an attempt to understand linguistic affairs. However, once we fail to differentiate between the practice of language and other human practices, it is difficult to see what remains from Habermas's speculative history.

What about the theory's attitude towards humans as historical beings? In view of the above discussion, the theory of communicative action is not merely an attempt to make us aware of the need to perfect communication but is also, and decisively so, an account which takes all extant acts of communication as, in principle, instances of miscommunication—each one of them is, we may say, a *fallen* instance of communicative action. This is so since the ideal speech situation is not a counterfactual in the usual sense of the term. It belongs, in principle, to an extra-historical realm—a realm beyond the reach of any concrete historical situation. By implication, all historical instances of communication must, in some sense or another, be distorted. Now, if we accept the view that humans are in essence communicative creatures, this, in effect, means that humans are 'always already' (past, present, and future) fallen creatures. Habermas, in other words, provides us with a secular version of a characteristically Christian story at the core of which is a view of human beings as fallen. His theory belongs to what Nietzsche calls 'the ascetic spirit', one which refuses to accept humans as they are; or one which places redemption outside the realm of historical possibilities.[21] Whether or not we accept Nietzsche's negative attitude towards these types of theories, one thing seems to be clear: Habermas's approach is more parochial, less universalistic, than it appears initially.

Habermas quite rightly emphasizes the need to overcome solipsistic, subjectivist, modes of understanding human nature. Nevertheless, the move from a subjectivist to an intersubjective conception of human nature does not have to take the form which he proposes. No one would deny the centrality of language in human affairs. But as the realist in spirit would allow, from that it does not follow that our modes of sociability are best understood in terms of communication or dialogue alone.[22]

Rousseau's conception of humans was perhaps just as parochial as that of Habermas. Like Habermas he thought that we are fallen creatures of a kind. Yet on this issue the contrast between the two authors could not be greater, since for Rousseau the move from a solipsistic to non-solipsistic understanding of human nature, including the nature of human rationality, comes at a price. For him, once reason is understood in social terms, its achievements can no longer be fully (or at all) trusted. The reasons for that are complex, but essentially they are related to the connection Rousseau makes, between, on the one hand, reason and human passions and, on the other, reason and social esteem. The psychological profile that arises from these discussions is of human beings as creatures that are characterized by *l'amour propre*—egocentric creatures whose sense of themselves is dependent on the esteem they command from others. Reason, including language as its medium, cannot rise above these egocentric psychological traits, but rather is a vehicle in their formation, as well as their amplification and institutionalization. As so vividly expressed in the *Discourse on the Origin and Foundations of Inequality Among Men*,[23] reason excites the imagination, giving rise to otherwise unimaginable passions, most of which cannot be satisfied. As a mechanism for compensating their inability to satisfy their ever-expanding passions, people's social status becomes the sole principle through which their sense of self is achieved.

Linguistic affairs play a crucial role in the introduction of status, whether it is captured in moral, cultural, or material terms. In fact, it would be impossible to imagine the rise of most aspects of social inequality, and in particular the institutionalization of private property, without the aid of reason. Thus, while Habermas stresses the significance of rational dialog in the process of increasing mutual respect or intersubjective recognition, Rousseau suspects that the recognition people espouse is irrecoverably hierarchical. This is why according to him only in very specific social circumstances could the use of reason help us achieve morally just and politically legitimate goals. Given the historical developments of his time, Rousseau thought that the circumstances required for achieving justice and legitimacy in the domestic domain no longer existed. But equally important to him was to stress the futility of thinking about the possibility of restoring justice and legitimacy thus understood on the international level.

As a realist in spirit, Rousseau compelled us to understand the human predicament as a feature of people's interdependence. In this sense, he was what we would now call a proponent of intersubjectivity. He thought, however, that if applied properly rational reconstructions—whether they are understood in terms of the state of nature, or in today's terms, the original position or the ideal speech situation—could help us realize the contrast between our historically constructed psychological, material, and institutional conditions and any of their idealizations. Thus, for instance, a rigorous portrayal of the state of nature would help us realize how little can be explained about the social world by attributing to people an elementary motivational structure which is premised on an atomized, Robinson Crusoe style, self-sufficiency: it will make us realize the existence of an unbridgeable gap, or an epistemological break, between the imagined history of creatures whose psychological make-up is that of *amour de'soi*, and the study of humans' actual history as an interplay between reason, passion, and circumstance. Clearly for him, any attempt to understand politics as well as envisage institutional reforms should be conceived in terms of the latter.

Like Kant and Hegel before them, Rawls and Habermas attempt to turn the table in favour of Dispassionate Reason. But the challenges posed by Rousseau and, as will be discussed later in this chapter, many of his contemporaries, do not fade easily.

11.3. CONTEXTUALISM IN POLITICAL THEORY

Rival accounts to both Rawls's and Habermas's theories focus primarily on developing more historically sensitive approaches to the study of moral and political ideas. In the following, I will concentrate on one such alternative, broadly termed as contextualism, namely, the view that moral and political concepts and ideas have an irreducible historical dimension. It is however important to emphasize from the outset that proponents of this way of thinking about politics do not constitute a single doctrine. I will focus, in particular, on the works of Alasdair

MacIntyre, Charles Taylor, and Richard Rorty. Nevertheless, in order to understand their respective positions, we need to change slightly the trajectory of the discussion.

In order to understand the contextualist approach, and identify its different forms, one has to trace its origins. Although they are in other respects opponents of Rawlsian and Habermasian modes of thinking, the contextualists share with both authors an animosity towards 'positivism'. In this respect, contemporary political theory is best understood as a debate regarding the appropriate response to (what is more accurately described as) the 'positivist spirit' and its deadening effects.[24]

This can be couched more concretely as a debate about the appropriate reaction to '*emotivism*'. Generally speaking: 'Emotivism is the doctrine that all evaluative judgements and more specifically all moral judgements are nothing but expressions of preference, expressions of attitude or feeling, in so far as they are moral or evaluative in character'.[25] For the sake of brevity, I will not rehearse Rawls's and Habermas's responses, but rather identify two main contextualist lines of argument. Corresponding to them are two conceptions of humans.

11.3.1. Emotivism Writ Large

In *After Virtue*, MacIntyre describes modern societies as governed by an emotivist culture. He argues that utilitarianism and Kantianism are both based on a conception of a (transcendental or nominal) self innocent of any history, which he labels the 'emotivist self'. Since this self is nothing but a fiction, both accounts are vulnerable to the Nietzschean critique of morality—of morality as an expression of the will to power in disguise. Emotivism, we may say, stems from the natural progression of a logic that is based on such a construction of self. Relieved from the 'chains' of any attachment to society (or nature) the emotivist self has nothing but its preferences to rely upon. This can be put slightly differently: emotivism is an expression of the modern culture of amnesia—a culture of self-deception—which denies its being a culture, or, in MacIntyre's terms, denies its being part of a highly specific tradition. Instead, it is conceived of as governed by abstract, universally valid, principles.

Through the study of our history, this allegedly distorted mode of self-understanding can be rectified. Once members of contemporary societies come to understand themselves as belonging to a specific tradition, what seems to be an inevitable conclusion—namely, emotivism—would be seen as only one possibility among others. Well, not really! Once members of our society become aware of the historicity of the Self, their choice will not be entirely up to them to make. The choice for Christians, as MacIntyre famously puts it, is a choice between Nietzsche and Aristotle. This is better understood as a choice between Weber and Freud (as disciples of Nietzsche) and Thomism (as a Christian version of Aristotle).

Clearly, here, we have a form of 'moral realism', one which attempts to overcome emotivism by reminding people that, whether they like it or not, they belong to certain traditions—modes of thinking and acting which have developed over time and space, and, importantly, *loci* through which moral and political rationality can be restored.

Is this a good solution? I do not think so. First, the concept of tradition is (to say the least) problematic. For instance, how are we to describe the tradition to which Baruch/Benedictus Spinoza belongs?[26] Can we, from the point of view of his life as a whole, make a clear-cut distinction between his Judaism and his Christianity? Upon reflection, I am not entirely sure what counts as the content and boundaries of the tradition to which I am supposed to belong. Second, yet not less important, traditionalism of that kind amplifies rather than eases the grips of emotivism: MacIntyre, we may say, sets out to combat emotivism in all its embodiments, yet he ends up substituting the emotivism of the self with emotivism of (or between) traditions. Evaluative statements are no longer statements of the preferences of individuals—they are statements of the preferences of ascriptive and deferent groups. MacIntyre's solution, in other words, is nothing but *Emotivism Writ Large*.

Although he is more charitable in his criticism of modern societies, Taylor's emphasis on 'cultures' suffers from roughly the same problem.[27] Both authors have certainly contributed much to our awareness of the outcomes of allegedly modern modes of practical reasoning, especially those based on atomistic and monological metaphysics. As such, they have contributed greatly to our understanding of the historical dimension of our modes of understanding ourselves and the world. But their emphasis on 'virtues' or 'the good' *alone* is still overly parochial; they remain committed, with Habermas and Rawls, to a narrow and unwarranted conception of consensus. The only difference is that, unlike Habermas's and Rawls's rationalist/universalist attempts, MacIntyre and Taylor have introduced a 'vernacular conception of consensus'. It remains, however, one which takes virtually no account of power relations and material circumstances.

11.3.2. Oblivious Emotivism

Instead of trying to suspend allegations of emotivism locally, one could ignore them altogether; especially if one does not accept the presuppositions on the basis of which theories of emotivism have been constructed. One can, as it were, be oblivious towards any such theory. Hereafter, such a strategy will be labelled 'oblivious emotivism'. This is Richard Rorty's strategy.[28]

Philosophically, terms such as 'culture', 'tradition', or even 'humanity', are treated by the 'oblivious emotivist' either as optional sets of 'heuristics', elective pragmatic tools, and/or as representations whose perspectival—aspectual nature cannot be overridden. The principal advantage of the 'oblivious emotivist' over proponents of 'emotivism writ large' is related to the fact that he or she does not confuse a commitment to some form of social as well as semantic holism with a commitment to any of its concrete articulations.

Nevertheless, an oblivious emotivist such as Rorty does not simply ignore emotivism, but, in a sense, introduces to it an *ironist twist*. For him or her, while the theory of meaning underpinning emotivism is unconvincing, emotivism can be seen as a powerful articulation of the phenomenology of (the use of) evaluative terminology. In their attempt to explain 'meaning' in purely logical terms, some analytical philosophers have tried to dispense with any reference to psychological states (emotions, feelings, and so on). Positivists, as well as non-cognitivists, found this emotive dimension of language baffling. But once one is no longer committed to the 'rigorization' of philosophy as it was understood by these schools of analytical philosophy, inability to dispense with psychology should not surprise us. On the contrary, it would be rather odd if statements of value would have no psychological equivalents or emotional bearings.

Rorty's project, and especially his insistence on seeing philosophy as an exercise in '*sentimental education*', is best understood as an attempt to incorporate such an insight.[29] Crudely put, once we accept the fact that nothing is simply given, either by fact or by reason, moral and political language-games are best understood as competing attempts to win the hearts and minds of fellow humans.

Peter Munz complains that Rorty's project is an attempt to make 'the world safe for rhetoric and for nothing but rhetoric' in an attempt 'to establish the hegemony of Rhetoric'.[30] Contrary to Munz, I believe this is—or, at least, could be—a welcome development. Yet as far as I can see, its lessons are not the ones which have been drawn by Rorty. If the choice we have to make is, as MacIntyre suggests, a choice between Nietzsche and Aristotle, Rorty is clearly on the Nietzschean side. However, for complicated reasons, he is unnerved by the tragic ramifications of his own valorization of Nietzsche as an epitome of the 'great poet', namely, one who introduces an entirely new vocabulary on the basis of which our worldview is radically altered. As perhaps the most significant 'great poet' of modern times, Nietzsche's critique, his radical revaluation of values, has shattered the foundations of Western moral and political thought. The ramifications of such a demolition enterprise are, according to Rorty, too dangerous. Subsequently, he focused on the 'habituation' or 'domestication' of what he saw as the dangers embodied in Nietzschean poetic tendencies. Against the intoxication of *Tragedy*, he introduces *Irony*, and thus succumbs to what can be termed a 'second order rationalism' or 'second order idealism'. This explains his subsequent alliance with both Rawls and Habermas, but most palpably, it explains his comradeship with Robert Brandom who stresses consensus among 'scorekeepers' in an 'idealized community' as the only community which can genuinely employ the term (say) 'we'.[31] Nothing could be more of an anathema to a Nietzschean than an alliance with these types of moral and political philosophies.[32]

Rorty's late interest in moral and political matters was undoubtedly a welcome development. However, as Richard Bernstein argues, his approach is poorly suited to redirecting the American left, the so-called cultural left, into 'real politics'.[33] For instance, based on his own approach—that is, based on his understanding of the battlefield of ideas as combat between different re-descriptions of the world— Rorty called for the left to re-engage itself in the political discourse concerning the appropriate content of 'patriotism'. Such a reengagement is of utmost importance if the American left wishes to have any significant impact on American politics.

Yet, as Bernstein argues, re-description without a programmatic dimension is nothing but spin. Engagement in 'real politics' requires, quite simply, admitting some sort of reality, which Rorty has spent most of his intellectual energy denying.

In what sense is oblivious emotivism of the kind propagated by Rorty a missed opportunity? Rorty's philosophical enterprise has been an exercise in making us aware of the intimate relations between our allegedly natural endowments, namely, our sentiments and emotions, and our intellectual capacities, namely, our capacity to converse and reason; an exercise in making us accept *Eros* and *Rationality* as basically two sides of the same coin, neither of which is innocent of a linguistic dimension. From that perspective, our ideas are those of natural creatures attempting to cope with an equally natural realm. In an intellectual atmosphere within which the divorce of reason from any emotional baggage is taken to be a mark of progress, the call for re-examining the intricate relations between reason and sentiment has been valuable. However, if we wish to follow Rorty in his quest to win hearts and minds, if we wish to involve ourselves in sentimentally educating others so that their moral and political convictions will be similar to ours, we need to understand them better. In other words, we have to take extremely seriously the reality of their beliefs and desires in order to make our so-called educational enterprise effective. For Rorty, the American left had retreated from genuine politics especially due to its sense of intellectual superiority and overwhelming self-righteousness. In their attempt to become politically relevant again, they may want to introduce hitherto unknown beliefs and values in order to reshape people's entire outlook and motivations. But even great poets such as Nietzsche or Freud, to the extent that we find them convincing, did not introduce a wholly novel vocabulary, if by novelty one means the introduction of an entirely unrecognized vocabulary or some sort of incommensurate terminology and modes of thinking. Rather, their call to revaluate our belief-systems was, in fact, a call to re-examine our extant beliefs and motivations as they expressed themselves in highly specific social and cultural settings.

11.4. POLITICAL REALISM AND THE REALISITC SPIRIT

Realism in IR has been sometimes dubbed immoral or amoral. As a number of contributors to this volume demonstrate, such labelling does not survive proper scrutiny. Realism, like any other conception of politics, needs an infusion of novel approaches if it wishes to maintain its practical relevance. But it seems that there is a common thread to all these attempts to understand the international domain, namely, a refusal to accept the remits of what was labelled by Bernard Williams as 'thin' conceptions of morality and politics.[34] Quite simply, in the terminology offered above, realists are those who are suspicious of conceptions of morality and politics which, if at all, only meagrely correspond to what otherwise are the 'surface phenomena' of political life. Put slightly differently, perhaps that common thread can be described as a refusal to accept any form of aprioristic conceptual distinction between moral, immoral, or amoral reasoning and action. By and large, the appeal of authors such as Machiavelli, Thucydides, Nietzsche, or even Rousseau for realists rests in their refusal to conform to a wholly aprioristic abstract discussion about the realms of morality and politics.

The discussion up to this point was meant to convey the idea that making a move towards a realistic approach to politics requires recasting our understanding of the relations between reason and sentiment. In order to avoid falling back into unhelpful and potentially detrimental abstractions for understanding politics, an investigation of the relations between reason and the sentiments should be historical in nature. What is required is a genealogy of the emergence, place, and disappearance of certain classes of sentiments. A genealogical undertaking of this kind should not be simply a history of terminological change, but rather a history of the emergence of different types of classifications of sentiments and modes of argumentation and their relations to reason, as well as the impact they are thought to have on individual and collective action as part of a wider social and political context. Writing a history of this kind is not an easy task, and the temptation to follow the footsteps of Habermasian speculative history, MacIntyre's and Taylor's versions of communitarianism or Rorty's irrealist pragmatism is great.

Given the current philosophical atmosphere, it is also important to avoid the temptation to surrender this type of analysis, namely, the attempt to recover the history of 'moral psychology', to what is nowadays conceived under the heading of theories of the mind. A realist historical reconstruction of this kind should be conceived of as part of practical rather than theoretical wisdom. One does not need to reject any effort to account for the relations between reason and sentiment on a theoretical level while continuing to insist on the existence of a categorical distinction between attempts to answer abstract theoretical questions regarding, say, the relations between mental and physical states, and attempts to answer the practical question of whether the history of sentiments can help us to make sense of people's behavioural repertoire and their propensity to judge and act in certain ways.

If one wishes to make any headway in answering the second question, one should insist on the autonomy of taking a practical interest in the realm of human sentiments and the irreducibility of practical concerns to purely theoretical ones. Thus, for instance, in recent years we have witnessed a surge of philosophical interest in human 'emotions'. This is a welcome development. Yet abstract analytical discussions on the nature of 'love', 'friendship', 'jealousy', and the likes have, if at all, only a remote bearing on the kind of investigation suggested here. In fact, it is more likely that the two types of investigations would remain in constant (preferably fruitful) tension with one another.

This is not the place to defend such an approach in detail. At its centre however is the view that depictions of sentiments, their significance and the impact they have on human behaviour, should be understood as one dimension (or a pole) in a triangulation whose other dimensions are reason and circumstance. According to such an approach, any attempt to depict 'people as they are' has to involve a description of the interplay between reason, sentiment, and circumstance. A change in the depiction of one of these poles means practically a change in the depiction of the others.

On this view:

(i) Questions of the form 'What is X?', where X stands for any particular sentiment, cannot be answered meaningfully *in abstractis*. Beyond heuristic or introductory purposes, attempts to offer definitions for sentiments tend to be uninformative or even detrimental for understanding their significance for and effects on human life. This is so, because

(ii) Sentiments, hence also their descriptions, tend to change over time. Thus, for instance, it would be natural to expect our experience of romantic love to change in relation to our particular circumstances (the particular subject of our love; the precise nature of our relations, and so on). Also, we have good reasons to believe that amorous relations in different societies, or past societies, take different forms.

(iii) A sentiment is most likely to be experienced or depicted as a part of a whole 'economy' of sentiments. For instance, it would be impossible to state what love is without considering the differences and relations between love, lust, respect, envy, friendship, and so forth.

I argued earlier that a proper investigation of moral sentiment would have to be historical in nature. To say this does not mean that the study of sentiments should be an investigation of the past alone, but to indicate the fact that, if (i), (ii), and (iii) are true, then any attempt to account for human sentiments needs to be context specific. Holistic depictions of sentiments of this kind are not simply identifications of psychological dispositions, especially if by the latter are meant those mental states that can be identified without reference to circumstance. Neither are they depictions of emotions *simpliciter*. Rather, from the point of view of practical wisdom, sentiments are best described as correlatives to specific modes of conduct.

An example of accounting for sentiments from the point of view of practical wisdom can be found in Aristotle's discussion of the nature and political implications of hubris.[35] As explained by David Cohen, hubris, for Aristotle 'involves ... conduct engaged in for the pleasure it brings'. For example, people may resort to violence as a consequence of anger or fear. In these cases, while their actions are instances of lack of self-restraint (*arkasia*), they are not necessarily pleasurable. By contrast, in hubristic behaviour, the pleasure involved in acting violently is related to the fact that the agent had a choice about the matter. Hubristic behaviour, in other words, is more likely to appear in cases of unequal relations, where the powerful parties of society assert their might. To be sure, hubristic behaviour may take many forms, not all of them violent. In the *Politics*, however, 'Aristotle advises the rulers above all to avoid two kinds of *hubris*: corporal punishment of free men and sexual abuse of boys and girls (1315a15–28).

These two forms of *hubris* should be shunned because they are most likely to cause attempt at revenge by the outraged families.'[36]

Hubris, therefore, is a general term used to denote a general psychological disposition. But without further elaboration on the specific cases in which hubris manifests itself, it remains essentially an empty concept. Thus, for instance, acts of a sexual nature could be thought of as originating in passions of one sort or another. On the whole, they are likely to be pleasurable, and therefore, *prima facie*, meet the conditions expressed in the definition of hubris. Pleasurable as they might be, however, it would be ridiculous to think of such actions as necessarily manifestations of a hubristic personality. Even in cases that are considered as instances of wrongdoing, say when individuals partake in adulterous relations, no hubris is necessarily involved. Rather, for an act of such a kind to be a mark of hubris, beyond the fulfilment of sexual desire, the pleasure it brings has to be related to external interpersonal or social conditions of unequal power.

Hubris has never disappeared from political life. Contemporary political theory however has nothing to say about this aspect of politics. Given what seems to be a rise in hubristic behaviour in contemporary politics, especially on the international level, the absence of any serious discussion on the nature and implications of hubris on political life is not merely a regrettable fact, but an indication of a serious theoretical impediment.

Yet, informative as it may be, indulging ourselves in the works of ancient authors such as Aristotle would not suffice for understanding modern politics. This may sound like a truism. What is needed however are not simply amendments to the existing frameworks of thought as they are presented by, among others, the authors mentioned above, but a radical shift away from the ways in which they discuss politics and the philosophical priority they give to notions such as 'freedom', 'justice', the 'good', and so on. Inspired by the work of Istvan Hont, the final section of this chapter indicates how we might think about investigating the role of sentiments in political theory.[37]

11.5. ANCIENTS, MODERNS, AND THE REVIVAL OF POLITICAL THEORY

Machiavelli and Hobbes are often seen as the founding fathers of modern political thought. But their theories can also be seen as admirable, yet not entirely successful, attempts to escape ancient modes of political thinking. This is so, since both failed to incorporate the reality of *commerce* into their theoretical accounts. In this respect, they are still *ancient* or at least pre-modern thinkers. The eighteenth century gave rise to a different and, at the time, an entirely novel set of questions, namely, 'What are the effects of Commerce on human sentiments?' What, in other words, are its effects on human modes of understanding themselves, their relations to other individuals, as well as other collectives?

Clearly, thus was the way in which Rousseau understood the task of 'taking humans as they are'. It would be a mistake, however, to understand this cluster of concerns as simply an attempt to recount the relations between 'pure' psychological traits and 'pure' economic reasoning. Regardless of their ideological affiliations, eighteenth-century authors understood the realms of commerce and politics as inseparable; they sought a 'political economy'. The emergence of the market economy, they claimed, could not be understood without the emergence of a new form of polity, namely, the modern state. Equally futile was the attempt to understand the modern state without the market. For this reason, debates throughout the century revolved around the question of how to modify Hobbes's theory of the state and Machiavelli's republicanism (especially his focus on *Grandezza*) in order to adapt them for understanding modern commercial societies. They were especially concerned with the pathological manifestations of the combinations between statecraft and economic reasoning. 'Hume, Smith, and their contemporaries wanted to explain how the conflation of the logics of war and trade arose in the seventeenth century and why it was so difficult to exorcise them afterward.'[38] Territorial conquest was by no means a new phenomenon. However, with the emergence of the market economy, competition among the European maritime superpowers of the time made it 'murderously intense': 'Making [territorial] increase a reason of state unleashed imperialism and a dramatic increase of trade with the extra-European world.'[39]

But the logics in question could not be discerned without appeal to the language of sentiments. What was needed was a better understanding of the kind of sentiments that are evoked as a result of the emergence of a new kind of politics marked by the fact that 'global market competition [turned into] a primary state activity'.[40] Such an epochal change went hand in hand with the emergence of a new 'economy of (individual as well as national) sentiments', and resulted in the formation of new incentives on both the interpersonal and the collective levels.

As was understood by the various protagonists, the effects of commerce are a mixed blessing. On the one hand, commerce gave rise to unprecedented wealth. On the other hand, the world witnessed a hitherto unknown degree of inequality. The repercussions of these developments were massive in both the domestic and international domains. Domestically, questions about the effects of 'luxury' on social cohesion and especially on patriotism or 'love of county' and the relations between 'love of country' and 'love of humanity' emerged. On the international front, questions concerning relations between poor and rich countries, absolute and relative advantages in the global market economy, or as already mentioned, competition between rich and powerful countries, took centre stage. In all cases, the discussions were neither simply empirical nor normative, but a mixture of the two, coupled with pragmatic recommendations regarding public policy and institutional reforms. As Hont argues, the participants in these debates were not simply interested in understanding the past, but 'also hoped to discern the future of international economic competition'. They understood however that what lies in the future of economic competition is very much dependent on the policies implemented at their time. Increasingly it had also become clear that thinking about domestic politics in isolation from international politics was no longer an option. Isolationism as a way to rectify the ills of the modern world could no longer be justified on either practical or philosophical grounds.

What throughout the eighteenth and nineteenth century had seemed to be the most pressing question in relation to modern societies—namely, how are we to understand the relations between commerce and moral sentiments, or how does this new 'economy of sentiment' of commercial societies play itself out in both the domestic and the international domain?—has lost its appeal. Marx and Weber were perhaps the last great thinkers to pose that same question.

The vocabulary of moral psychology attached to this way of thinking has largely vanished. Today most political theorists take the language of 'Jealousy of States' or 'Jealousy of Trade' and their combined effect on 'Reason of State' to be anachronistic. Nothing seems to (many of) us more alien than the question of whether commerce enhances conducive modes of *jealousy* (e.g. fair competition; industrious tendencies, emulation, and so on) among individuals as well as collectives (especially states), or else throws us into the abyss of a destitute state characterized by a destructive dynamic of *envious* relations. The irony is that generically premodern discussions of legitimacy, liberty, freedom, equality, and so on—which take no account of (or only derivatively discuss) the effects that the emergence of commercial societies had on our sentiments, and therefore our disposition to act and judge in certain ways rather others—sound more familiar, less anachronistic. How are we to understand such a state of affairs? At least in part, the answer has to be related to the fact that the relatively recent 'revival' in political theory has been a revival of pre-modern, pre-commercial, modes of thinking about politics.

What lies in the future for humans as historical beings in a commercial reality—humans whose sense of being and relations to others are based on what Rousseau labelled as *amour propre*—remains, however, the most acute and modern question of all. Commerce is neither purely domestic nor international. Ignore it and Reality will bite!

NOTES

I wish to thank Duncan Bell, Raymond Geuss and David Palfrey for their useful comments.
1. J. J. Rousseau, 'The State Of War', in Victor Gourevitch (ed.)', *The Social Contract' and Other Later Political Writings* (Cambridge, MA: Cambridge University Press, 1997), p. 162.
2. Cora Diamond, 'Realism and the Realistic Spirit', in *The Realistic Spirit: Wittgenstein, Philosophy and the Mind* (Cambridge, MA: MIT Press, 1995), pp. 39–40.
3. For a defence of the 'project of normative theory', see Andrea Sangiovanni's Chapter 12 in this volume.
4. Rousseau, 'The Social Contract', p. 41.
5. Rawls, *A Theory of Justice* (Cambridge, MA: Harvard University Press, 1999 [1971]); Rawls, *Political Liberalism* (New York: Colombia University Press, 1993); and Rawls, *The Law of Peoples* (Cambridge, MA: Harvard University Press, 1999).

6. Nagel, 'The Problem of Global Justice', *Philosophy & Public Affairs*, 33 (2005), p. 147.

7. Nagel, 'The Problem of Global Justice', p. 126.

8. Sandel, *Liberalism and the Limits of Justice* (Cambridge, MA: Cambridge University Press, 1998), esp. p. 87.

9. Onora O'Neill, *Constructions of Reason: Explorations of Kant's Practical Philosophy* (Cambridge, MA: Cambridge University Press, 1989), p. 210. On the differences between abstraction and idealization, see her *Towards Justice and Virtue* (Cambridge, MA: Cambridge University Press, 1996).

10. Geuss, 'Neither History Nor Praxis', in his *Outside Ethics* (Princeton: Princeton University Press, 2005), pp. 33, 34.

11. Rawls, *The Laws of Peoples*, p. 11. Note the use he makes in this quote of terms such as 'ordinarily' and 'us'.

12. Charles Beitz, 'Bounded Morality: Justice and the State in World Politics', *International Organization*, 3 (1979), pp. 405–25; Thomas Pogge: *Realizing Rawls* (Ithaca: Cornell University Press, 1989); and Pogge, 'An Egalitarian Law of Peoples', *Philosophy and Public Affairs*, 23 (1994), pp. 195–224.

13. Bernard Williams: 'Moral Luck', in *Moral Luck* (Cambridge, MA: Cambridge University Press, 1981), pp. 20–40; and Thomas Nagel, 'Moral Luck', in *Mortal Questions* (New York: Cambridge University Press, 1979), pp. 24–38. Within political theory, many of the discussions on this matter are couched in terms of 'arbitrariness' and 'contingency', which to my mind obscure the significance of investigating the role luck plays in morality, and, more importantly, in politics.

14. Justifications of the need to rectify 'bad luck' are labelled in the literature 'luck egalitarianism'. Cf. Elizabeth Anderson, 'What Is the Point of Equality', *Ethics*, 109 (1999), pp. 287–337.

15. Habermas, *The Theory of Communicative Action: Reason the Rationalization of Society*, Vol. I (Boston: Beacon Press, 1984), esp. pp. 273–339; Habermas, *The Theory of Communicative Action: Life World and System*, Vol. II. (Boston: Beacon Press, 1987); and Habermas, *Communication and the Evolution of Society* (Boston: Beacon Press, 1991), esp. pp. 50–68.

16. Habermas, 'Comments on John Searle: Meaning, Communication and Representation', in Ernest Lepore and Robert Van Gulick (eds.), *John Searle and His Critics* (Oxford: Blackwell, 1993), p. 17.

17. Searle, 'Response', in Lepore and Van Gulick (eds.), *John Searle and His Critics* p. 92.

18. For a more detailed critique of Habermas's theory, see Ze'ev Emmerich, 'Towards a Needs-Based Conception of Intersubjectivity', *South African Journal of Philosophy*, 25 (2006), pp. 249–57.

19. For a critique of the concept of practice, see, Stephen Turner, *The Social Theory of Practice* (Cambridge, MA: Polity Press, 1994).

20. For Theodore Schatzky, practices are loci of 'doings and sayings': *Social Practices* (Cambridge, MA: Cambridge University Press, 1996).

21. Nietzsche, in Keith Ansell-Pearson (ed.), *On the Genealogy of Morality* (Cambridge, MA: Cambridge University Press, 1994).

22. For a critique of Habermas's ideal of deliberative democracy, see Andrew Kuper, *Democracy Beyond Borders* (Oxford: Oxford University Press, 2004), pp. 47–74.

23. Rousseau, 'Discourse on the Origin and Foundations of Inequality Among Men', in Victor Gourevitch (ed.), *The Discourses and Other Early Political Writings* (Cambridge, MA: Cambridge University Press, 1997), p. 218.

24. The effect positivism had on political philosophy was famously articulated by Peter Laslett's phrase 'For the moment, anyway, political philosophy is dead', in Peter

Laslett and W. G. Runciman (eds.), the introduction to *Philosophy, Politics and Society*, Vol. 1 (New York: Macmillan, 1956).

25. MacIntyre, *After Virtue: A Study in Moral Theory* (London: Duckworth, 1985), pp. 11–12.

26. See also the comments in Duncan Bell's introduction to this volume, pp. 3–6.

27. Taylor, *The Malaise of Modernity* (Concord: Anansi, 1991); and Taylor, 'Irreducibly Social Goods', in *Philosophical Arguments* (Cambridge, MA: Harvard University Press, 1995), pp. 127–45.

28. The following discussion is based especially on: Richard Rorty, *Philosophy and the Mirror of Nature* (Princeton: Princeton University Press, 1979); Rorty, *Contingency, Irony and Solidarity* (Cambridge, MA: Cambridge University Press, 1989); Rorty, *Truth and Progress: Philosophical Papers* (Cambridge, MA: Cambridge University Press, 1998); and Robert Brandom (ed.), *Rorty and His Critics* (Oxford: Blackwell, 2000).

29. Rorty, 'Human Rights, Rationality and Sentimentality', in *Truth and Progress: Philosophical Papers* (Cambridge, MA: Cambridge University Press, 1998), pp. 167–85.

30. Peter Munz, 'The Rhetoric of Rhetoric', *Journal of the History of Ideas*, 51 (1990), p. 130.

31. Brandom, *Making It Explicit* (Cambridge, MA: Harvard University Press, 1994), pp. 641–5.

32. In the name of attentiveness to 'concept-use', a view has emerged where my saying that 'We (say, me and you) had a conversation' is taken to be a 'fallen' mode of expressing the fact that a conversation had taken place. This way of thinking about 'we-ascriptions' is at odds with a Rortian vocabulary and mode of argumentation: recall the frequent, some would say obsessive, use made by Rorty of 'we-ascriptions' to describe his belonging to a like-minded community of 'Wittgensteinians', 'liberal-ironists', 'postmodernist bourgeois liberals'.

33. Bernstein, 'Rorty's Inspirational Liberalism', in Charles Guignon and David R. Hiley (eds.), *Richard Rorty* (Cambridge, MA: Cambridge University Press, 2003), pp. 124–38.

34. Williams, *Ethics and the Limits of Philosophy* (Cambridge, MA: Harvard University Press, 1985).

35. See also the discussion in Richard Ned Lebow's Chapter 2 in this volume.

36. Cohen, 'Sexuality, Violence, and the Athenian Law of Hubris', *Greece and Rome*, 38 (1991), p. 173.

37. See especially Hont, *Jealousy of Trade: International Competition and the Nation-State in Historical Perspective* (Cambridge, MA: Harvard University Press, 2005).

38. Hont, *Jealousy of Trade*, p. 8.

39. Hont, *Jealousy of Trade*, p. 17.

40. Hont, *Jealousy of Trade*, p. 6.

12

Normative Political Theory: A Flight from Reality?

Andrea Sangiovanni

12.1. INTRODUCTION

In this essay, I first seek to characterize what I conceive to be some of the most difficult objections to the project of systematic normative reflection about politics, and then to work towards their assessment. These objections are at the heart of several forms of contemporary political realism and have quite wide-ranging implications for how to think about the possibility of normative political theory, including much of contemporary international political theory. My aim will not be to defend systematic normative reflection about politics *per se*, but to assess how the force of these objections, when properly understood, should alter the way we think of the justification and formulation of political values—justice, human rights, solidarity, liberty, equality, and so on—in contemporary political philosophy.

12.2. NORMATIVE POLITICAL THEORY

Let me begin by stating more precisely what I mean by 'systematic normative reflection about politics', or, as I shall sometimes refer to it, the 'project of normative political theory'. This project is closely associated with Rawls and post-Rawlsian philosophy, and includes philosophers whose interests are as diverse as Brian Barry, Allen Buchanan, Joshua Cohen, G. A. Cohen, Ronald Dworkin, David Miller, Robert Nozick, Susan Okin, and Philippe Van Parijs.[1] What characterizes the project in which they participate, along with a significant majority of other political philosophers, is a set of defining features. I emphasize that these are defining features rather than necessary and sufficient conditions for identifying the project: there might be cases that clearly seem to be instances of systematic normative reflection in a post-Rawlsian vein, but which do not share at least one of the features included below.[2] The representative members of the project, we might say, bear a family resemblance.

There are four features relevant for our purposes. Post-Rawlsian political philosophy is *action-guiding, idealizing, moral,* and *liberal.* We focus on these features in particular because they form the tacit background of assumptions that, I believe, raise the most problems for realists. I also take it that they are of interest in their own right, since there has been relatively little discussion of them in the literature. Indeed, for those raised in the project, they may seem patently obvious starting points for anyone who wants to think clearly about politics in a philosophical vein. The main aim of this article is to see whether this is in fact the case.

12.2.1. Action-Guiding

The point of setting out systematic accounts of political values is to guide action. The aim is to put us in a position not only to appreciate, as spectators, the goodness, rightness, beauty, or usefulness of actions and states of affairs but also to engage our will as participants in the forms of life at stake.

12.2.2. Idealizing

When I say that the point of the project is 'to engage our will as participants in the forms of life at stake', which forms of life are 'at stake'? Put another way, who is the intended audience of a particular piece of post-Rawlsian political philosophy, and what is its purported domain? At its most ambitious, the project is meant to address anyone that can have an impact, however small, on political outcomes. If the political value is 'justice', then the political outcomes include the organization of policy, law, and administration, as well as broader societal norms. In some cases, the societal norms could be as encompassing and informal as the particular social ethos pervading a political community.[3] So the principles articulated in the theory should be capable of guiding

(a) a citizen contemplating which party to vote for or whether to vote at all;
(b) a legislator contemplating how to vote on a bill;
(c) a judge deciding a hard case;
(d) a civil servant facing a discretionary decision on whether to deport an illegal immigrant and his family;
(e) someone contemplating violent forms of political resistance in a democracy;
(f) someone contemplating violent forms of political resistance in a non-democracy;
(g) a subject of a non-democracy contemplating various ways to organize resistance to the current leader, without toppling the state;
(h) a teacher contemplating her curriculum and her general approach to marking;
(i) a novelist deciding whether to publish her (politically controversial) book;

(j) a development economist contemplating what advice to give to a state of which he or she knows little;

(k) a citizen contemplating how much time to spend on various forms of political action;

(l) a couple deciding how to divide resources between their daughter and their son.

This list may seem to reflect a misunderstanding. What theory could possibly propose to guide action across each of these very different contexts? In response, one may be tempted to restrict the scope of the theory by, for example, stipulating that contemporary theories are addressed, at most, to decisions that have a direct impact on the 'basic structure' or the 'social ethos', on the way, that is, in which the main social and political institutions of a society or its predominant ethos shapes the distribution of social benefits and burdens. But how would this serve to strike candidates off the list? It seems difficult to deny that each of the decision situations depicted here potentially has an impact on how major institutions and social ethi will end up shaping the overall distribution of benefits and burdens. To be sure, each decision, taken individually, may have a small, even negligible impact on the shape of the society in question, but this should not matter. The point is that *cumulatively* decisions of each sort *will* have such an impact, and that seems to be all that is required.[4]

To allay this worry about the seemingly implausible scope of the targeted audience, we need a further distinction, crucial to the post-Rawlsian project, namely, the distinction between ideal and non-ideal theory.[5] The aim of ideal theory is to formulate principles for the governance of a society in which everyone complies with those principles, and that compliance is common knowledge. The aim of non-ideal theory, by contrast, is to articulate lower-level principles, precepts, and rules to guide decision-making in circumstances—our own—in which there is only partial compliance with principles. The key point is that our actions in non-ideal circumstances must ultimately be justifiable in light of the principles and ideals identified by ideal theory; principles formulated for a perfectly just society should function as a regulative ideal for us here and now:

A conception of justice must specify the requisite structural principles and point to the overall direction of political action. In the absence of such an ideal form for background institutions, there is no rational basis for continually adjusting the social process so as to preserve background justice, nor for eliminating injustice. Thus ideal theory, which defines a perfectly just basic structure, is a necessary complement to non-ideal theory without which the desire for change lacks an aim.[6]

To be sure, the principles that should govern an ideal society cannot directly regulate our actions here and now. While ideal theory is necessary for non-ideal theory, it is not sufficient. Not only might it not be clear (as an empirical matter) what acting on, say, the 'difference principle' would require, but it might also not be prudent to do so. Put another way, in non-ideal circumstances, our aim is to bring about the just society. But it is left open both whether some courses of action involving *prima facie* injustice might be necessary in achieving that goal and, if such courses of action were allowed, which constraints would have to be recognized in pursuing them. It may be, for example, that policies that would be unjust if implemented in the ideal society may be permissible for us here and now. Non-ideal theory, in turn, is required to identify and guide judgement in the presence of such complicating features.

How does the division of labour between ideal and non-ideal theory help us to allay our initial anxiety about the audience? In each of the cases listed above, what is at stake is non-ideal rather than ideal theory. So the philosopher can say that *ultimately* his or her aim is to guide action in non-ideal circumstances (including the cases listed above), but that his or her aim *qua* philosopher is merely to articulate the principles that should govern an ideal society (in which the complexities of the above-listed cases are only contingently relevant). How to implement that ideal in the 'real world' is left to those with more specialized knowledge of the empirical, sociological, and historical facts affecting feasible paths of reform. The ideal theorist does not claim to address individual action *directly* but only *indirectly*.

The project of normative political theory is, in sum, *idealizing*. An essential precondition for doing political philosophy in a Rawlsian vein is to abstract away from circumstances that affect problems of implementation and application, and hence to focus attention on the idea of a 'perfectly just society', even if we have little confidence that such a society could ever arise.[7] Without the projection of such a perfectly just society, our desire for change, Rawls claims, would lack an aim.

12.2.3. Moral

The study of political philosophy is the study of political *morality*, or the attempt to understand the variety of ways in which we can wrong one another through various forms of political action, the nature of our remedial obligations in rectifying wrongs for which we are responsible, and, as we have already discussed, the analysis of the ways in which a society organized according to the correct moral-political principles should and would operate. Political values such as justice, of course, are not the whole of morality, but only one significant part of it. Furthermore, while non-moral values such as, for example, well-being or efficiency or prudence may enter into the justification of moral-political values, such as justice, they are never the conclusion of any particular bit of political theorizing. The project is also not understood to answer the question—'What is the best life for me (or us) to lead?' Rather, it aims to tell us what moral constraints we should recognize in organizing our cooperation whatever the (non-moral) goals we have set ourselves.

12.2.4. Liberal

The project aims to set out principles and values that are, in some sense, *liberal*.[8] There is wide and persistent disagreement about what exactly liberalism is, and I do not intend to try and settle that disagreement here. But it seems uncontroversial to say that all those involved in the project are self-described liberals. It is an interesting question whether any pre-Rawlsian liberals would have subscribed to the three features with which we began. Some have argued that they would not have.[9] If that is true, then these features highlight a way in which contemporary liberal political philosophy is a significant departure from previous treatments in part precisely *in virtue* of the aforementioned features.

12.3. OBJECTIONS

Let us now draw up a list of what I conceive to be some of the most important realist objections to the project of normative political theory understood in the way I have just suggested. Each objection is, I will claim, ultimately unsuccessful, but each one contains partial insights that should change the way we think of the project. I also believe there is a kind of synthesis that can be constructed out of the objections taken together, which I will sketch at the end of this article. I should note that though each of these objections could be fitted into a realist tradition, I will not try to do so here. Nothing should hinge on the success or failure of that further task. The objections would be serious ones even if they cannot be successfully shoehorned into a realist canon.

12.3.1. Feasibility

The first objection receives its clearest and most far-reaching form with regards to the project's contributions to the global justice debates (though it could be pressed with respect to their involvement with domestic issues as well). Realists worry that the circumstances are not right for justice to be done at the global level. Indeed, because the circumstances are not right, the pursuit of justice—when it is pursued—is likely to lead to a kind of blindness to the *facts* of global interaction, most important of which is the absence of a sovereign. And by overlooking the *verità effettuale* of global politics, the moralizing politician, in so far as he or she is persuaded by any of the project's claims, will overshoot their mark, destabilizing an already precarious order in the pursuit of a vain ideal.[10] By seeking justice, the moralizing politician will produce its opposite.

Those eager to defend the project's involvement in the global justice debates have a respectable reply. They can claim that the realist *accepts* that there is an ideal worth defending, but only questions the circumstances in which it can be realized. The sceptic has identified reasons to be wary of how to *implement* principles of justice in international relations, but he has not put in question the project, or, for that matter, offered an alternative account of either the scope or content of any specific set of principles. Seen in this light, the disagreement is less stark than it might have first appeared; it begins to look like merely a disagreement about what circumstances are most likely to favour just policies, or about the best means for achieving justice, than about the nature of the project itself. The disagreement leaves entirely open the question to which the project seeks an answer, namely, what justice, solidarity, and so on, in fact *are*, rather than how they should best be implemented, or in what conditions they are most likely to be in fact implemented. At best, the realist's charge can therefore be understood as a demand for doing more non-ideal theory (while keeping in place the claim that ideal theory, and hence the project, is necessary for non-ideal theory).

It is no coincidence that, within the global justice debates, the force of the realist critique is often reduced to a concern about 'feasibility'.[11] But when discussing principles of justice, feasibility is a very weak constraint. This is because feasibility is best understood as a virtue of *public policies* rather than of *conceptions of justice*. It is a virtue which obviously requires attention in 'designing' social and political institutions, but principles of justice themselves are not immediate candidates for rejection on the basis of their 'infeasibility'. Take a radical principle of egalitarianism such as the global extension of Rawls's difference principle as it is presented in, for example, Thomas Pogge's *Realizing Rawls*.[12] If any principle of global justice is to be rejected as 'infeasible', the globalized version of the difference principle would be, for obvious reasons, a prime candidate. But consider the way Pogge presents the principle. The difference principle tells us to select, among the *set of feasible institutional schemes*, the one that optimizes the position of the worst-off representative global citizen. Once put in this way, it is clear that the disagreement between our defender of the ideal and the realist has been relocated from an argument about the nature of justice to an argument about the boundaries of the set of feasible institutional schemes.[13] And once again, this leaves the debate about the correct conception of global justice entirely open. Notice that this is not a peculiarity of Pogge's own early version of global justice. The same rider could be attached to *any* conception of justice: for any principle of justice J, J tells us to select, among the set of feasible institutional schemes, the one which, all else being equal, most closely approximates J.

It may seem that the realist's critique can be safely laid to rest, and indeed most theorists of global justice have done precisely that. But they would be wrong to do so. The form the objection takes, however, needs to be recast: 'feasibility' is a red herring.

12.3.2. Ideal Theory is Neither Necessary nor Sufficient

'Feasibility' turns out to be a weak basis from which to critique the project of normative political theory. A defender can very easily embed the concern with feasibility by stating ideal principles as instructing us to choose, from among the set of all feasible institutional schemes, the one that most closely approximates J. But this response, if left in this form, is obscure. What does it mean to 'approximate' J? How can we tell which feasible institutional scheme is 'closest' to satisfying whatever set of principles one favours? In a recent article, Amartya Sen has made much of this puzzlement. In this section, we aim to evaluate his objections to the project of ideal theory.

Sen summarizes his own argument as follows (Sen calls ideal theory in the Rawlsian mold 'transcendental'):

A transcendental approach cannot, on its own, address questions about advancing justice and compare alternative proposals for having a more just society, short of proposing a radical jump to a perfectly just world. Indeed, the answers that a transcendental approach to justice gives—or can give—are quite distinct and distant from the type of concerns that engage people in discussions on justice and injustice in the world, for example, iniquities of hunger, illiteracy, torture, arbitrary incarceration, or medical exclusion as particular social features that need remedying. The focus of these engagements tends to be on the ways and means of advancing justice—or reducing injustice—in the world by remedying these inequities, rather than on looking only for the simultaneous fulfillment of the entire cluster of perfectly just societal arrangements demanded by a particular transcendental theory.[14]

There are two main planks to Sen's critique. The first is that ideal theory is not sufficient for what is really needed, namely, a theory that allows us to compare courses of action, policies, and reforms available to us here and now. The reason is that, because ideal theory aims to identify a perfectly just society, it gives us no way of assessing comparative 'distances' from the ideal. Different feasible courses of action, policy, and reform will typically involve both gains and losses with respect to justice. How can a theory designed to issue in what Sen calls 'spotless' justice help us in identifying which trade-offs bring us closer to justice and which lead us farther away? 'To consider an analogy', Sen writes, 'the fact that a person regards the *Mona Lisa* as the best picture in the world, does not reveal how she would rank a Gauguin against a Van Gogh.'[15] Let us suppose that in a Rawlsian ideal society, everyone has as much liberty, educational opportunity, self-respect, income, and wealth as can be hoped for consistent with Rawls's two principles. But now suppose that we face a decision among two (and only two[16]) feasible policies in our own non-ideal circumstances: we can pursue a policy that will slightly increase equality in educational opportunity, but significantly decrease the income of the worst-off, or we can pursue another policy which will maintain the (slight) inequalities in educational opportunity, diminish the social bases of self-respect, but increase, over time, the income of the worst-off. Which course of action would the Rawlsian urge us to choose? Whatever our answer to this question, it seems clear that in cases like this knowing what the distribution of primary goods would be in an ideal society (or the structure of trade-offs faced there) is of little help to us here and now. Of what use would it be to know that in an ideal society, we would have much more income, educational opportunity, and self-respect than we do now or that policies increasing equality in educational opportunity would raise both income and self-respect for everyone?

The second plank of Sen's critique is that 'transcendental' theory is not necessary for assessing the justice of feasible courses of action, policy, and reform. The reason is that we can make assessments of comparative injustice in our non-ideal circumstances without knowing what an ideal society would be like. According to Sen, in 'arguing for a Picasso over a Dali we do not need to get steamed up about identifying the perfect picture in the world, which would beat the Picassos and the Dalis and all other paintings in the world'.[17] We do not need a complete specification of an ideal society in order to identify improvements in justice here and now. Indeed, searching for such a complete specification will distract our attention from the more concrete and less controversial steps towards justice that we can achieve. As long as a conception of justice can identify such concrete steps, it is none the worse for being incomplete or even indeterminate with respect to wide areas of policy and practice. To switch analogies, a map of the entire globe is neither necessary nor sufficiently detailed to aid us in getting from Newcastle to London. So, if what we need to do in politics is to get from Newcastle to London, then planning, researching, and creating new global projections is, quite simply, a waste of time.

I see no reason to doubt that ideal theory is not sufficient for comparing courses of action here and now. It seems obviously true that we need much more empirical information in reaching a concrete judgement in non-ideal circumstances. But it is also obvious that further moral reflection (not already contained in the ideal theory or any merely subsumptive extension of it) is required to identify both constraints on the realization of the ideal, including permissible forms of injustice, and further principles for evaluating more fine-grained trade-offs that arise only in non-ideal cases (e.g. between self-respect and income, or between small increments in educational opportunity vis-à-vis large increases in the income of the worst-off). This strikes me as uncontroversial.

The important point is the second one, regarding whether ideal theory is necessary for identifying real-world reforms that improve justice. Sen's argument, however, rests on an ambiguity, which, when resolved, defeats the objection. The ambiguity is this: does the idea of an 'ideal society' refer to a specific set of institutions, or to the principles of justice that, once internalized by its citizens, are intended to guide it? If the aim of ideal theory were in fact the former—if ideal theory were modelled on works such as Thomas More's *Utopia* or Fourier's plans for a socialist republic—then the objection would hit its mark. It would be, indeed, absurd to suppose that identifying improvements in the justice of our own society required the prior construction of an ideal institutional arrangement of such specificity. The problem with the objection is that ideal theory does not in fact aim to make assessments of current institutions against a template defined by an institutional ideal.[18] The aim is rather to set out the *principles* of justice, solidarity, and so on, that would operate in such a society *whatever it would turn out to look like in practice*. The implications for institutional reform here and now are determined in *non-ideal* theory, in which the full range of constraints and limits imposed by politics, social technology, and so on will play a role. Returning to the analogies deployed by Sen to motivate the claim that ideal theory is not necessary, the relevant extension should not be from 'ideal societies' to specific works of art but from principles of justice that aid us in evaluating institutional arrangements to principles of aesthetics that aid us in ranking—or, more appropriately, interpreting—works of art. But once we make this clear, the analogies no longer work to motivate the objection. After all, the evaluation of works of art *does* require, even if they are never explicitly articulated, a background of values and principles against which such evaluation and interpretation occurs. A theory of aesthetic interpretation would provide us with those principles and their justifications, just as a theory of justice would provide us with the principles and premises that should guide our judgement of institutions, states of affairs, and courses of action.

It might be thought that I have not addressed the underlying thrust of Sen's argument, which is to set forth a new kind of political theory, namely, comparative theory, as an alternative to ideal theory. Whether or not I am right that his critique of ideal theory is successful, comparative theory deserves to be taken seriously on its own terms. But what does such comparative theory look like, and how is it different from ideal theory? We know that comparative theory is specifically designed to provide standards with which to compare alternative policies here and now, and we know that it does not reason from what ideal institutional arrangements would look like. But we know very little else. On the account I have been offering of the aims and structure of ideal theory, ideal theory neither eschews the attempt to guide judgement here and now—though it recognizes that it does not offer sufficient conditions for such judgement (but does comparative theory?)—nor does it reason from ideal institutional arrangements. It is revealing that all of the examples Sen gives of comparative principles are principles with a wide basis of already existing support. For example, he writes:

The comparative approach does not require an 'all or nothing' extremism, and it allows the world to come to grips with intense issues of global injustice (such as famines, widespread hunger, rampant illiteracy, or needless deaths from preventable or manageable diseases), on which consensus may be easier to obtain, without waiting for a full agreement on more contentious evaluations.[19]

The thrust of the argument in passages like this one seems to be that we should not waste our time worrying about principles that stand little chance of acceptance. Instead, we should focus on how principles that are widely shared can aid us in identifying feasible courses of action and reform. This kind of ecumenicism has much in common with Thomas Pogge's recent project, with which I think it can usefully be compared. Independently of one's theoretical starting point in ideal theory (whether right libertarian, left libertarian, or liberal egalitarian), Pogge argues that we are committed to the conclusion that we are currently harming the global poor and that we must take various achievable, determinate steps to stop such harming. The aim of Pogge's project is not to justify any one theory against the others, but to show how they all, when appropriately understood, commit us to determinate courses of action, such as reform of the international borrowing and resource privileges.[20] But if ecumenicism is indeed at the root of Sen's view, then it becomes unclear what the difference between comparative and ideal theory is really meant to be. The distinction seems to reduce to the difference between theories that seek to justify principles, and those that seek to draw the implications of principles that are already widely accepted. But what is (philosophically rather than strategically) wrong with trying to give grounds for holding a given set of premises and principles and drawing inferences at a high level of abstraction from them? Ecumenicism is a wise political strategy, but it does not give one any reasons to reject justificatory approaches as incoherent and inconsistent ways of grasping the nature or content of justice (or, indeed, of any other political value). If the comparison to Pogge is apt, it is relevant that Pogge does not consider himself to be offering a rejection or even alternative to ideal theory; in fact, as I have said, his project presupposes a background of ideal theories—libertarian, egalitarian, and so on—from which he then reasons to determinate conclusions regarding global reform.

12.3.3. The Liberalism of Fear

Among the most incisive and unquestionably 'realist' critiques of the project are those flying under the banner of the 'liberalism of fear'. Included in their ranks are Judith Shklar (who first hoisted it), Bernard Williams, and Raymond Geuss.[21] Against the 'intense moralism of much American political and indeed legal theory', they defend a negative liberalism that eschews an approach to politics and political philosophy as 'applied morality'.[22] Calling upon an earlier tradition of liberalism (Constant, Mill, Tocqueville, Humboldt, Berlin), they seek to show that current liberal ideal theorizing is a turn decisively in the wrong direction.[23] Justifications of liberalism are at their best when they point to the importance of avoiding 'what is universally feared: torture, violence, arbitrary power, and humiliation' and at their worst when they try to paint edifying fantasies of what political life would be like were everyone to be 'reasonable'.[24] This hard-edged critique of the project has surprisingly triggered little attention from those wedded to ideal theory.[25] This section aims, if nothing else, to begin the discussion. I will focus on Bernard Williams and Raymond Geuss's specific versions of it because they are the most developed *qua* critiques of the project.[26]

The fundamental claim, in a nutshell, is that the 'intense moralism' of the project leads its champions to misunderstand the nature, limits, and possibilities of politics.[27] This claim can be parsed into two main objections. First, the project suffers from a misconceived understanding of the relationship of 'morality' to political life. This is true, claims Williams, for both of the modes of 'political moralism' typical of normative political theory. According to what he calls the 'enactment model', the role of the political theorist is to formulate ideals, concepts, and principles. The role of the political *actor*, on the other hand, is to realize those ideals, concepts, and principles in actual politics. Politics is understood as an instrument of morality. The paradigm of such a model is utilitarianism. According to the 'structural model', on the other hand, the role of the political philosophy is to set conditions on the just exercise of political power in circumstances of coexistence under coercive authority, and the role of the actor is to respect those constraints in political action. The paradigm is Rawls in both *A Theory of Justice* and *Political Liberalism*.

The problem in both cases is the same. To be truly 'action-guiding', political philosophy cannot offer solely moral guidance justified from a point of view cleansed of political struggle. Political philosophy must first be based on a correct understanding of politics as a distinct realm of activity: 'the project of taking seriously in political theory an understanding of what modern social formations are is very fundamental.'[28] If the aim of this understanding is to orient political judgement, it must be based on something more than a well-attuned moral sense. According to Geuss, similarly,

...understanding a political philosophy involves taking account of a wide variety of factors that have no parallel in the case of strictly empirical theories. These include hidden structural features, various assumptions the people who are going to act on the theory make, and the actual institutional, economic, and political reality of the world into which the theory is trying to allow us to intervene (even if that intervention is at the level of a mere normative assessment).[29]

This understanding, in turn, cannot be achieved without a more developed historical sensibility: 'political projects are essentially conditioned, not just in their background intellectual conditions but as a matter of empirical realism, by their historical circumstances.'[30] Because the project lacks a sense of the historical conditions that have made its defence of liberalism possible, it lacks an adequate sense of its own function and purpose in political life. Putting liberalism is its historical place will have, it is claimed, profound and wide-ranging effects on our conception of it, and on the place of political philosophy in relation to it. In particular, a sense of the contingency of liberalism's emergence will lead us to focus negatively on those elements of politics that could undermine the most basic freedoms held dear by liberals, and less on ideal theoretical devices of justification like the original position. Armed with a historical sense of what are very much *our own* concerns about politics, we will come to see that the only real universals in politics are more basic—the 'desire to be free from want, domination, oppression'—and that the high-flying demands of political 'morality' might be relevant, but only in much more local and contingent contexts 'now and around here'.

The second objection questions the 'action-guiding' pretensions of the project. The very elements that make the project unique—namely, its abstract, moralizing, systematic, and idealizing character—ensure its disconnection from the real world of political struggle, and hence its irrelevance. Instead of accepting the fact that politics is irreducibly dominated by conflict, by disagreement about power and the use of violence, the project pins its prospects on an absurd hope, namely, that political philosophy, when correctly carried out, could resolve such conflict once and for all. According to Geuss, for example, 'What is characteristically liberal is the attempt always to see society *sub specie consensus*. This approach, however, is completely misguided.'[31] By publicly stating, justifying, and arguing for a set of moral norms for the regulation of social and political activity, political philosophy can promote the emergence of a lasting consensus that would finally end fundamental political disagreement. This hope is sustained by the notion that political conflict is possible only as a function of mistakes in moral reasoning, which can be corrected through the idealizing exercises pursued by the project. Were everyone, for example, to reason in accordance with the correct set of moral and prudential constraints (as participants in Rawls's original position do), disagreement would cease. This is wrong-headed not only because it is hopelessly implausible but also because, politically, opponents are treated as malignly ignorant rather than as mere losers in a struggle for power.[32]

The first objection hits its target (with an important qualification to be registered in a moment), but the second is wide of the mark. In the rest of this section, I will discuss where I believe the second objection fails; the next section considers to what extent the first objection is on target, and whether the project of normative political theory should be abandoned as a result.

The second objection rests on three premises:

(1) Political philosophy must be responsive to the nature of political disagreement and conflict, which is (a) centrally to do with the coercive, and often violent, exercise of power, (b) basic and unavoidable, and (c) not solely the product of mistakes in moral reasoning.

(2) The project assumes that a discursively achieved consensus on the correct set of moral norms for the regulation of political and social activity is both possible and desirable, and that this consensus would end basic political conflict (although less divisive conflict over means and lower-level affairs might persist). This hope is sustained by the thought that all fundamental political and social conflict is a result of faulty, corrigible moral reasoning.

(3) Normative political theory can play a role both in stating what such norms are and, via their public statement and justification, in contributing to their realization.

(4) Therefore, the project is not appropriately responsive to the nature of political disagreement and conflict, and is for this reason both implausible and irrelevant. Politically, furthermore, it has unsavoury consequences for the way opponents are viewed and treated.[33]

I am happy to grant (1) and (3), and accept that the conclusion follows correctly from (1) to (3).[34] The trouble with this argument is (2), which is not required by any participant in the project. To be sure, holding the belief that a set of norms is justified for the regulation of political affairs entails the belief that others should not reject the set of norms as a basis for such regulation. What it does *not* entail is that others must come to affirm the set of norms in question as the best set available. Someone might say: 'I accept that this set of norms is a justifiable basis on which to exercise political power, but I believe there is another set of norms which would be even better.' Indeed, given the possibility that any stable and ongoing 'consensus' in politics in often the product of sometimes veiled, often unveiled coercion, one would be justified in presuming that a thorough-going consensus on political values, were it to emerge, ought to be mistrusted.[35] Any participant in the project can, as a result, affirm the belief that there is basic, irreducible conflict and disagreement in politics, not all of which is a product of moral disagreement, or corrigible by moral argument.

It might be thought that (2) cannot be denied so easily, given the reliance on models of 'hypothetical agreement' rife in normative political theory. Does not the original position model a consensus among parties to it? And does not Ronald Dworkin's 'equality of resources'—which holds that equality requires outcomes that are 'envy-free', namely, outcomes where no one is willing to exchange their bundle of resources for anyone else's—also model a kind of hypothetical agreement, since everyone is presumed to be happy with the lot they end up with?[36] What about Barry's adaptation of Scanlon's 'reasonable rejection' test, which states (simplifying) that a set of rules for the regulation of social and political affairs is just only if no one could reasonably reject it?[37] In each of these cases, the role or appeal of hypothetical agreement neither presupposes a belief that political disagreement and conflict can be ended once and for all, nor, similarly, does it presuppose wide seas of consensus.[38] The basic idea is another. Models of hypothetical agreement are best understood as trying to capture the thought that, for the exercise of political power to be legitimate, it must be capable of being justified to each person in terms they could accept.[39]

This, I believe, can also in part explain the idealizing character of normative political theory. Recall that the aim of ideal theory is to formulate principles for the governance of a society in which everyone complies with those principles, and that compliance is common knowledge. It should now be clear why this makes sense. The idea of 'full compliance' is not meant to describe a desired or possible utopia; it is not intended, I have argued, to represent an ideal institutional arrangement. Rather, the condition of 'full compliance' is meant, again, to model the idea that political power could be justifiable to each person. If a set of proposed principles justifies the exercise of political power to each person, then we should be able to imagine a society in which everyone complies and knows that everyone else complies with the very same principles. Imagining the operation of such a society helps us to check whether our proposed principles are in fact justifiable to each person; the imaginative exercise is a heuristic device supplementary to models of hypothetical agreement such as the original position. If, for example, it turns out that the operation of such a society would require, say, traits of character that are not in large supply (and that would not be in large supply even in a just society), or if such a society would require great sacrifices by some for the good of the rest, then there may be grounds for rejecting the principles in question.[40]

To be sure, one can disagree whether such models actually *do* help to illuminate the question—under what conditions can the exercise of political power be justified to each person?—but that requires arguments of quite a different kind. The important point, for our purposes, is that any such argument would be speaking on the same terms as the project, and would have little to do with whether actual consensus is likely or possible or desirable. It is revealing that Bernard Williams seems to agree. His 'basic legitimation demand' (BLD) states a condition on the legitimate exercise of all political power, namely, that it must be justifiable 'to each subject'. Williams goes on to ask 'whether the BLD is itself a moral principle'. Rather than explicitly deny that it is (which would seem implausible[41]), he writes: 'If it is, it does not represent a morality which is prior to politics. It is a [moral?] claim that is inherent in there being first a political question, namely, a question, to put it bluntly, regarding who is to wield power and who is to submit to it.'[42] Understood in this way, I do not see any reason why a participant in the project need deny this way of putting the 'demand for justification'.[43]

12.4. JUSTIFICATION AND HISTORICAL CONTINGENCY

In this section, we turn to the first objection, namely, the objection that the project has no sense of liberalism's historical contingency. I shall argue that this objection, when properly understood, hits its mark, but that it does not serve to justify the further claim that normative political theory (and the politics that is said to follow from it) should limit itself to preventing the worst, rather than achieving the best (this is the qualification mentioned above). I shall then outline how I believe the objection should force us to reconsider the aims and methods of normative political theory generally.

The force of the objection lies in its demand to refocus attention on the role political values like democracy, solidarity and so on, play in the actual circumstances of politics. Liberalism, for example, is not simply the political expression of the truth about a universal, timeless morality. It is a congeries of different demands that have taken historical expression through the contingent outcomes of particular social and political struggles. This is not to deny that liberalism is the best justification for the exercise of political power here and now. It may be, but its content, scope, and justification must be understood in terms of its political point and purpose, which in turn cannot be understood without a more historical sense of its function. Like Nietzsche, the value of any morality—including a liberal one—must be assessed in terms of its role in organizing specific constellations of power.

Williams, once again, provides a good example of both the promise and the limits of this objection. After presenting the basic form of the BLD, Williams goes on to discuss the actual content that might be given to it: what conditions on the use of political authority would satisfy the BLD? Williams's central concern is to demonstrate the contingency of liberalism as a particular demand of the BLD. While the BLD applies universally, Williams claims that liberalism becomes the only way to satisfy the BLD in 'certain historically contingent circumstances' closely tied to 'the nature of modernity', which include 'organizational features (pluralism, and so on, and bureaucratic forms of control), individualism, and cognitive aspects of authority (*Entzauberung*)'.[44] It is only in these circumstances, he says, that liberalism 'makes sense' to us 'now and around here'. Outside of these circumstances, liberalism ceases to apply as a demand of 'basic legitimation'. But nowhere does Williams explain how we get from 'the nature of modernity' to liberalism; nowhere does he give us a mapping from the current 'circumstances of politics' to the conditions for the exercise of legitimate authority. Why, for example, does liberalism count as the correct account of the BLD 'now and around here'? Why and how does it 'make sense' to us, other than being very popular in Western societies at the moment? These questions are not intended as criticisms of Williams's account; they merely suggest that we need to go further. In the conclusion to this article, I outline how.

Above, I mentioned that we should accept the force of the first objection, with a qualification. The qualification is this: there is little warrant for concluding that the energies of political theorists and practitioners should be expended in merely preventing the worst. This further claim would have weight if it were true that any attempt in politics to go beyond securing freedom from fear, want, cruelty is likely to end in disastrous results. I do not want to deny that there is some truth to this charge, but it is surely overstated. There is a risk to accepting the 'liberalism of fear' as the last word in politics. There are places and times where such a narrow focus on bare physical and psychological security is exactly what is required, and we do well to keep it in mind in such circumstances. But the argument does not generalize well. Should we abandon our concern for more high-reaching political values—such as, say, social equality—in, for example, relatively stable, rich constitutional democracies? To cope with questions like these, the liberalism of fear might try to point to more articulated (and controversial) conceptions of domination, for instance. But the more content and scope the liberalism of fear tries to pack in to its restricted range of values, the less it will be distinguishable from the project's attempts to articulate its own range of political values.

12.5. CONCLUSION

Let us take stock. I began with an account of some of the defining features of normative political theory, which often attract criticism. I then identified a number of more specific objections to normative political theory that could be broadly classified as 'realist'. I concluded that concerns about the feasibility of the political values championed by the project are not warranted. Similarly, I argued that Sen's salvoes against ideal theorizing are misdirected. It is uncontroversial that ideal theory is not sufficient for identifying which courses of action and policies to undertake in fully specified circumstances. And, once we see that the aim of an ideal theory is, in the first instance, to set forth principles rather than ideal institutional arrangements, there is no reason to suppose that ideal theory is not necessary for adequately assessing the justice of courses of action and policies here and now. Both objections evince a concern with what we might call the high-mindedness of current normative political theory, namely, its propensity to moralize unconstrained by any reference to real-world contexts of political action.

That underlying concern is best conveyed, however, in another way, namely, via the 'liberalism of fear'. Focusing specifically on the work of Bernard Williams (and to a lesser extent Raymond Geuss), I canvassed two challenges that champions of the liberalism of fear put to the project of normative political theory. The first, regarding the role of consensus in the project, is less incisive than the second, regarding the role of history and historical reflection in political philosophy.

The conclusion I believe we should draw from the discussion is this. Political values—even political values at a very high level of generality, such as justice—cannot be articulated in isolation from the political contexts within which they are intended to operate. Put another way, we need some conception of their function within those contexts in order to make sense of them, and to evaluate any specific interpretation of them.[45] In many instances, this will require a historical account of their emergence or transformation—the social and political needs the values were intended to fulfil, the constellations of power they were meant to justify, and so on. On this view, it is a mistake to think of institutions and practices solely as instruments in the realization of moral values whose justification is given independently of them. But none of this means that we must abandon normative political theory as I have outlined it. What it means is that we need to rethink the way it is normally done.

In particular, it encourages a divide between those who hold that fundamental political values can receive a full justification independently of contingencies of place and time, and those who do not; between those who hold that the aim of political philosophy is to uncover basic, practice-invariant moral commitments underlying our political judgements, and those who believe that such basic moral commitments cannot be justified without articulating them in light of the institutions and practices they are meant to govern. Elsewhere I have referred to this distinction as the distinction between 'practice-independent' and 'practice-dependent' views.[46] There are three crucial questions that must be faced by the latter if it is to be plausible. First, what role should a historical *cum* interpretive account of a political value play in its *justification*? How do we go, that is, from the 'is' implicit in the interpretation of an actual political context to the 'ought' sought by the normative political theorist? It is crucial, in understanding this question, that it be understood as a question *within* ideal theory. It does not ask how we might go about *applying* an already given set of principles. No one, after all, disagrees that contingent facts about political contexts are required in understanding how a political value is to be implemented. The question asks how, according to a practice-dependent view, we should integrate our interpretive understanding of a political context in the articulation and defence of a political value. How, for example, should facts about the current international system affect the content, scope, and justification of the principles of justice that apply to it?

Second, practice-dependent views must determine *which* contexts—cultural, institutional, and so on—are relevant to the articulation of a political value. For example, some believe that the social meanings of goods, such as leisure, health, and money, should affect our understanding of the political values governing their distribution. For a view of distributive justice like this, cultural meanings play a powerful role in defining the constraints that the justification of a conception of justice must respect. Other views give a greater place to formal institutions and practices—such as, for example, the state, the WTO, the UN—in shaping and conditioning first principles of distributive justice, and relatively minor role to cultural meanings. Which is the more plausible view? And, if neither, what alternatives might there be?

Third, how can a conception of a political value be sufficiently *critical*, given the more historical, context-bound interpretation role that it is intended to play? The challenge here is to explain how practice-dependent views can avoid arbitrarily favouring the status quo. Should not the articulation of a value like justice, after all, help us to 'get outside' our current institutions and practices, and to evaluate them from a point of view free from the historical injustices congealed in existing forms?

This is not the place to answer these questions. It is enough if we have identified a strategy for defusing realist misgivings regarding contemporary normative political theory, while showing how, properly understood, they can help us to rethink how to go about doing it.

NOTES

1. Jürgen Habermas's later work might also be classified in this camp. See, for example, Habermas, *Between Facts and Norms: Contributions to a Discourse Theory of Law and Democracy*, trans. William Rehg (Cambridge, MA: MIT Press, 1996). On Habermas, see Ze'ev Emmerich, 'Political Theory and the Realistic Spirit', this volume.
2. For example, for Nozick, rights are side constraints on all transactions, whether or not they occur in just conditions. See Robert Nozick, *Anarchy, State, and Utopia* (New York: Basic Books, 1974). Another example might be G. A. Cohen, who has recently argued that political philosophy should not aim to be 'action-guiding': principles for guiding action will need to take into account facts about existing circumstances, which are, Cohen claims, irrelevant to the justification of a conception of justice. See G. A. Cohen, 'Facts and Principles', *Philosophy & Public Affairs*, 31 (2003), pp. 211–45.
3. See, for example, Thomas Pogge, 'On the Site of Distributive Justice: Reflections on Cohen and Murphy', *Philosophy & Public Affairs*, 29 (2000), pp. 137–69.
4. The division between 'private' and 'public' decisions cannot help us here, since the division (if there is one) will itself have to be identified from within the theory.
5. Cf. Henry Sidgwick, *The Methods of Ethics*, 7th edn. (London: Macmillan, 1907), pp. 15–22. It is a question of no small importance how much, indeed, utilitarianism was in fact a precursor of the Rawlsian project, or, indeed, from this perspective how much the Rawlsian project is indebted to the structure of thinking about political morality used by classical utilitarianism. I cannot discuss this further here. But if it is true, then the objections to be considered will also apply to classical utilitarianism.
6. John Rawls, *Political Liberalism* (New York: Columbia University Press, 1993), p. 285.

7. Cf. Onora O'Neill, 'Abstraction, Idealization and Ideology in Ethics', in J. D. G. Evans (ed.), *Moral Philosophy and Contemporary Problems* (Cambridge, MA: Cambridge University Press, 1988), pp. 55–69; and O'Neill, *Towards Justice and Virtue* (Cambridge, MA: Cambridge University Press, 1996), pp. 38–44. But see also Robert E. Goodin, 'Political Ideals and Political Practice', *British Journal of Political Science*, 25 (1995), pp. 37–56.

8. This is true also of those who either were part of or were influenced by the Marxism of the 'September Group', such as G. A. Cohen and Philippe Van Parijs.

9. Raymond Geuss, *Outside Ethics* (Princeton: Princeton University Press, 2005), pp. 15–17.

10. See, for example, George F. Kennan, 'Morality and Foreign Policy', *Foreign Affairs*, 64 (1985), pp. 205–18; Edward Hallett Carr, *The Twenty Years' Crisis, 1919–1939* (London: Macmillan, 1946); and Hans J. Morgenthau, 'The Twilight of International Morality', *Ethics*, 58 (1948), pp. 79–99.

11. Charles Beitz, *Political Theory and International Relations*, 2nd edn. (Princeton: Princeton University Press, 1999), Afterword.

12. Pogge, *Realizing Rawls* (Ithaca: Cornell University Press, 1989).

13. Hence the force of the often-avowed distinction between moral and political cosmopolitanism. See Thomas Pogge, 'Cosmopolitanism and Sovereignty', *Ethics*, 103 (1992), pp. 48–75.

14. Sen, 'What Do We Want from a Theory of Justice?' *The Journal of Philosophy*, 103 (2006), p. 218.

15. Charles Beitz, 'International Liberalism and Distributive Justice', *World Politics*, 51 (1999), p. 221.

16. Doing nothing, let us say, is not a feasible option.

17. Sen, 'What Do We Want from a Theory of Justice?' p. 222.

18. This is true even of Part II of *A Theory of Justice* (Cambridge, MA: Harvard University Press, 1999), in which Rawls describes a 'basic structure that satisfies' justice as fairness. Rawls writes: 'I do not argue that these arrangements are the only ones that are just. Rather my intention is to show that the principles of justice, which so far have been discussed in abstraction from institutional forms, define a workable political conception, and are a reasonable approximation to and extension of our considered judgments' (p. 171). The aim, in other words, is to demonstrate the plausibility of the two principles by showing how their (idealized) implementation would not violate any of our considered judgements. The aim is not to present an ideal form against which to rank our own social and political arrangements.

19. Sen, 'What Do We Want from a Theory of Justice?' p. 235.

20. See, for example, Thomas Pogge, 'Real World Justice', *The Journal of Ethics*, 9 (2005), pp. 29–53.

21. See, in particular, Shklar, 'The Liberalism of Fear', in Nancy Rosenblum (ed.), *Liberalism and the Moral Life* (Cambridge, MA: Harvard University Press, 1989); Shklar, *Ordinary Vices* (Cambridge, MA: Harvard University Press, 1984), esp. ch. 1; Shklar, *Legalism* (Cambridge, MA: Harvard University Press, 1986); Geuss, *Outside Ethics*, esp. chs. 1 and 2; Geuss, *History and Illusion in Politics* (Cambridge, MA: Cambridge University Press, 2001); Williams, in Geoffrey Hawthorn (ed.), *In the Beginning Was the Deed: Realism and Moralism in Political Argument* (Princeton: Princeton University Press, 2005); and Williams, *Truth and Truthfulness: An Essay in Genealogy* (Princeton: Princeton University Press, 2002), esp. chs. 9 and 10. The reference to Geuss as a 'liberal' should not be misconstrued. Geuss is one of the most ardent

critics of contemporary liberalism writing today. That said, he allows that, *faute de mieux*, the 'liberalism of fear' is our best hope, given our circumstances, for assuaging the more general 'discontent with liberalism'. See Geuss, *Outside Ethics*, p. 28.

22. Bernard Williams, 'Realism and Moralism in Political Argument' in *In the Beginning Was the Deed*, p. 12.
23. Geuss, *Outside Ethics*, pp. 16, 28.
24. Williams, *Truth and Truthfulness*, p. 208. See also Williams, 'The Liberalism of Fear' in *In the Beginning Was the Deed*, p. 59.
25. An important exception is Leif Wenar, 'Review of Raymond Geuss, *Public Goods, Private Goods*', *Ethics*, 112 (2002), pp. 151–4.
26. The Shklar pieces mentioned in note 21 are not intended specifically as a critique of ideal theory as I have identified it, though they quite clearly have implications for it. Including a discussion of Shklar's rich writings on legalism, liberalism, and the avoidance of cruelty would take us far beyond the purposes of this chapter.
27. See also Brian Leiter, 'Classical Realism', *Noûs*, 35 (2001), pp. 244–67.
28. Williams, 'Realism and Moralism in Political Argument', p. 10.
29. Geuss, *Outside Ethics*, p. 36.
30. Williams, 'In the Beginning was the Deed', in *In the Beginning Was the Deed*, p. 25; and Geuss, *History and Illusion in Politics*, pp. 12–3, 160.
31. Geuss, *History and Illusion in Politics*, p. 4.
32. For the latter point, see Williams, 'Realism and Moralism in Political Argument', p. 13.
33. This last point, though much less thorough-going, echoes Berlin's earlier concerns with the authoritarian consequences of 'positive liberty' in politics. See, for example, Geuss, *Outside Ethics*, p. 17, for the idea that Kantian morality *qua* political philosophy is the very epitome of anti-liberalism. The demand for consensus and respect for the 'moral law' is here interpreted as 'authoritarian'. In a similar vein, cf. what Mirabeau had to say about Robespierre at the beginning of the Revolution: 'That man will go far, for he believes everything he says.'
34. It is worth pointing out that even Williams and Geuss must hold some version of (3). This is clearer with Williams, who believes that the 'liberalism of fear' could form the basis of such a system of norms, and that its articulation in books and articles can contribute to its realization. But even Geuss should accept it, with the caveat that the emphasis would not be on identifying any set of norms that should govern a society, but on critique of the current dominance of debilitating ideological forms (such as liberalism). The important point is that, in the latter case, the aim cannot be solely negative: enlightening individuals to the stifling, fettering, enslaving circumstances in which they live obviously has implications—though they are never spelled out in any detail—for how they *should* live.
35. Cf. Geuss, *History and Illusion in Politics*, p. 5.
36. Brian Barry, *Justice as Impartiality* (Oxford: Oxford University Press, 1995).
37. Ronald Dworkin, *Sovereign Virtue* (Cambridge, MA: Harvard University Press, 2000), ch. 2.
38. To be sure, some existing agreement on premises, paradigmatic cases, or 'considered judgments' is required to get the discussion started (how could it be otherwise?), but, if the argument is a good one, these shared premises should be as weak and uncontroversial as possible. See, for example, Rawls, *A Theory of Justice*, p. 16; and Rawls, in Samuel. Freeman (ed.), *Collected Papers* (Cambridge, MA: Harvard University Press, 1999), p. 394.

39. Cf. Nagel:

   The unanimity in question is neither actual unanimity among persons with the motives they happen to have, nor the kind of ideal unanimity that simply follows from there being a single right answer which everyone ought to accept because it is independently right, but rather something in between: a unanimity which could be achieved among persons in many respects as they are, provided they were also reasonable and committed within reason to modifying their claims, requirements and motives in a direction which makes a common framework of justification possible

   Nagel, *Equality and Partiality* (New York: Oxford University Press, 1991), pp. 34–5. It should also be mentioned that this requirement, shared in one form or another by much of the project, emerges in an attempt to define a plausible alternative to consequentialism, in which acts or rules are assessed solely in terms of their contribution to the goodness of outcomes. For a useful contrast, which brings this feature of the project out very clearly, see Derek Parfit, 'Justifiability to Each Person', *Ratio*, 16 (2003), pp. 368–90.

40. Cf. Rawls, *Theory*, Part III. It should be emphasized that this kind of heuristic is different in character than the one used in models of hypothetical agreement such as the original position or the reasonable rejection test. In the former, we ask: would the favoured principles of justice, when institutionalized, be able to generate and sustain support for them? In the latter, the question is broader: what principles of justice would be selected by individuals in a fair choice situation?

41. The BLD is not, for example, merely a description of how most political systems work. It does not merely indicate that most political systems demand and expect compliance as a matter of right from each person. Rather, it explicitly states a *normative* claim regarding what any political system ought to do. I see no other way of understanding the presumptive force of this 'ought' than in moral terms.

42. Williams, 'Realism and Moralism in Political Argument', p. 7.

43. One might wonder: could not one deny that there *is* an answer to the question raised in the text, namely, under what conditions political power is justifiable to those subject to it? This can mean one of two things. First, it might mean that political power cannot be justified. This is an anarchist position, and has many good arguments for it; the important point is that it accepts the premise that political power must be justifiable in order to be legitimate. Anarchists simply believe that no such justification is available. Second, it might mean that it is senseless or meaningless to ask whether political power can be justified to each person. Our attitude towards political power should not be a moral one. Rather, it should be a prudential one: treat the exercise of political power as you would treat a lion in your garden. Much more argument would be required to make this possibility an intelligible one, so I simply leave it aside.

44. Williams, 'Realism and Moralism', p. 8.

45. Cf. Raymond Geuss, *Public Goods, Private Goods*, 2nd edn. (Princeton: Princeton University Press, 2003), pp. 113–4, where he discusses how one might construct the distinction between private and public:

   . . . so I wish to suggest that to make a *practically significant* distinction between public and private, a distinction, that is, that deserves to have moral, existential, social, or political standing, we first need a clear idea of the use to which we wish to put the distinction when we have made it. The first question is this: *Why* exactly do we want to distinguish private and public? What are our purposes and values? Because we can have a variety of different (legitimate) purposes, we can have a legitimate plurality of different ways of distinguishing between the two. From the fact that we do not begin with an ontologically realist account of the distinction *as a single, unitary distinction*, it does not follow that we cannot come to a rationally well-supported view that gives us reason to distinguish them for particular purposes in particular contexts. It follows only that the 'reason' we will use will be a contextually located human power, not some abstract faculty of reading off the moral demands of the universe from the facts of the case. To put the same thing another way, it is not as if there were simply *nothing* for our concepts and theories to track in the case of 'the private' and 'the public', in the sense that there is nothing for zoological theories of unicorns to track. Rather, there are many *different* things to track, but tracking them distinctly requires knowing why you might want to catch them, and failure to distinguish will lead into a dismal conceptual swamp from which it will be very difficult to extricate oneself unmuddied.

See also Geuss, *Outside Ethics*, p. 232; and Geuss, *History and Illusion in Politics*, pp. 159–60. It is relevant here that Geuss is not arguing that the distinction between 'private' and 'public' makes no sense; rather, he is arguing that the particular polemical uses to which it is put by liberalism obscures its contextual nature.

46. Andrea Sangiovanni, 'Justice and the Priority of Politics to Morality', *Journal of Political Philosophy* (forthcoming).

Index

Printed and bound by CPI Group (UK) Ltd, Croydon, CR0 4YY